Perspectives in American History

No. 20
ALBERT GALLATIN BROWN
RADICAL SOUTHERN NATIONALIST

ALBERT GALLATIN BROWN

(Photograph by Hiatt Studio, Jackson, Mississippi, from painting in Department of Archives and History, the State Capitol, Jackson, Mississippi.)

ALBERT GALLATIN BROWN

Radical Southern Nationalist

BY

JAMES BYRNE RANCK, A.M., Ph.D.

PROFESSOR OF HISTORY, HOOD COLLEGE

PORCUPINE PRESS
Philadelphia 1974

Library of Congress Cataloging in Publication Data

Ranck, James Byrne.
  Albert Gallatin Brown, radical Southern
nationalist.

  (Perspectives in American history, no. 20)
  Reprint of the ed. published by D. Appleton-
Century Co., New York.
  Bibliography: p.
  1. Brown, Albert Gallatin, 1813-1880.
2. Mississippi--Politics and government. 3. Slavery
in the United States. I. Title. II. Series:
Perspectives in American history (Philadelphia) no. 20.
F341.R88R36 1974   976.2'05'0924 [B]   73-16349
ISBN 0-87991-347-9

First edition 1937
(New York: Appleton-Century Co., 1937)

Reprinted 1974 by
PORCUPINE PRESS, INC.
1317 Filbert St.
Philadelphia, Pennsylvania 19107
by arrangement with James Byrne Ranck

Manufactured in the United States of America

TO
MY WIFE
DOROTHY SCHWIEGER RANCK

PREFACE

The importance of a study of Albert Gallatin Brown as a typical radical Southern nationalist was suggested to the late Dr. John H. Latané of the Johns Hopkins University by Dr. Frederic Bancroft of Washington, D. C. This work was commenced under the direction of Dr. Latané and was developed and concluded under the guidance of Dr. W. Stull Holt of the Johns Hopkins University. The author wishes to express his appreciation and thanks to Dr. Holt for his stimulating criticism and continual encouragement.

Much of the material for this work was collected at the Department of Archives and History of the State of Mississippi, where the Director, Dr. Dunbar Rowland, was most cordial and helpful. The author is grateful for the courteous assistance given by officials of the Library of Congress, and of the Libraries of the Universities of Minnesota and of Chicago. To his wife the author is also indebted for much valuable criticism and aid.

JAMES BYRNE RANCK.

INTRODUCTION

From the foothills of the older South in the early decades of the last century a large class of people found that society was becoming more and more stereotyped about them, that nearly half the population were slaves,[1] and that the short-staple cotton plants were quickly wearing out the soil. The few white men who could find durable soils remained, but "the rest were logically right in thinking that better lands lay beyond the horizon and resolving to win them; right also in believing that acquiring or maintaining well-to-do status in the wilderness depended upon a quick exploitation of the best-favored localities, upon getting ahead of the crowd." These more aggressive spirits set out for the true realm of cotton in the newer frontier in Alabama and Mississippi. Here, in the lower South, "they obtained a small tract of land, bought a negro with their first crop of cotton, and set up as planters 'on the make.' "[2] To this group Albert Gallatin Brown's father belonged, and to the traditions of this class as "the most ardent advocates of the institution of slavery"[3] Albert Gallatin Brown succeeded. Reared in poverty, he identified himself with the small slaveholders and the non-slaveholders of the poor piney-woods and sea-shore sections of eastern and southern Mississippi. In the seven years preceding the War of Southern Nationalism Brown was the most influential leader of these classes in Mississippi and was surpassed only by Jefferson Davis in the leadership of the Democratic party in the state.

Although Brown can not be considered a great man in any sense and was not a man of broad cultural interests, his career, neglected heretofore, is of much interest and significance. He held an elective

[1] Since the transition from tobacco to cotton culture in the 1790's, slaves in the South Carolina piedmont counties had increased each decade by 70 per cent, 90 per cent, and 50 per cent to 1820 when they constituted two fifths of the population. (Ulrich B. Phillips, *American Negro Slavery*, p. 161.)

[2] William E. Dodd, *The Cotton Kingdom*, p. 8. Phillips, "Georgia and State Rights," *Annual Report of the American Historical Association, 1901*, II, 136–137. Phillips, *Life and Labor in the Old South*, pp. 94–99. Avery Odell Craven, *Edmund Ruffin, Southerner: A Study in Secession*, pp. 74–76. Phillips and Craven describe this western movement from Georgia and South Carolina.

[3] Dodd, *The Cotton Kingdom*, p. 8.

INTRODUCTION

office every year from 1832 to 1865 without suffering a single defeat. These offices were military, legislative, executive, and judicial and were served under County, State, National, and Confederate governments. Such a uniformly successful career for a generation as a representative of public opinion is significant in itself in a democracy.

But the career of Brown is of greater importance as illustrating the radical pro-slavery and Southern nationalistic views and measures which it was necessary for him to advocate in order to win and to retain the support of the poor whites who had the least property in cotton and Negroes to lose by the abolition of slavery or by the dissolution of the Union. As Cleo Hearon has pointed out: "He was the faithful spokesman of the small slaveholders and the non-slaveholders among his constituents. This made him an interesting contrast to Jefferson Davis, who from disposition and position, represented the planting element in the Democratic party. Reflecting the sentiments of the classes for whom he spoke, Brown was more outspoken in his views and more radical in the measures he advocated than Davis." [4]

During his early career Brown adjusted his political views to the developing consciousness in his community that there were economic and social interests which were peculiar to the South, and he proved himself to be a most adroit and skillful politician in following the popular lead. He worked in harmony with Jefferson Davis during the crisis of 1850–1851 which made it clear that a distinctive Southern nationalism was emerging, but Brown was more unrestrained in expression. Both Davis and Brown, however, found themselves in advance of public opinion in 1851, when all the leading advocates of Southern rights were forced to retreat because of the weakness of Southern nationalism in its first major test. But Brown alone among the prominent Southern-righters in Mississippi was able to save himself from defeat in 1851 because he represented the economic interests of the poor whites who favored the most aggressive pro-slavery policies.

When the slavery issue came to the fore again in 1854, when the Kansas-Nebraska bill was introduced in the Senate, Brown, always more concerned with preserving the rights of the South as a whole than those of Mississippi as such, was no longer a mere follower, but was the acknowledged leader of the radical Southern nationalists in

[4] Cleo Hearon, "Mississippi and the Compromise of 1850," *Publications of the Mississippi Historical Society*, XIV, 33.

Mississippi, while the aristocratic Davis was the conservative party chief. Although there is very little direct evidence of the attitude of Davis towards Brown, the major cleavage in the Democratic party in Mississippi between the conservative forces of Davis and the radical forces of Brown has been developed for the first time in a published work from Brown's correspondence in the Claiborne Collection and from the newspapers of the time. Davis could sit in a Cabinet, work in harmony with national administrations, conciliate Northern Democrats, and finally be chosen president of the Confederacy as a conservative; Brown was only for brief intervals in sympathy with the administrations of Pierce and of Buchanan and saw more and more clearly the impossibility of maintaining friendship with Northern Democrats without sacrificing his principles of Southern nationalism. As the slavery agitation increased in bitterness and in intensity during the years immediately preceding the War of Southern Nationalism, Brown took positions more and more extreme, until in 1860 he was well in advance of his party. Motivated much more than in his earlier years by the principles in which he believed, he refused to retreat by yielding to the demands of party regularity, and as a result he dared to risk political annihilation.

But the career of Brown before 1861 has a far larger significance than that of throwing light on the causes of political radicalism in Mississippi and on the career of Jefferson Davis. Brown is most important as a type of Southern radical, who, together with the abolitionists in the North, was largely responsible for the failure of pacific means in settling the perplexing issues between the sections. The statements of William Garrott Brown a generation ago that "it is . . . somewhat surprising that the pro-slavery agitators are generally neglected by the historians of their times" and "of the pro-slavery agitators, properly so called, we know very little" are still largely true, in spite of the works in recent years on Edmund Ruffin of Virginia and Robert Barnwell Rhett of South Carolina.[5] Stephenson in 1931 rightly called attention to the need of a more thorough study of the radical leaders of the Southern movement.[6] Many more radical leaders need to be studied, and reinterpretations of John Quitman of Mississippi and of William Lowndes Yancey of Alabama must be made before a synthesis of the forces which created and sus-

[5] William Garrott Brown, *The Lower South in American History*, p. 115.
[6] Nathaniel W. Stephenson, "Southern Nationalism in South Carolina in 1851," *American Historical Review*, XXXVI, 314-335.

tained Southern nationalism can be attempted.[7] At the present time it is not possible to draw from the economic forces at work in Mississippi conclusions which would be true for the South as a whole. For instance, it has been known for a long time that the poorer whites in the piney-woods regions of other states were radical pro-slavery advocates. But it would be erroneous to infer that these economic groups in other states followed men of Brown's plebeian type rather than conservative aristocrats like Davis, since a number of the radicals, as Rhett and Ruffin, were aristocrats.[8]

It is clear, however, that positions formerly considered radical became dominant when passions became more and more inflamed and warfare threatened to be the arbiter of the dispute between the sections. And finally, the election of Lincoln, which led so directly to secession and to the outbreak of war, brought the South up to the radical positions of Brown, Rhett, Ruffin, and Yancey and seemed to justify the logic of their advanced State-rights and Southern-rights views.[9]

During the War of Southern Nationalism Brown had an opportunity to put his Southern patriotism to the test, and he acquitted himself well as an officer in the army and as a senator from Mississippi. In the latter office particularly he proved the consistency of his Southern nationalism by rising above his earlier enmity against Davis when he insisted on the necessity of a strong executive in order to maintain the Southern nation. In his advocacy of strong measures by the central government, such as the control of cotton production, universal conscription without exemptions, and the determination of legal tender, he proved that he did not belong to the particularistic State-rights school of Governors Vance of North Carolina, and Joseph Brown of Georgia or of Yancey. And finally, during the last few months of the war, when the Confederacy was forced to face the terrible dilemma of a choice between the emancipation of conscripted Negroes and the existence of the nation, Brown did not hesitate to sacrifice the institution of slavery for the cause of Southern nationalism.

During the Reconstruction period the sub-title, "Radical Southern

---

[7] Craven entitles his first chapter on Ruffin, "A Gentleman of the Old South," and stresses the need of further study of the southern radicals in the Preface, pp. vii–viii.

[8] Laura White, *Robert Barnwell Rhett: Father of Secession*, pp. 161–162.

[9] The author has not attempted to estimate the extent of Brown's influence in the North.

Nationalist" obviously does not apply to Brown. The fact is, Brown quickly became a reconstructed nationalist and was one of the leading advocates of conciliation with the radicals in Congress. This former fire-eating pro-slavery man constantly urged that the Negroes be given full political and economic rights, and after the Democrats got control of the government in Mississippi following the Revolution of 1875 Brown proved the sincerity of his post-war principles by continuing to defend the legal rights of the Negroes and by denouncing the Democrats for discriminating against them.

The author does not claim to have explained satisfactorily the reasons for this transfer of loyalty from the vanquished Southern nation to the reestablished United States. It would have seemed more logical for an extremist like Brown to have committed suicide as Ruffin did, or to have followed Rhett in hoping for the reestablishment of the Southern nation at some distant day. The lack of personal correspondence makes an attempt to disclose the psychological causes of Brown's viewpoint after 1865 very untrustworthy. Nevertheless, the author will risk the judgment that the policies which Brown favored after his career as an office-holder was over were the most statesmanlike of his whole life. Many festering evils and bitter hatreds could have been mitigated if policies of cooperation and of conciliation had been adopted towards the victorious nation and towards the former slaves. But it was almost too much to expect the South, which had been led by radicals like Brown into the War of Southern Nationalism, to follow a moderate course of cooperation and conciliation during the tragic era of Reconstruction.

CHRONOLOGY OF ALBERT GALLATIN BROWN

1813, May 31, born in Chester District, South Carolina
1823, moved to Copiah County, Mississippi
1832, elected a colonel of militia
1834, admitted to bar; elected a brigadier-general of militia
1835–1839, in House of Representatives of Mississippi
1839–1841, in federal House of Representatives
1841–1843, circuit judge of Mississippi
1844–1848, governor of Mississippi
1848–1854, in federal House of Representatives
1854–1861, in federal Senate
1861–1862, captain in Confederate Army
1862–1865, in Confederate Senate
1865–1880, retired on his farm near Terry, Hinds County, Mississippi
1880, June 13, died

CONTENTS

MAPS

ALBERT GALLATIN BROWN
RADICAL SOUTHERN NATIONALIST

CHAPTER I

EARLY CAREER—FOUNDATIONS OF RADICAL SOUTHERN NATIONALISM

Albert Gallatin Brown was born on May 31, 1813, in Chester District, South Carolina, along the foothills of the Appalachians. He was the second son of Joseph Brown, a poor farmer, who in 1823 joined in the march of the more aggressive spirits to the newer frontier lands in Mississippi. He settled in Copiah County, which had been separated from Hinds County this same year, and became a planter "on the make." [1] The next year he became Justice of the Peace [2] and in 1825 was the third largest slave owner and taxpayer in the county. Yet he could not be considered a man of wealth. Indeed, the primitive condition of the county is illustrated by the fact that Joseph Brown owned only eighteen slaves and paid a tax of $14.25, while the richest among the six hundred and twenty-five land owners had only twenty-two slaves and paid a tax of only $17.25. [3]

Little is known of the boyhood and youth of Albert except that he worked on his father's farm, attended the inferior public schools of the neighborhood, and entered Mississippi College in February, 1829. In the winter of 1832 he transferred to Jefferson College, but was dissatisfied and left after six months. He was eager to attend Princeton or Yale, [4] but his father, although now owning 1,600 acres and twenty-three slaves, [5] was unable to provide the necessary funds.

Much chagrined, Brown entered the Gallatin law office of E. G. Peyton, one of the leaders of the Mississippi bar. Before he was of eligible age he was examined and admitted to the bar by the Supreme Court of Mississippi, [6] and on January 10, 1834, his card as an attorney-

[1] M. W. Cluskey, *Speeches, Messages, and Other Writings of the Hon. Albert G. Brown*, p. 5.
[2] Dunbar Rowland, *Encyclopaedia of Mississippi History Comprising Sketches of Counties, Towns, Events, Institutions, and Persons*, II, 713.
[3] MS. Mississippi State Archives, Auditor's Series, G, No. 67.
[4] Cluskey, p. 6.
[5] MS. Mississippi State Archives, Auditor's Series, G, No. 78.
[6] Cluskey, p. 6.

at-law in Gallatin appeared in the Jackson *Mississippian*,[7] About the
same time his father started him off by giving him a town lot assessed
at $1,200 and one slave.[8]

The earliest settlement in the State in which Brown started his career
had been made by the French in 1699 at Biloxi on the Gulf of Mexico,
but Natchez on the Mississippi River became the chief settlement and
trading center. Not until 1795 did the United States secure undisputed
possession of Natchez when Spain yielded up the area between the
latitude of 31° and the mouth of the Yazoo River. Three years later
Mississippi Territory was formed with a government modeled after the
Ordinance of 1787, but with the significant exception that slavery
should not be prohibited.

Already the cotton industry, destined to give Southern slavery a
new lease of life, had been established. The first gin was introduced
in 1795, two years after its invention, and two years later cotton was
recognized as king in the fertile lands of the Natchez district. The
population of the territory increased by leaps and bounds, more than
quadrupling from 1800 to 1810, and in 1820 the population of the western part of the territory, established in 1817 as the new State of Mississippi, had nearly doubled itself. During this same period the slave population more than increased proportionately, forming 38 percent of the
population in 1800, 42 percent in 1810, and 43 percent in 1820.[9]

During the decade of the 1820s, when the great migration following
the War of 1812 and the Panic of 1819 was in full tide, the population
again nearly doubled itself, while the proportion of slaves increased to
48 percent. Mississippi had become entirely an agricultural community
dependent on slave labor. In seven of the twenty-six counties, including all the six counties along the Mississippi River, the slave population was over 50 percent. The Choctaws and Chickasaws still occupied
over half the State, although their entire population was less than
25,000. In 1830 the Choctaws in central and eastern Mississippi were
removed by the federal government, and two years later the Chickasaws
gave up their lands in northern Mississippi.

In spite of the great increase in population in the southern half of
the State, west of this region was still a frontier community during the
early 1830s. All except southwestern Mississippi, west of the Pearl

[7] *The Mississippian,* Jan. 10, 1834.

[8] MS. Mississippi Archives, Auditor's Series, G, No. 81.

[9] Hearon, "Mississippi and the Compromise of 1850," pp. 7–9. Total population
of Mississippi: 1800—8,850; 1810—40,352; 1820—75,448; 1830—136,621. Slaves:
1800—3,389; 1810—17,088; 1820—32,814; 1830—65,659.

River, was beyond the frontier limit of six people per square mile, and the general average (excluding the Indian lands) was less than three per square mile.[10] Along the Mississippi River were the wealthiest counties (Claiborne, Jefferson, Adams, and Wilkinson), each having over 9,000 population, more than half of whom were slaves, and land values of over $200,000. The poorest counties were in the piney-woods region of the eastern and southeastern part of the State. Seven of these counties had a population of less than 3,000 each, less than one third of whom were slaves, and each had land values of less than $75,000. Copiah County was one of the poorer—but not one of the poorest— counties, with a population of 7,001, of whom 1,754 or 25 percent were slaves, and land values of $128,756. As Joseph C. Baldwin pointed out in his *Flush Times in Alabama and Mississippi,* such a frontier community, with its "cheering and exhilarating prospects of fussing, quarreling, murdering, violation of contracts, and the whole catalogue of crimen falsi—in fine, of a flush tide of litigation in all of its departments civil and criminal" was a Utopia for the young lawyer. The region was "peopled by a race of eager litigants only waiting for the lawyers to come on and divide out to them the shells of a bountiful system of squabbling. . . . Every lawyerling (of real talent and energy —and who isn't at the start) who comes to the bar in the course of five or six years with anything like moderate luck, make (*sic*) expenses, and surviving that short probation on board wages, lay (*sic*) money up ranging from $250 to $500 according to merit and good fortune." [11]

Brown was quick to take full advantage of his opportunities. In 1832, when Copiah County elected him a colonel of militia,[12] he had already commenced his remarkable career as a public officeholder— a career which he followed for thirty-three years without a single defeat and which has no counterpart in Mississippi history.[13] And in 1834, a little over a month after he started work at his profession

[10] See "Map of Indian Lands and of Total Population and Proportion of Slaves of Rest of State, 1830," based on "Abstract of the Returns of the Fifth Census," House Document No. 283, 22nd Congress, 1st sess. *Statistical View of the Population of the United States from 1790 to 1830, Inclusive,* Department of State. William MacDonald, *Jacksonian Democracy,* map opposite p. 178 on "Removal of Indians," and map opposite p. 258 on "Frontier Line in 1830." Also see "Map of Land Values, 1833," based on MS. Mississippi State Archives, Auditor's Series, G, No. 94.

[11] Joseph C. Baldwin, *Flush Times in Alabama and Mississippi,* p. 48.

[12] Cluskey, p. 7.

[13] Dunbar Rowland, "Political and Parliamentary Orators and Oratory of Mississippi," *Publications of the Mississippi Historical Society,* IV, 379.

of the law, he announced his candidacy and won the election for brigadier-general of the first brigade, comprising four counties.[14]

At the same time Brown thrust himself into the active political struggle. Although his father was a Whig, he threw in his lot with the Democrats, who were predominant in the more recently developed poorer sections of southern and eastern Mississippi. During this winter of 1833–1834 the price of cotton was much depressed, and yet, as a correspondent wrote to Senator George Poindexter, "the mania for possessing land and negroes continues with unabated violence." [15] This combination of low prices and speculation caused immense pecuniary distress, and as a result many of the warmest friends of President Jackson looked to the central government for aid and demanded the recharter of the United States Bank as the best method of securing a stabilized currency.[16] At a public meeting at Gallatin, Brown was on a committee which drew up resolutions denouncing Jackson for removing the deposits of the government "from their legitimate and constitutional depository in the Bank of the United States and its branches to the vaults of other banks not known to be solvent." The President, it was felt, had assumed a power given neither expressly nor impliedly in the Constitution, and therefore "dangerous to the liberties of the people, calculated to create feelings of jealousy and distrust which should never exist in any government and is in fact a gigantic stride towards DESPOTISM !" [17] The struggle between the wealthy Mississippi valley and the poorer piney-woods sections over the banking issue was foreshadowed by the complaint that the Gallatin lawyers who controlled this meeting were willing to see Copiah County governed by "Nicholas Biddle and his stiff backed agents in Natchez. . . . We Piney Woods boys are not to be bought up like cotton, we are poor, very poor, but the Bank has not got money enough to buy us." [18]

[14] *The Mississippian,* Feb. 28, 1834.

[15] MS. J. F. H. Claiborne Collection, Vol. A, No. 14, letter of A. Campbell to Poindexter, Jan. 1, 1834. The diagram in Phillips, *Life and Labor in the Old South,* p. 177 shows that there was an abrupt halt in the rise of the price of upland cotton at New York in 1834, but that the price of slaves continued to rise in the Southern markets.

[16] MS. J. F. H. Claiborne Collection, Vol. I, No. 9, letter of Caldwell to Poindexter, Jan. 29, 1834.

[17] *The Mississippian,* March 28, 1834. Although Brown was a Democrat, he was not "a most ardent *Jacksonian* Democrat," as Riley states in his article on Brown in the *Dictionary of American Biography,* III, 100.

[18] *The Mississippian,* May 9, 1834, correspondence. It is not surprising that there was prejudice against Natchez, situated in Adams County, the richest in the State.

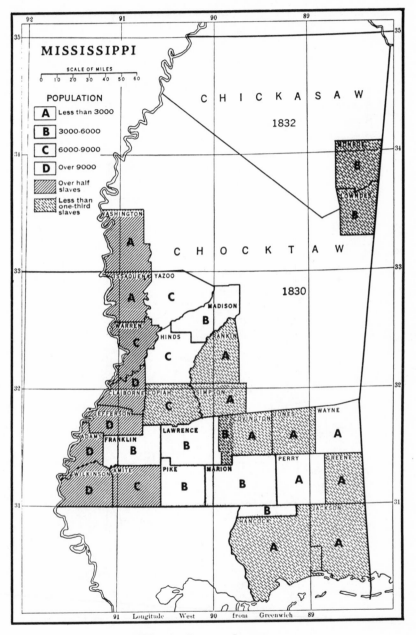

MAP 1. INDIAN LANDS
Total population and proportion of slaves of remainder of State, 1830

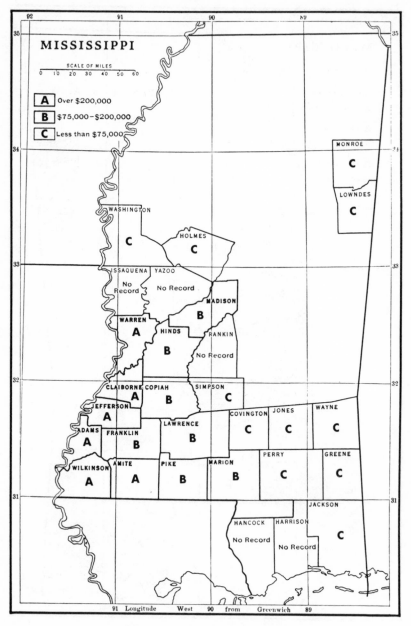

MAP 2. LAND VALUES, 1833

Thus Brown started out in politics by relying upon the central government to stabilize the chaotic finances of Mississippi. On the issue of nullification, which South Carolina had thrust upon the attention of the South in 1828, he likewise took a nationalistic position—this time in entire harmony with that of President Jackson. When this issue arose Mississippi, comprising 31,074,234 acres, depended upon the national government to remove the troublesome Indians from the 16,885,760 acres which they occupied and to sell on favorable terms these vast Chickasaw lands, together with the 11,514,517 acres still in the possession of the United States. Mississippi, more a part of the West than of the South, showed the ardent nationalism of the typical frontier community and did not yet evince the sharp cleavage between North and South which was already apparent in the seaboard States.[19] Thus, in 1829 Governor Brandon, although questioning the policy of encouraging industry by protective tariffs, yet rejoiced that threats of determined and hostile resistance had not been followed. The legislature in both 1829 and 1830, while condemning the tariff of abominations of 1828, gave no encouragement to the movement for nullification as outlined in the South Carolina Exposition of Calhoun.[20] In January, 1833, at the height of the crisis in South Carolina, Governor Scott, of Mississippi, in his annual message to the legislature, expressed sympathy for South Carolina. However, a committee of the House of Representatives reported resolutions strongly condemning secession, declared nullification "contrary to the letter and spirit of the Constitution, and in direct conflict with the welfare, safety, and independence of every State in the Union,"

In 1831 the Natchez bank was made a branch of the second bank of the United States, and the city became an important banking center. In 1832 the New Orleans, Mobile, and Natchez branches issued one fourth of all the notes of the United States bank, and after 1832 the New Orleans, Nashville, Louisville, Mobile, and Natchez branches did over four fifths of all the exchange business of the West and Southwest. When the branch banks were sold in 1836, the one at Natchez sold for $1,043,278, which was the seventh highest value of the twenty-eight branches. Of the Western branches, the one at New Orleans sold for over three times this amount, the Louisville and Mobile branches for only slightly more, while the Lexington and Nashville branches sold for a less amount. (Ralph C. H. Catterall, *The Second Bank of the United States*, pp. 143, 368, 384, 411.)

[19] Hearon, "Nullification in Mississippi," *Publications of the Mississippi Historical Society*, XII, 38. "Distinction between north and south did not as yet exist in the trans-Alleghany region. The difficulties of the pioneer of the old Northwest in hewing a clearing out of the hard woods of his region were matched by the trials of the Mississippi pioneer in wrestling with the pine forests of the south."—Arthur Meier Schlesinger, *New Viewpoints in American History*, p. 202.

[20] Hearon, "Nullification in Mississippi," pp. 41–42.

and called upon President Jackson "to maintain, unsullied and unimpaired, the honor, the independence, and integrity of the Union." These resolutions were accepted by the House by a vote of thirty to three and also passed the Senate. Mississippi refused to join South Carolina, Georgia, and Alabama in recommending a general convention of all the States to amend the Constitution, and Governor Lynch of Mississippi, in a message to the legislature in November, 1833, condemned the course of South Carolina.[21]

However, there was an able minority, led by Chancellor John Quitman and Chief Justice William Sharkey, both Whigs, who organized a State-rights party and called a convention which met at Jackson on May 19, 1834. A committee, of which Quitman was chairman, drew up an address asserting the doctrines of State sovereignty and nullification and condemning the Congressional force bill.[22] Interest now centered on the position which the Democratic party would take at its convention on June 9.

Brown did not wait for the answer of his party, but on May 31 served on a committee of three in Gallatin to draw up resolutions for an anti-nullification meeting. Nullification was declared to be an unconstitutional remedy because this mode of redress was not specified in the constitution itself. It was therefore resolved "that we look upon the doctrine of nullification as delusive in its character, dangerous in its tendency, and totally inadequate as a remedy for unconstitutional and oppressive legislation." Brown was elected by this meeting to be a member of the State Anti-Nullification Convention which met at Jackson on the same day as the Democratic State Convention.[23] Brown was on the majority side, for the Democratic State Convention took the same position as the Anti-Nullification Convention when it declared on June 9 that "the doctrines of nullification . . . are repugnant to the vital principles of our political system, . . . the extension, adoption, and enforcement of which must inevitably terminate in anarchy and civil war" and "that the constitutional right of secession from the Union . . . is utterly unsanctioned by the federal constitution, which was framed to establish, and not to destroy the Union of the States." [24] It was evident that it would require an issue

[21] Hearon, "Nullification in Mississippi," pp. 49–51, 54.
[22] Ibid., pp. 55–59.
[23] The Mississippian, June 27, 1834, from Gallatin Intelligencer.
[24] Hearon, "Nullification in Mississippi," p. 66. James W. Garner, "The First Struggle over Secession in Mississippi," Publications of the Mississippi Historical Society, IV, 90.

more vital than the tariff to wrench this new State from its loyalty to the Union.

For years the leading politician in Copiah County had been Franklin E. Plummer, who, according to J. F. H. Claiborne, the Mississippi historian, "became virtually sheriff, clerk and county judge, though the commissions of course were held by three respectable citizens." He was a most picturesque character. With little or no education, he was hale-fellow-well-met to all, ingratiating, humorous, and plausible, and "knew exactly how to play upon the emotions of his constituents." Although he knew very little law, he was most successful at the bar because he had the most consummate audacity and knew how to influence his juries. He built up a political machine among the poor piney-woods farmers of eastern Mississippi and with the aid of his demagogic slogan, "Plummer for the people, and the people for Plummer," won his way into the State legislature and into the national House of Representatives.[25] There is a typical picture of him from his campaign for Congress in 1830. Six weeks before the election he was not seriously considered in Hinds County, but two or three weeks before election "he came around making stump speeches and saying he was the people's man . . . and that he was opposed at every point by the members from the Mississippi. . . . One week after he was here there was no person spoken of but Plummer." [26] His appeal was made to the small farmers of central and eastern Mississippi and was especially effective when he dubbed the rich planters along the Mississippi River as "swelled heads" and "bloated bondholders." Judge Powhatan Ellis lost all influence in eastern Mississippi when Plummer charged him with effeminacy and Natchez dandyism.[27]

But in 1835 the national banking interests were at the height of their popularity and Senators George Poindexter and John Black and Representatives Harry Cage and Plummer, all elected as Jackson men, had turned against the anti-bank administration.[28] Charles Lynch, the leading Democrat in eastern Mississippi, was the anti-Jackson candidate for governor. Plummer, campaigning for the Senatorship, met at Gallatin the impassioned appeal of Governor Runnels,

[25] J. F. H. Claiborne, *Mississippi as a Province, Territory, and State*, pp. 424–425.

[26] MS. J. F. H. Claiborne Collection, Vol. B., letter G. H. Holliman to Quitman, Aug. 12, 1830.

[27] Paul H. Buck, "The Poor Whites in Ante-bellum South," *American Historical Review*, XXX, 53.

[28] Claiborne, p. 411.

the administration candidate for governor, in a calm, pleasing manner, and carried this strong Democratic county for Lynch.[29] Brown, a disciple of Plummer, was running for the lower house of the State legislature as an anti-Jackson Democrat.[30] In conducting his first political campaign he showed that he was an apt pupil in the Plummer school by making a stronger appeal by catch phrases "than by the solid reasons he may have offered." [31] Of the nine candidates for the three representatives to be chosen from Copiah County, Brown received next to the highest number of votes. In the legislature Brown immediately recognized his indebtedness to Plummer, his political mentor, by casting his vote for Plummer for Senator on all five ballots.[32] But all to no avail, for Plummer was defeated by Robert J. Walker, "The Wizard of Mississippi," a far more versatile and more clever politician than Plummer or Poindexter, the anti-Jackson candidates.[33]

Once elected, Brown immediately took the course which was to be the keynote of his political career by championing the interests of the small farmers of southern and eastern Mississippi against the wealthy planters along the Mississippi River valley. When the legislators from the Mississippi River districts opposed the construction of the New Orleans and Nashville Railroad west of the Pearl River Brown objected that it was an effort to foster Natchez at the expense of the poor yeomanry of the interior. The western part of the State, he claimed, "with all her wealth, pomp, and affluence," adds insult to injury by proclaiming in substance "that our Eastern brethren were but a set of cow-hunters and paupers, dependent upon the bounteous resources of the great west." He urged the East to legislate wisely so as soon to "burst the fetters that have so long bound in humble poverty her industrious and enterprising sons." [34] This energetic young legislator challenged Sargent S. Prentiss, recognized as the leading orator in Mississippi, to a debate on this issue, and also crossed swords with this eminent Whig when he sought to delay the admission of the representatives of ten new northern Chickasaw counties from the newest frontier of the State which were sure to add to Democratic strength.[35]

29 Claiborne, p. 426.
30 *The Mississippian,* May 22, 1835.
31 Wiley P. Harris, Autobiographical sketch, typewritten copy, pp. 10–11.
32 *The Mississippian,* Jan. 12, 1836.
33 Dodd, *Robert J. Walker, Imperialist,* pp. 16–17.
34 *The Mississippian,* Feb. 19, 1836.
35 *Ibid.,* Jan. 6, 1837.

During the session of 1837 Brown secured a recognized position in the legislature. At the previous session his bill extending the powers of the justices of the peace had become law,[36] and now he was placed on the judiciary committee. He was made chairman of the special committee on the militia and secured the passage of a bill which recognized the state militia.[37] When the legislature reconvened in April Brown was put in nomination for the speakership. He was not elected, but shortly afterwards was chosen speaker *pro tem* by acclamation when Vennerson, the incumbent, became ill. Brown thus became the youngest speaker of the House of Representatives which Mississippi has ever had.[38] *The Mississippian,* the leading Jackson paper, showed its favor towards Brown shortly after the end of the session by printing a communication strongly praising him and urging him for the next speakership.[39]

In Mississippi, as in any frontier community, the farmer was insistent in his demand for credit to enable him to pay for his new farm and to finance it for the first few years until it could become self-supporting. Since Eastern capital was not invested in Western development, the westerners turned enthusiastically to the United States bank and to state banks for credit. During the boom years of emigration to the West, with their over-speculation in land and high prices, the demand for paper money increased. When the long financial debauch in the country came to its end in 1837 Mississippi suffered the financial collapse common to the prostrate Western States.[40] So great was the demand for paper money that the legislature chartered the Mississippi Union Bank which aided insolvent debtors and the people at large by issuing bank notes as loans on land mortgages. At a special election in July for Mississippi's two congressmen-at-large, when the normally Democratic County of Copiah voted for General E. L. Acee, a Whig, against Colonel Gholson, a Democrat, Brown attributed it to the fact that Gholson was represented as advocating an exclusive gold and silver currency.[41] The growing popularity of Brown was proved by his reelection to the legislature in November, even though Copiah voted by large

[36] *Ibid.,* Mar. 4, 1836.
[37] *Ibid.,* Jan., 1837.
[38] This is based on the authority of Dr. Dunbar Rowland, State Historian of Mississippi.
[39] *The Mississippian,* July 28, 1837.
[40] Frederic L. Paxson, *History of the American Frontier, 1763–1893,* pp. 226–228, 311–322.
[41] *Mississippi Free Trader,* Sept. 5, 1837.

majorities for a Whig governor and for Whig congressmen,[42] and by the fact that he was strongly recommended for speaker by the *Eastern Clarion* of Paulding, the leading Democratic paper in the eastern part of the State, a section which had only two Whig members in the lower house of the legislature.[43]

Brown was the leader of his party in the House of Representatives in 1838. Although Dr. King of Rankin County, a Whig, defeated Brown for the speakership, the Democrats succeeded in organizing the House. Brown was chosen chairman of a committee to act with the Senate to secure speedy action on Pray's Code of Mississippi Laws and also chairman of the Ways and Means Committee.[44] But his most noteworthy accomplishment during this session was his report as chairman of the special committee to deal with the retiring Governor Lynch's remarks in favor of a national bank. Brown started his career, as we have seen, as a nationalist, and in the contest for the speakership was sharply contrasted with King, who was described as "a red hot nullifier." [45] But in this report Brown showed that he was following his party into the State-rights school and outlined the main principles of the policies which were to be most distinctive of his later career as a State-rights man and as an advocate of Southern nationalism. He first attacked a national bank upon constitutional grounds. Any other policy than that of strict construction "produces a tendency to consolidation and absolute anarchy alarming to state sovereignty, and at once subversive of the best interests of the American people." The commerce clause gave Congress the right to regulate commerce, but not to regulate a means of carrying on commerce, such as a national bank; nor can the general welfare clause be used, "like a mantle of charity . . . to cover a multitude of political sins." Here one notes the growing influence of the slavery question over his thought—an influence which later became dominant and which led him to identify State rights with Southern rights. If Congress, he argued, was the exclusive judge of the degree of necessity for legislating for the common good, then the abolitionists of the North, "whose strength, disguise it as you will, is increasing with frightful rapidity," could abolish slavery in the District of Columbia and in the Southern States.

The bank was not only unconstitutional, it was also inexpedient.

---

[42] *The Mississippian*, Nov. 17, 1837.
[43] *Southern Star*, Dec. 16, 1837.
[44] *The Mississippian*, Jan. 12, 1838.
[45] *Mississippi Free Trader*, Feb. 6, 1838. *Southern Star*, May 19, 1838.

If specie were obtained from abroad, the foreigner would fatten on our labor, would control our politics in peace times with his money, and would dominate our commerce both in peace and in war. If the bank's stock were based on state bank notes, it would force the state banks to resume specie payments which would bankrupt them. He did not neglect the political argument of charging the bank faction with the purpose of bringing the Van Buren administration into disrepute among the people. Nor did he forget an appeal to his poor constituents. Cotton was worth only twelve cents a pound from 1827 to 1830, when the bank was at its zenith; in 1836, when the bank was disbanded, it was worth from sixteen to twenty-two cents. Satisfied with the mere statement of these sweeping generalities, he concluded that the bank "is an institution which makes the weak weaker and the potent more powerful, ever filching from the poor man's hand to replenish the rich man's purse." [46]

This report won the warmest praise from the anti-bank forces.[47] *The Mississippian* lauded it, but was outdone by the *Mississippi Free Trader* which had severely criticized Brown a few months before.[48] This paper hailed the report as a truly Jeffersonian document—a second Declaration of Independence, which would be reechoed by the Democracy of the Union, "rending away, a second time, the chains which the aristocracy of wealth were silently riveting upon the body politic to secure a conquest by stealth which the aristocracy of power had failed to achieve by force over the patriots of '76." [49]

A series of political events now added to Brown's prestige. In July, 1837, Governor Lynch called a special election for members of Congress to serve for the special session called by Van Buren to deal with the financial crisis. The governor's call specifically stated that the elected members were to serve "until superseded by the members chosen at the regular election on the first Monday and Tuesday in November." As the depression caused a decided reaction against the Democrats in the country, the Democratic House of Representatives, fearing a loss of the House, declared in October that J. F. H. Claiborne and Gholson were elected for a full term. As a result of this decision Claiborne and Gholson renounced their candidacy for reelection in November, and the Whigs, Prentiss and Word, were

---

[46] Cluskey, pp. 19–26.
[47] *Ibid.*, p. 8.
[48] *The Mississippian*, Jan. 26, 1838. *Mississippi Free Trader*, quoted by *Natchez Courier*, Sept. 7, Oct. 26, 1837.
[49] *Mississippi Free Trader*, Feb. 12, 1838.

elected. In defending his right to a seat, Prentiss "stigmatized the October action of the House as a gross legislative usurpation." He spoke two hours on each of three days and by his brilliant defense confirmed his reputation as one of the greatest orators of his time. Although Claiborne and Gholson were unseated, the House by the casting vote of Speaker Polk also rejected Prentiss and Word, thus illustrating a second time the dictum of Alexander—"if a majority, without need of recruits, wantonly unseats opponents simply to gratify partisan prejudices, it is certain to disregard all semblance of fairness when control of the House hinges on its action." John Quincy Adams called this contest "one of the most remarkable conflicts between honest principle and party knavery that I have ever witnessed." [50]

Brown, on the other hand, saw the issue only from the viewpoint of a blind partisan. He was secretary of a Claiborne-Gholson meeting at Jackson in January, 1838, and thus dispelled the charge of the *Natchez Free Trader* that he was opposed to Gholson.[51] A new election was set for April 23 and 24. The *Southern Star* of Gallatin, Brown's organ, placed the names of Brown and Roger Barton at the head of its editorial columns and insisted that Brown was the first choice of southern and eastern Mississippi.[52] Here was an excellent opportunity for Brown to gain influence by declining, and he was astute enough to grasp it. In a letter, full of florid, resplendent bombast, to Editor Kiger he betrayed, all too clearly, demagogic tendencies worthy of Plummer himself. Congress, by a lawless and disgraceful act, had become the mere pander of federal usurpation and had "not only insulted, but attempted to disgrace a sovereign member of this republican confederacy," and showed to the world "the most glaring and disgraceful inconsistency that ever stained the annals of American Legislation. . . . The laurel wreath which has been woven for our native Claiborne and Gholson, would but illy deck another's brow." They were persecuted because they dared to go forth to free their countrymen from an unwilling captivity to a soulless and unrelenting monied aristocracy. He implored the enlightened freemen of Mississippi not to bow before the golden image; changing his metaphor, he pictured the bank as Circe, touching the people, who awoke "to find the owners and favorites of the Bank the lords and masters

[50] De Alva Stanwood Alexander, *The History and Procedure of the House of Representatives*, pp. 316–319. Alexander quotes the J. Q. Adams statement from Adams' *Diary*, IX, 488.

[51] *Natchez Courier*, Jan. 24, 1838.

[52] *Southern Star*, Mar. 3, 17, 1838.

of the land, and they, the people, the veriest beasts of drudgery."
The editor accepted Brown's declination, praised him for his patriotic course, and prophesied that he would soon be elected to Congress.[53]

In his debate with Prentiss at Gallatin on April 4, he showed clearly that the bank controversy and the growth of abolitionism in the North had led him fully into the State-rights camp, which he now identified with the Democratic party and with the rights of the South. No honest State-rights man, he insisted, could support the Whig candidates, for their triumph "would be hailed by the bank federalists of the south and the abolitionists of the north with equal joy." [54] Brown gave evidence that he was an unsafe guide for the people by his sweeping, unreasoned charges against Clay. Because Clay had upheld the right of the abolitionists to petition Congress, he "encouraged and promoted the objects and views of those northern fanatics." Therefore, by a *non sequitur* Brown made the sweeping charge that Clay was an abolitionist and that Prentiss, in following Clay, encouraged abolition.[55] The tragedy of it was that such a bold appeal to the emotions was believed and that Brown gained praise and prestige by it. The indignant voters of Mississippi administered a stinging reproof to the unjust tactics of Congress by reelecting Prentiss and Word by an overwhelming majority.[56]

The *Southern Star* returned to prophesying for its favorite son. Because of his able report on a national bank, his magnanimous refusal to run for Congress, and his aggressive stumping for the Democracy it was certain that the people of the southern section of the State would call him at no distant day to represent them in Congress.[57] But a further test at the polls was required before this prophecy was fulfilled. In the summer of 1838 Brown took a trip to Boston. During his absence the Whigs drew up a petition signed by a majority of the voters in Copiah County, demanding that Brown and J. B. Reid, their representatives, vote for a pro-bank senator at the next legislature or resign. Brown immediately resigned upon his return and made eight speeches in a campaign for reelection.[58] The Democratic press supported him and he was vindicated by a

[53] *Mississippi Free Trader*, Mar. 15, 1838.
[54] *Ibid.*, April 12, 1838.
[55] *Ibid.*, April 23, 1838. *Southern Star*, April 14, 1838.
[56] Alexander, p. 319.
[57] *Southern Star*, June 2, 1838.
[58] *Ibid.*, Nov. 16, Dec. 7, 1838. *Mississippi Free Trader*, Nov. 24, 1838.

large majority, winning nine of the eleven precincts in the county.[59]

On January 8, 1839, Brown was nominated for Congress by the Democratic State-Rights Convention at Jackson to represent the southern part of the State, while Jacob Thompson of Pontotoc County was chosen to represent the northern part, both, however, running on a State-wide ticket.[60] His legislative activity at the session of 1839 may be considered as part of his campaign for election. He had won and was sure to secure further popular acclaim by advocating railroad extension. In January, 1837, he had moved that a select committee be formed to memorialize Congress to allow his State to invest a portion of the proceeds from land sales in Mississippi in the Mississippi and Alabama Railroad.[61] In March, 1838, Brown, together with E. G. Peyton and J. B. Reid, were superintendents for selling $250,000 worth of stock in the branch of the Mississippi Railroad bank at Gallatin, and when the books were opened on April 2 the entire amount was subscribed in three hours.[62] On January 4, 1839 he was chosen a director of the Gallatin branch of the Grand Gulf Railroad and Banking Company.[63] On February 14 in the legislature he opposed all riders and amendments to the bill which ensured the completion of the road running from Natchez through Copiah County, Jackson, and on to Canton, in Madison County. He spoke of this bill enthusiastically as "among the most important bills presented to this Legislature, and . . . calculated to place our State in an enviable situation among our elder sisters." [64]

During this legislative session Brown crossed swords on two issues with Henry S. Foote, who became his most powerful political antagonist during the years immediately following the slavery crisis of 1850. Foote, a Whig, wanted an immediate election of a senator who would take office on March 4, 1840, while Brown urged a delay until after the fall elections, when the Democrats hoped for a greater chance of success. The Whigs won their point and elected John Henderson.[65] We shall see the method of electing a senator rise to be an issue of major importance between Foote and Brown in 1853,

[59] *The Mississippian,* Dec. 14, 1838. *Piney Woods Planter,* Dec. 15, 1838, Jan. 5, 1839. *Southern Star,* Jan. 4, 1839. Cluskey, pp. 9–10.
[60] *Mississippi Free Trader,* Jan. 24, 1839.
[61] *Ibid.,* Jan. 19, 1837.
[62] *Southern Star,* Mar. 17, April 14, 1838.
[63] *Mississippi Free Trader,* Jan. 19, 1839.
[64] *Ibid.,* Feb. 16, 1839.
[65] *Sentinel and Expositor,* Jan. 19, 26, 1839.

when their campaigns for the senatorship arrested public attention.
The other issue was of more immediate concern. As money was
still scarce Foote introduced a resolution that the Union Bank, established by the legislature in 1837 and 1838 with $15,500,000 capi-
tal—more than that of the five other state banks combined,[66] be permitted to issue $10,000,000 of bank notes at 5 percent, redeemable
in one or two years. Brown proposed an amendment that the responsibility for the amount to be issued be left with the banks and that
the issue run for only one year at not less than 6 percent.[67] He pointed
out that Tennessee's bonds had been refused in the market at 6 percent and was convinced that Mississippi's bonds would be refused
at 5 percent. Brown had voted for an amendment to the Union Bank
bill the year before to allow the issue of bank notes, but he insisted
that the notes have sufficient collateral behind them.[68] The present
resolution, he claimed, would authorize bills of credit, forbidden to
the States by the federal constitution, and he spoke of State's duties—
a worthy line of argument for a State-righter: "If the States wished
not to have their dominion invaded by the federal power, the first
lesson to be learned by them, was not to invade the dominion of that
power." Indeed, in elaborating his views in favor of a sound money
standard, he rose far above the mere politician or demagogue. He
condemned "this whirlwind of popular feeling . . . gotten up by
knaves desirous of speculating on its paper," and warned that the
bank could not sell its bonds at par value, as it was bound to do by
its charter, merely by securing the good opinion of its friends or by
State credit. The Foote bill would force upon them a miserable shinplaster currency, drive the banks to suspend specie payments, and
drain the country of every dollar of good money. The laboring man
in his constituency knew that he would be cheated out of one fourth
of his earnings by the resultant depreciation, which could only benefit
a very small proportion of the people.[69] Here was clear, statesmanlike
thinking. And he stood by his convictions. When his amendment was
voted down and the legislators yielded to the speculative mania by
passing Foote's bill Brown voted against it, although it was favored

[66] H. E. Van Winkle, *Nine Years of Democratic Rule in Mississippi*, pp. 40–41.
Samuel Proctor McCutchen, *The Political Career of Albert Gallatin Brown*, p. 9,
points out that the force of the depression of 1837 did not strike Mississippi until
1839 and 1840. This unpublished dissertation was consulted only after the present
work had been submitted to the Carnegie Revolving Fund Committee.

[67] *Sentinel and Expositor,* Aug. 6, 1839.

[68] *Natchez Courier,* Feb. 12, 1838.

[69] *Mississippi Free Trader,* April 24, 25, 1839.

by Governor McNutt,[70] now the Democratic candidate for reelection.

The Whig press carried on a constant attack against Brown during 1839. Even his personal appearance was criticized. The *Courier* pictured him as "a flippant gentleman, who sports a pair of whiskers, a large guard chain, and gold headed cane, and who if he had more *ton,* would pass on Broadway as a dandy of the first water." [71] The campaign itself was full of mud-slinging, and Brown was forced to defend his entire political career on the stump. When he called the banks "slaving shops, swindling machines, and their paper filthy, spurious trash, and rotten rags," it was pointed out that he had favored bank note resolutions in 1837, 1838, and to a limited extent, in his own resolution at the last legislature, thus making him guilty of "double dealing" and "political gambling." [72] When Brown eulogized Andrew Jackson and denounced a national bank his resolutions of March 13, 1834, were unearthed in which Jackson was termed despotic for removing the deposits from the United States Bank,—resolutions now hailed by the (Whig) *Yazoo Banner* as expressing genuine Whig sentiments.

Whether Brown's earlier career proved him to be "perhaps guilty of as much duplicity and shifting as any other two men of his age, in this or any other clime" [73] or not, his staunch and loyal support of the existing administration could not be questioned. While charging Harrison with being an abolitionist, he excused Van Buren's opposition to the admission of Missouri as a slave State as "nothing more than other distinguished men would have done and did do." [74] He encouraged criticism by his statement that he would at once drop his advocacy of the sub-treasury scheme if Van Buren were no longer to support it. And he was criticized, for he was dubbed "the supple tool, the slave, the vassal, the cringing and willing instrument of the President." [75] In his answer to these charges Brown showed clearly that no principle or policy had yet demanded his allegiance above the claims of party loyalty. He was content to play safe, to keep his ear to the ground in order to detect the direction party loyalty demanded. "Young men, like myself," he asserted, "must follow, not lead, on these great national questions. . . . For myself, I would never be

[70] *Mississippi Free Trader,* Aug. 1, 1839.
[71] *Southern Star,* Feb. 9, 1839, from *Natchez Courier,* Jan. 25, 1839.
[72] *Yazoo Banner,* Aug. 16, 23, 1839.
[73] *Ibid.,* Oct. 25, 1839.
[74] *Aberdeen Whig,* Oct. 5, 1839.
[75] *Whig Advocate,* Sept. 7, 21, 1839.

found bringing forward a question on our side after it was abandoned by my party." [76] Quite true, but the slavery issues had not yet become dominant in politics!

The Jackson Democratic press supported Brown, but not wholeheartedly. Volney E. Howard, editor of *The Mississippian*, thought the ticket rather weak, with Thompson the stronger candidate.[77] After all, Brown was only twenty-six, just above the eligible age for Congress. The *Independent Journal*, while admitting that he was "a gentleman of pleasant and agreeable manners in the social circles of life, and most genteel in his personal demeanor," yet felt that he had not enlightened the bar or bench profoundly nor greatly illumined the State legislature and had no hopes that in his youthful days he would prove to be a brilliant star in Congress.[78] The Democratic press outside the capital supported him more enthusiastically, particularly that of the southern part of the State, where there were few slaves and small cotton production.[79] He was praised for resisting bank corruption and shinplaster establishments which encouraged speculation and his loyalty to the doctrine of State-rights was no longer questioned.[80] At Paulding Brown made an effective appeal to the poor farmers by charging that Clay attempted to cast odium upon the hardy pioneers of the forest who had exposed themselves to all the hardships incident to the settlement of a new country by refusing to grant cheaper public lands. Clay would crush to the earth "a weak and defenseless portion of his fellow-countrymen . . . in order to extend his popularity with a more powerful and influential class of his fellow-citizens." [81] This effective *argumentum ad hominem* led the Paulding *Clarion* to predict that Brown would receive "the united opposition of the aristocracy." [82] The election returns showed that he had won by well over 2,000 majority. The result proved that Brown's greatest strength did lie in the poorer sections of the State [83]

[76] *Southern Star*, Nov. 3, 1839, letter to C. M. Price, editor of *The Mississippian*.

[77] MS. J. F. H. Claiborne Collection, Vol. B, No. 58, letter Howard to Quitman, Jan. 14, 1839.

[78] *Independent Journal*, Sept. 7, 1839.

[79] See map, "Abstract of Census Returns of State of Mississippi for 1840," from *Journal of the Senate of the State of Mississippi, 1841*, opposite p. 22.

[80] *Sentinel*, Mar. 19, April 23, 1839. *Piney Woods Planter*, Oct. 12, 1839. *Southern Star*, June 15, 1839, from *Columbus Democrat*.

[81] *Southern Star*, July 3, 1839, from *Eastern Clarion*.

[82] *Southern Star*, June 15, 1839.

[83] Brown secured 18,602 votes; Bingaman, the leading Whig, won 16,215. (Rowland, *Encyclopedia of Mississippi History*, I, 610; II, 433. Election returns

—the political significance of which was by no means overlooked by Brown.

Brown waited long before making his maiden speech in Congress— so long that he was likened to the boy at a party who had not a word to say.[84] But on April 17, 1840, he rose to defend the administration while the House was in committee of the whole on the general appropriation bill. The speech was restrained and conciliatory in tone as befitted a new member and was free from the passionate bombast which he found so effective on the stump in Mississippi. He had, indeed, mastered the primary qualification of a speaker, for he knew how to adjust himself to his audience. After modestly explaining his aversion to engaging in the general scramble for an opportunity to speak, he adverted to his favorite theme in explaining the reasons for the heavy postoffice expenditures. They were due to "the existence of banks, the redundancy of paper money, a species of devouring reptile, which, like the locusts of Egypt, has overrun and laid waste the entire country," and especially Mississippi, "a state upon which the evils of the day have fallen with more severity than upon any other portion of the Union, or of the world." [85] He put the initial blame for

---

map based on MS. Secretary of State Archives, Series F, No. 51.) Compare with slave and cotton production map of 1840. Brown secured a plurality of votes over both the Whig candidates and over his own running-mate, Thompson, in fifteen of the twenty-two counties in which the number of slaves per male white poll was less than one and in nine of the fifteen counties which produced less than 1,000 bales of cotton. Thompson's greatest strength was in a group of counties in northeastern Mississippi, while Brown carried the poorer counties in north-central, eastern, and southern Mississippi. The contrast with the Whig vote is marked. The Whigs won eighteen counties, including all the eight counties in which over 25,000 bales of cotton were produced and all the six counties in which the number of slaves per male white poll was over five. They carried only one county (Perry) in which both less than 1,000 bales were produced and less than one slave per male white poll were combined, while the Democrats carried nine such counties.

[84] *Yazoo Banner,* Mar. 6, 1840.

[85] The diary of W. H. Wills vividly depicted these evil conditions in 1840. "Speculation has been making poor men rich and rich men princes. . . . A revulsion has taken place. Mississippi is ruined. Her rich men are poor, and her poor men beggars. . . . We have seen hard times in North Carolina, hard times in the east, hard times everywhere; but Mississippi exceeds them all." Lands formerly worth from $30 to $50 an acre had declined in value to $3 or $5, while lands worth from $10 to $20 were sold at sheriff's sales for fifty cents an acre. Many farms were deserted, even after crops had been planted. "I had prepared myself to see hard times here, but unlike most cases, the actual condition of affairs is much worse than the report." (Phillips, *American Negro Slavery,* pp. 372–373, quoting Wills' diary from *Southern Historical Association Publications,* VIII, 35.) The diagram between pages 370 and 371 (also in his *Life and Labor in the Old South,*

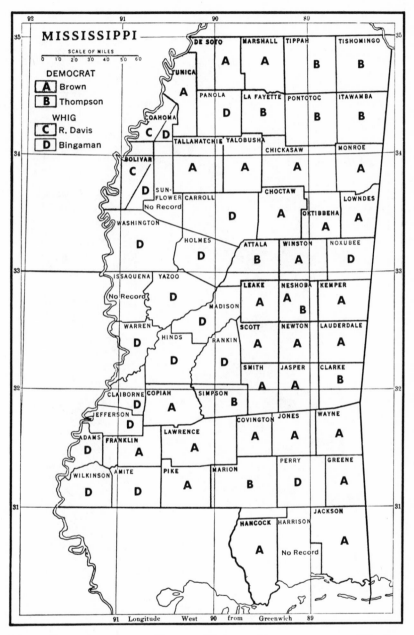

MAP 3. ELECTIONS FOR THE FEDERAL HOUSE OF REPRESENTATIVES, NOVEMBER, 1839

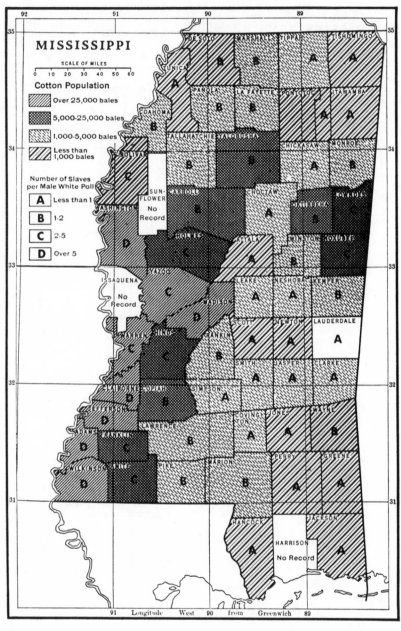

MAP 4. COTTON PRODUCTION AND NUMBER OF SLAVES PER MALE WHITE
POLL, 1840

this condition on the eastern merchant companies who speculated on "wild lands" in the hope of selling at twice the purchase price of $1.25 an acre. But Brown was no unreasoning apologist for his own State, and was fair enough to apportion part of the blame to citizens of his own State who became "regularly installed into all the mysteries of living without work." Thus money was lost to real business, and more banks and paper issues were demanded. The landholder was sued and became bankrupt: "at this point he turns Whig, curses General Jackson, swears that Van Buren is the greatest scoundrel that ever lived, and starts to Texas." Brown heartily favored the sub-treasury scheme, for he had no faith that Congress could exercise any effective control over the $50,000,000 bank which Clay proposed.

Brown supported Van Buren as a Northern man with Southern principles. He refrained from attacking the abolitionists. He condemned the Whigs for making a military hero of Harrison and for concealing his political views. If "log cabin and hard cider" are the only qualifications necessary for the President, he offered to supply Presidents from his State for 500 years at $500 apiece, and thus effect the economy which the Whigs demanded.

Brown ended his maiden speech with a rhetorical eulogy of the great triumvirate. Although differing from Webster politically "as wide as the extremities of earth," he could contemplate him with pride and exultation. He was like a deep and placid lake that never moves but in a storm, "and then, foaming and casting high the billows of passion, sentiment, and wit, he seems from the very bottom of his soul to be throwing up the collected contents of a thousand years." Clay was no longer an abolitionist, but "one of nature's noblest, greatest works, a man whose name is commensurate with the ends of the earth, and whose fame is as boundless as eternity itself." But his highest praise was reserved for Calhoun, "the noblest son of the sunny South," as "one nearer my heart, one whose sentiments are in unison with my own." He was "the political Niagara of America" who "will stand

---

p. 177) shows the continuous decline in slave and cotton values between 1837 and 1845. J. F. H. Claiborne, in letters to newspapers, described deserted villages in southeastern Mississippi, "all around vestiges of the people departed and dispersed," or towns like Perry, tumbling to pieces, "some twelve or fifteen crumbling tenements—the wrecks of by-gone days! Not a tree stood in the gaping square for the eye to rest upon; the grass was all withered up; the burning sun fell on the white and barren sand . . . and was reflected back until the cheek scorched and the eyes filled with tears." (Phillips, *Life and Labor in the Old South*, p. 101, quoting *Publications of Mississippi Historical Society*, IX, 489–538.)

through all after time no less the wonder than the admiration of the world."

The cogency of this first speech was somewhat lessened immediately afterwards when Jenifer of Maryland forced Brown to admit that he would give up the sub-treasury scheme if Van Buren abandoned it and that he had given a reluctant support to the post note system in Mississippi.[86]

This speech was printed verbatim in his Gallatin organ, which regarded his respect, courtesy, and liberality towards his opponents as its most distinguishing feature.[87] His eulogy of Calhoun was praised in his native State,[88] but the contrast between his abuse of Clay during his campaign and his honeyed words in his maiden speech did not escape notice.[89]

In June Brown sent a letter to his constituents in which he strongly favored the preemption bill then before Congress—a bill sure to appeal to his log cabin constituents as being against a "purse proud aristocracy." In supporting the bankruptcy bill against his own better judgment he showed that he construed his function narrowly, that he considered himself a follower, not a leader. In carrying out the superior judgments of his constituents, he wrote, "I but carry out my original pledge, to obey their wishes, whenever they be ascertained. I vote for them, not for myself." As the presidential campaign was in progress, Brown used the most effective argument against Harrison—the inflammatory and unfounded charge that Harrison was supported by the abolitionists and that he had heard that Harrison had given secret pledges to support them.[90] Little did he know what dynamite he was handling so carelessly!

Brown was not alone in taking an alarmist position. He signed for Mississippi an address to the people of the slaveholding States by the Democratic Republican members of Congress. This address complained that four Northern State legislatures passed resolutions favoring trial by jury for fugitive slaves, that votes were being given to Negroes, and that Congress received abolition petitions. An urgent plea was made that the South support the Northern Democrats as an alternative to destruction. Southern Democrats must vote for Van

[86] *Congressional Globe,* 26th Cong., 1st sess., appendix, 385–390. Cluskey, pp. 27–46.

[87] *Southern Star,* June 13, 1840.

[88] *Ibid.,* June 27, 1840, from *Charleston Mercury,* May 22, 1840.

[89] *Natchez Courier,* July 23, 1840.

[90] *Southern Star,* Aug. 8, 1840, letter from Washington, D. C., June 18, 1840.

Buren and thus "repudiate in a voice of thunder this odious and unholy union of Northern Whigs with the abolitionists. . . . Solemnly impressed at the rapid and alarming strides of legislative abolitionism," the signers were convinced that "the true course of the south is to reject and repudiate all connection, direct or indirect, with abolition and its allies." [91] The slavery question was clearly becoming the major political issue in Brown's mind.

In accordance with instructions from the Mississippi legislature,[92] Brown spoke in favor of Jacob Thompson's amendment to the general appropriation bill, which provided that federal clerks, attorneys, and marshals in the federal district courts in each State should receive the same fees as the corresponding officers in the highest State court receive. There was a peculiar fitness, he held, in leaving this regulation to the State legislatures because these services were worth more in sparsely than in densely settled sections, while litigants in sparsely settled States were least able to pay high fees. Equality of fees throughout the union was but "a system of legalised plunder." Fees were abstracted from the pockets of his indebted constituents into the federal treasury to build light-houses, harbors, and to make other improvements in the Eastern States. Mississippi, he claimed, had already been forced to pay five times her just quota under the tariff and land laws of the United States. Since these fees really affected the States unequally, they were unconstitutional, and he should expect this ill-gotten gain, wrung from the unfortunate debtor "to turn to shiny reptiles and to hissing adders that would besmear the vaults of your treasury with their filth, and sting, as with a deadly poison, each hand that dared to remove them." [93] This speech illustrated the dangers of extreme statements into which his bombastic style led him. It showed how jealous Brown had become of the rights, not so much of his State as of his section of the Union, and how quick he was to take offense at any action by the federal government which he thought unfair to Mississippi or to the South.

A month before he delivered this speech Brown had been renominated for Congress by his party,[94] but in April he declined because of financial embarrassment.[95] Indeed, for this year, he was assessed only

---

[91] *Mississippi Free Trader,* Oct. 16, 17, 1840.

[92] MS. Executive Journal, Governors McNutt, Tucker, Brown, p. 128, Feb. 25, 1840.

[93] *Congressional Globe,* 26th Cong., 2nd sess., p. 160.

[94] *The Mississippian,* Jan. 29, 1841.

[95] *Ibid.,* May 7, 1841, letter from Gallatin, April 24, 1841.

for a $100 watch and one slave.[96] But he did decide to run for judge of the fourth judicial circuit, and he defeated Judge Thomas A. Willis, the incumbent, by a majority of three to one.[97] Brown was the outstanding leader in the southern part of Mississippi and was considered by the chief historian of the State as the most popular man in the State.[98]

By this time Brown had laid the foundations of his later radical Southern nationalism. He had started as an American nationalist, for in the early 1830s Mississippi was still "a part of the Jacksonian West," and, experiencing the nationalizing influences of the frontier,[99] opposed the secession movement in South Carolina. However, the rush of settlers to the best cotton lands during the boom years when the Indian titles were being extinguished subtly changed Mississippi into a part of one of those sections which invariably became solidified into potential nations behind the ever forward-moving frontier. Thus, Mississippi was drawn more and more closely to the neighboring States to the east and northeast by the common economic ties of cotton and slavery, and this Southern section was fast becoming, potentially, a nation in itself.[100] We are interested in seeing how Brown became a leader in transforming this potential nation into an actual new nation.

But the South must not be thought of as a region having undiversified economic interests during this period. In Mississippi, as in other States, "speculators and combinations among buyers . . . usually forced the small squatter to abandon his claim on the good cotton soils of vacant lands or to sell and remove to rougher and poorer soils." [101] These poor whites in the South, "an original pioneer stock,

[96] MS. Mississippi Archives, Auditor's Series, G, No. 103.

[97] In 1843, when Brown ran for governor, Willis was again elected as judge (Cluskey, p. 11). Samuel Proctor McCutchen, "The Political Career of Albert Gallatin Brown," pp. 30–31, believes that Brown's "private interests" for refusing to run for Congress were only an excuse for avoiding the necessity of taking a definite stand on the issue of repudiation of the bank bonds and that the judicial position provided an ideal storm cellar where he would be safe from attack.

[98] J. F. H. Claiborne, *Mississippi as a Province, Territory, and State,* p. 433. Brown was married in October, 1835, to Elizabeth Frances Taliaferro of Virginia, who lived only five months after the marriage; in 1841 he married Roberta E. Young, daughter of General Robert Young of Alexandria, Va. Their first son, Robert Young Brown, was born this same year. (Cluskey, pp. 7, 11.)

[99] Frederick Jackson Turner, *The United States: 1830–1850. The Nation and Its Sections,* p. 213.

[100] *Ibid.,* p. 1.

[101] *Ibid.,* pp. 211, 228.

drained by the westward movement of its most energetic and ambitious elements," [102] formed a separate economic group along the foothills of the Appalachians and in the piney-woods regions of the gulf States. They constituted "the illiterate slums of the South." [103] In some States there were quite distinct, well-defined groups, living in significant isolation in districts by themselves. Buck defines this piney-woods area in Mississippi: "East of the Pearl River a barren section of pine woods formed a distinct portion of the state known as East Mississippi, the home of the 'hill-billies,' 'sand-hillers,' and 'clay-eaters.' " [104] Large numbers of these unfortunate people were physically disabled by the hookworm and malaria, and mentally crippled by illiteracy, "without schools, without reading, without contact with the outer world." [105] Morally, many possessed rugged virtues such as personal honesty and a rude hospitality, but their isolation, lack of cultural interests, and mental starvation made them subject to excessive emotional stimulation. We are not concerned with their response to this stimulation as expressed in religious emotionalism except to note in passing that it provided a powerful religious sanction for the defense of the slavery system, facilitated, as it was, by the use of proof texts from the Bible.

We are, however, directly interested in the way their economic and social condition aroused their emotions. Economically, the poor whites were superfluous as a productive factor. There was "no position that the poor white could fill that was not already being satisfactorily filled by others." [106] The existence of Negro slavery made work appear degrading for white people. Now, the fact that the poor whites were forced by their poverty to work brought them into direct economic

[102] Arthur C. Cole, *The Irrepressible Conflict,* pp. 38–39.

[103] Turner, p. 155. Paul H. Buck, "The Poor White in the Ante-bellum South," *American Historical Review,* XXXI, 46, calls the poor whites "the slum element of the South." 514,000 poor whites were illiterate in 1850 (Albert Bushnell Hart, *Slavery and Abolition, 1831–1841,* p. 74).

[104] Buck, p. 42. Hart, p. 73.

[105] Hart, p. 74. French Ensor Chadwick, *Causes of the Civil War,* p. 24. Mrs. Susan Smedes, in *Memorials of a Southern Planter,* p. 113, described the piney-woods people along the road from her father's estate in Hinds County to Pass Christian as "almost totally uneducated. They had but little use for money, subsisting on the products of their little patches, and cows, pigs, and fowls. They were frequently 'squatters,' living on government lands." Lewis Cecil Gray, *History of Agriculture in the Southern United States to 1860,* Vol. I, p. 483, spoke of the poor whites as "aimless, shiftless, utterly lazy . . . a definitely inferior class."

[106] Buck, p. 49.

competition with the slaves, many of whom were little below the cultural level of the poor whites.[107]

The poor whites, moreover, were extremely sensitive to the least indication of a paternalistic attitude on the part of the large planters. Mrs. Susan Dabney Smedes explained how her wealthy father, Thomas Dabney, was considered cold and haughty and was misunderstood and misjudged by the plainer classes in Mississippi, who, unlike the same groups in Virginia, aspired to social equality, and "resented anything like superiority in breeding." She narrated how two poor farmers disliked the services of twenty of her father's slaves at a frontier house-raising and at the clearing of a field "in the grass." The first service was considered "a serious offense to the recipient," and Thomas Dabney was invited to no more house-raisings. The following explanation of the resentment which these services aroused is very illuminating and helps us to understand the wide gulf which separated the wealthy planters from the poor whites: "The man said that if Colonel Dabney had taken hold of a plough and worked by his side he would have been glad to have his help, but to see him sitting up on his horse with his gloves on directing his negroes how to work was not to his taste. He heard a long time after these occurrences that he could have soothed their wounded pride if he had asked them to come over to help him to raise his cabins. But he could not bring himself to call on two or three poor white men to work among his servants when he had no need of help." [108]

This inferior economic position of the poor whites in relation to the planters made them all the more jealous of their superior social position in relation to the Negroes. Thus, the poor whites, who had least to gain economically by the use of slaves, had most to lose socially by the destruction of the slavery system, for then the actual economic equality of poor whites and Negroes would have been patently acknowledged. Meeting "on all sides an overwhelming distrust of their capacities," despised alike by the great planters and by many of the slaves as "po' white trash," they were, nevertheless, ready to defend the "peculiar" institution of slavery to the death.[109] The social self-

[107] Buck, p. 51, states that under the slavery system "the economic barrier between the poor white and the negro was weak and only artificially maintained." Cole, p. 39, expresses the same viewpoint. The poor whites would not "have been willing to toil alongside the slave, whom they thoroughly scorned, but over whom they could not always show a marked superiority."

[108] Smedes, *Memorials of a Southern Planter*, pp. 67–68.

[109] Hart, *Slavery and Abolition, 1831–1841*, p. 76. Buck, p. 47. Chadwick, p. 24, expressed this succinctly: "These people, however, were fiercely southern in

interest of the poor white was expressed emotionally in a bitter hatred for the Negro and a deep conviction that slavery was essential. Buck pointed out that northern and southern economists "recognized the strength and depth of the poor white's attachment to slavery. . . . To their undisciplined minds the possible emancipation of the despised negro presented social and economic dangers far greater than the continued superiority of the planter class." [110]

These anomalous economic and social conditions largely determined the political viewpoints of the poor whites and made it easy for agitators like Brown to fan the flames of discontent against both the wealthy planters and the Negroes and at the same time to instill hatred against the anti-slavery North. The poor whites found compensation for their low economic and social status in a passionate belief in the principle of democracy, which recognized their political equality with the planters of western Mississippi. They were most eager to assert their belief in the slavery system. Small wonder, then, that they were the prey of fire-eating demagogues, that "the politician who sought the votes of the poor white class would be keen to urge violent resistance to the enemies of slavery, to flatter the poor white by condemning the slave !" [111]

Brown, as we have seen, threw in his lot with these small slaveholding and non-slaveholding farmers of the eastern and southern sections of Mississippi. Finding that political shibboleths which appealed to the emotions often proved more effective than well reasoned arguments, he did not hesitate to play the demagogue by making broad, unfounded assertions. He was led to identify himself more and more with the State-rights, particularistic position of his constituents by his opposition to a national bank fostered by the "moneyed aristocracy." Of much greater significance was the fact that he had discovered the potency of the plea against abolitionism and was beginning to discern a group of Southern interests quite distinct from those of the North. In thus identifying the interests of his constituents with those of the entire South, he laid the foundations for developing his State-rights radicalism into the more comprehensive principle of Southern nationalism upon which he was to base his leadership of the radical secessionists in Mississippi.

---

feeling through the ever-present need of asserting the superiority of their white blood, which was all they had to differentiate them in social consideration from the lowliest black." Gray, I, 487, called them "the outcasts of Southern society, and even the Negroes regarded them as beneath contempt."

[110] Buck, pp. 52, 54.
[111] *Ibid.,* p. 52. Turner, p. 155.

CHAPTER II

Governor—Ardent Southern Expansionist

Brown spent the entire year 1843 in seeking the governorship. On January 4 he wrote a confidential letter to J. F. H. Claiborne, editor of the *Mississippi Free Trader,* in which he angled for support. While asserting that he was not and would not be a candidate against Governor Tucker, as he had told Tucker himself, yet he declared, "I will say to you, what I have never said to any man before and I say it in the most confidential manner—that Tucker cannot and will not get the party strength and in a doubtful contest against a popular adversary his nomination would hazzard (*sic*) the success of the cause." He added that many sterling Democrats in the East vowed to him that they would not vote for Tucker even if he got the nomination, and that, having recently traveled in Copiah and four neighboring counties, he knew that Tucker could not get the party strength in these counties. Brown was obviously seeking to undermine Tucker and prepare the way for his own nomination, for he expressed his willingness to run if "others are brought forward having no *greater* claims than my friends suppose me to have." [1] Brown sounded out Tucker and reported to Claiborne that Tucker would run only if there was an almost unanimous demand for him.[2] Already the Paulding *Eastern Clarion* had come out for Brown,[3] but Brown leaned most heavily upon the support of the editor of the *Mississippi Free Trader.* Claiborne himself was strongly urged by John D. Freeman, the attorney-general, to run for governor in case Tucker could be induced by his friends in the northern part of the State to become senator. "Tucker's place must be filled and I *know* that east and south would prefer you to Brown." Freeman suggested that four newspapers "might all be started on this *trail* in a short time. What do you say?" [4] Claiborne did not yield to this temptation to be-

[1] MS. J. F. H. Claiborne Collection, Vol. A, No. 71, letter Brown to Claiborne, Jan. 4, 1843.

[2] *Ibid.,* Vol. A, No. 72, Jan. 23, 1843.

[3] *The Mississippian,* Jan. 6, 1843.

[4] Claiborne MSS., Library of Congress, letter Freeman to Claiborne, Feb. 3, 1843.

come a candidate for governor. A week earlier the *Mississippi Free Trader* had stated that it was generally conceded that Tucker would not become a candidate for reelection and that Brown was favored, especially in the central, southern, and eastern counties, which it felt he could carry without opposition.[5]

Brown revealed his accomplished talent as a political manipulator in his next letter to Claiborne. He regretted that the nominating convention would meet on February 22 since he and his friends had felt that the unsettled political situation could be turned to his advantage by a delay to June 1. Brown planned to attend the convention, and earnestly urged Claiborne to come to aid him. "It will be highly necessary to have some old & experienced tacticians on the ground. We have a multitude of captains now & some of them very unskillful ones. Without men of influence & character are present (*sic*) to govern & controll in some manner the action of the convention, we shall have a stormy & disastrous time of it. . . . Your country never needed your services more than at this time. . . . You can do much, very much, in giving a right direction to things." In his last letter to Brown, Claiborne had intimated a willingness to serve Brown, and Brown was not reticent in indicating how this could be done. "If you were present at the Convention & my name should be brought forward, it might be in your power to serve me in more ways than one, by keeping down competition & by preventing an unjust combination among other aspirants. I shall have many warm friends in the Convention, but I know of no one possessing a sufficient amount of *skill* and experience to keep the *ship righted in a gale.*" Brown felt "the utmost delicacy in writing to any one" because of his understanding with Tucker that he would not be a candidate against him, but he expressed the greatest confidence in the aid of Claiborne, to whom he had "written more & said more . . . ten to one than to any other man in the state." Brown asserted that he would adhere "most religiously" to his private agreement with Tucker, and yet he urged Claiborne to write letters in his behalf to some of his leading friends who were delegates to the convention.[6]

Claiborne and his paper continued to support Brown. The *Mississippi Free Trader* stated that it was generally conceded that Tucker would not run and that Brown was favored, especially in the central, southern, and eastern counties, which it felt he could carry without opposition. This powerful paper supported Brown enthusiastically,

[5] *Mississippi Free Trader*, Jan. 27, 1843.
[6] Claiborne MSS., Library of Congress, letter Brown to Claiborne, Feb. 6, 1843.

praising him as "a gentleman of fine education, eminent legal attainments, a ready and polished debater, a stern and unflinching advocate of democratic principles." [7]

On February 23 the State convention met with two thirds of the counties represented.[8] Brown was in an excellent "available" position, since, as a judge, he had not been involved in the growing bitterness over the issue of the repudiation of the bonds of the Union and of the Planters' banks.[9] On the first ballot Brown received twenty-one of the sixty-eight votes cast, a plurality of four votes over Tucker, who had not withdrawn. Tucker now withdrew from the contest and Brown was nominated by two to one over Taylor of Hinds County on the eighth ballot.[10] There was great dissatisfaction with the convention because it sought to shelve all controversial issues: no nomination was made for United States senator, a resolution for Van Buren and Walker for President and Vice-President was tabled and, most important of all, the convention refused to commit itself on the payment of the Union bank bonds.[11]

The State's share of these bonds ($5,000,000), provided in the supplemental bill of 1838, had been sold in August of that year to Nicholas Biddle. In 1840 Governor McNutt repudiated these bonds because they had been sold below par,[12] a position which Brown also accepted in 1841 when the people voted to repudiate them.[13] The Democratic party was split into the factions which favored the payment of the Union bank bonds by the State and that which urged their repudiation. Volney Howard, a bond-payer of influence, sought the withdrawal of the Democratic candidates, for he considered the anti-bond-paying faction "low and beastly and in the way of every *gentleman*

---

[7] *Mississippi Free Trader,* Jan. 27, Feb. 9, 1843.

[8] *Ibid.,* Feb. 27, 1843.

[9] McCutchen, "The Political Career of Albert Gallatin Brown," p. 42. Brown had urged Claiborne to use his influence to prevent the extortion of a pledge from the candidates on the question of the repudiation of the Planters' Bank bonds because this exciting question would be sure "to create divisions & heart burnings if persisted in. It is not a legitimate party question. We are now upon high ground, & it will be madness to abandon it to follow the fortunes of this *will o' the wisp.*" (Claiborne MSS., letter Brown to Claiborne, Feb. 6, 1843.) A month after Brown was nominated and had expressed himself in favor of the payment of these bonds, there was complaint because he "was perfectly voiceless during the last canvass." (Claiborne MSS., Azel B. Bacon to Claiborne, Mar. 19, 1843.)

[10] *Mississippi Free Trader,* Feb. 27, 1843.

[11] *Ibid.*

[12] Joseph D. Shields, *Life and Times of Sergeant S. Prentiss.* Lowry and McCardle, *History of Mississippi,* p. 291.

[13] *The Mississippian,* June 18, 1841.

in the party." He urged John A. Quitman to become a candidate and endeavored to align the press in favor of paying the bonds.[14] Quitman refused to enter the contest, but a few days later Thomas H. Williams, a former United States senator, wrote to Howard that he would become a candidate as a bond-payer on an independent ticket.[15]

Another cause of dissension within the Democratic party was the feeling in the northern part of the State from which Tucker came that Tucker had been thrust aside by the Jackson convention in which eight northern counties were not represented, and another convention at Pontotoc was proposed to nominate him. It was charged that Brown would not have been nominated if these counties had been represented, although *The Mississippian,* edited by Volney Howard and opposed to Brown, admitted that ten unrepresented eastern and southern counties would undoubtedly have voted for Brown.[16] Brown refused to resign his candidacy in March,[17] but in May he yielded to the attacks within his own party and withdrew from the contest, urging at the same time the calling of a new convention, and insisting that the bond question was not an issue.[18]

The new convention met on July 10 at Jackson, and Brown, supported by the southern and eastern counties, easily won over Tucker, forty-seven to twenty-six, while Tucker was conciliated by being nominated with Jacob Thompson for Congress.[19] The *Statesman,* Whig journal of Jackson, charged that this ticket was prearranged by intimate friends of Brown and Tucker, and kept up charges until Brown categorically denied them.[20] On August 4 Brown published an address to the people in which he dubbed federalism as a monstrous political heresy and defined his own political creed in two words, "Madison's report," for he now considered the Virginia resolutions of 1798 as "the very quintessence of Republicanism." He took a most advanced liberal position by urging the establishment of schools "in which every poor white child in the country may secure free of charge, the advantages of a liberal education," and praised the enlightened population of New England as "a most striking commentary on the advantages of a free school system." But of more immediate consequence was his

[14] MS. Claiborne Collection, Vol. B, No. 91, letter Howard to Quitman, Mar. 1, 1843.

[15] *Ibid.,* Vol. C, No. 36, letter Williams to Howard, Mar. 17, 1843.

[16] *Mississippi Free Trader,* April 1, 1843, from *The Mississippian.*

[17] *Ibid.,* letter Brown to C. M. Price, March 20, 1843.

[18] *Ibid.,* June 5, 1843. *Natchez Courier* (June 6, 1843).

[19] *Mississippi Free Trader,* July 15, 1843.

[20] *Statesman,* July 29, Oct. 14, 1843.

repudiation of the resolution of the convention and his own former position against a commitment on the payment of the Union bonds by declaring that the bonds were unlawfully sold below par, thus relieving the people of the necessity of redeeming them by taxation if the bank itself could not redeem them.[21] Since the Union bank had failed,[22] the payment of the bonds by State taxation thus became the principle issue of the campaign, with Williams, independent Democrat, and Clayton, a distinguished Whig lawyer, both favoring the payment of the $5,-000,000 bonds held by the State.

Brown now had to face the charge of inconsistency in his attitude towards the State bank issue as he had to do towards the national bank question in 1839. He admitted that he had borrowed $150,000 from the Union bank in order to pay loans to friends, whom he endorsed lavishly without distinction as to party.[23] He wistfully suggested that all the Whigs he had endorsed who skipped off to Texas come back and vote for him, and he objected to his liberality, from which he had suffered so much financially, being made a means of wrecking his political fortune also.[24] Because Brown had thus taken full advantage

[21] *Mississippi Free Trader*, Aug. 4, 1843. Cluskey, pp. 50–54. F. L. Riley, *School History of Mississippi*, p. 245.

[22] Failure was inevitable. The bank issued loans on mortgages of real and personal property for twelve months, but the loans were renewable for eight years if the interest and one eighth of the principal were paid at the end of each year. The $15,500,000 bonds were to be paid in four installments in twelve, fifteen, eighteen, and twenty years. This arrangement required that $750,000 interest be paid each year from the profits (!) of the bank. As Lowry and McCardle remark, such financing "would have wrecked the bank of England. . . . Nothing can better expose the blind fatuity of the legislators of that day, or the mad, reckless temerity of the so-called financiers of the time." (p. 287.) Here was typical wild-cat western finance!

[23] Three years before, in 1840, Brown had owed the Union Bank $16,000, and endorsed for $50,647.05; his brother owed $11,625, and endorsed for $38,215.50; and his father owed $8,240.51, and endorsed for $33,561.79. (Quoted by McCutchen, p. 18, from "Legislative Report of 1840," reprinted in *Natchez Courier* Aug. 23, 1843.)

[24] *Free Trader*, July 26, 1843. Claiborne, *Life and Correspondence of John A. Quitman*, I, 164, gives us a vivid picture of the high cost of campaigning in Mississippi. "Candidates," he tells us, "were expected to indorse their 'friends,' to loan indiscriminately, to pay any price asked for entertainments, and to establish and support newspapers, besides sundry other outlays." McCutchen, p. 50, shows that Brown was such a campaigner and was accused of extravagance and of luxurious living. Brown's reply was characteristic: "I have never had many of the luxuries of this life, unless living in an obscure country tavern, and feasting on bacon and cornbread, dried herring and small potatoes, can be called luxuries. It would make a Stoic laugh to hear of luxuries about the little pine-girdled village of Gallatin." (Quoted from *The Mississippian*, Sept. 27, 1843.)

of the privileges of the Union bank, it was felt that he showed rather poor grace to attack its legality. Although voting against the supplemental bill which authorized the State to assume the $5,000,000 bonds, he had been a majority member of a committee of the legislature in 1839 which recommended that the $10,500,000 bonds authorized in the original charter be issued and voted for this issue even after it was vetoed by Governor McNutt. Brown was called a contemptible demagogue for running for governor as a repudiator, "after voting in the legislature for more bank charters, state bonds, and post notes than would shingle a meeting house. Go it humbug!"[25]

While Brown was being criticized by the Whig press for allowing his views to adjust themselves too easily to the changing popular opinion against banks, national and State, and was scorned as a man without acquisitions, cultural or literary,[26] the Democratic press of Jackson and Natchez supported him. Again the issue was viewed as a contest between the large planters and the poor farmers. The Whigs "court the favor of the wealthy nabobs of the old river counties," while Democracy will go among the humbler settlers of the North, and of the Piney Woods, and of the country in all divisions of the State, and from them it will receive support." *The Mississippian* saw no reason why Brown, a poor man, should not express his opinions against the bonds because he had the misfortune to be in debt to the bank. In any case, it pointed out, he did not repudiate *his* debt to the bank.[27]

That the people were vitally concerned in the banking issue is evidenced by the fact that nearly 4,000 more votes were cast than in the gubernatorial election in 1841. The people were clearly opposed to the payment of the Union bonds by the State, for Brown won a plurality over Clayton of 3,713 votes, while Williams secured only a handful of votes.[28] The *Courier* was convinced that Brown would have beaten Williams if the Whigs had supported him by one or two thousand more votes than he actually secured against Clayton and Williams together.[29] Brown had swept the poorer sections of the State, was the

[25] *Statesman*, Oct. 7, 1843.

[26] *Ibid.*, Aug. 5, 19, Sept. 30, Oct. 7, 14, 1843. *Natchez Courier*, July 26, 29, Oct. 3, 1843. *Yazoo Banner*, Sept. 2, 1843.

[27] *The Mississippian*, Aug. 3, 10, 1843. *Mississippi Free Trader*, Aug. 9, 1843.

[28] MS. Secretary of State Archives, Mississippi, Series F, No. 58. In 1841 there were 35,832 votes cast while 39,700 were cast in 1843, Brown won 21,035, Clayton 17,322, and Williams 1,343.

[29] *Natchez Courier*, Nov. 25, 1843.

acknowledged leader of the Democracy, and probably the most popular man in the State.[30]

Governor and Mrs. Brown were the first to occupy the present governor's mansion in Jackson, but proper arrangements had not been
made for their comfort. Thirty-one years later Brown, in contrasting
his governorship with the extravagant and corrupt administration of
Adalbert Ames, told of his first experiences in the executive mansion.
"Very little had been wasted on furniture for the mansion. I shall never
forget my first night in that house. My wife slept on a shuck mattress,
without sheets, and rested her head on a carpet sack. It was a bitter
cold night in January, and she used woolen garments as a substitute
for blankets. I remained in the Mansion four years and in all that time
there was never appropriated one dollar to furnish it. I did not ask it,
and would not have allowed it if it had been offered until the State
was out of debt." [31]

As was to be expected, Brown devoted most of his inaugural address to the State bond question. Although asserting that the people,
when correctly advised, will always do right and that their unbiased
opinion may always be trusted, he insisted that an act passed by a
majority of their representatives could not be legal if passed in violation of the State constitution. The representatives of the people have
no more right (under Article seven, Section nine of the constitution
of 1832) "to issue, or cause to be issued, bonds in the name of the state,
without first obtaining the consent of the people, than a man employed
to labor would have by indenture, to sign away his employer's liberty
for life." He felt the necessity of defending his position, not only against
the bond-payers within the State, but against "the extremely harsh and
unwarrantable attacks made on the state by citizens of other states, and
of foreign nations." By the speedy liquidation of the Planters' bank
bonds he believed that the State could show that it was not actuated by
mean or sordid principles in rejecting the Union bank bonds. He urged

[30] Rowland, *Mississippi History*, I, 634. See map based on MS. Secretary of
State Archives, F, No. 58. By comparing this result with the map following p. 21
of cotton production and number of slaves per male white poll in 1840, it is found
that the Whigs carried all the wealthy cotton counties of the Mississippi and
Yazoo River regions except Claiborne, while Brown won all the counties of
which there is a record in the eastern half of the State except Lowndes and
Noxubee in the eastern cotton belt, and the poor county of Perry which he lost
in 1839. The result was a sorry commentary on frontier standards of financial
honor.

[31] *Clarion*, Jan. 21, 1875.

new taxation of the rich by a levy on gold and silver plate, marble mantels, costly furniture and homes.

As in his address during the campaign, he made a strong appeal for free, common schools modeled after the New England system. Of greater significance for our purposes is his reason for the establishment of a State university because it illustrates his growing feeling that his State and section have peculiar institutions which must be jealously guarded. Young men must be discouraged from being educated in other sections of the Union, for they are likely to contract unfortunate habits and to grow up with false prejudices against home institutions and laws. The greatest menace to these institutions is abolition; the greatest immediate danger comes from England, which is seeking to acquire Texas and to establish abolition there. Brown warns his fellow citizens not to stand idly with folded arms "whilst Texas, and with her our own institutions are drawn inch by inch into the meshes of a wily nation that has never failed to do us injury." The South in self-defense must exert every energy to secure Texas in order to maintain that equilibrium in the Senate "so absolutely essential to the safety of our domestic institutions." [32]

The legislature enacted the administration program. A bill was passed incorporating the University of Mississippi, located at Oxford, but little progress was made in establishing a public school system.[33] The assignees of the defunct Union bank turned over the $5,000,000 bonds which were cancelled [34] and have never been paid—their payment, as well as the $2,000,000 Planters' bank bonds being specifically repudiated in the last two constitutions of Mississippi of 1875 and 1890, although complaint against this repudiation has constantly been made.[35] Brown had not been able to carry all of his party with him in urging the payment of the Planters' bank bonds, and yet much difficulty was experienced in securing the surrender of the franchise and the

[32] MS. Executive Journal, 1838–1845, pp. 416–425. Cluskey, pp. 56–66.

[33] Rowland, *Mississippi History* I, 636. Franklin L. Riley, "Life of Colonel J. F. H. Claiborne," *Publications of the Mississippi Historical Society*, VII, p. 200. Virginius Dabney, *Liberalism in the South*, p. 148.

[34] *The Mississippian*, April 17, 1844.

[35] This complaint has been particularly vocal in recent years on the part of the British and French Council of Foreign Bondholders, who have felt that the insistence of the United States upon the payment of the British and French World War debts has given them a stronger claim to consideration. Furthermore, the repudiation of Mississippi has repeatedly been referred to in the general discussion of the World War debts problem. See, for instance, the Jackson *Daily News* (July 23, 1929) and *New York Times* (Dec. 11, 18, 1932).

$47,000 assets of this bank as required by an act of this legislature. When the stockholders at Natchez refused to allow the commissioners of the sinking fund to surrender the franchise and to appoint a commissioner, Brown wrote a strong letter to Attorney-General John D. Freeman, declaring "these high handed proceedings unparalleled in the annals of Bank audacity," and demanded prompt and decisive action "as to the rights of the state, and the authority of these men openly to plunder and rob her," [36] and showed much irritation later in the year when legal action against the bank had been delayed.[37] But the anger and exasperation of Brown against this rich-man's institution was outdone by the Democratic Association of Jackson which resolved to "repudiate all banking institutions as in themselves inimical to human liberty; violative and derogatory to the constitution of the United States, not necessary for trade or commerce; corrupting and demoralizing to society; and odious to all republican institutions." [38]

The banking experience of Mississippi is typical of the finance of frontier States so vividly described by Paxson: "The development of social institutions provided a new financial resource for the pioneer at the moment of the great migration, and for two decades banks played a double role upon the frontier stage. Cast as the hero in the first act, ready and able to save the heroine from distress, the bank in the second act became the detected villain on the verge of strangling the confiding victim, only to be foiled as the curtain fell by the protective efforts of a new wave of fundamental democracy. Each of the parts played by the banks was inevitable; together they form a contrast that reveals much of the western spirit in its two phases of hopefulness and despondency." [39] By 1844 in Mississippi the second act ended in a fit of unreasoning despondency.

While Governor Brown was maintaining his popularity by his action against the banks, he was turning his State-rights theories into action in a contest with the federal government. The preemption law of 1841 had given 500,000 acres to Mississippi. It was found that 60,000 acres of this land were already claimed under article fourteen of the treaty of Dancing Rabbit Creek, made with the Chocktaw Indians in 1830. This

[36] MS. Governors Archives, Mississippi, Series E, No. 35, letters Brown to President and Directors of Planters' Bank, Feb. 23, 1844, Brown to Freeman, April 24, 1844.
[37] *Ibid.,* Nov. 27, 1844. McCutchen, p. 65, note 27, gives the interesting information that two years later Brown was able to secure $2,250 for the great poet, William Wordsworth, who had held $9,000 worth of Planters' Bank bonds.
[38] *The Mississippian,* April 10, 1844.
[39] Frederic L. Paxson, *History of the American Frontier, 1763-1893,* p. 228.

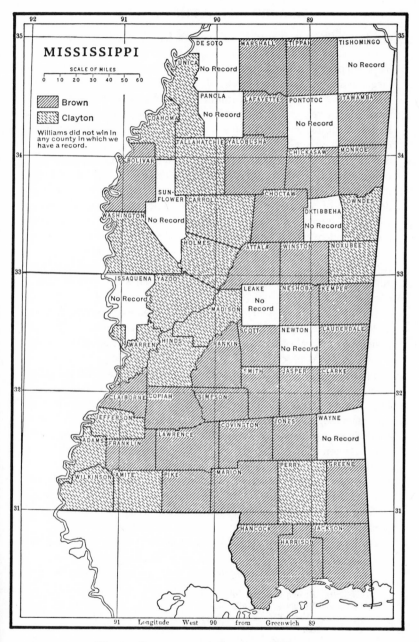

MAP 5. ELECTION FOR GOVERNOR, 1843

article permitted each head of a Chocktaw family who became a citizen of the United States within six months to secure 640 acres. As entry had been granted *after* six months, Brown insisted that the grants were illegal and complained to Thomas H. Blake, Commissioner of the General Land Office when Mr. Girault, the Federal Register, recognized these Indian grants and refused to register these lands.[40] Brown also sent a much longer and detailed letter to George M. Bibb, Secretary of the Treasury, citing numerous authorities to prove his case, and maintaining that the Indian was a mere catspaw for the white speculator, demanding whether the federal government "will give up these lands to the speculators in solemn mockery of her legislation and in derogation of Mississippi's rights." [41] He went further and employed Phillip R. Fendall, a Washington attorney to represent him, promising a liberal reward if he succeeded in establishing the claims of Mississippi.[42] As a result of this vigorous action by Brown and his attorney the decision of the register was reversed, and Brown sent an agent to superintend the registration, thus saving between $300,000 and $400,-000 for the State.[43]

During the summer a large barbecue was given for Governor Brown at Washington, Adams County, the old capital of the State. This occasion was typical of that indispensable political institution of the old South. A large procession of 1,100 marched to the open-air picnic grounds. After a salute of twenty-six guns—one for each State—felicitous resolutions were read by J. F. H. Claiborne. The Governor, hailed as the first orator of the Democracy, was introduced by General Quitman and, we are told, "charmed, thrilled, delighted, and convinced that immense audience for the space of two hours." After another flourish of cannon and a march played by the orchestra, "the social rights of hospitality and festivity" began. The pigs, which had been turning over the fires for hours, were served to 1,000 seated at the tables which were filled two or three times. After the dinner, there was more speechmaking for three and one half hours and the assembled multitude departed.[44]

At the end of the year the Democratic press in all parts of the State

[40] MS. Governors Archives, Mississippi, Series E, No. 35, letter Brown to Blake, July 1, 1844.

[41] *Ibid.*, letter Brown to Bibb, July 27, 1844.

[42] *Ibid.*, letter Brown to Fendall, July 29, 1844.

[43] *Ibid.*, letters Fendall to Brown, Sept. 26, 1844, Brown to Register at Grenada, Oct. 28, 1844.

[44] *Mississippi Free Trader*, Aug. 17, 1844.

rallied whole-heartedly to support the renomination of Governor Brown.[45] Even *The Mississippian* believed there was no dissatisfaction with his administration in any part of the State, looked forward to his renomination by acclamation, and doubted whether the Whigs could find a suitable man to oppose him.[46] But before the nominations were made Brown risked his chances of success by joining with Robert J. Walker, the master of political manipulation who dominated the national Democratic machine,[47] in a species of political jobbery entirely discreditable to him. On March 5, 1845 *The Mississippian* announced that Brown had appointed Jacob Thompson as senator to succeed Walker who became Secretary of the Treasury in Polk's cabinet.[48] At the end of April a letter of Thompson's of April 12 to Brown was published, stating that he had just received the appointment on the previous day, although he had been appointed on February 21, and the appointment was to take effect on March 10. Thompson made no complaint of this delay, but declined it.[49] It was immediately suspected that the appointment was "no doubt dependent upon contingencies . . . intended to preserve the ascendency of the democratic party in the Senate in the event of Mr. Walker's withdrawal." [50] Since such a contingent appointment was considered illegal, there was a growing demand, even in the Democratic press, that all the correspondence in the case be published.[51] In the meantime Brown was nominated by acclamation in July.[52] He refused to publish the correspondence until after his reelection by an overwhelming majority—the largest recorded up to that year.[53] Only a resolution of the State House of Representatives in January, 1846, forced Brown to produce the correspondence. It was found that Senator Walker sent in his resigna-

[45] *The Mississippian*, Dec. 25, 1844, quoting *Mississippi Democrat, Columbus Democrat, Sentinel*, and *Winston Banner*.

[46] *The Mississippian*, Dec. 11, 1844.

[47] Dodd, *Robert J. Walker*, pp. 20–23. Dodd, *Jefferson Davis*, pp. 65–66.

[48] *The Mississippian*, Mar. 5, 1845.

[49] *Mississippi Free Trader*, April 29, 1845.

[50] *Ibid.*, May 24, 1845.

[51] *True Democrat*, Sept. 3, 1845, from *Sentinel*.

[52] *The Mississippian*, July 30, 1845.

[53] Rowland, *Mississippi History*, I, 646. Map based on MS. Secretary of State Archives, Mississippi, Series F, No. 61. Brown won 28,310 votes, Thomas Coopwood, 12,852, and Isaac N. Davis, 1633. Although the official records for this election are even more defective than those of his first election as governor, it appears that Brown carried all the counties he won in 1843, and gained the Whig counties of Lowndes and Noxubee in eastern Mississippi and Jefferson, Yazoo, and Carroll in western Mississippi.

tion on February 11, 1845 to take effect on March 10. Accompanying this resignation was a letter written "in confidence of friendship,
personal and political *and for your eye alone.*" On March 4, he explained, there would be twenty-five Democrats, twenty-four Whigs,
and three vacancies in the Senate. If he were to withdraw to the
cabinet without a Democratic successor at hand to take his place, the
Democrats would most probably fail to elect a public printer. Therefore, argued Walker, it is imperative that Brown should immediately
appoint some one now in Washington. At the request of some of the
special friends of President Polk, Dr. William M. Gwin, later a senator
from California, agreed to accept the appointment temporarily "only
to prevent the defeat of Col. Polk's administration in the election of a
printer." Brown fell in with this scheme, but appointed Representative Thompson instead of Dr. Gwin.[54] However, he refused to accept
Walker's resignation till he heard from him again and admitted that
"nothing but the state of things in the Senate which you represent"
could have induced him to act. At the same time Brown wrote to
Thompson and suggested that he might not want to surrender his seat
in the House for a doubtful election to the Senate. In the meantime,
since the "contingency" did not arise, Walker did not send the commission to Thompson until the Senate had adjourned. Brown showed his
moral bluntness by seeking to defend Walker from any unworthy motive and in claiming, even in opposition to Walker, that the new commission was legal without the acceptance of Walker's resignation. Although the *Mississippi Free Trader* tried to whitewash both Walker
and Brown,[55] the *Sentinel,* the leading Democratic paper of Vicksburg, condemned the duplicity of Walker in the strongest terms and
claimed that Brown's popularity was gone and that "he has only to
thank his own double-dealing and attempts to conceal and deceive." [56]

[54] McCutchen, pp. 33–53, pointed out that Gwin and Walker belonged to the
faction which had favored Tucker for governor. In 1840, when Brown was in
Congress, Gwin had been very friendly to Brown and Thompson, and was closely
allied with J. F. H. Claiborne. He helped Claiborne to secure the *Mississippi Free
Trader* and appointed him a deputy marshal. (J. F. H. Claiborne MSS., Vol. I,
Library of Congress, letter Gwin to J. F. H. Claiborne, Feb. 1 and 21, 1840.) An
undated letter from Gwin to Claiborne in Vol. II of this collection, but evidently
written in 1848 or 1849, indicates that cordial relations between Gwin and Brown
had been restored. The author regrets that he has not been able to consult the
photostats of the memoirs of Gwin of his period of service as senator from California, 1850–1861, in the Library of Congress.

[55] *Mississippi Free Trader,* Feb. 5, 1846.

[56] *Natchez Courier,* Feb. 11, 1846, from *Sentinel.* McCutchen, p. 88, believed
that the Lost Commission affair made it inexpedient for Brown to seek the senatorship in 1847.

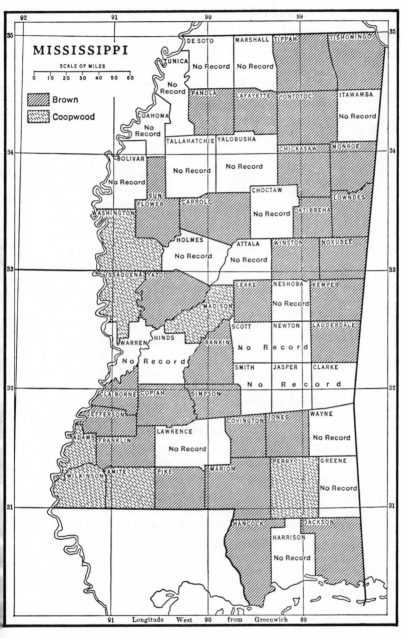

MAP 6. ELECTION FOR GOVERNOR, 1845

The period of depression following the Panic of 1837 was now passed, and Brown was fortunate to be governor during a period of general prosperity throughout the State. This prosperity was reflected in his annual message to the legislature in 1846. By careful economies the State debt had been reduced in two years from $614,743.84 to $271,707.07 and a surplus of over $100,000 was confidently expected for the coming year.[57] A few days later, in his second inaugural address, Brown defended the State against the accusation, made by residents of other States, of bad faith for repudiating the Union bank bonds. He was proud of the attitude of Mississippi before the world, "of the noble bearing which she exhibits amid the reproaches and contumely cast upon her," and lauded "the independence which marks her conduct regardless of the opinions and conduct of others." He made a fine plea that these charges of bad faith could best be answered by vindicating the State constitution, not only by not paying the Union bank bonds but also by taxing the people to pay the Planters' bank bonds.[58] Not so wise was the lesson he drew from Mississippi's banking experience, for it illustrates his proneness to accept an extreme position when difficult problems arise in which passions are aroused. While the recollection of the events of the banking mania was still fresh in the minds of the people he proposed to make "an enduring record of the hostility they have engendered to banks and banking; and to this end I advise an amendment to the constitution, forever prohibiting the establishment of banks in this state." [59]

By far the most constructive part of his legislative program was his concrete plan for public education. He had given much thought to this problem. Nearly a year before he sent circular letters to the governors of the several States in which he asked for the most detailed information concerning the founding, financing, controlling, and organization of schools in their respective States.[60] He also wrote to Lyman Cobb, the noted educator of New York City,[61] and invited Judge James Thacher to aid him in drawing up plans for Mississippi.[62] Brown now recommended that $200,000 be set aside as a permanent education

[57] Cluskey, pp. 66–82. Prices of slaves and cotton declined from 1837 to 1845, but steadily increased after the latter date. (Phillips, *American Negro Slavery*, diagram between pp. 370 and 371; also his *Life and Labor in the Old South*, p. 177.)

[58] Cluskey, pp. 87–90.

[59] *Ibid.*, p. 82.

[60] MS. Governors Archives, Mississippi, Series E, No. 35, Feb. 19, 1845.

[61] *Ibid.*, March 18, 1845.

[62] Cluskey, p. 97, mentioned in last annual message to legislature, Jan. 3, 1848.

fund, the interest to be expended for the State university and for ten high schools. But more important were the common, free schools, which should be under a board of school commissioners in each county, and supervised by State officers. He estimated that $75,000 a year could be granted from State fines and licenses to the counties which needed aid; he recognized the difficulty and expense due to sparse population in many counties, but urged that teachers be employed for at least three months a year—"if we can not do everything, surely it is not a valid reason why we should do nothing." Finally, he expressed his willingness to support any other plans which would give a reasonable promise of success.[63] Some felt that this plan would provide education only for the sons of the wealthy in the university and high schools, and that only a small number of townships which had a few sixteenth sections of fertile and well-timbered lands would set up public schools.[64] On the other hand, his scheme elicited enthusiastic support from some Whig quarters.[65]

But national, not State, issues were destined to dominate Brown's second administration and, indeed, his whole later career. As in 1836, when he roused to the highest pitch of enthusiasm his brigade of militia, in anticipation of war with Mexico in order to aid Texas [66] to secure her independence, so now he was eager to prepare for a war with Mexico which would retain Texas within the Union and add new territory into which Southerners could go with their slaves. As early as August 13, 1845, Brown wrote to Marcy, Secretary of War, a rather saucy letter, tendering to the United States, in case of war, "such aid as she may be willing to *accept* at our hands." Citizens of Mississippi who voted against the admission of Texas will be as eager to defend it as those who voted for it, he claimed.[67] Less than a month later John A. Quitman, as the oldest major-general of the State, requested Brown to put him in charge of any volunteers that might be called for. Brown promised to give him the first command, but informed him that Marcy "does not encourage the hope that Mississippi will get any part of the glory of the struggle if it occurs," and further sought to stir up animus against Marcy by charging that he would favor Texas, Louisiana, and Alabama before Mississippi.[68]

[63] *Ibid.*, pp. 71–76, Jan. 6, 1846.

[64] *Mississippi Free Trader*, Jan. 15, 22, 1846.

[65] *Natchez Courier*, Jan. 20, 1846.

[66] *Ibid.*, Mar. 3, 1840, from *Southern Sun.*

[67] MS. Executive Journal, Governors Brown–McRae, p. 9, letter Brown to Marcy.

[68] Claiborne, *The Life and Correspondence of John A. Quitman*, I, 223–224.

In his annual message to the legislature and in his second inaugural in 1846, Brown anticipated war also with England over the Oregon question. He felt certain that the war would be fought in the Southern States and urged that Congress be asked to grant alternate sections of land for the construction of a railroad from Vicksburg, through Jackson to the Alabama line as a means of speedy and safe transportation of troops and munitions of war. The leading Whig paper taunted him with accepting Whig principles on internal improvements,[69] but he sought further aid from Congress to defend the Southern coast with light-houses, arsenals, and forts and demanded to know if the Southern States were "strangers to the sisterhood of states, that our interests are thus neglected and our safety set at nought." Although believing in a thorough preparation for a war against England, he hoped it would not occur as it would "give impetus to New England manufactures, and open new and profitable markets for western produce" while bringing only blight and desolation to the South. Brown feared the political results of the economic cooperation of the manufacturing East and the agricultural West, but he did not seek to attract the West by developing manufactures in the South or to form an economic bond with the East by developing a diversified agriculture. He accepted the cotton-economy doctrines which the large Negro labor supply forced on his section, and declared cotton to be "the axis on which the commercial world revolves." [70] Indeed, two years earlier, when a J. H. Robb urged the cultivation of hemp in Mississippi, claiming that more could be raised per acre than in Kentucky, Brown feared the cost of production would be greater than in Kentucky and that short crops would be frequent. But these fears were subsidiary to his main argument: "You will, however, pardon me when you reflect what has been the policy pursued in Mississippi for ten or fifteen years—that of raising cotton and buying everything else." [71]

[69] *Natchez Courier,* Jan. 14, 1846.

[70] Cluskey, pp. 69–70, 89–90.

[71] *The Mississippian,* March 20, 1844. Brown was certainly not fully aware of the economic necessity which forced on the South this concentration upon the raising of cotton. Paxson, in his *History of the American Frontier,* sums up admirably the conclusions of modern scholars like Dodd, Phillips, and Stone on the economic results of the slave system. Since the Negroes did not have the training or capacities which diversified farming and manufacturing demanded, the planters were forced to enlarge the extent of the cotton kingdom in order to keep the large numbers of Negroes busy. The unfortunate result of this economic necessity is well expressed by Paxson: "The southern planter owned his slaves, but in as true a sense they owned him and bound him to a narrow repetition of unprofitable operations." p. 200.

During the early part of May, 1846, Brown was in New Orleans where the war spirit against Mexico was rife.[72] On his way back to Mississippi, on May 6, he sent a demand to the quartermaster-general of the State militia to have all arms and accouterments ready for immediate service, and made a plea for volunteers in case war should be declared.[73] Soon after the declaration of war on May 13, twenty companies offered their services to the governor.[74] Pleas were urgently made for more volunteers, and the energetic governor prepared for a draft, and appealed to the president to call the troops into the national service. Brown was much disappointed that only one regiment of infantry, comprising ten companies of eighty privates each was called. He informed the press that he had expected 2,500 men to be called,[75] but saved his wrath for Marcy himself, as he did not dare to condemn the Democratic administration publicly. He said that there was general dissatisfaction because only one regiment had been called, while three were called from the President's State of Tennessee, whose people were neither braver nor better, and which did not have three times the population of Mississippi. He demanded to know upon what principle Mississippi was discriminated against and asked, "Was it because we had shown any backwardness in this struggle? . . . We shall never rest satisfied until we know how it is and why it is that a part of this fight is transferred to Tennessee and other States." [76] Four days later he again appealed to Marcy that a regiment of cavalry be called,[77] and he urged upon Polk the appointment of Quitman as brigadier-general, as he had promised.[78]

In the meantime the companies were collecting at Vicksburg, but found that the federal government had not provided funds for their subsistence and transportation. Brown sent an urgent request "To the People" for funds, promising his utmost exertions to have it refunded by the federal or State government.[79] Again he expressed his real feelings privately—this time to General A. C. Bennett. He declared that the liberality of Vicksburg in subscribing $28,000 for the troops

---

[72] *Natchez Courier*, May 5, 1846.

[73] *Ibid.*, May 13, 1846, Brown to Major R. Elward.

[74] MS. Executive Journal, Governors Brown–McRae, p. 71, Brown to Marcy, June 7, 1846.

[75] *Natchez Courier*, June 2, 1846, from *The Mississippian* Extra of May 30, 1846.

[76] MS. Executive Journal, p. 61, letter Brown to Marcy, June 3, 1846.

[77] *Ibid.*, p. 71.

[78] *Ibid.*, p. 64, letter Brown to Polk, June 5, 1846.

[79] *Mississippi Free Trader*, June 4, 1846.

"contrasts strangely enough with the miserable halting and jotting and niggardly policy of the Government at Washington who with ten millions at its disposal has not sent us money enough *to mend a soldier's breeches.*" He hopes these gifts "may stir up the head of the War Dept. to a little effort at reflection if such a thing ever does reflect." [80]

While Brown, in his eager impatience, was berating the national government he himself was blamed for masterly inactivity and satirically commended for restraining the people in their warlike propensities. "Were he to come among us, not a cannon would be fired, as that would horrify him with an idea of a battle wherein some of his fellow-citizens . . . might get hurt." [81] Because it was impossible to accept more than ten companies, indignation meetings against Brown were held in communities whose troops were not received. The Jefferson County Volunteers went so far as to break out into song:

The Requiem of Governor Brown

Our Gov'ner has betrayed his trust,
He has disgraced our name.
And for his treacherous acts we have
Condemned him to the flame.

We found him in an humble sphere,
And honored him with trust;
But he has faithless proved, and we
Consign him to the dust.

Alas! let this hereafter be
A warning to the rest.
We love a brave and valiant man,
A coward we detest.

Now while these circling flames enclose,
His faithless, impure heart,
Let's give three cheers, three noble cheers,
Three cheers to Captain Clark.[82]

The Natchez Fencibles outdid the other disappointed companies by marching to Jackson to stage a hostile demonstration in front of the governor's mansion. Even the *Natchez Courier* deprecated their burning Brown in effigy and declared him blameless in not calling out the

[80] MS. Executive Journal, p. 65, letter Brown to General Bennett, June 5, 1846.
[81] *Natchez Courier*, June 3, 1846 (also from *Vicksburg Intelligencer* of May 25, 1846), June 10, 1846.
[82] *Natchez Courier*, June 24, 1846.

Fencibles, and Brown denounced their actions in the strongest terms.[83] A Democratic paper declared that one might as well "endeavor to stop the waters of the Mississippi as to screen A. G. Brown from the justly merited contempt of a free and spirited people." [84] But when the *Memphis Eagle* used similar language in expressing "shame, deep, burning and *everlasting shame* to her governor," the *Natchez Courier,* which led this insane war-mad attack on Brown, complained that it was not entirely agreeable to hear strangers attack the governor of Mississippi.[85]

After the first frenzied months were over Governor Brown was able to prove that he was not a slacker, but a leader in warlike activity. Immediately upon hearing the news of the victory at Monterey, he again wrote to Marcy to call for more troops from Mississippi, so that she would have her just quota in the field, and reminded him that he was under promise to do ample justice to Mississippi.[86] On November 27 a call was sent for another regiment of infantry by December 18 for service "during the war," and Brown seized this favorable opportunity to challenge the disappointed volunteers and congratulated them "on the present favorable opportunity of entering their country's service." [87] But now, it seems, the war spirit had cooled. Two weeks later Brown was forced to write to Marcy that it was impossible to have

---

[83] *Ibid.,* July 7, 1846 (also letter of Brown to F. L. Claiborne of June 26, 1846). *Ibid.,* July 22, 1846. *Mississippi Free Trader,* July 28, 1846. A generation later Frank A. Montgomery, who had joined this company, gave his explanation of the dissatisfaction against Governor Brown. "It was charged openly it was due to the desire of the state administration to keep a place open for a company from some other part of the state, which was always true to the Democratic party of the time, that Captain Clay's company was not mustered in, it being from a staunch Whig county." General Duffield at Vicksburg rejected Montgomery and another man from the company because they were under age. "Having thus reduced the company below the minimum, he promptly rejected it. We were all indignant, as were many prominent citizens, and it was decided to go to Jackson and lay our case before Governor Brown, . . . but the Governor was reported sick and could not be seen. . . . We did not get to see him, but we had a high time. Any number of speeches were made, and it was openly charged that he was keeping a place for a favored company for political purposes. There was great excitement and danger of personal difficulties, but happily these were avoided." (Frank A. Montgomery, *Reminiscences of a Mississippian in Peace and War,* pp. 12–13.)

[84] *Natchez Courier,* July 22, 1846, from *Hernando (DeSoto County) Backwoodsman.*

[85] *Ibid.,* June 24, 1846.

[86] MS. Executive Journal, Governors Brown–McRae, p. 104, letter Brown to Marcy, Oct. 6, 1846.

[87] *Natchez Courier,* Dec. 2, 1846.

the regiment completed on time because it was feared "during the war" might mean from two to five years.[88] On December 18 only seven companies were ready, and the time limit was extended to January 1, 1847. On December 24 the regiment was completed, and Brown reasserted his confidence that it would prove an over match for any three Mexican regiments and urged Marcy to send it "to that point where there is to be the hardest fighting." [89] A few weeks later he wrote in the same vigorous and aggressive vein, offering to have Mississippi fill the quotas of such delinquent states as Massachusetts, Connecticut, and Rhode Island, which hesitated because they feared an extension of slavery. "Mississippi entertains no such scruples and she will with great pleasure cross the line or do whatever else the Administration may ask in the vigorous prosecution of this just and righteous war," was Brown's proud boast.[90] In April Congress asked for ten new regiments from the country. When only one company was asked from Mississippi, Brown flared up again. It was a clear intimation, he felt, that Mississippi was slow in performing her duty, and was playing the sluggard in the war, and, considering it "an unjust imputation on the chivalry and patriotism of our people, injurious to our volunteers now in the field and unjust to our citizens at home, *I solemnly protest against it.*" He was most eager to impress on Marcy his conviction that the people of his State were at one in favoring and continuing the war until Mexico begged for peace and that they would respond as long as a man was left who could bear arms.[91]

But when five companies of infantrymen were called for in July Brown had to sound a less aggressive note. He wrote to Marcy that he expected them to be ready by August 25, but asked what he should do if he lacked one or two companies.[92] His fears were realized, and on August 26 he issued a second call and extended the time to September 25.[93] Another urgent appeal was sent out in October,[94] but by the middle of November only three companies had been raised. Brown was now weary and disgusted with promises to raise companies. Two counties now promised companies, but he complained that he had very little prospect of getting either. "About every other man wants a com-

---

[88] MS. Executive Journal, p. 121, letter Brown to Marcy, Dec. 12, 1846.
[89] *Ibid.,* p. 123, letter Brown to Marcy, Dec. 24, 1846.
[90] *Ibid.,* p. 132, letter Brown to Marcy, Jan. 11, 1847.
[91] *Ibid.,* pp. 154–155, letter Brown to Marcy, April 14, 1847.
[92] *Ibid.,* p. 176, letter Brown to Marcy, July 30, 1847.
[93] *Ibid.,* p. 190, letter Brown to Marcy, Aug. 26, 1847.
[94] Rowland, *Mississippi History,* I, 684.

mission and the intermediate ones care but little about going in any way." [95] No one could now criticize the governor for his energetic prosecution of the war. He was much praised even by the Whig press for securing permission for the returned soldiers of the first regiment to retain their arms, and for appointing its wounded commander, Colonel Jefferson Davis, a senator in place of General Speight who had died.[96]

Brown was urged to campaign against William Sharkey, a Whig, for Judge of the High Court of Errors and Appeals, but he declined, rightly feeling that he was better fitted for a political office. When F. L. Claiborne, in favor of Brown, declined to become a candidate for Congress for the fourth district, which included the southern part of the State, Brown sought the nomination, but insisted that it be determined by a district convention, and not by the State convention which formerly chose congressional nominees.[97] The convention met at Monticello, was addressed by Brown, nominated him by acclamation on the first ballot, and adjourned. Only one other name, that of Powhatan Ellis, had been proposed, and that was withdrawn at Ellis' own request.[98] But the ease with which Brown secured the nomination did not mean that all was to be smooth sailing. Almost immediately one of the strongest papers in the eastern part of the State, the Paulding *True Democrat,* edited by O. C. Dease, started a vigorous campaign against Brown which was, of course, eagerly seconded by the Whig press.[99] Dease claimed that the Monticello convention was quite unrepresentative of the people of the district, but was an ingeniously devised fraud made possible by the apathy of the voters. Col. William B. Trotter, who nominated Brown, represented Clark County, although he admitted that no meeting had been held to choose a delegate, and yet he cast the votes of Wayne and Jones Counties also. In other counties, a Mr. Learned had Trotter appointed a delegate by a few men without giving public notice. The *Natchez Courier* declared that the Monticello Convention "bids as fair to become as notorious for corruption and intrigue as any known to political history." [100] The Paulding *Clarion* defended Brown in general terms, but did not at-

95 MS. Executive Journal, Governors Brown–McRae, p. 213, letter Brown to General John M. Duffield, Nov. 19, 1847.

96 *Sentinel,* Aug. 12, 1847. *Vicksburg Whig,* Aug. 25, 1847. MS. Executive Journal, p. 185, letter Brown to Jefferson Davis, Aug. 10, 1847.

97 *Mississippi Free Trader,* May 13, 1847. *Vicksburg Whig,* May 18, 1847.

98 *Natchez Courier,* Aug. 4, 1847. *Mississippi Free Trader,* Aug. 5, 1847.

99 *True Democrat,* Aug. 11, 18, 1847.

100 *Natchez Courier,* Aug. 25, 1847.

tempt to answer any specific charge made by the *True Democrat,* which challenged Brown to rebut its charge of fraud.[101] A few days later at Paulding, Brown admitted that six counties were unfairly represented, but insisted that he still had a majority in the convention when he waived their votes.[102] In spite of this admission of dubious political manipulation, no Democrat could be found to run against him, and by October the storm had subsided. Even the *Natchez Courier* now admitted that he was an excellent fellow, and that, since "he came off triumphantly with the spoils, we suppose no one has a right to complain."[103] Neither could the Whigs find a candidate to oppose Brown, and Brown won the election with 8,115 votes against 491 votes cast for Quitman, who was not a candidate.[104]

Since our chief interest in Brown during the rest of his political career will be in his attitude towards the slavery issues, it is important to note his views while governor. We find him to be quite lenient in administering the State slave code. In two instances he remitted the fines imposed upon masters for "having more than six slaves quartered more than a mile from his residence without an overseer or other competent white person to direct and control." In two cases he freed individuals for selling spirituous liquor to slaves, although he insisted in one of these that it must not be considered a precedent because he regarded this offense "one of the most flagrant of all the minor offences: compassion has no place in my mind for a man who for a paltry gain of a few coppers inflicts the most serious injury on his neighbor's property and endangers the safety of society itself."[105]

As was to be expected, Brown was not so lenient towards the attitude of the North in favor of the Wilmot proviso. In a letter to William Smith, governor of Virginia, he praised the resolutions of the Virginia legislature which condemned the Wilmot proviso and hoped they would "check our Northern friends in their mad career and cause them to reflect before they force the South to the last extremity . . . and de-

[101] *Natchez Courier,* Sept. 1, 1847.

[102] *Ibid.,* Sept. 11, 1847, from *True Democrat.*

[103] *Ibid.,* Oct. 13, 29, 1847.

[104] MS. Secretary of State Archives, Mississippi, Series F, No. 65. The only effective opposition to Brown came from wealthy Wilkinson County where 306 votes were cast for Quitman and 303 for Brown. Although the Democrats carried the first three congressional districts, there was a large Whig vote in each of them.

[105] MS. Executive Journal, 1838–1845, pp. 460, 477, 478, 479. MS. Executive Journal, Governors Brown–McRae, pp. 109, 143.

fend our rights with those means which God and nature has placed in our hands." Although suggesting the ultimate use of force, his more immediate proposals were more mild. "We have not asked for partial Legislation to protect our labor, we have only asked to be let alone." He was quite sure the North would yield to this reasonable request. If this should not be done, he did not suggest secession, but only insisted that the South must be united in opposing any Whig or Democratic candidate for the nominations or election for President in 1848.[106]

At the beginning of his first term the State treasury was bankrupt, and employees of the State were paid with auditor's warrants;[107] in his last annual message Brown reported a net surplus in the treasury of $78,718.60, and outstanding auditor's warrants were accepted at face value. He again urged the necessity of a more effective common school law and recommended the establishment of a normal school. The last legislature had passed a law to encourage the manufacture of cotton goods, but the superintendent of a mill which had been established complained of the difficulties in selling the cloth except at a loss,[108] and Brown was not inclined to encourage this industry any further as he heartily favored the specialization in the production of cotton, as we have previously seen. On the slavery issue he took the squatter sovereignty position which had just been announced by Lewis Cass in his famous Nicholson letter. Any attempt of the free States to exclude the slaveholding States from full participation with their slaves in the territories "would be as preposterous as if the latter were to assume, through the agency of Congress, to establish the institution of slavery throughout such acquired territory. . . . The question in the territories, it seems to me, must be left, as in the states, to be settled by the people who inhabit them." If Congress can exclude slavery from the territories, "why may not the friends of slavery exclude such applicant until she admit and establish the institution of slavery?" Both alternatives, he claimed, were unconstitutional. And now his threat of secession is more immediate than in his letter to Governor Smith of Virginia. Should the Wilmot proviso be passed "our federal government will have ceased to be one of confederate states, and each member must assume its original, sovereign, and independent position.

---

[106] MS. Executive Journal, Governors Brown–McRae, pp. 155–156, letter Brown to William Smith, April 15, 1847.

[107] Cluskey, p. 13.

[108] MS. Governors Archives, Mississippi, Series E, No. 36, letter J. W. Wade to Brown, Nov. 25, 1847.

Whether we shall be forced to this extremity, depends upon the councils which shall govern at Washington." [109] That Brown was not more extreme than his party is evidenced by the unanimous resolutions passed by the Democratic State Convention two weeks later. They declared that territory must be secured from Mexico if the United States is not to admit itself wrong in going to war. The question of the introduction of slaves into the territory to be secured "belongs exclusively to the citizens of such territory—and that, if Congress should interfere it would be a gross violation of the constitution and dangerous to the existence of our glorious Union." [110] Backed by these resolutions on the supreme problem of the time, Brown proceeded to Washington to take his place again in the House of Representatives.

By this time Brown's particularist views, which we saw developing in his earlier career, were well formed. Depending upon the poorer sections of the State, he had increased his popularity during his governorship by his anti-bank position which appealed to their prejudice against a moneyed aristocracy; but it was of far greater significance that he was in accord with their growing consciousness that the South represented interests quite different and distinct from those of the North when he prevented the federal government from closing public lands from sale, when he struggled for Mississippi's full share in the Mexican War against a jealous national administration, and, more particularly, when he took the position that the South must prepare to defend its peculiar institution from the attacks of the more powerful, aggressive North.

Although Brown was an able and efficient governor, he appealed to popular prejudice and played the politician in his appointment of Thompson as senator and in his conduct of the Monticello convention in a way which made him a rather dangerous leader for the critical times ahead in which statesmanship of the highest order was demanded.

[109] Cluskey, pp. 92–105, document of Jan. 3, 1848.
[110] *Sentinel,* Jan. 19, 1848.

CHAPTER III

THE COMPROMISE OF 1850

Up to this point there has been occasion to mention Jefferson Davis only once—when Governor Brown appointed him a senator; but from this period their careers touch each other increasingly. During the critical years of the conflict over the compromise of 1850 they worked in harmony, but during the middle and later years of the 1850s, when Davis led the conservative faction of the Democratic party in Mississippi and Brown led the radical wing, their antagonistic temperaments prevented them from working together.

These differences in temperament and viewpoint can be partly explained by the sharp contrast in the earlier training of the two men. Davis was born in Kentucky five years before Brown; like Brown, he moved during early childhood to Mississippi. While Brown's father was poor and settled in the piney-woods county of Copiah, Samuel Davis, the father of Jefferson, settled in the wealthy county of Wilkinson along the Mississippi River and soon became one of the wealthiest planters in the State. Unlike Brown, Davis was given the advantages of a formal education at Transylvania College in his native State and at West Point, where he graduated in the class of 1828. He served in the army until 1835, taking an honorable part in the Black Hawk War in 1832. In 1835, when Brown was elected to the legislature for the first time and entered into the rough and tumble of politics, Jefferson Davis settled down to the more quiet pursuits of a gentleman planter on the estate which his elder brother, Joseph, presented to him at Briarfield along the Mississippi River in Warren County. During the next ten years Davis devoted much time to study and became a polished, cultured aristocrat.

In 1843 Davis emerged from his retirement, "a fearless and haughty spirit, proud to the verge of arrogance, but perfectly devoted, perfectly sincere," [1] and entered the political field. In the campaign in which Brown was elected governor, Davis ran for the State legislature as a Democrat, but failed because Warren County was a Whig stronghold. In this campaign Davis, representing the moneyed interests, re-

[1] Stephenson, *The Day of the Confederacy*, p. 32.

51

fused to be considered as a repudiator. He took a position half-way between the bond-payers and the anti-bond payers by urging that the issue of the payment of the Union bank bonds be left to the courts and not to the electorate, as Brown wished.

Two years later, in 1845, Robert J. Walker sponsored the nomination and election of Davis to the National House of Representatives.[2] He resigned the next year to lead a regiment in the Mexican War. After his brilliant military career was ended by a wound at Buena Vista, Brown appointed him to the Senate. Davis was rather surprised by the cordiality of Brown and acknowledged it graciously on a number of occasions.[3] Although there was some opposition by the Democratic press in the northern part of the State to the election of Davis to a full term to the Senate,[4] he was elected unanimously by the Mississippi legislature to continue in that position. The prevailing sentiment was well expressed by the leading opposition Whig journal: "Jeff. Davis has done enough for the State of Mississippi to entitle him to the Senatorship until doomsday."[5] Davis, like Brown, had already shown marked State-rights tendencies. He had refused to accept a commission over volunteers from President Polk because he claimed such an appointment could be given only by State authorities;[6] he looked with foreboding to the meeting of the Democratic National Convention, favored withdrawal from the convention unless the Wilmot proviso were disavowed, and felt that "it might become necessary to unite us southern men, and to dissolve the ties which have connected us to the northern democracy."[7] Like Brown, he had "the philosophy of state rights on his lips, but in his heart that sense of the Southern people as a new nation."[8]

Brown, "destined," as Cleo Hearon has recognized, "to become after Davis, the most influential leader from Mississippi in the slavery con-

[2] Dodd, *Robert J. Walker*, pp. 27–28.

[3] Rowland, *Jefferson Davis, Constitutionalist. His Letters, Papers, and Speeches*, I, 88, letters Davis to Stephen Cocke, July 15, 1847; p. 89, Davis to John Jenkins, Aug. 4, 1847; pp. 93–94, Davis to Brown, Aug. 15, 1847; p. 178, Davis to Brown, Oct. 24, 1847. The friendly relations between Davis and Brown at this time are shown by the willingness of Robert Barnwell Rhett to inform Calhoun of the political views of Taylor as expressed by letters Davis to Brown, Rhett to Calhoun, June 21, 1847 (*Annual Report of American Historical Association, 1899*, II, 1120).

[4] *Natchez Courier*, Dec. 16, 1847.

[5] *Ibid.*, Jan. 14, 1848.

[6] Rowland, *Jefferson Davis*, I, 86, letter Davis to Polk, June 20, 1847.

[7] *Ibid.*, pp. 95–96, letter Davis to C. J. Searles, Sept. 19, 1847.

[8] Stephenson, p. 32.

troversy," [9] took his seat in the House on January 24, 1848, nearly two months after the session had commenced.[10] He immediately presented resolutions and bills to secure new post routes and sections of public lands in the State and for improving rivers,[11] and on February 10 he made an extended address on the issues before the country.[12] The occasion for his speech was the Whig vote of censure against the declaration and conduct of the Mexican War. As we have observed in former instances, strong opposition led him to take an extreme jingoistic position. There is none of the carping against the conduct of the war which we noticed while he was governor. He insisted that the war "has been vigorously prosecuted thus far, for wise and proper ends; and . . . it should be so prosecuted, until we have the amplest reparation for past wrongs, and the fullest security that our rights as a nation are to be respected in future." His main concern, however, was not in defending the conduct of the war, but in justifying its declaration. It made no difference to him if Mexico claimed to the Nueces River because the Mexican province of Texas did not extend beyond it. So long as negotiations continued with Mexico, the United States had a right to consider the Rio Grande as the boundary because the Republic of Texas made that claim and to repel any hostile invasion beyond the Rio Grande. This, he believed, justified Taylor's occupation of Corpus Christi and his turning guns on Matamoros on the other side of the Rio Grande. Brown justified this provocative action by the United States, but strongly condemned Mexico when her army "came upon our soil [in the disputed area], in all the panoply of war, burning our houses, plundering and murdering our people before our face, threatening desolation to the country, and menacing our little army with a total overthrow." He taunted the Whigs with lack of patriotism for opposing heavier taxation to prevent "the merciless spoliations of Mexico," while this party at the same time sought to tax the poor man's necessities of life in order to pay tribute to "your lordly manufacturers. Take our property for the defense of our national honor, but do not plunder us to make a rich man more rich." This address was printed in the Democratic press of Mississippi and hailed as "a most triumphant vindication of the course of the administration." [13]

9 Hearon, "Mississippi and the Compromise of 1850," p. 33. This book completely supercedes the earlier "The First Struggle over Secession in Mississippi," by Garner in *Publications of the Mississippi Historical Society,* IV.

10 *Cong. Globe,* 30th Cong., 1st sess., I, 223.

11 *Ibid.,* I, 268–269.

12 *Ibid.,* I, 333–336.

13 *Mississippi Free Trader,* June 15, 17, 1848.

Brown, at this time in agreement with the majority of Southern Democrats, was not prepared to accept the radical Alabama Platform adopted by the Alabama State Convention. This platform opposed the choice of any Democratic nominee who favored either the Wilmot proviso or an interpretation of squatter sovereignty which would allow the people of a territory to exclude slaves from their territory.[14] But he did aid in holding up the immediate admission of Oregon as a free territory so that its admission could be used by the Southerners in bargaining for slave territories for the lands secured from Mexico.

On June 3 Brown took full advantage of the Oregon bill to make his first extended speech on slavery in the territories [15]—a speech which illustrates the main outlines of his position throughout the remainder of the long controversy. Although he believed that "there is not one man in Congress who desires or expects that slavery is ever to exist in Oregon, or in any other territory above 36° 30'" because nature had erected an insuperable barrier against the introduction of slavery, yet he felt it so necessary to use every available means to counteract the anti-slavery forces that he strongly opposed article twelve of the Oregon bill which extended the anti-slavery article of the Ordinance of 1787 to Oregon. He questioned the consistency of the North, so lately recovered from the "moral leprosy" of slavery, in taunting and jeering the South for its continued existence there, "seeing that they brought it among us, cherished and cultivated its growth, and finally sold it to us for gold and silver." The very fact that no power was given to Congress to extend the Ordinance of 1787 over newly acquired territory was "presumptive evidence that it was not intended to delegate to the Federal power authority such as is now claimed over the territories." Article four, section three of the constitution gave Congress power to legislate only for the territories as property, but did not imply the far greater power of regulating the political institutions of the territories. The Missouri Compromise, in extending the principle of the Ordinance of 1787 was "a fungus, an excrescence, a political monstrosity . . . the first, greatest, and most fatal error in our legislation on the subject of slavery." Since the South gave everything and received nothing, the compromise lacked all the elements of mutuality which render a contract binding, and it was, therefore, void.

Brown showed his inability to grasp the doctrine of squatter sovereignty. In his last annual message as governor a few months before,

[14] Hearon, "Mississippi and the Compromise of 1850," pp. 27–28. John W. Du Bose, *Life and Times of W. L. Yancey*, pp. 212–214.
[15] *Cong. Globe,* 30th Cong., 1st sess., Appendix, 645–649.

he had accepted the doctrine and had insisted that the question of the admission of slaves into the territories must be left, as in the States, to be settled by the inhabitants. But now, fearing that the inhabitants might take action against the slaveholders, he vigorously attacked the doctrine of squatter sovereignty. He insisted upon the sovereignty of the people *by States* and that no sovereign power to exclude slavery existed in the people of a territory. "The vote by which this foul wrong is consummated," he warned, "will unhinge the Constitution, and leave our country at the mercy of the winds and waves of popular fury." Mississippi, he was sure, "never will submit to a wrong like this; no sir, never, never, never!" Should this despotic power be used, "the tocsin will sound; the spirit of Washington will depart; the Constitution will pass away as the baseless fabric of a vision; anarchy will reign triumphant. May God, in His mercy, preserve us from such a calamity!"

Later in the session Brown elaborated upon the desire of the North to discriminate between slave and other property. When Schenck of Ohio claimed that the slave States had an undue and disproportionate influence in the House because three fifths of their slave population was represented, Brown denied the charge and complained because the other two fifths were not counted. Since over half the population of Mississippi were slaves, her political influence was diminished by one fifth. When Schenck pointed out that none of these slaves had a vote Brown replied that the right to vote was not the basis of representation in the House. Thus, Schenck represented all the women, children, and free Negroes in his district, none of whom had a vote, while Brown represented only three fifths of the Negroes in his district. But Schenck had a ready answer. He showed how Brown always spoke of the slaves as property which could be taken by the Southerners into a territory just as any Northerner could take any of his goods there; but now, when asked whether he did not represent three fifths of the slaves in his district as *property,* Brown was forced to admit that he was now considering them as *persons* also, for "at present they have a mixed character; they are property, it is true; but, then, they are *persons.*" [16] Brown, in his confusion was thus forced to admit the anomalous and paradoxical character of the slavery system.

Although accepting the advanced Calhoun theory as expressed in the "Alabama Platform," Brown was not yet prepared to act in accordance with it. Indeed, the character of Brown forms a marked con-

[16] *Cong. Globe,* 30th Cong., 1st sess., p. 1023.

trast to that of his chief prototype in Alabama, William Lowndes Yancey. Yancey, like Brown, was a native of South Carolina, born one year after Brown.[17] Both men started their careers as nationalists by opposing the nullification movement in South Carolina in 1833, and both became the leaders of the radical wing of the Democratic party in their States. But Yancey, true to his convictions, withdrew from the Democratic Convention when it refused to accept his Alabama Platform and refused to support Cass.[18] By refusing to sacrifice his principles for the sake of expediency, Yancey had the courage to risk his political life and to remain in the background of practical politics until 1860.

But not Brown! He not only supported Cass whose doctrine of squatter sovereignty he had denounced, but he voted at the end of the session of Congress to extend the hated 36° 30' line to the Pacific as Polk desired.[19] In the subsequent presidential campaign Brown canvassed his district energetically for his party during September and October, seeking to prove the existence of an alliance between whiggery and abolitionism in the North.[20] The voters in Brown's district were confused, as was Brown, by the doctrine of squatter sovereignty. It was not clear whether the people of a territory could determine the status of slavery while still under the territorial government or only when they formed a State constitution. As a result of distrust in this rather ambiguous doctrine, Cass received a small majority of only 298 votes in the fourth congressional district of Mississippi.[21]

Soon after the reconvening of Congress, many Southern representatives became alarmed by the attitude of the House in regard to slavery, and, under the leadership of Calhoun, drew up "The Address of the Southern Delegation in Congress to their Constituents." Although it was a cautious and moderate statement, aimed to unite both parties in the South, and recommended no action if Southern grievances were not redressed, only forty-eight of the 110 Southerners signed it. Only two Whigs signed—one being Tompkins of Mississippi. It was obvious that the South was not united in its opposition to the North, and it was not without significance that the only States whose representatives

[17] Yancey moved to Alabama when the poisoning of a spring killed his slaves and forced him into bankruptcy in 1839. Phillips, *American Negro Slavery*, p. 381.
[18] John W. Du Bose, *The Life and Times of William Lowndes Yancey*, p. 219. Brown, *The Lower South in American History*, pp. 117–118, 131–149.
[19] *Cong. Globe*, 30th Cong., 1st sess., p. 1062.
[20] *Natchez Courier*, Sept. 1, 19, 1848. *Port Gibson Herald*, Oct. 20, 1848. *Mississippi Free Trader*, Nov. 7, 1848.
[21] *Columbus Democrat*, July 7, 1849.

gave their undivided support to the Southern movement were South Carolina and Mississippi.[22]

On December 21 the House passed a resolution of Gott of New York asking the Committee for the District of Columbia to report a bill prohibiting the slave trade in the District.[23] Although this resolution was later rescinded, the committee reported a bill to prohibit the importation of slaves for sale.[24] Brown, a member of the District committee, pointed out that the bill was almost a literal transcript of the bill which he drew up and introduced into the legislature of Mississippi on January 14, 1837 and which became a law. This law imposed a fine of $500 and from one to six months in jail for importing slaves into the State as merchandise or for sale. It did not affect slaves in transit or slaves bought out of the State and brought in.[25] Such bills, he pointed out, had been passed by almost all the slave States and did not involve the question of the abolition of slavery. These bills had been passed because the border States of Maryland, Virginia, Kentucky, and Missouri were being drained of their slaves and there was fear that they would abolish slavery as the northern States had done—and at a time when the extreme South desperately felt the need of assistance from the border States. This fear was well expressed by Vernon of Madison County in the Mississippi legislature a few days before Brown's speech in Congress. If the emigration of slaves from the border States continues, Vernon declared, "we, of the extreme south will have aided in bringing about a catastrophe which not even the annexation of all the territory between our southern boundary and Patagonia would begin to remedy." [26]

Although Brown sought to prevent the emigration of slaves from the border States into the District of Columbia, he opposed the present bill because it forbade any citizens to leave the District to buy a slave for use within the District. He also opposed the abolition of slavery in the District, which had been proposed by Palfrey of Massachusetts on December 13, for he was convinced that such a policy would make the District a receptacle for all the free Negroes in the country. In the same speech Brown took occasion to justify the Southern Address. The Southerners "stood for protection against annihilation. . . . When a sleepless and dangerous enemy stood at our doors, we felt the neces-

[22] Hearon, "Mississippi and the Compromise of 1850," p. 39.
[23] *Cong. Globe*, 30th Cong., 2nd sess., p. 84.
[24] *Ibid.*, p. 216.
[25] *The Mississippian*, Jan. 20, May 19, 1837.
[26] *Natchez Courier*, Feb. 7, 1849.

sity of acting together. . . . So long as you keep up this pressure, these endless, ceaseless, ruthless assaults upon us, we must stand together for defense. In this position we must regard you as our enemies, and we are yours." [27]

On February 10 Brown replied to Hunt, a New York Whig who hailed the victory of Whig principles in the election of Taylor. Brown pointed out that Cass and Van Buren, who both opposed a national bank and other old Whig principles, got 152,000 more votes than Taylor. But Brown, as a political realist, insisted that the old issues, in any case, were dead—"summon the old issues if you like. Call them from their tombs of martyrdom. But let me tell you, the new ones will not down at your bidding." He chided Hunt with speaking about nearly everything *not* the issue and with ending seven minutes before his hour was up "without alluding, in the smallest degree, to the only question that *was* in issue—I mean the question of Free-soil." He charged the Whigs with a double-faced attitude on this one vital issue. Taylor was represented in the North as "a better Free-soil man than even Van Buren himself, and in the South as the very prince of slave-holders . . . all things to all men." Brown was resolved to face the paramount issue of slavery in the territories squarely, come what may. On the new phase of the problem which was now rising to the fore, that of admitting New Mexico and California as States, he declared he had reached no satisfactory conclusion, but he was inclined to counsel delay until they had a larger population, particularly of cotton, sugar, and tobacco growers who had not yet started on their journey.[28]

Although, as we have seen, Brown clearly visualized slavery as the paramount issue and expressed himself vigorously in warlike phraseology, he did not neglect other matters which concerned his constituency during the Thirtieth Congress. He succeeded in having the location of a proposed marine hospital changed from Louisville to Natchez and in having the appropriation increased.[29] He introduced a bill to require Congressmen to send public documents to all the counties of their districts for public use. The bill was lost, but Brown sent the *Congressional Globe* to each clerk of a county court in his district and to the newspapers, for which service he was highly praised by the press of both parties.[30]

[27] Cluskey, pp. 145–149. *Cong. Globe,* 30th Cong., 2nd sess., pp. 421–422.

[28] Cluskey, pp. 149–161. *Cong. Globe,* 30th Cong., 2nd sess., pp. 120–124.

[29] *Mississippi Free Trader,* June 15, 1848; Feb. 7, 1849.

[30] *Cong. Globe,* 30 Cong., 1 sess., p. 730. *Port Gibson Herald,* Jan. 5, 1849. *Mississippi Free Trader,* April 14, 1849.

Brown urged that liberal rewards be given to the veterans of the Mexican War and spoke in favor of a bill to give 160 acres to each soldier who had served for over a year. Son of the frontier himself, he wanted the land granted on the most liberal terms. If the government received what the land had cost to put it on the market he thought the government was amply compensated and should depend on other revenue. Seven dollars a month seemed to him to be a poor dole for a soldier. A small portion of the hundreds of millions of acres of land could very well be given for homes for the men who had won it all. Not only to the soldiers, but to all, he would give a free homestead. "To my mind," he asserted, "there is a national nobility in a Republic's looking to the comfort, convenience, and happiness of its people; there is a national meanness in a Republic selling a poor man's home to his rich neighbor because that neighbor can pay a better price for it." [31] Thoroughly understanding the typical frontier psychology, he had already introduced a resolution that the committee on public lands be instructed to inquire into the expediency of graduating the prices of public lands, and that after July 1, 1849, there should be a reduction each year of twelve and one half cents for all land unsold after five years "and all lands not sold within twelve months after the price is reduced to twelve and one half cents per acre, should be relinquished to the States within which they lie, respectively, for the purposes of education: Provided, That no fee or reward shall be paid by or accepted from any pupil for tuition at a school supported in whole or in part by the lands thus relinquished." [32]

Brown constantly gauged his policies so as to appeal to the poorer classes among his constituents. His radical and aggressive attitude on the slavery issue did not antagonize the poor whites who had little property to lose by a conflict between the sections, while his aggressive defence of slavery made a particularly powerful appeal to those very classes whose social status would be most endangered if the Negroes were set free, and his advocacy of cheap lands and of free, popular education appealed directly to the personal interests of the "pineywoods boys." Brown himself made no special attempt to attract the wealthy Whig planters in the western part of his district. With their property at stake, they feared a conflict with the North and sought security in a conservative and conciliatory policy. Indeed, he thought of the Whig party as distinctly the party of wealth. Their motto, he de-

[31] *Cong. Globe,* 30 Cong., 1 sess., Appendix, p. 547.
[32] *Cong. Globe,* 30 Cong., 1 sess., p. 505.

clared, "has always been, Let the government take care of the rich, and the rich will take care of the poor." [33]

And his constituency responded to this appeal. The general attitude towards Brown was rather naively expressed in a letter in the *Mississippi Free Trader* urging his renomination for the next Congress. "He is entirely a self-made man . . . unaided by *wealth* and *royal blood.*" He is not supported by *"big* men, royal ancestors or the aristocrats of the land. Against these he has had to contend all his life. His friend has always been the farmer—the laborer—the working man—the poor man. . . . In social life he is a kind, clever man—feels at home with all, and looks upon every respectable man as his equal." In the same issue the *Mississippi Free Trader* urged his renomination, declaring that no man would represent the interests of the farming and working class more faithfully or more ably.[34] Democratic county meetings strongly endorsed Brown,[35] and no one could be found to oppose him, although a number of leaders were suggested.[36]

The Democratic Convention of the fourth congressional district met at Monticello on June 26 and resolved, "That our confidence in the principles of the democratic party is undiminished and that we are more than ever convinced that the true prosperity of the country is to be secured only by their success." Brown was renominated without a dissenting vote.[37] Even O. C. Dease, who so strongly opposed Brown for packing the convention in 1847, was a delegate and supported Brown.[38] His renomination was hailed as usual, as a victory for the poorer classes. In his speech of acceptance Brown expressed his conviction that both houses of Congress would pass the Wilmot proviso and that Taylor would sign it.[39] His own congressional activity was lauded, and he was hailed in the Democratic press as "more zealously devoted to the interest of the South and Southern institutions than any man in the House of Representatives" and as "universally acknowledged . . . the best Representative we have ever had." [40]

[33] Cluskey, p. 161.

[34] *Mississippi Free Trader,* March 24, 1849.

[35] Jasper County (*Natchez Courier,* April 11, 1849), Clark County (*Columbus Democrat,* April 21, 1849), Adams County (*Mississippi Free Trader,* May 9, 1849).

[36] General Cooper, General Stanton, J. J. McRae, J. F. H. Claiborne (*Mississippi Free Trader,* May 9, 1849).

[37] *Mississippi Free Trader,* June 30, 1849.

[38] *Natchez Courier,* April 11, 1849.

[39] *Mississippi Free Trader,* July 25, 1849.

[40] *Ibid.,* July 25, Aug. 1, 1849, from *Free Press.*

Even the Whig press was not unfriendly. Indeed, the Whigs had the greatest difficulty in securing a man to oppose Brown. Colonel Alonzo G. Mayers of Jasper County was suggested,[41] but he declined in August.[42] It was not until the end of August that a candidate—and a most interesting one—was found. It was the Rev. Dr. William Winans of Wilkinson County, an eminent slaveholding Methodist minister who had taken a major part in securing the secession of the Methodist Episcopal Church, South, in 1844. In the New York General Conference of that year he had been the first to openly threaten the secession of the Southern Methodists if Bishop James O. Andrew were asked to resign because he was a slaveholder. He was a member of the first and second committees of nine which drew up the Plan of Separation, and he called to order the first General Conference of the Methodist Episcopal Church, South, at Petersburg, Va., in 1846. Here, indeed, was a worthy pro-slavery antagonist for Brown.[43]

Brown canvassed his district vigorously,[44] even throwing himself open for the first time to the charge of a tendency towards disunion sentiments,[45] but Dr. Winans, because of his clerical position, did not take the stump. The Whigs hailed Dr. Winans as a worthy "champion of the honor and interests of the South, understanding fully our rights, appreciating properly our condition and knowing thoroughly the motive and nature of the assaults upon the South." They took courage and hoped to wipe out the narrow Democratic majority of 298 of the previous year and to send Brown outside the fourth district where they felt he belonged, to the plantation he had just bought near Terry, Hinds County, in the third district.[46]

But a flaw was found in the loyalty of Dr. Winans to the South. In 1846 before the Colonization Society in New York he had admitted that slavery was a great social evil. He now explained that he did not mean that slavery was a *moral* evil or sin, that sudden freedom would be worse than slavery, that he but followed Wash-

---

[41] *Southron*, July 20, 1849. *Natchez Courier*, July 25, 1849.

[42] *Natchez Courier*, Aug. 15, 1849.

[43] J. M. Buckley, *A History of Methodists in the United States*, pp. 416–417, 432–433, 442–443, 693–697. Alexander Gross, *A History of the Methodist Church, South*, pp. 29–32, 44. John Nelson Norwood, *The Schism in the Methodist Episcopal Church, 1844*, pp. 60, 80, 83–84.

[44] *Natchez Courier*, Sept. 5, 1849. *Mississippi Free Trader*, Sept. 1, 1849. *Southron*, Sept. 21, 1849.

[45] *Port Gibson Herald*, Sept. 7, 1849.

[46] *Southron*, Sept. 21, 1849. *Natchez Courier*, Sept. 26, 1849.

ington, Jefferson, and Cass, in thinking slavery an evil, and that he had been known since 1824 in the North as an uncompromising advocate and defender of Southern rights. He believed that the federal government had no right to legislate concerning slave property in the territories or with respect to the slave trade between the States or in the District of Columbia, and he wanted to see all free Negroes removed to Africa.[47]

But so far had his district been committed to slavery as a positive good and so critical was the position of slavery felt to be that all his explanations did not prevent Dr. Winans from being classed with the Northerners who "inspire our slaves with the hope of freedom and thereby incite them to rebellion," and even many Whigs felt it would be imprudent if not dangerous to elect him.[48] In the election Brown carried every county except the three wealthy river counties of Jefferson, Adams, and Wilkinson. The *Mississippi Free Trader* was filled with amazement at the overwhelming majority Brown received,[49] and "his bold and manly vindication of their rights" was compared with "the uncertain policy of Parson Winans." [50]

In the meantime, on May 7, 1849, a bi-partisan meeting in Jackson, led by Chief Justice Sharkey and Jefferson Davis, had expressed the Southern grievances and had called a State convention for October. The resolutions were moderate, and declared, "We meet not to agitate—not to act; but to prepare for action when the occasion may be forced upon us." [51] The bi-partisan State convention met in October, called a convention of the Southern States to meet at Nashville on the first Monday in June, 1850,[52] and issued an address which was "the first formal expression in Mississippi looking to secession as a final resort in defense of slavery." [53] Although the two parties seemed to be united in defense of Southern rights, the

---

[47] *Southron,* Sept. 28, 1849, letter of Dr. Winans, Sept. 17, 1849. Also in *Natchez Courier,* Sept. 26, 1849.

[48] *Mississippi Free Trader,* Oct. 20, 27, 1849.

[49] *Ibid.,* Nov. 10, 1849. Map based on MS. Secretary of State Archives, Mississippi, Series F, No. 68. Brown secured 8,000 votes, Winans 3,906. The Democratic majority of 289 was increased to 4,094. Brown won the fourth river county, Claiborne, by only two votes, 392 over 390.

[50] *Columbus Democrat,* Dec. 8, 1849.

[51] Hearon, "Mississippi and the Compromise of 1850," pp. 46–48.

[52] *Natchez Courier,* Oct. 10, 1849.

[53] Hearon, "Mississippi and the Compromise of 1850," pp. 63–68. "Address of the Committee of the Mississippi Convention to the Southern States 1849," pamphlet, Library of Congress.

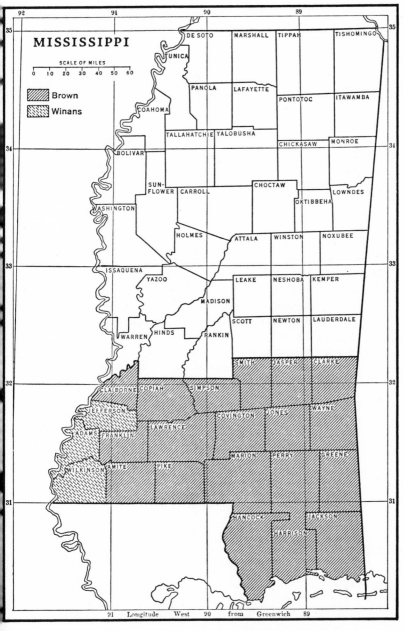

MAP 7. ELECTION IN THE FOURTH CONGRESSIONAL DISTRICT FOR THE
HOUSE OF REPRESENTATIVES, NOVEMBER, 1849

Democrats took the more extreme position and elected Quitman as governor, all the representatives in Congress, and an overwhelming majority in both houses of the State legislature.

The famous Thirty-first Congress started with a prolonged contest over the speakership in which the free-soilers held the balance of power. Brown followed his fellow Democrats in voting for Howell Cobb of Georgia, and then for W. J. Brown of Indiana until it was found that he had bargained with Wilmot over committee appointments.[54] A. G. Brown then offered a resolution declaring Cobb speaker. He was a Democrat who had refused to sign Calhoun's Address of the previous January and so was considered a compromise nominee and was finally elected on December 23, but only after a rule had been passed allowing election by plurality vote.[55]

The next day President Taylor announced that California was about to seek admission into the union as a State. The people had already drawn up their State constitution which excluded slavery. The California issue was the one problem on which the October convention in Mississippi had not been able to unite. A majority report had declared against admission as a free State, but such a strong minority report [56] was drawn up by three leading Whigs, Thomas Dabney, George Winchester, and John I. Guion that no statement on the issue was made in the final resolutions. On January 21, 1850, all the senators and representatives from Mississippi sent a joint letter to Governor Quitman asking for "such expression of opinion by the legislature, the Governor, and if practicable, by the people, as shall clearly indicate the course which Mississippi shall deem it her duty to pursue in this emergency." They expressed their own viewpoint, however, that "the proposition to admit California, as a State, under all the circumstances of her application" was "an attempt to adopt the Wilmot proviso in another form." [57]

[54] *Mississippi Free Trader,* Oct. 20, 27, 1849.

[55] Du Bose, p. 240. Hearon, "Mississippi and the Compromise of 1850," pp. 75–76.

[56] This minority report illustrated the more conservative attitude of the Whigs. The question of California, they insisted, had not been presented to the people of Mississippi or of any other slave State. They had doubts whether the Southern people would object to the admission of California. In any case, they believed that the majority report, which stated that the admission of California would be a fraud upon the slave States, would weaken the effect of the resolutions as a whole, and would "place the slave states upon a less lofty attitude of clear and indisputable right." (Hearon, "Mississippi and the Compromise of 1850," pp. 66–67.)

[57] Hearon, "Mississippi and the Compromise of 1850," pp. 76–77. *Southron,* Feb. 15, 1850.

But Brown did not wait for further instructions. On January 30 he made an extreme, fire-eating speech in which he claimed that "the fibres of the great cord which unites us as one people are giving way, and that we are fast merging to ultimate and final disruption." He showed no spirit of compromise. He had passed clearly beyond the doctrine of State-rights to the more comprehensive doctrine of Southern nationalism. He fully identified the interests and rights of Mississippi with those of the South. The South favored unrestrained extension of slavery in the territories; the North was committed to restraining slavery. These were positions "from which one or the other must recede, or a conflict, dangerous to liberty and fatal to the Union, will certainly ensue." The South did not interfere when the Northern States emancipated their slaves, but the North has been disturbing the peace of the South by attacking slavery for twenty years. Long years of outrage upon the feelings of the South and disregard of their rights had awakened in every Southern heart a feeling of stern resistance. Brown warned the North not to entertain the delusion that the South was not in earnest. "If the North embrace it the Union is gone," he cried, for the South "will resist your authority, and to the last extremity." So far did Brown extend the doctrine of State sovereignty as to insist that the United States was a mere agent for the States, holding certain of their political powers in trust. More concretely, Brown held that there could be no people of the United States because the people had political existence only as citizens of a particular State, and that, 'technically, the United States as such did not acquire the new territory from Mexico.[58]

Just a little over a week before, the leading Democratic paper in Brown's district had made the statement, quite extraordinary as late as 1850, that "the evil, the wrong of slavery is admitted by every enlightened man in the Union." [59] But not Brown! "For myself," he continued, "I regard slavery as a great moral, social, political, and religious blessing—a blessing to the slave and a blessing to the master." The imagination, by its utmost stretch, could hardly "measure the elevation to which the Southern slave stands above the African in his native jungle . . . a race of cannibals, roasting, eating men as we do swine and cattle." The South, with its exports of rice, cotton, and tobacco, produced by this slave labor, exceeded the ex-

[58] Cluskey, pp. 162–164. *Cong. Globe,* 31st Cong., 1st sess., pp. 257–261.
[59] *Mississippi Free Trader,* Jan. 19, 1850.

ports of the North, and, with its internal exports to Northern States, nearly equaled the entire national exports. This favorable economic situation meant that the South need not fear dissolution from a Union which no longer challenged devotion as it did before the era of Northern aggression, for "as a separate independent confederacy we should have the heaviest agricultural export of any people on the face of the earth." The whole civilized world may be opposed to Southern slavery, but an independent South need not fear foreign disfavor. "We know how much British commerce and British labor depend for subsistence on our cotton. . . . When the looms stop, labor will stop, ships will stop, commerce will stop, bread will stop. England will not interfere with southern slaves. Our cotton bags are our bonds of peace." Brown's thought even proceeded a step further to consider the probable attitude of the North towards an independent South. He was convinced that the North would be only too glad to be rid of the troublesome South, but warned the North to make all things ready if it wanted a fight.

And yet, despite all the extreme language he had used, Brown denied that he harbored sentiments of disunion. He did not favor immediate disunion even if the North succeeded in excluding slavery from the territories or in abolishing slavery or the slave trade in the District of Columbia. These actions would be only the initial steps which would lead to the mastery of the North over the South; *later* steps of aggression would lead to disunion and the creation of an independent Southern nation.

Finally, Brown turned to the immediate issue of the admission of California. He considered the California constitution "unwise, unpatriotic, sectional in its tendencies, insulting to the South, and in the last degree despicable." He condemned President Taylor for sending General Riley to California to secure delegates for a convention for which he claimed slaves, Mexicans, foreign adventurers and interlopers voted. Only Congress had the authority to authorize a convention, and this Congress had refused to do. The President was simply aiding the North to reach its ultimate goal of securing a two thirds majority of free States. Brown suggested that an adjournment be forced without the admission of California and that the Nashville Convention then devise means for vindicating the rights of the South. He hoped this convention would urge slaveholders to carry their slaves "into all of southern California, as the property of sovereign states, and there hold them, as we have a right to do; and if molested, defend them, as is both our right and duty. We ask you to give us our rights by *Non-Intervention;* if you refuse, I am for taking them by *Armed Occupation."* [60] With this threat he ended this fiery speech. Surely there was little hope of peaceful settlement of the slavery question if Brown's counsels prevailed.

By this speech Brown definitely placed himself in the company of Toombs of Georgia, Colcock of South Carolina, and Clingman of North Carolina as the leading Southern fire-eaters in the House of Representatives.[61] The *Mississippi Free Trader* praised the speech in the highest terms, declaring that "not a man imbued with one spark of Southern feeling but would feel a rush of blood to his heart at Governor Brown's challenge to the invaders." [62] On the other hand, the *Natchez Courier* clearly presaged the coming conflict in Mississippi by declaring, "If he imagines that the voters of the fourth Congressional District of Mississippi will sanction his treasonable calculations he is as badly mistaken as it is possible for any man to be. . . . If Governor Brown's constituents have made any calculations about the Union at all, it is to defend and perpetuate it. They know its value to be priceless—to be incalculable, and they are determined to maintain it." [63]

In February Brown was undeceived as to the position of Cass on the squatter sovereignty issue and unhesitatingly turned against the Democratic standard-bearer of the last presidential election. He confessed that he had interpreted the Nicholson letter as allowing the people of a territory to decide for or against slavery only when admitted as a State with some misgivings, but now he found Cass sustaining the people of California and claiming that they could even exclude slavery while still a territory. This latter doctrine, Brown declared, "though he might stand alone, without one other southern representative to sustain him, he would protest against . . . to the last." [64]

In the meantime, the legislature of Mississippi did not give the Mississippi senators and representatives the unequivocal guidance on the California issue which they had asked for. The joint standing Committee on Federal and State Relations presented resolutions

[60] *Cong. Globe,* 31st Cong., 1st sess., p. 261 ff. Cluskey, pp. 164–176. Henry Wilson, *The Rise and Fall of the Slave Power,* II, 224.
[61] Hearon, "Mississippi and the Compromise of 1850," pp. 76, 104.
[62] *Mississippi Free Trader,* March 23, 1850.
[63] *Natchez Courier,* April 10, 1850.
[64] Cluskey, pp. 177–178. *Cong. Globe,* 31st Cong. 1st sess., pp. 336–337.

which reaffirmed the position of the October convention, and, like that convention, omitted any expression of opinion about California. However, when the request of the Mississippi delegation in Congress was received, it was impossible longer to evade the issue. Although Governor Matthews, in his farewell address, spoke against the admission of California,[65] the new legislature, in spite of being overwhelmingly Democratic in both houses,[66] did not instruct the Mississippi delegation in Congress to oppose the California bill. Instead of accepting their view that it represented the Wilmot proviso in another form, the legislature took the evasive and ambiguous attitude of instructing them to resist the admission of California if they had reliable evidence that fraud and improper influences had been used in the election.

The Whigs, as usual, were more conservative. Five Whigs presented a minority report from the joint standing Committee on Federal and State Relations in which they favored the admission of California and denied that her constitution presented the Wilmot proviso in another form.

It was clear that the Whigs were not strongly opposed to the admission of California and that the Democratic party was not ready to commit itself to resistance to the admission of California, although its representatives in the legislature appropriated $220,000 to pay the expenses of the delegates to the Nashville convention and to be used, if necessary, to defend the State. Indeed, large meetings were held in Jackson and in Natchez to praise the position of Cass and to declare that "the clause of the Constitution of California prohibiting the domestic relation of slavery should form no obstacle to her admission and that we do not deem such admission a question of unconstitutional aggression by the non-slaveholding states." [67] Thus, the Congressional letter, as Hearon points out, served to defeat the objects of its authors by revealing and accentuating the real divisions in the State in regard to California.[68]

This division of opinion over California in Mississippi was typical of other Southern States. The legislatures of Alabama, Maryland, and Virginia remained silent, the legislature of Tennessee took a

[65] Hearon, "Mississippi and the Compromise of 1850," p. 78.

[66] There were twenty Democrats and ten Whigs in the Senate, sixty-two Democrats and thirty-six Whigs in the House. (Hearon, "Mississippi and the Compromise of 1850," p. 69.)

[67] *Southron,* Feb. 22, 1850. *Natchez Courier,* March 12, 1850.

[68] Hearon, "Mississippi and the Compromise of 1850," pp. 80–85.

neutral position, while Georgia alone included the admission of California among the issues that would require redress.[69]

During March and April the Committee of Thirteen was working out the compromise measures and reported to the Senate on May 8.[70] Jefferson Davis, who had just been elected on the second ballot for a full six-year term beginning on March 4, 1851,[71] had opposed the separate measures and now rejected the compromise. The greatest concession he would make was "the drawing of the line 36° 30' through the territories acquired from Mexico with this condition, that in the same degree as slavery is prohibited north of that line, it shall be permitted to enter south of the line; and that States which may be admitted into the Union shall come in under such constitutions as they think proper to form." [72] The bitter antagonism between Senators Davis and Foote had expressed itself in an exchange of blows more than two years before,[73] and was now continued when Foote took a leading part in securing the appointment of the Committee of Thirteen and earnestly defended the compromise which it presented. All the Mississippi congressmen upheld the position of Davis.

That Brown was thoroughly aware of the significance of the issues involved is shown in a letter to the editor of *The Mississippian* urging the people to buy the *Congressional Globe*. "The debates in Congress during the present session," he wrote, "are confessedly the most important and interesting since the adoption of the Federal Constitution. They will increase in interest as the years pass on." [74] On May 13 he wrote a lengthy letter to his constituents which "may be regarded as expressing not simply his own views in regard to the compromise, but those of his colleagues as well," and, indeed, "of the Southern Democrats, generally, in both the Senate and the House." [75] As this letter outlined the position of the Southerners opposed to the compromise, and affords a key to their position during 1850 and 1851, it will be necessary to examine it in some detail.

Brown dealt first with the phase of the problem which had caused most division of opinion—the admission of California. Although the

[69] Hearon, "Mississippi and the Compromise of 1850," pp. 89–90.

[70] *Ibid.*, p. 115. *Cong. Globe*, 31st Cong., 1st sess., p. 946.

[71] *Natchez Courier*, Feb. 19, 1850.

[72] *Cong. Globe*, 31st Cong., 1st sess., p. 531.

[73] Dodd, *Jefferson Davis*, p. 125.

[74] *The Mississippian*, May 17, 1850, letter of Brown, April 21, 1850.

[75] Hearon, "Mississippi and the Compromise of 1850," p. 133.

legislature had refused to declare that the abolition of slavery there was the Wilmot proviso in another form, Brown reasserted that he held this viewpoint "as religiously . . . as the existence of an over-ruling Providence. . . . The northern people understand this, and to a man they are for her admission." Following the instructions of the legislature, Brown felt it incumbent upon him to prove that undue and improper influences had been exerted in California. He had written to Buchanan and Marcy and secured denials of the charge that they had advised General Riley to take steps to hasten the admission of California into the Union, thus seeking to place the blame exclusively on the Taylor administration.[76] Now he again sought to show that basely fraudulent means had been used by the administration. He quoted Secretary of State Clayton's letter of April 3, 1849, to Thomas B. King who was sent as agent to California— "You are fully possessed of the President's views, and can with *propriety suggest* to the people of California the ADOPTION of measures best calculated to give them effect. These measures must, of course, originate solely with themselves." This letter, Brown claimed, clearly showed that King was sent on a political mission detrimental to slavery. He denied the assertion that California was not adapted to slavery, on the assumption that slave labor was never more profitably employed than in mining. Furthermore, New Mexico and Deseret sent agents to Congress to ask for territorial governments, while California, "in contempt of the modest example of her two neighbors, . . . sends . . . up two senators and two representatives, with a bold demand for instantaneous admission into the Union. Why is California favored? I'll tell you, fellow citizens. Deseret and New Mexico did not insult the South by excluding slavery." And yet, despite these objections, Brown declared that he would favor the entire compromise measures if the South could get a fair equivalent for surrendering its rights in California.

But Brown believed that the other measures dealing with the territories secured from Mexico were also entirely unfair to the South. Whether $5,000,000 or $15,000,000 were paid to Texas for the land she gave to New Mexico—land nearly twice the size of Mississippi, "to me, it is not a pleasant thing to sell out slave territory, and pay for it myself; and I confess that this much of the proposed bargain has not made the admission of California a whit more palatable to me." New Mexico, in any case, said the opposition, was sure to be a

76 *Mississippi Free Trader,* March 20, 23, 1850.

free territory. Even if Webster was not correct in thinking that the laws of God made slavery unprofitable there, as he stated in his famous Seventh of March Speech, the laws of Mexico, according to Clay, excluded slavery. He believed the views of both Webster and Clay incorrect. And always the Wilmot proviso stood over the South as a threat. Some argued that the South could get no better compromise. "In God's name, can we get anything worse? . . . Like the fatal Missouri compromise, it gives up everything and obtains nothing; and like that and all other compromises with the North, it will be observed and its provisions maintained, just so long as it suits the views of northern men to observe and maintain them, and then they will be unscrupulously abandoned. . . . My head, my heart, and every thought and impulse admonish me that I am right, and I cannot doubt or hesitate. Your fellow-citizen. A. G. Brown." [77]

The Whig press in Mississippi attacked this letter vigorously. The Jackson *Southron* declared that Brown would but excite the derision of serious-minded men by his charges against the honesty of President Taylor. It did not doubt that Brown "has allowed himself, under the promptings of a rankerous and malignant party spirit, to give utterance to that which he not only does not know to be true, but which he would not dare, in a moment of cool reflection, to assert in the presence of men whose respect is deemed worthy of consideration." [78] The *Natchez Courier* devoted over a column in each of four numbers to answering Brown's letter. It was particularly caustic in assailing his willingness to surrender the rights he claimed for the South in California if an equivalent could be obtained elsewhere. "You place then a market value upon the rights of property and unconstitutional enactments! . . . The proviso is unconstitutional, but pay us for it, and we acquiesce." Even more telling was its criticism of Brown for not having placed the blame on Cass during the last few years "for the heresies begotten and cherished by your great democratic leader. . . . You wilfully, and with your eyes open, deceived yourself. And what induced you? *Party, sir, party.* Nothing else." [79]

In Brown's later speeches in Congress during the session he made it even more clear that he had lost all confidence in the fairness and

[77] Cluskey, pp. 178–190.
[78] *Southron*, May 31, 1850.
[79] *Natchez Courier*, June 7, 11, 18, July 2, 1850.

good faith of the Northerners in Congress. He committed himself thoroughly to a policy of resistance to Northern aggression. His language becomes more extreme. If "the Union is to be used for these accursed purposes, then, sir, by the God of my fathers, I am against the Union; and so help me Heaven, I will dedicate the remnant of my life, to its dissolution. . . . We will invoke with one voice the vengeance of Heaven upon such a Union—we will pray unceasingly to the God of our deliverance that he will send us a bolt from heaven to shiver the chain which thus binds us to tyranny and oppression." [80]

In the meantime, the Southern convention had met at Nashville. This convention, called by the Mississippi convention of October, 1849, had at first been hailed with enthusiasm by all the slaveholding States. The legislature of Mississippi gave the Nashville convention a more formal recognition by disregarding the delegates appointed by the October convention and appointing others to be paid by the State. But the compromise measures in Congress acutely divided southern opinion on the advisability of holding the convention. Cleo Hearon claims that public sentiment seemed to favor the convention in only South Carolina and in Mississippi. [81] Although Brown and Davis felt that the convention should meet in order to warn the North not to take further aggressive measures against the South,[82] there was much opposition to the convention in Mississippi. Senator Foote, who later admitted that "it was through me, in the first instance, that Mr. Calhoun succeeded in instigating the incipient movements in Mississippi, which led to the calling of the Nashville Convention" was now a leading advocate of the compromise measures and opposed to the convention.[83] And Chief Justice Sharkey, chairman of the October convention, also favored the compromise, and was convinced that "the convention movement would result in a total failure." In a letter to Foote he expressed his opposition to the admission of California, but not on constitutional grounds. He had no other objections to the other compromise measures and so was willing to accept all the measures as the best the South could get.[84]

[80] Cluskey, pp. 190–192. _Cong. Globe,_ 31st Cong., 1st sess., p. 1197.

[81] Hearon, "Mississippi and the Compromise of 1850," pp. 117–118.

[82] Rowland, _Jefferson Davis,_ I, 323, letter Davis to F. H. Elmore, April 13, 1850.

[83] Dallas Tabor Herndon, _The Nashville Convention of 1850,_ pp. 203–208.

[84] _Natchez Courier,_ June 18, 1850.

The Nashville convention, therefore, met with its prestige decidedly lowered. It took the same position as Davis in opposing the compromise measures, resolving "to acquiesce in the adoption of the line 36° 30′ north latitude, extending to the Pacific Ocean, as an extreme concession," and resolved to reassemble six weeks after Congress adjourned to decide on a course of action. Robert Barnwell Rhett of South Carolina drew up the address of the convention to the Southern people and took Brown's position that the admission of California was the Wilmot proviso in another form,[85] but when he returned home he went far beyond Brown's position in declaring that South Carolina should secede even if she could not get the cooperation of other Southern States.[86] Brown had committed himself to Southern nationalism, while Rhett remained a State-rights advocate.

Brown, thoroughly committed to the holding of the Nashville convention, wrote from Washington on June 10 to the *Mississippi Free Trader:* "We are in trouble here. Clay's bill, I think, will fail. What next, God only knows. If the Nashville Convention stand up firmly for 36–30, we can get it. Less than this we ought never to take." [87] The leading Democratic papers in Mississippi upheld Brown, but the *Port Gibson Herald* (Whig) remarked that "the cogitations and recommendations of the late Nashville Convention seem to have brought about a remarkable change in Governor Brown's mind relative to the Missouri Compromise line, which in his late letter to his constituents he *denounced* so *bitterly,*" [88] while the *Southron* even hoped that he would lose sight of party ends and support the compromise measures.[89]

On July 9 President Taylor died and Millard Fillmore succeeded him. It was evident that the new President would support the compromise when he appointed Webster as Secretary of State. On August 6 Fillmore urged the passage of the compromise measures in a message to Congress. He pointed out that there was imminent danger of a clash between Texan and federal forces in the territory

---

[85] Hearon, "Mississippi and the Compromise of 1850," pp. 123–128.

[86] Dallas Tabor Herndon, "The Nashville Convention of 1850," *Transactions of the Alabama Historical Society,* V. p. 208. N. W. Stephenson, "Southern Nationalism in South Carolina in 1851," *American Historical Review,* XXXVI, 314 ff.

[87] *Mississippi Free Trader,* June 29, 1850.

[88] *Port Gibson Herald,* July 12, 1850.

[89] *Southron,* July 5, 1850.

in dispute between New Mexico and Texas, and therefore urged immediate action on the Texas bill.[90] There was danger in delaying further the solution of the problem.

Since it was most probable that New Mexico would be free territory, any addition to its territory which had been claimed for the slaveholding interests was looked upon as a direct blow to the South. A month before the leading Democratic paper in Mississippi had declared that the South would "never suffer Texas to be stripped of her territory from any indifference on our part. Shall the federal government seek to usurp the territory of Texas, we are ready to see our sons mount their rifles and draw their sabres in her behalf." [91]

If Brown had been bitterly hostile to Taylor, his indignation at Fillmore passed all bounds. On August 6 he attacked Fillmore's message as the most extraordinary which had ever emanated from an American President. It was extraordinary "for its bold assumptions; for its suppression of historical truth; for its warlike tone; and still more extraordinary for its supercilious defiance of southern sentiment." He showed his utmost scorn of the new President, tossed by accident into power, who acted like a King or despot in threatening the South with fire and sword. "When Jackson threatened, there was dignity in the threat. When Taylor threatened, it was not quite contemptible; but for Millard Fillmore, a mere come-by-chance, a poor little kite, who has fallen by accident into the eagle's nest— when he attempts to play the hero, and to threaten the South, one scarcely knows what limit to fix to contempt and scorn." Brown declared ominously if Texas struck for her honor, "I warn her oppressors that she will not strike alone." Jefferson Davis had said that he had a superstitious reverence for the constitution, but Brown, ever more radical and less restrained than Davis, now declared the day had passed "when I and my people can cherish a superstitious reverence for mere names . . . [a constitution] that can only shield Northern people and Northern property—we will *spurn* it." [92]

The next day the Texas bill passed the Senate and the other bills followed. In the House the Mississippi delegates joined in a movement to defeat the measures by parliamentary obstruction, but they could not obtain sufficient support.[93] Before the session ended Brown wrote to the Mississippi press making clear the position he would

[90] *Cong. Globe,* 31st Cong., 1st sess., pp. 1525–1526.
[91] *The Mississippian,* July 5, 1850.
[92] Cluskey, pp. 200–207. *Cong. Globe,* 31st Cong., 1st sess., pp. 1548–1550.
[93] Hearon, "Mississippi and the Compromise of 1850," p. 145.

take when he returned home. He saw the prospects of the South "growing more dim and gloomy every day. I fear we shall submit, in the end, to a humiliating and disgraceful surrender. . . . If God gives me life and strength, I will take the mask off this infamous transaction before my people and expose its hideous face to the honest men of Mississippi." [94] In the final vote McWillie and Thompson voted for the passage of only the fugitive slave bill and the Utah bill, while Foote alone voted for all the compromise measures and Davis, Brown, and Featherston voted only for the fugitive slave bill.[95] It was clear that these senators and representatives from Mississippi had staked their future political careers on the positions they took on the compromise measures. Of these six men, Brown had expressed himself most vehemently and had taken the most radical position. Would he be sustained by the small planters and farmers of southern Mississippi upon whom he depended for support?

What was true of Mississippi congressmen applied to the representatives from all the Southern States. The issues touched the most sensitive nerves and aroused the most powerful emotions. They were far more important and called forth deeper convictions than those which determined party loyalties. Since the issues of submission or resistance to the compromise measures cut across old party lines they caused the formation of temporary new political alignments.

The tone of the leading Democratic papers in Mississippi certainly supported the extremists. *The Mississippian* believed that the State's representatives in the House truly represented their constituents and would not have any opposition if elections were held in the fall.[96] In August this paper proposed a slave colony in California south of 36° 30' as eminently feasible. Masters should sell slaves to those willing to take them to California where they would form companies armed and equipped to protect their property. If they were attacked, "there would be a rush to their support from the Southern states that would very soon beat down all opposition." [97] When *The Mississippian* heard that California had been admitted, it could hardly contain its fury. "Never in the history of the world, did one people perpetrate so foul a wrong as that now consummated at Washington, upon another, without having to make a bloody atonement. It will be marvelous if strife does not grow out of this unparalleled

94 *Mississippi Free Trader*, Sept. 14, 1850. *Woodville Republican*, Sept. 17, 1850.
95 Hearon, "Mississippi and the Compromise of 1850," p. 145.
96 *The Mississippian*, July 26, 1850.
97 *Ibid.*, Aug. 23, 1850.

injury to the Southern people." Feeling confident that the Southern States had means far superior to the Northern States for independent existence, it believed that the South was not forced by economic consideration to make concessions to the North. The consequences of disunion were not to be feared, for "resistance sooner or later to the usurpation of the North must be considered as essential to the existence of the South." It called upon Governor Quitman to convoke the State legislature "to lead us out of infamy, bondage, and impending ruin." [98]

The *Mississippi Free Trader,* the leading Democratic paper in Brown's district, declared for secession, and took a house-divided-against-itself attitude. "Slavery and the Union cannot long continue to exist together," it asserted. "Hereafter in arguing the matter, we will term the two parties Secessionists and Submissionists, for we believe that those are the only issues before the country." And a week later—"when we declared ourselves in favor of the Southern States singly or collectively seceding from the Union, we were fully aware of the responsibility we assumed." [99] The *Woodville Republican* of Wilkinson County, which had urged the secession of the wealthy counties of southwestern Mississippi from the poorer sections of the State in 1846,[100] now applied the same doctrine to a larger field when it asserted, "We must and will secede from this Union! Either we must submit to disgrace, and soon to abolition, with all its horrors, or we must prevent it. There is but one way to prevent it, and that is by Secession!" [101]

Governor Quitman, who had been a consistent defender of the rights of nullification and separate State secession since the nullification controversy of 1832–1833, naturally took the leadership of the ultras as the most extreme and uncompromising of the State-rights leaders.[102] He wrote to John McRae that he believed there was no effectual remedy for the evils before the South but secession. He communicated with the State-rights leaders in South Carolina and, as was to be expected, at the end of September called a special meeting of the legislature to meet on November 18 and wrote to Governor Seabrook of South Carolina that, as he had no hope

[98] *Ibid.,* Sept. 13, 27, Oct. 4, 1850.

[99] *Mississippi Free Trader,* Sept. 25, Oct. 2, 1850.

[100] *Natchez Courier,* March 17, 1846, quoting from *Woodville Republican* of March 14, 1846.

[101] *Woodville Republican,* Sept. 17, 1850.

[102] Hearon, "Mississippi and the Compromise of 1850," p. 201.

of any remedy for the present evils, his views of State action would look to secession.[103]

The Union men, as those who favored the acceptance of the compromise measures were called, were no less active in holding public meetings than were those whom they dubbed disunionists. They were satisfied to take a moderate course, denounced both Northern and Southern zealots and fanatics, and declared themselves "alike opposed to Northern and Southern ultraism." [104] The *Natchez Courier*, which had joined with the *Woodville Republican* in demanding the secession of the southwestern counties in 1846,[105] was now the leading Unionist journal; it insisted that the Unionists were as loyal to the South and as true to her interests as any disunionists. It considered the calling of the legislature to discuss secession "the most audacious usurpation of authority," for there could be no constitutional, peaceful secession. Secession, it held, was nothing but revolution. New York has as much right to say that the federal compact is not broken as Mississippi to say that it has been broken. All the other States have "the same right to preserve it unbroken, as she to break it. . . . Who is the umpire between sovereign States? There is none, except the sword. Where then is *peaceable* secession?" [106]

When Brown returned to Mississippi and found strong opposition to accepting the compromises, he did not think it necessary to moderate his views or his belligerent language. He was second only to Quitman in his aggressive attitude. It is little wonder that the *Natchez Courier* accepted the unfair statement of the *Baltimore Patriot* "that Mr. Brown is among the last men in Congress who wish to see the slavery agitation at an end, and the country in a state of peace and tranquillity. . . . Certain southern fire-eaters wish . . . to stir up the South to an overt act of disunion." [107]

On October 12 Quitman and Brown addressed a meeting in the hall of the House of Representatives in Jackson. Brown's language was highly inflammatory. He pronounced the Texas boundary a fraud upon the Southern States and cried out, "So help me God, I am for resistance; and my advice to you is that of Cromwell to his colleagues, 'pray to God and keep your powder dry.' " Quitman told of his own willingness to send his slaves to southern California and

---

[103] *Ibid.,* pp. 161–163.
[104] *Southron,* Sept. 20, 1850.
[105] *Natchez Courier,* March 17, Sept. 23, 1846.
[106] *Ibid.,* Sept. 10, 24, Oct. 1, 18, 1850.
[107] *Ibid.,* Sept. 20, 1850.

claimed that 1,000 Negroes would have been sent from his neighborhood in order to win this region for slavery. *The Mississippian,* in an extra edition, praised these speeches in the highest terms and was probably correct when it claimed that if they were made on every stump in the State, "there would be a flow of popular excitement fanned into existence, which would never cease to burn until the South forced from her enemies the recognition of every right under the Constitution, or freed herself from a yoke which none but vassals can wear." [108]

Brown spoke also at many meetings in his own district, and, if we may believe the friendly paper, *The Mississippian,* he was received everywhere with open arms and congratulations.[109] His most important address was delivered at Ellwood Springs, near Port Gibson, on November 2 at an adjourned meeting of citizens of Claiborne County who supported the Nashville convention and the Southern-rights movement. Brown, in accepting the invitation, asserted that he would come "to receive instructions as to the best mode of preserving our rights in the Union, or if the Union must be destroyed, the best mode of preserving those rights out of the Union." [110]

Brown began his address by reviewing the events leading up to the Nashville convention and denounced aspiring politicians who sought to dub the convention an assembly of conspirators, treasonably bent on the destruction of the Union. He next launched into a severe castigation of the compromise measures. The irregularities in California were a positive outrage upon the slaveholding States since they were permitted only because California prohibited slavery. More than half these Forty-Niners who voted in California, he claimed, had now returned to their families in the East. The South had no alternative but to choose between a humiliating submission and "a severance of the bonds which unite us to the North." The cup of Southern degradation was filled when the North seized one third of Texas for a $10,000,000 bribe. When this act was passed with the aid of one half the Southern votes, the House gave "one long, loud, wild, maniac yell of unbridled rejoicing—the South was

[108] *The Mississippian,* Oct. 18, 1850. *Southron,* Oct. 18, 1850. James W. Garner, *Reconstruction in Mississippi,* p. 2.

[109] *The Mississippian,* Nov. 1, 1850.

[110] *Port Gibson Herald,* Oct. 25, 1850, letter of Brown, Oct. 19, 1850, accepting invitation. Also in *The Mississippian,* Nov. 15, 1850.

prostrate, and Free Soil rejoiced. . . . It was a night of riot and revelry." The Southern shepherd was unfaithful, so another lamb was taken. This time it was the prohibition of the slave trade in the District of Columbia. The prohibition of this trade, which Brown had urged in Mississippi in 1837 and had looked upon with favor in January 1849, he now dubbed "to all intents and purposes, an act of abolition." But, it was argued, the North *gave* the South an effective fugitive slave law. In Brown's opinion, the North gave nothing, for "no man who had sworn to support the Constitution could refuse to vote for an efficient law for the surrender of fugitive slaves unless he was willing to commit wilful and deliberate perjury. . . . If it has really come to this, that the Southern States dare not assert and maintain their equal position in the Union for fear of dissolving the Union, then I am free to say that the Union ought to be dissolved. . . . So help me God, I believe the submissionists are the very worst enemies of the Union. . . . If the Union cannot withstand a demand for justice, I shall rejoice to see it fall. . . . By a submission you may secure, not a union, but a *connection* with the North," such as that of Ireland to England or of Poland to Russia. "The North will inflict all that the South will bear even to a final emancipation of the negro race. She will inflict nothing that you will not bear. . . . I am for resistance. I am for that sort of resistance which shall be effective and final." Brown, of course, heartily approved the calling of the special session of the legislature on November 18, and hoped it would call a State convention and that South Carolina, Georgia, Alabama, and Florida would "meet us on a common platform, and resolve with us to stand or fall together."

But Brown was not content simply with fiery and provocative generalizations; he outlined specific demands which he thought should be made as the price of remaining in the Union. The laws of Texas should be extended over the territory given to New Mexico so that slave property could be carried and protected there; slave property should be admitted in *all* the territories and given the same protection that is given to the property of Northerners; Congress should not interfere with slavery in the territories, in the District of Columbia, in the States, on the high seas, or anywhere else except to protect it—demands which were to split his party in a few years and to break it in 1860; an effective fugitive slave law must be retained; and, finally, no State should be denied admittance because her constitution tolerated slavery. "If the demands here set forth, and such others as would most effectually secure the South against further disturbance, should be denied, and that denial should be manifested by any act of the Federal Government, we ought forthwith to dissolve all political connection with the Northern States." Brown closed this flaming manifesto which took an hour and a quarter to deliver by confessing his exclusively sectional viewpoint— "Wholly and entirely southern in my sentiments and feelings, I have never debated with myself what course it were best for me to pursue. . . . Her destiny shall be my destiny. If she stands, I will stand by her, and if she falls, I will fall with her." [111]

That Brown had not advanced beyond the position of his audience was shown by the rousing cheers at its close, but more particularly by the resolutions of the meeting, which called for the dissolution of old party ties and declared that "the issue is forced on the slaveholding States, of separation from the non-slaveholding States, or ignominious submission and abolition of slavery. Let our motto then be the union of the South for the independence of the South." Secession, as an inherent and reserved right of the States, should afford no cause for war, but, if war should ensue, confidence was expressed in the ability of the South to defend itself against aggression from all nations. [112]

Jefferson Davis had also been invited to address this meeting, but he received the invitation after the event. In his letter expressing his regret he declared himself a friend of the Nashville convention, but, as usual, expressed himself with more caution and reserve than Brown. [113] In answer to a letter which a group of citizens sent to the senators and representatives, demanding whether they favored a dissolution of the Union now or hereafter, the establishment of a Southern confederacy, or of any kind of resistance, Foote, of course, gave an emphatic "no," Brown simply referred to his specific demands in his Ellwood Springs speech, while Davis contented himself with more general recommendations. He vigorously denied that he sought immediate disunion, but favored the plan of a State convention "to consider of and decide on our present condition and future prospects" and to prepare to defend the State. This convention should propose a convention of all the slaveholding States, but he

111 Cluskey, pp. 246–261.
112 *The Mississippian*, Nov. 15, 1850.
113 *Port Gibson Herald,* Nov. 29, 1850, letter of Davis, Nov. 7, 1850.

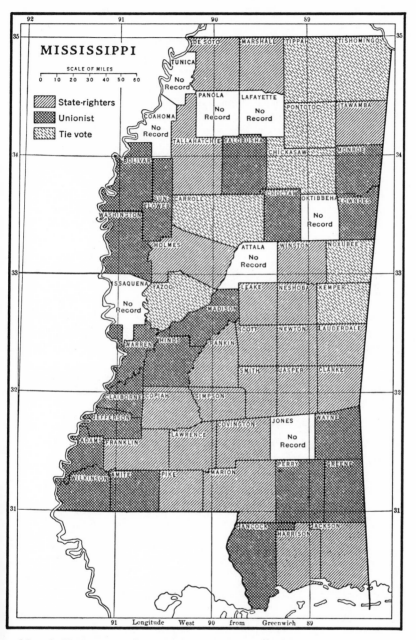

MAP 8. NOVEMBER, 1850, VOTE OF MISSISSIPPI HOUSE OF REPRESENT-
ATIVES ON ATTITUDE OF MISSISSIPPI DELEGATION IN CONGRESS TO COM-
PROMISE MEASURES

did not specify the demands which either the State or the Southern convention should make.[114]

While the leading Democratic papers supported the disunionists,[115] many, although opposed to the compromise measures, yet favored submission and claimed large majorities in their counties opposed to secession.[116] On November 11 the second session of the Nashville convention met and Mr. Davenport of Mississippi claimed that a majority of the people of his State favored the radical resolutions he introduced calling for a Southern convention to arrest further Northern aggression or to secede from the union.[117]

The first test of the sentiment of Mississippi came the next week when the legislature met at Jackson amidst intense excitement. On the opening day, November 18, Senator Foote addressed a large mass meeting of Unionists at which the Union party was formally organized, and Jefferson Davis, Brown, and General Huston spoke at a Southern-rights meeting.[118] The new slavery issues had broken down the old lines of division into Whig and Democratic parties. In the legislature the State-righters were victorious, for resolutions were passed censuring Foote and approving the course of Davis and the four representatives,[119] and calling for elections on the first Monday and the day following in September, 1851, for a State conven-

---

[114] *Flag of the Union* (formerly the *Southron*), Nov. 22, 1850. The change in name of this Whig journal is significant. Party lines were shifting, and the leading Whig journals, the *Natchez Courier* and the *Southron* (*Flag of the Union*), became the leading Unionist papers.

[115] *The Mississippian. Mississippi Free Trader. Southern Press.*

[116] The *Natchez Courier*, Nov. 8, 1850, cites *Kosciusko Chronicle* (Attala), *Columbus Republican, Monroe Democrat, Lexington Advertiser* (Holmes).

[117] Herndon, p. 231.

[118] *The Mississippian*, Nov. 22, 1850. Hearon, "Mississippi and the Compromise of 1850," pp. 178–179.

[119] These resolutions were passed in the House by the close vote of forty-three to thirty-seven. *The Mississippian*, Nov. 29, 1850; *Flag of the Union*, Nov. 29, 1850. Checked with list of members with party affiliations, *The Mississippian*, Dec. 21, 1849, this vote shows clearly how doubtful was the issue of submission or resistance in Mississippi a few months after the passage of the compromise measures. The northern half of the State was almost evenly divided, since the representatives of seven counties were Unionists, six were State-righters, and six were tied. Of great significance for Brown was the fact that half of the twenty-four State-rights counties were in the fourth congressional district. This vote also illustrates the fact that during this crisis a large majority of Whigs became Unionists, while most Democrats became State-righters. All the wealthy Whig Mississippi-River counties whose representatives voted favored the Unionists. Only one Whig voted to uphold the State-rights representatives in Congress, while twenty-six of the thirty-seven who favored Foote were Whigs.

tion to meet the second Monday in November, 1851.[120] It was obvious that the final attitude of the State would not be decided for another year and that the year 1851 would be one long contest between the new Unionist and State-rights parties.

During these critical years, 1848–1850, we have seen that Brown's earlier extremist tendencies reached a culmination in radical and, all too often, in unrestrained expression. He was usually a step ahead of the official position of his party in Mississippi, as evidenced by his objection to the admission of California and by his repudiation of Cass. Although his constituency responded favorably to his position, Brown was astute enough not to alienate his party by taking the most extreme stand in favor of immediate Southern secession and he did not make any statement which favored separate State secession without the cooperation of other Southern States. Upon this cooperation, it was clear, depended the success of the resistance policy. In fact, to a large extent, the name of the new State-rights party was a misnomer because its principles sought primarily not State but Southern rights, and most of its leaders, including Davis and Brown, were thinking in terms of sectional, and not of State rights.

[120] Hearon, "Mississippi and the Compromise of 1850," pp. 180–181.

CHAPTER IV

Retreat, 1851–1853

It was generally understood that the border States would favor resistance, if at all, only if the initiative were taken by the cotton States. Mississippi had taken the lead in calling the Nashville convention and a State convention for November, 1851. If these measures were to lead to united action by the slave States, it would depend largely on what steps the lower South would take. Even before the special session of the Mississippi legislature met in November, 1850, it was evident that Alabama could not be relied on. Both Senators William R. King and Jeremiah Clemens favored submission and mass meetings made it evident that a large majority of the Whigs and at least a large minority of Democrats were opposed to resistance. The question whether Alabama would provide any effective resistance to the compromise measures was finally answered in the negative when the governor refused to call an extra session of the legislature.[1]

The State-righters entertained greater hopes of success in Georgia. In October, 1849, the Democrats had wrested control of the legislature from the Whigs and had reelected Towns, a radical, as governor. The first message of Towns to the legislature in November, 1849, clearly placed him "in the front rank of those Southern-rights leaders who were demanding action as well as words." In Georgia, as in Mississippi, the wealthy planters of the Black Belt were politically and economically more conservative than the poorer farmers of the Pine Barrens. The planter had a direct economic interest in the welfare of his slaves and felt no economic competition or social jealousy towards the Negroes as the poor "crackers" did. The wealthy planter, therefore, was a Unionist, for "while ready to lead in the defence of his slave property in any crisis, he was inclined . . . to deprecate any excitement over the slavery question that seemed unnecessary to its defense." When Governor Towns called an election on November 25 to elect delegates to a State convention the

---

[1] Hearon, "Mississippi and the Compromise of 1850," pp. 188–189.

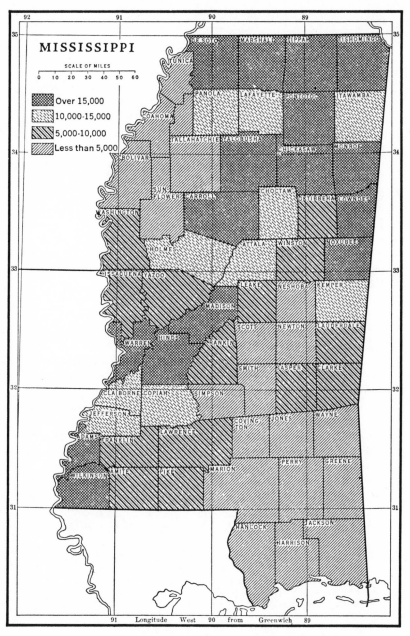

MAP 9. TOTAL POPULATION, 1850

counties of the Black Belt united with those of upper Georgia, where the majority of the farmers owned no slaves and had little feeling against Negroes, to defeat the race-conscious State-righters of the pine-barren counties. The convention met at Milledgeville on December 10 and was dominated by Cobb and Stephens, staunch Unionists. The Union party had an overwhelming majority and drew up the Georgia platform opposed to resistance to the compromise measures.[2]

The State-rights party in Mississippi could find encouragement in South Carolina alone after the adverse decision of Georgia. In December, 1850, the South Carolina legislature recommended the calling of a Southern congress to meet at Montgomery, Alabama, in January, 1852; and in February, 1851, the extremists who favored separate State secession chose a large majority of delegates to a State convention called for February, 1852, to act on the recommendation of the proposed Southern congress.[3] The legislature of Virginia, desiring to calm her more radical Southern neighbors, with but one dissenting vote, thereupon "earnestly and affectionately" urged South Carolina "to desist from any meditated secession upon her part." [4]

Despite this possibility of action by South Carolina the State-rights party of Mississippi was placed in a very awkward position by February, 1851. "Resistance" now could not mean cooperative action by the Southern States against Northern aggression, for such action was impossible. Since the boundaries of South Carolina were not coterminous with those of Mississippi and thus would prevent the establishment of a contiguous Southern Confederacy, "resistance" now meant that any demands these two States might make would most probably be rejected and would lead to the most extreme position of separate State secession. Although Governor Quitman, like Rhett in South Carolina, still favored separate State action and urged South Carolina to secede first,[5] the other leaders of the State-rights party realized that it would be impossible to carry the State

[2] Richard Harrison Shryock, *Georgia and the Union in 1850,* pp. 66–67, 69, 72–76, 111, 209–212, 219, 237–238, 296, 308, 320, 323.

[3] The Southern congress never met, and a State convention in April, 1852, resolved by a vote of 136 to 19 to submit "from considerations of expediency." (Hearon, "Mississippi and the Compromise of 1850," p. 220. Stephenson, "Southern Nationalism in South Carolina in 1851, *American Historical Review,* XXXVI, 323–335.)

[4] Hearon, "Mississippi and the Compromise of 1850," pp. 188–198.

[5] *Ibid.,* p. 198, quoting letter of Quitman to John S. Preston, March 29, 1851.

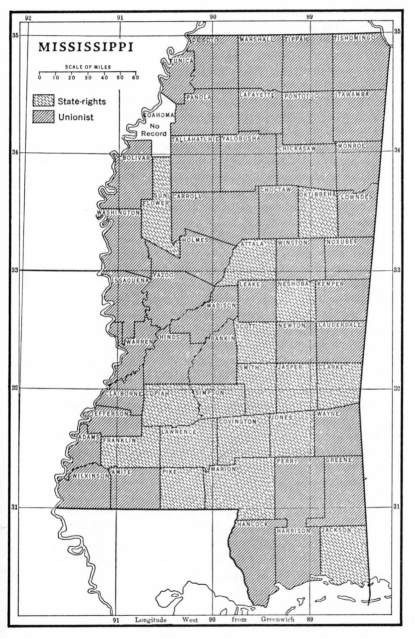

MAP 10. ELECTION FOR DELEGATES TO STATE CONVENTION, SEPTEMBER, 1851

with them in pursuing such a suicidal policy. They were cruelly deceived in their faith that the growing consciousness of Southern nationalism was strong enough to express itself in united action by the Southern States against the North.

Especially was this true of northern Mississippi, where the leading Democratic papers insisted on a moderate course. The *Columbus Democrat,* "the time-honored organ of the democracy in North Mississippi," [6] supported Unionist candidates for the State convention, objected to Quitman's demanding an amendment to the Federal Constitution and the division of California or the secession of Mississippi from the Union, as these demands went beyond the requirements of the convention of October, 1849.[7] The *Southern Standard* declared against both secession and submission. It opposed the demand for an amendment to the Federal Constitution because it would be impossible to secure it. "Success," it asserted, "depends as much on *moderation* as on *harmony.* We have cast anchor in the calm waters of conservatism. We cannot consent quietly to submit nor can we adopt the ultra position of South Mississippi." The Unionist party, it claimed, was held together only because it could "taunt us with the prospect of being swallowed by the Secession party as they style our southern friends of that section. . . . What is true in this is true in a tier of ten counties in this section. And what is true in regard to these, may be taken as a good index of the rest in North Mississippi, three or four counties excepted." [8] The positive aspect of this more moderate State-rights policy was well expressed by resolutions of the party in Lowndes County, which specifically declared an unwillingness to secede from the Union and declared that the November convention should remonstrate with Congress and, if Congress refused to modify the compromise laws, to instruct the State legislature "to raise our revenue from such articles as are manufactured in the offending States . . . at the same time taking the tax off of the industry of our own people." Thus, the ultimate threat proposed was not secession, but a tariff war with the North on control over interstate commerce.[9] Considering this lack of cooperation on the part of all the Southern States except South Carolina and the positive opposition of northern Mississippi, the State-righters were forced to hedge, to compromise.

[6] *Natchez Courier,* April 4, 1851.
[7] *Columbus Democrat,* May 29, 1851.
[8] *Southern Standard,* April 5, 1851.
[9] *Ibid.*

The Unionists, on the other hand, found their position much strengthened when they could point out the dangers in the statements of their extreme opponents. The new Unionist paper, the *Flag of the Union,* could not tell from Brown's Ellwood Springs speech whether he was for resistance or not, but it had no doubt that "secession is to be the finale to this 'peaceable' and 'bloodless' drama." [10] To the *Natchez Courier,* the hot-headed resisters of Mississippi and of South Carolina were in the same class with the Boston mob which resisted the enforcement of the fugitive slave law, for it considered both extremes as revolutionary in spirit. This paper attacked the argument that a Southern Confederacy could be economically prosperous. New taxes and prohibitory tariffs would have to be imposed which would place an insupportable burden on the State. How tragically prophetic of reconstruction times was its belief that secession would surely lead to civil war which "would certainly end in subjugation or despotism, after the mountain wave of blood had swept over the land." [11]

In the meantime Governor Quitman had been indicted in New Orleans for aiding filibustering expeditions against Cuba and had resigned as governor. Brown wrote a most cordial letter from Washington to Quitman. "I approve your course with all my heart, and have never doubted that our people will sustain you most triumphantly." He was convinced that the administration had hoped Quitman would resist arrest so that "an indignant community would lose sight of the treachery and imbecility of an administration which either will not or cannot arrest a fugitive slave in Boston." [12] This same month Brown expressed his belief that the perfect calm in Congress over slavery issues was as deceptive as there was reason to fear it would be short-lived. He pointed to the open rebellion against the fugitive slave law and free-soil gains in elections in Vermont, Massachusetts, New York, and Ohio as evidence that "the agitation is not over. The *wind* has subsided but it will swell again into a more fearful storm. May the South be ready to meet it!" This was belligerent enough, but with his usual keen perception of the trend of public opinion he now realized the necessity of trimming his sails, for he asserted, "I am not, and never have been for disunion or secession. . . . I may *submit*. It may be that I can do nothing

[10] *Flag of the Union,* Dec. 6, 1850.
[11] *Natchez Courier,* Dec. 10, 1850; Jan. 31; March 4, 1851.
[12] Claiborne, *Life and Correspondence of John A. Quitman,* II, 73, letter Brown to Quitman, February —, 1851.

else." [13] This last statement marked the beginning of Brown's strategic retreat from his fire-eating radicalism of 1849–1850.

When Brown returned to Mississippi after the end of the short session of Congress he immediately started his campaign for reelection and for the election of State-rights members in the November convention. At Port Gibson he met in debate General John D. Freeman, who had been attorney-general during Brown's administration, but was now a Unionist. Although Brown endorsed Quitman and praised South Carolina, he did not urge Mississippi to follow their course. Instead, he informed his audience that he was one of the best Union men in the world, that the Southern-rights men disapproved of the compromise, but if like measures should be again passed by Congress, they would favor, not secession, but giving the "assurance . . . that our quiet and hearty acquiescence . . . is not to be relied upon or anticipated." [14] Even the *Mississippi Free Trader* admitted that the Unionists were considerably dumbfounded at his attitude.[15] Freeman ironically congratulated Brown on his sound and wholesome Union doctrines, but expressed his surprise at such a change in Brown, "who last fall was so full of resistance, extra sessions of the legislature, conventions, Quitmanisms, Ellwood Springs speeches, etc." His conclusion was that Brown was "the queerest Union man whom he had ever met in the South." The *Flag of the Union* took the position that Brown "was . . . and constantly had been . . . an out and out secessionist and in favor of a Southern Republic." [16]

Although Brown found it expedient to modify his speech on the secession issue, he did not put checks on his language in discussing the national administration. He denounced Fillmore for hounding Quitman out of office; he said that Fillmore was ready enough to send an army into Texas, but "when the fugitive slave law has been flagrantly set at defiance by a mob of free negroes in Boston, he comes whining to Congress with doubts as to the extent of his powers!" [17]

After Brown spoke in Jackson on April 14 the *Flag of the Union* tried to pin him down on specific issues. It refused to accept the

[13] *Mississippi Free Trader*, Feb. 26, 1851, quoting letter from Brown, Feb. 8, 1851.
[14] *Port Gibson Herald*, Apr. 11, 1851. *Flag of the Union*, Apr. 18, 1851.
[15] *Mississippi Free Trader*, April 16, 1851.
[16] *Flag of the Union*, Apr. 18, 1851. *The Mississippian*, Apr. 18, 1851.
[17] *The Mississippian*, April 18, 1851.

question Brown presented, "are the people of Mississippi satisfied with the acts of adjustment?" It insisted that this question presented no issue at all because no one in Mississippi was satisfied with it. "We concede the question. We believe every Union man in Mississippi will also concede it." The vital question, "Mississippi, dissatisfied with the compromise, what is she to do? Secede—go out of the Union?" Brown had evaded this question in his public address. He was attempting a dignified retreat and wanted to speak or hear no more of secession. The crux of the matter, of course, was whether Mississippi would support South Carolina. The editor claimed Brown "was willing to see South Carolina take an attitude of unconditional secession . . . and as soon as the people of Mississippi or some other State could be brought up to the South Carolina standard, he was willing of course *to see them go out together.* . . . It will not be difficult now, in our judgment, for the public to perceive very clearly, *what kind of a Union man* Gov. Brown is." [18]

This definition of his position for him brought a long letter from Brown in which he calmly and judiciously outlined his views. He had sought a guarantee for slave property in all territory south of 36° 30′ as "but a meagre return for the blood and treasure lavished by the Southern people in the acquisition of the common territory." The denial of this guarantee he regarded as evidence of a hostile feeling against the South. This hostile feeling was particularly dangerous for the South because of the growing disproportion of relative strength of the North and South in both House and Senate. Although the South could not object to the mere possession of this growing power of the North, when the North evinced a disposition to use her preponderance to the prejudice of the South, he was startled and alarmed and convinced that "if its use were continued contrary to our remonstrances, we should be driven out of the Union." With respect to the immediate situation, Brown hoped South Carolina would not secede alone, but he "expected to see her take the position that the *causes* for secession were ample, and that she was ready to secede. . . . I never said that I was *willing* to see her secede alone or with other States. . . . I did not say or intimate that I was willing to see Mississippi or any other State go out with South Carolina. I stated my apprehensions—my fears for the future." He answered the question, "Mississippi, not satisfied, what is she to do?" by asserting, "The answer is plain and easy. *She should say*

[18] *Flag of the Union,* April 25, 1851.

so through her Convention." [19] In this letter Brown omitted any suggestion of threats against the North. He has changed from a fire-eater to a simple protester. But his enemies refused to accept his conversion to a policy of moderation and insisted on judging him by his past record. The *Flag of the Union* still maintained that "there is abundant testimony to be drawn from his published letters and speeches, to convict him, in the very teeth of his denials to the contrary, of being to all intents and purposes . . . an unqualified and unquestionable disunionist." Even though Brown, like Foote, would propose no more than the Georgia resolutions or Virginia's resolutions at the November convention, his general course, evincing a tendency to advocate extreme measures in a crisis, was felt to lead towards ultimate secession when the time would again be ripe for action.[20]

At the same time the *Natchez Courier* was more specific in attacking the course of Brown in Congress. He had denounced the Missouri Compromise as a fatal step and yet sought to extend the compromise line to the Pacific; he had voted, together with abolitionists, against the Utah bill which did not prohibit slavery although it was north of 36° 30' and yet ended his speech with "So help me God, I am for resistance." [21] Brown, in answering this last charge, admitted that the Utah bill was the least objectionable and that if California and New Mexico had been placed on the same footing he might have voted for all the bills. He explained that his reference to "resistance" applied, not to the Utah bill, but to the compromise measures as a whole.[22]

On the first Monday in May the Union party convention met at Jackson, nominated its leader, Senator Foote, for governor and unanimously adopted as a platform the resolutions of the Union mass meeting held at Jackson on November 18, 1850.[23] During May and June Davis and Brown stumped the State. Davis could retreat more gracefully than Brown because he had not used such unrestrained language as Brown. Davis did not think it wise for South Carolina to secede and felt that Mississippi should interfere only in case the federal government should attempt to coerce South Carolina

---

[19] *Flag of the Union,* May 16, 1851, quoting Brown's letter of May 1, 1851.
[20] *Ibid.*
[21] *Natchez Courier,* April 22, 29, 1851.
[22] *Ibid.,* May 20, 1851, quoting Brown's letter of May 3, 1851.
[23] Hearon, "Mississippi and the Compromise of 1850," p. 201.

if she did secede. Although opposed to any immediate political action against the North, Davis favored economic "non-intercourse with the North to every extent practicable." [24]

In Lawrence County, where Brown was very popular, an unfriendly critic noticed that Brown refused to stand upon the radical Quitman platform; "in leaving the Quitman wreck, the governor [Brown] declared himself, strange as it may seem, *a Union man!*" He was not convinced of Brown's sincerity because he made frequent allusions to the people of the North as Yankees "in the most sneering terms of irony and contempt . . . and his endeavors to promote feelings of hostility and bitterness between us and them." [25] In Clark County Brown created the same impression. He was now described as a gentle dove, a tamed lion, "that Southern fire which was then [1850] glowing in his bosom had gone out—almost." [26]

There was much truth in the explanation of the *Flag of the Union* that Brown and other leading State-righters now appeared as Union men because the people had been heard from. "They have given up their object because they can't attain it. . . . Their desire to cover their retreat from disunion by *resistance* in the shape of remonstrance, is merely to cover their disgraceful backing out, and to save themselves with the people." [27] Brown, in moderating his views, was upheld by the leading Democratic papers in central and southern Mississippi: *The Mississippian* of Jackson, the *Mississippi Free Trader,* the Vicksburg *Sentinel,* and the *Paulding Eastern Clarion.* The *Mississippi Free Trader,* which as late as February had urged secession, now in a lengthy eulogy of Brown explained that "he never contemplated armed resistance." [28] The wisdom of a policy of masterly retreat was evident on every hand.

[24] Rowland, *Jefferson Davis,* II, 78, 80–81, speech of Davis at Aberdeen, May 26, 1851. Montgomery, writing his reminiscences a generation later, declared, "I remember one thing Mr. Davis said which was applauded both by those who supported him and those who did not. Mr. Davis said, if that state [South Carolina] did secede, and the Federal government attempted to coerce her, he for one would shoulder his musket and go to her aid. The sentiment was loudly applauded, for none in this country at that time denied the right of a state to secede and set up a government of its own if its people desired, with or without reason." It is interesting to note that Montgomery "thought Mr. Foote the superior of Mr. Davis on the stump." (Montgomery, p. 9.)

[25] *Flag of the Union,* May 9, 1851.

[26] *Ibid.,* May 30, 1851.

[27] *Ibid.,* Aug. 29, 1851.

[28] *Mississippi Free Trader,* Feb. 5, 1851; June 7, 1851.

Brown, realizing that success could lie only in the moderate Davis position, which stressed *Southern* rights rather than *State* rights as such, steered clear of committing himself to the extreme Quitman view of whole-hearted cooperation with South Carolina. He declined to attend a dinner in honor of Quitman and wrote ambiguously, "His fault, if fault he has committed, has been a too ardent defence of Southern rights." [29] A week before the Democratic State-rights Convention met the Aberdeen *Independent* noted that "Quitman doctrines never took well with the masses; and for several weeks we have seen a general disposition among his followers to desert him to save themselves. . . . This letting down of ex-Governor Brown disposes of Governor Quitman." [30]

But Quitman was not so easily disposed of. The Democratic State-rights Convention, which met in June, was reluctant to nominate Quitman, although he was the logical candidate because of his resignation under fire. Since the resistance movement had already failed in every State except South Carolina, where the issue was still in doubt, the more practical leaders realized that their only chance of success lay in favoring the lowest point short of acquiescence and short of abandonment of Southern rights. The nominating committee sought the withdrawal of Quitman so that Davis, the leader of the moderates, could be nominated. But Quitman refused to withdraw, so there was nothing to do but nominate him in order to prevent an open split in the party. [31] Brown was a delegate and a member of the committee on resolutions, which left to the November convention "to estimate the wrongs we have suffered and to indicate the mode and measure of redress." [32] Davis himself drew up the resolution which asserted the right of secession, [33] thus directly reversing the position of the Democratic party in June, 1834, when nullification and secession were roundly denounced. [34]

In Brown's district a Union convention at Monticello chose Judge A. B. Dawson to run against Brown for Congress. Judge Dawson was a native of Georgia, a graduate of the University of North Carolina, who had come to Mississippi in 1841 and had settled in Clark County. He was a dangerous candidate because he was a Democrat

[29] *The Mississippian,* June 6, 1851.
[30] *Independent,* June 7, 1851.
[31] Hearon, "Mississippi and the Compromise of 1850," pp. 204–205.
[32] *The Mississippian,* June 20, 1851.
[33] Hearon, "Mississippi and the Compromise of 1850," p. 205.
[34] Quoted by *Flag of the Union,* May 16, 1851.

and was popular in the eastern part of the district where Brown's greatest strength lay.[35] Brown was so obviously the favorite of the State-righters that it was thought sufficient for the leading papers to announce him by acclamation and without any official formality, so a district convention was dispensed with.[36] Thus, the stage was set in Mississippi for the campaign for the election of delegates for the November convention, a campaign which was to be "one of the bitterest and most exciting in the history of the state." [37]

Giles Hillyer, the able editor of the *Natchez Courier,* led the Unionist attack in 1851 and all through this decade until secession was an accomplished fact. Hillyer felt that the course of Brown, if sustained by the people, must end in the dissolution of the Union. True, his resistance platform did not call for immediate disunion for the reason. which Brown well knew, that that course would be disastrous. But since Brown defended all his speeches, he was an *ultimate* secessionist. Therefore, there was only one way of escape— "If he would free himself from the charge of being a disunionist, let him openly confess that no aggressions have been made" by the North against California, Texas, or the District of Columbia; "if they were such, he stands self-confessed a disunionist!" Since Brown was a disunionist at heart, only waiting for a more favorable change of circumstances, he was thus "as little to be trusted as those who are ready at once to declare for immediate secession." [38] At Natchez, where both Davis and Brown spoke on July 2, Brown sought to minimize the influence of Hillyer, who had gone so far as to call him a traitor, by disposing of him contemptuously as "a venturer amongst us of whom nobody either knows or cares." [39] But Hillyer continued to charge that Brown had come down on a sliding scale from "dissolution" to "resistance," and finally, after not knowing what he wanted, to "acquiescence." At Holmesville Brown was reported as confining his resistance to besieging Congress with petitions. The *Natchez Courier* comments, "He is for resisting by petitioning Congress, by begging for redress. Who are the submissionists?" [40]

---

[35] *Natchez Courier,* June 13, 1851; June 20, 1851, quoting from *Port Gibson Herald.*
[36] *Mississippi Free Trader,* June 25, 1851. *Woodville Republican,* July 1, 1851.
[37] Hearon, "Mississippi and the Compromise of 1850," pp. 205–206.
[38] *Natchez Courier,* June 24, 27, 1851.
[39] *Ibid.,* July 4, 1851. *Mississippi Free Trader,* July 5, 1851.
[40] *Natchez Courier,* July 8, 11, 15, 25, Aug. 1, 1851.

The *Natchez Courier* and other Unionist papers kept up a constant attack against Brown's speeches in Congress.[41] As a result of these attacks the *Mississippi Free Trader,* although criticizing the *Natchez Courier* for publishing only the most extreme portions of Brown's speeches, yet admitted that "Gov. Brown's speeches may now appear intemperate." It condoned this intemperance, however, by pointing to "the provocations, the taunts, and jeers of the abolitionists, and even the more temperate northern men. . . . There was indeed scarcely a Southern man who could keep his temper about the time Brown's speeches were made."[42] To all of which the *Natchez Courier* responded, "His friends have crawfished for him and now apologize, extenuate and take his words back!"[43]

Although Quitman was nominated, he was felt to be a liability, since he favored separate State action and was not much concerned about the joint cooperation of the Southern States.[44] He was too much of the direct action, Garibaldian type, to pay attention to the nuances of tact and diplomacy which political leaders must follow. Although there is no proof that he was guilty of the charges against him of aiding the Lopez expedition to Cuba, it is clear that he was involved later. His letters of June and August, 1851, written after President Fillmore had issued a proclamation against filibustering, show clearly that Quitman was dealing then with the Cuban Junta in New Orleans and arranging for another demonstration against the island, and there are many letters sent to Quitman offering aid in an expedition.[45] While Quitman was engaged in these dubious activities it was noted that Brown seemed to desire to keep as far distant from Quitman and his confederates as possible.[46] At Shieldsboro, in Hancock County, where his Unionism was challenged because he favored Quitman, Brown refused to indorse Quitman, but asserted that "he did not hold himself responsible for the opinions

[41] *Independent,* June 14, 1851. *Port Gibson Herald,* July 18, 1851. *Flag of the Union,* July 18, 25, 1851.

[42] *Mississippi Free Trader,* July 26, Aug. 2, 1851.

[43] *Natchez Courier,* Aug. 5, 1851.

[44] Stephenson, "Southern Nationalism in South Carolina in 1851" in *American Historical Review,* XXXVI, 314–335.

[45] John S. Everett, *John A. Quitman's Connection with the Cuban Filibusters,* typewritten, pages not numbered. MS. John A. Quitman Papers, 1851–1858, letters, J. L. O'Sullivan to Quitman from New Orleans, June 20, 1851; W. J. Bunch to Quitman from Jackson, Aug. 18, 1851.

[46] *Port Gibson Herald,* Aug. 1, 1851.

of any man or set of men; he was only responsible for his own opinions." [47]

Brown, driven hard to find an issue less embarrassing than those raised in 1849–1850, sought to appeal to the old Democratic party-loyalty. The State-rights party, in full retreat, recognizing the wisdom of reforming its lines on the basis of the old majority party, at its June convention, had added "Democratic" to its title. But Brown had difficulty in dubbing the opposition in his own district as Whigs because Dawson, his opponent, was a Democrat. (Brown did have a definite advantage, however, for Dawson was prevented from campaigning because of ill-health and the death of two of his sons.) [48] Brown struck a more sympathetic chord when he followed the leadership of Davis [49] and others [50] in shifting the issue from the political issue of secession to the more fundamental social problem, by claiming that the compromise measures tended "either to ultimate overthrow of the institution of slavery, or the extinguishment of the white race." [51]

George T. Swan, who accompanied Brown during July, reported enthusiastically to Quitman on the prospects in the southwestern counties and threw an interesting light on the attitude of the Democratic voters. He found them "seemingly anxious for light and desirous to know really whether we were for immediate secession. Their countenances brightened and they looked cheerfully when they . . . saw that the cry of disunion is only the same old song of Federalism sung by that party in 98 and 99,[52] when resistance was proclaimed to its noted acts of that era." And, as the event proved, the southern part of the State was the only section which trusted the State-righters, for nearly every State-rights delegate to the November convention came from the southern part of the State, and nearly all counties carried were poor counties with few Negroes and all producing less than 10,000 bales of cotton.[53] As in Georgia, the piney-

[47] *Flag of the Union*, Sept. 5, 1851.

[48] *Port Gibson Herald*, Aug. 1, 1851. *Natchez Courier*, Aug. 19, 1851.

[49] Rowland, *Jefferson Davis*, II, 73, 74, 76, speech of Davis at Aberdeen, May 26, 1851. Shryock, pp. 66–67.

[50] As, for instance, the Columbus *Southern Standard*, August 23, 1851, which asserted that "the Political Issue is but as a feather in the balance beside the Social Issue."

[51] *The Mississippian*, Aug. 29. 1851.

[52] MS. J. F. H. Claiborne Collection, letter G. Swan to Quitman, July 18, 1851, Vol. C.

[53] Hearon, "Mississippi and the Compromise of 1850," map opposite p. 10. Cluskey, p. 16.

woods farmers voted for the State-rights ticket, while the State as a whole was won by the Unionists by the large majority of 28,402, to 21,241.[54]

Thus, after the September elections the State-righters were in even a weaker position than before. Quitman, recognizing that Davis and Brown refused to countenance separate State action and that resistance was dead, now resigned as candidate for governor and Jefferson Davis, who could yield to a victory of the Submissionists with more grace than Quitman, took his place. Quitman himself, at Davis' home after his withdrawal, clearly summed up to Davis the difference between their attitudes, "I carry my State-rights views to the citadel; you stop at the outworks." [55] The leading Democratic papers, as was to be expected, now urged more strongly than ever the reestablishment of strict party lines in order that the normal large Democratic majority in the State might reassert itself.[56]

Brown had retreated so far that he had completely reversed his position during the last year. Brown publicly recognized that Mississippi had decided that submission to or acquiescence in the compromise measures was her true policy, and he continued vigorously the struggle for reelection, which now became more embittered. The *Natchez Courier* published and circulated two pamphlets, each entitled *"The True Issue Stated,"* aimed directly at Brown's congressional and Ellwood Springs speeches. Brown prepared an elaborate answer, full of anger and invective: "The intention of this writer is to show that I am a Disunionist. To this charge I give the LIE direct. . . . The charge laid against me that I was, or ever had been, for *disunion* or *secession,* was and is FALSE and SLANDEROUS." Brown asserted that the

[54] See map, based on the *Whig Almanac and U. S. Register, 1852,* p. 57 and checked with incomplete records MS. Secretary of State Archives, F, No. 71. Cf. Hearon, "Mississippi and the Compromise of 1850," map opposite p. 208. Hearon, "Mississippi and the Compromise of 1850," p. 209. Population map based on *Tenth Census of U. S.,* I, 67–68. A more detailed analysis of the returns bears out the statements made above. Fourteen of the seventeen counties which gave State-rights majorities came from the southern half of the State. Nine of the State-rights counties had populations of less than 5,000 and six between 5,000 and 10,000, while the State-righters did not win any of the sixteen counties with populations of over 15,000. They won only three (Oktibbeha, Sunflower, and Franklin) of the twenty-six counties which had a Negro population of more than 50 percent. Eleven State-rights counties produced less than 2,500 bales of cotton, six between 2,500 and 10,000 bales, while not one of the nineteen counties producing over 10,000 bales was won by the State-rights party.

[55] Mrs. Varina Howell Davis, *Jefferson Davis. A Memoir,* I, 470.

[56] *The Mississippian* and *Mississippi Free Trader,* noted in later references. Aberdeen *Independent,* Oct. 18, 1851.

accusations against him were such as he would expect from the Natchez aristocracy.[57] The *Natchez Courier* continued the attack, centering attention on Brown's desertion of Quitman, and asserted that the reason was that he "has never yet been known while a candidate to repudiate that, for which he believed there was a majority of supporters among the people." [58]

At the end of September Brown was alarmed. In a letter to his close friend, J. F. H. Claiborne, marked "Confidential," he confessed that "matters do not look as well as I desire but I think with the help of my friends I can be elected but I will have nothing to spare." But Brown was in his element in a campaign and was always ready with some new method of attack. In this same letter he enclosed a sketch of an article he wanted published in both French and English in the *New Orleans Courier* and ordered the paper sent to persons whose names he enclosed. He expressed confidence that this article would secure his election.[59] From this article, especially directed to the seashore and piney-woods counties, reprinted in *The Mississippian* and in the *Mississippi Free Trader,* we can clearly see how astute Brown was in shifting the issue of the campaign to his personal claims for reward because of his diligence in caring for the interests of his poor white constituents. "The poor man," he wrote, "can never forget Brown's effort to have the price of public lands reduced to ten cents per acre. . . . The settlers on public lands will remember Brown's bill now before Congress to grant every man the privilege of residing on and cultivating public lands as long as he chooses without paying anything." He claimed that the seashore counties owed the coast survey, light-houses, and mail facilities to him and showed how he had sought aid for the navigation of their rivers. "If he has a fault as a politician, it is his too great attachment to his own State." The extent of his shift on the slavery issue is illustrated by his claim that "in the late exciting contest in Mississippi for delegates to the State convention, Governor Brown's position was eminently conservative. . . . The idea of separating her [Mississippi] from her sister States never was for a moment entertained by him." [60]

Dawson now took the stump and campaigned with Brown. Dawson saw the humor in Brown's retreat and "cautioned the Governor against coming out too strong on the Union side, as the Southern-

[57] Cluskey, pp. 233–246.
[58] *Natchez Courier,* Sept. 19, 1851.
[59] MS. Claiborne Collection, A, No. 73, letter Brown to Claiborne, Sept. 26, 1851.
[60] *Mississippi Free Trader,* Oct. 11, 1851. *The Mississippian,* Oct. 10, 1851.

rights party might bring out a candidate and beat them both." [61] Brown evidently did not omit the *argumentum ad feminam,* for a correspondent claimed that he had embraced every mother and kissed every child in the piney woods of Mississippi. Brown tried to steer clear entirely from the slavery issues. He refused to attack Foote or to defend Quitman. The *Natchez Courier* insisted that this "death-bed repentance" should not avail him, since "even in the event of Mr. Brown's becoming a submissionist, we know not how quickly one who has already made so sudden a change, will make another." [62] But it did avail Brown, and Brown alone, for he was the only State-rights congressman elected, and the Unionists carried both the governorship and the legislature.[63] A few days later the State convention resolved "that we perceive nothing in the above recited legislation of the Congress of the United States which should be permitted to disturb the friendly and peaceful existing relations between the Government of the United States and the Government and people of the State of Mississippi," and, by a vote of seventy-three to seventeen, reasserted the position of 1834 that the right of secession was "utterly unsanctioned by the Federal Constitution . . . and that no secession can in fact take place, without a subversion of the Union established, and which will not virtually amount in its effects and consequences to a civil revolution." [64]

Thus ended the controversy over the Compromise of 1850 in Mississippi with a conclusive victory for those who favored acquiescence, and, even in the case of Brown, the interpretation of the hostile *Flag of the Union* was largely correct: "No doubt, his success is owing to the fact that he everywhere claimed himself to be a *Union* man of the first order." [65]

[61] *Sentinel,* Sept. 16, 1851. *Natchez Courier,* Oct. 3, 1851.

[62] *Natchez Courier,* Oct. 10, 21, 1851.

[63] See map, based on *Whig Almanac and U. S. Register,* 1852, p. 57 and checked with incomplete records MS. Secretary of State Archives, F, No. 71. *The Mississippian,* Nov. 14, 1851. Brown carried fifteen of the twenty-two counties in his district, losing Harrison, Perry, and Wayne in the east, and all the four wealthy river counties in the west—Wilkinson, Adams, Jefferson, and Claiborne. Brown won over Dawson by a vote of 7,304 to 5,444, while Foote defeated Davis by 29,358 to 28,359. Foote carried every county in the State along the Mississippi River except Jefferson—the only county in Brown's district which supported Dawson but failed to vote for Foote.

[64] Hearon, "Mississippi and the Compromise of 1850," pp. 215–217, quoting from *Journal of the Convention of the State of Mississippi, 1851,* pp. 33, 47–48. Nine of the seventeen minority votes came from Brown's district, representing eight counties, every one of which Brown carried.

[65] *Flag of the Union,* Nov. 14, 1851.

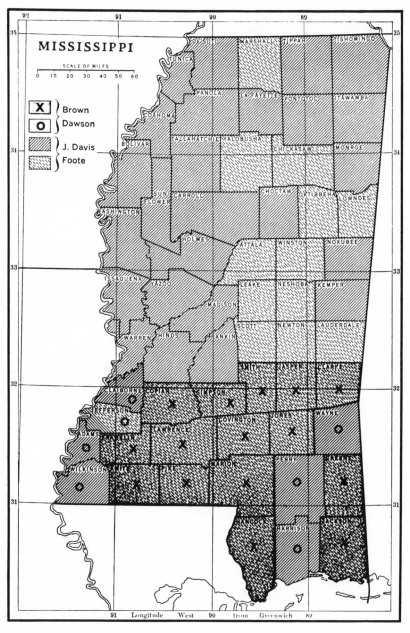

MAP 11. ELECTIONS FOR GOVERNOR AND FOR CONGRESSMAN IN THE FOURTH
CONGRESSIONAL DISTRICT, NOVEMBER, 1851

Brown's victory did not bring him peace. He found it necessary to write to Quitman to explain the constant charges that he had deserted him. He had heard that this story had "made an unfavorable lodgment on your mind." Brown declared categorically, *"I never did abandon your defense. I never on any occasion attempted to throw you off."* However, he showed that he was so busy defending himself that he had no time to turn aside to defend any one else. During the campaign, he explained, he had refused to defend Quitman unless his assailant would defend Foote. Brown's letter is really an admission that he *had* been most luke-warm in supporting Quitman as his enemies believed, for he declared himself committed only to Quitman's "general course and present position. I did not commit myself to *all* that you haid (*sic*) said or written. I took this position to avoid the thousand and one attacks made on your message, the defense of each one of which seperately (*sic*), would have left me no time for anything else. . . . The man does not live who can with truth and justice assert that my course has not been as is herein stated." [66]

Brown's peace was also disturbed by the confusion in which the bitter contest left the Democratic party in the State. The deep wounds which had led to the temporary break-up of the party were slow to heal. As late as August 1, 1851, *The Mississippian* urged Southern Democrats to keep out of the national Baltimore convention because "we opine the Southern Democracy have experienced enough of Northern perfidy. . . . Hereafter let us take counsel among ourselves." [67] But now that the Democratic State-rights wing had lost and yielded to the submissionists, there was nothing to do but seek to join the Union Democrats and get onto the national party bandwagon again. However, the reconciliation of the two wings of the party was no easy task. Rival conventions met to choose delegates for the Baltimore convention. On January 5, 1852, the Union Democrats met at Jackson, condemned secession as a dangerous heresy, and reasserted the finality of the compromise measures. Three days later the Democratic State Convention met. But the Unionists felt that this convention was dominated by secessionists, and the one delegate chosen specifically as a Union Democrat refused to serve and others who had favored the Unionists withdrew from the convention. [68]

[66] MS. J. F. H. Claiborne Collection, Vol. A, No. 74, letter Brown to Quitman, Nov. 13, 1851.
[67] *The Mississippian*, Aug. 1, 1851.
[68] *Columbus Democrat*, Jan. 31, 1852. *Natchez Courier*, Feb. 3, 1852.

In February, 1852, the legislature of Mississippi chose two Union Democratic senators, Walter Brooke and Stephen Adams, to fill the unexpired terms of Davis and Foote,[69] thus leaving Brown as the only one who had fought in the campaign as a State-righter from Mississippi in either branch of Congress. On March 5 Brown gave official notice of the attitude of his wing of the Democratic party by voting with the large majority of Southern Democrats for a resolution of Fitch, a Democrat of Indiana, which recognized the binding efficacy of the compromises of the constitution and deprecated "all further agitation . . . of the questions embraced in the acts of the last Congress known as the compromise and of questions generally connected with the institution of slavery, as unnecessary, useless, and dangerous." But it is even more significant that Brown did not follow the majority of Southern Democrats in voting for an amendment by Hillyer of Georgia to the effect that the compromise measures "are regarded as a final adjustment and a permanent settlement of the questions therein embraced, and should be regarded, maintained, and executed as such." Both the resolution and the amendment passed the House, and *The Mississippian,* the leading State-rights organ, hoped that this action would put a stop to all further discussion and agitation. "Henceforward," it asserted, "all attempts by schismatics and traitors to revive the controversy will be indignantly frowned down." [70]

How keenly sensitive Brown was to reminders of his former expressions of disunionism is well illustrated by a dramatic incident in the House on March 12 which secured nation-wide prominence. Brown made a lengthy speech explaining the whole course of the Southern movement since 1849. He showed how the Whigs and Democrats had worked together until the introduction of the compromise measures caused many early and sturdy advocates to fall off. "With the passage of the compromise I mark the first distinct evidence of its decay"; while the first Union convention at Jackson on November 18, 1850 marked the downfall of the Southern movement in Mississippi, "a fall which was rapidly succeeded by its downfall elsewhere." The Unionists were made up largely of Whigs, while the State-righters never left the Democratic party, and the entire Democratic press except the *Columbus Democrat* supported them. Therefore, Brown insisted upon his Democratic orthodoxy and threw

---

[69] *Mississippi Free Trader,* Feb. 25, 1852. *Independent,* Feb. 28, 1852.
[70] *The Mississippian,* March 15, April 16, 1852.

this question at his colleague, John A. Wilcox of Monroe County, who had been elected a delegate to the Baltimore convention by the January 5 Union Democratic Convention: "Who seems from these facts to have been getting out of the Democratic party—my colleague, who is sustained by the Whig press, or I, who have been and am yet sustained by the Democratic press?" Brown insisted that the convention of January 8, 1852 was the true Democratic convention whose principles were based on the old party issues.[71] Wilcox in answer quoted Brown's statement that "this Disunion or Secession party in Mississippi . . . is only a chimera, a mere phantom—that there is no party of disunion or secession in Mississippi, or in the United States" and then remarked, "I thought that gentleman had too high a regard for truth to make a declaration so baseless of truth." To which Brown replied, "Do you mean to say that what I have said is false?" And Wilcox, "If you say that there is no party in Mississippi in favor of secession or disunion, you say what is false." Here debate ceased abruptly, for Brown, standing near, struck Wilcox in the face; Wilcox struck back. Most of the members rushed to separate the fighters, and, amid great excitement, there were loud cries for the sergeant-at-arms, who was absent at the time, to come and arrest the parties. After some minutes the members succeeded in separating the contestants, and order was restored. Both men were forced to apologize to the House for the unseemly scuffle. Challenges for a duel were exchanged and seconds chosen, but friends interfered and prevented bloodshed, and Major Polk, the second of Wilcox, announced to the House "that they now occupied the same position of friendship which existed between them previous to the unfortunate affair." [72]

The press of Mississippi took sides according to its political bias. Thus, *The Mississippian*, although deprecating the affair, asserted that no one could place the least blame on Brown "whose long public career is marked throughout by the most honorable and knightly bearing to his political adversaries," [73] while the *Yazoo Democrat* did not see how Brown could have acted otherwise than to repel upon the instant the gross and unprovoked insult.[74] On the other hand, the

[71] *Cong. Globe,* 32nd Cong., 1st sess., pp. 734–736. Cluskey, pp. 261–272.

[72] *Ibid.,* March 15, 26, 1852. *Southern Standard.* April 3, 1852, *Flag of the Union,* March 19, 1852. *Natchez Courier,* March 19, 1852. Ben: Perley Poore described this fight in his *Perley's Reminiscences of Sixty Years in the National Metropolis,* I, 394–396, and included a picture, p. 395, of "A Row in Congress."

[73] *The Mississippian,* March 26, 1852.

[74] *Yazoo Democrat,* March 24, 1852.

Aberdeen *Independent* (Whig) declared that Brown's denial of the existence of secessionists among the State-righters was the "bold act of a genuine demagogue," and that Wilcox was on the defensive and could not be blamed. The action of Brown, it believed, "only proves the utter want of capacity in the secession party to unite the Union democrats with them, or their deep hatred and aversion for them." [75] The *Hinds County Gazette* (Whig) took a similar view and also pointed out the wide-spread interest in the fight. It was reported in nearly all the London papers, and a translation of the *New York Herald's* account appeared in the Paris papers. [76]

Brown's humble bid for a quiet healing of the breach in the Democratic fold was hailed by the *Vicksburg Sentinel,* [77] but called forth a bitter rebuke from the *Flag of the Union,* which regretted "that the ex-Governor did not perceive that during the whole canvass of '51 he was contending for a *rapidly declining movement* which had already received a mortal wound!" After the State-righters ratified the proceedings of the Nashville conventions, declared for 36° 30' or fight, and followed such fire-eaters as Rhett and Hammond of South Carolina, they alone, with Brown among its leaders, were responsible for the continued agitation. Since the Union Democrats were guiltless, they must have their full share in the Democratic organization. [78]

Brown was soon forced to defend his actions again from an attack by John D. Freeman of the third district of Mississippi, who had twitted Brown for saying that his party was dead. Brown exclaimed, "I said the 'southern movement was dead'; and so it is; but I said explicitly that it was not the movement of my friends or of any party," but of all parties in Mississippi. He had to point out again that his Ellwood Springs speech was not a violent harangue, that resistance was not synonymous with secession, and that he could not be proved to be a secessionist from statements in the State-rights press any more than Freeman, a Democrat, could be proved to be a Whig by reference to the Unionist Whig press. He insisted that the Democratic party in Mississippi must be free to shape its own policy as it did when it was laughed at for favoring the election of judges in 1832, or when Democrats in other States were horror-stricken when it repudiated the Union bonds in 1840. So, in 1850–

[75] *Independent,* March 27, April 10, 1852.
[76] *Hinds County Gazette,* March 25, May 20, 1852.
[77] *Sentinel,* April 17, 1852.
[78] *Flag of the Union,* April 9, 1852.

1851, the espousal of resistance to the compromise made Democrats no less loyal to the party.[79]

The *Flag of the Union* now dubbed Brown a member·of "the secessio-acquiescent party" and considered his anxious desire to get back into accord with the Northern Democracy, which he had so heartily denounced, as a masterly travesty or a gigantic practical joke. "Ordinary impudence is offensive," it continued, "but when it reaches the gigantic height of a week (*sic*) and powerless minority, offering spoils to the victors, disclaiming *partiality* in their distribution, we are lost in admiration of the intrepidity of the joke." Although the *Flag of the Union* resented Brown's implication that it was advocating the Whig party and supporting Fillmore,[80] its opposition to the State-righters was so bitter that in May it did gravitate back into the Whig fold, (where it had been before 1849 as the *Southron*), when Dr. Edward Pickett, the Democratic editor, resigned, leaving Thomas Palmer, a Whig, as sole editor.[81] Another indication of the reshaping of old party lines is shown by the return of the *Columbus Democrat*, the outstanding Unionist Democratic paper, to supporting Brown and to seeking his favor.[82] But the most dramatic evidence of rapprochement was the appearance of both Brown and Wilcox as speakers at a Democratic meeting at Monument Square, Baltimore, on August 20.[83]

Brown was even willing to work with Democratic free-soilers and gave hearty, even enthusiastic, support to the conciliatory Democratic nominees of the Baltimore convention, Pierce and King, and to the party platform, which was better than he expected. In a letter to the *Eastern Clarion*, he reported that "every section and all divisions of the party are united and harmonious. . . . More than one plank in the National platform was taken from the *pine woods of Mississippi. I am as well pleased with it as if I had constructed the whole of it myself.*" His remarks about Pierce, whom he has known for

[79] *Cong. Globe*, 32nd Cong., 1st sess., pp. 355–359.
[80] *Flag of the Union*, April 9, 1852.
[81] *Ibid.*, May 7, 1852.
[82] *Columbus Democrat*, May 29, 1852.
[83] *The Mississippian*, Sept. 3, 1852. The early reconciliation of Brown and Wilcox was undoubtedly aided by the qualities of Wilcox described by Senator Phelan of Mississippi at the time of his death in 1864: "His distinguishing trait was humor—social, congenial humor. He had the strongest sense of the ludicrous —the keenest sense of the ridiculous of any man he ever knew. . . . He had as little of the spirit of opposition based upon ill-will as any man he ever knew." (*Richmond Whig*, Feb. 9, 1864.)

twelve years, are particularly significant and worth noting in view of Brown's hostile attitude towards him during his administration— "On the question of State Rights, he is as reliable as Calhoun himself; and on the subject of slavery he stands far above *all* suspicion. Of all men living I do not know one who comes nearer up to the standard of perfection, than Franklin Pierce." [84] However extreme Brown might be, however much he might bolt from the control of the party machine, he always managed to be "regular" in presidential election years.

The value of the support of this radical pro-slavery man was recognized by the campaign managers of Pierce. Pierce was embarrassed before Southerners by a speech he had made at New Boston, New Hampshire, in which he "had characterized the fugitive slave law as inhumane and opposed to moral right." Although Pierce never specifically denied this statement, he tried to excuse himself by the claim that he was unwell at the time, and that his remarks had been distorted and misrepresented. A statement from Brown was solicitated by Charles H. Peaslee, the campaign manager in Washington, and Brown was willing to write Pierce a letter for publication, stating that the South was satisfied with his position on slavery. [85]

Quite in contrast was the attitude of Quitman, who was, most assuredly (like Yancey, his radical counterpart in Alabama and a poor politician) much more concerned with principle than with political expediency. Even before he knew the result of the nomination he wrote that he would not be for Pierce if he accepted the Compromise of 1850; "let us not write ourselves down as asses or rogues. How would Col. Davis, Governor Brown, or I appear, vindicating, defending, and approving such a platform?" A month later, when asked by a Jackson committee to speak for Pierce, he was true to his convictions and refused because the finality of the compromise had been accepted in the party platform. [86]

In the middle of September Brown returned to Mississippi after the long session of Congress to take part in the campaign for Pierce. He addressed the people of Jackson in the City Hall, where he was very well received by a large crowd. Brown congratulated his party

[84] *The Mississippian,* June 25, 1852, quoting Brown's letter of June 6, 1852. *Flag of the Union,* July 9, Oct. 15, 1852.

[85] Roy Franklin Nichols, *Franklin Pierce. Young Hickory of the Granite Hills,* pp. 210–211.

[86] Claiborne, *Quitman,* II, 166, 168.

in the State for the union and harmony so happily restored and trusted that nothing might occur in the future to disturb it. *The Mississippian* declared that Brown's "long and consistent public services have won for him the esteem and confidence of the Democracy of Mississippi and to a degree which few enjoy." [87] A few weeks later further evidence that the battle-axes of 1850–1851 had been buried was provided when both Brown and Foote addressed a Grand Democratic Rally at Jackson. Foote especially urged Union Democrats and Union Whigs to support Pierce. "In fact," we are told, "his whole speech was directed to the Union Party, to show that they had every incentive to urge them to support, with zeal, the democratic ticket." [88]

All this jubilation over the perfect harmony in Democratic ranks, was, of course, gall and wormwood to the opposition. The *Flag of the Union* even harped back to his earliest political career and put into his mouth, "I was a Whig and Copiah was Democratic. It was easier for me to go to Copiah than for Copiah to come to me, therefore I was pleased to be a Democrat." The planks in the platform which Brown found were taken from the piney woods would be found "so thickly varnished with free-soil dirt that it will be difficult . . . to distinguish one from another," and even Pierce was charged with being a free-soiler.[89] The great contrast with Brown's attitude when he returned home in 1850 was not overlooked.[90] Perhaps the comment of the *New Orleans Courier* in praising a speech Brown gave in New Orleans, and particularly the first clause, was not far from the truth: "The grand secret of his success is his unflinching fidelity to his party, and the broad benevolent and radical democracy he has ever advocated." [91]

Pierce won in Mississippi by a large majority,[92] and both branches of the Democratic party looked forward to presenting a reunited front in the State elections of 1853,[93] little suspecting that the wounds, caused by the contest of 1851, had not healed, and that the struggle, with all its bitterness, was to be fought out again, although

[87] *The Mississippian*, Sept. 17, 1852.
[88] *Ibid.*, Oct. 8, 1852. *Yazoo Democrat*, Oct. 13, 1852. *Primitive Republican*, Oct. 21, 1852.
[89] *Flag of the Union*, July 9, 1852.
[90] *Ibid.*, Sept. 17, 1852.
[91] Quoted in *The Mississippian*, Oct. 29, 1852.
[92] *Ibid.*, Nov. 26, 1852.
[93] *Southern Standard*, Nov. 13, Dec. 4, 1852.

on different issues. In 1851 the major contest was for the governorship in which Foote, "one of the best stump speakers of his day," [94]
won a notable victory over Quitman and Jefferson Davis; in 1853
the major contest was to be between Foote and Brown for the United
States Senate.

In the November elections of 1851 the Whig-Unionist coalition
elected a majority in the State House of Representatives, but there
were enough hold-overs in the State Senate for the Democratic State-
rights party to retain a majority there. In February, 1852, a select
committee of the Senate recommended, and the Senate passed a
resolution against electing a senator until after the elections of 1853,
thus making it impossible for the newly elected senator to serve during six weeks of the regular session of Congress, starting in December, 1853. The reason given for this unseemly delay was the propriety of referring the issue of the senatorial election to the people
in 1853, since this was not an issue in the campaign of 1851.[95] The
more obvious cause was the fact that the Unionists would have a
majority of twenty-six on the joint ballot; the hope of the Democrats
was to reinstate themselves in popular favor in the elections of 1853
so that they could then control a majority of votes in a joint Democratic caucus and thus in a joint session of the two houses. Further
preparations for the future were made in October, 1852, when the
legislature met to remake the congressional districts, since a fifth
district had been added as a result of the census of 1850. The House
passed a bill for three Democratic, one Whig, and one doubtful district, but the Senate, again hoping for a better gerrymander after
the next election, defeated the bill.[96]

Early in 1853 the leading Democratic journals in Brown's district
declared for Brown for the Senate.[97] General Robert Stanton was
suggested, but his refusal to run against Brown was announced in a
widely published letter of F. L. Claiborne, in which it was asserted
that Brown's withdrawal from the national legislature would be a
calamity for the State, for "if he has a fault, it is in too great devotion to Southern Rights and Southern institutions. If he has erred

[94] Hearon, "Mississippi and the Compromise of 1850," p. 208.
[95] *Flag of the Union*, June 24, 1853, quoting letter of Foote.
[96] *Ibid.*, Sept. 2, 1853. *Natchez Courier*, Oct. 19, 1852. *Independent*, Aug. 13, 1853.
[97] *Mississippi Free Trader*, Jan. 29, 1853, quoting *Monticello Journal. Natchez Courier*, Feb. 19, 1853, quoting *Port Gibson Reveille*. March 3, 1853, quoting *Holmesville Southron. Southern Reveille*, March 2, 1853.

in Congress, it has been on the side of his constituents." [98] After Jefferson Davis was appointed Secretary of War by President Pierce the senatorial contest was narrowed down to Brown, McRae, and Foote. John J. McRae came from the eastern part of Brown's district and was, like Brown, an ardent State-righter. In November, 1850, when speaker of the House, he was reported to have written the resolution which approved the course of the State-righters in Congress and censured Foote for upholding the compromise measures.[99] In 1852 he regretted the delay in the success of the filibustering movement against Cuba and expressed his "sympathies . . . with everybody who is for taking Cuba." [100] Thus, there was danger of the State-righters dividing their energies. Stanton and J. F. H. Claiborne felt that there was no necessity for a conflict between them, and Stanton proposed "that mutual friends should take the necessary steps to avoid a result that must prove disastrous to both." Since both men must be accommodated, "the supporters of Brown all express themselves willing to give their aid to McRae for Governor." [101] There was no such desire to reconcile the conflicting claims of Brown and Foote, although many Unionists felt that Foote should have a prior claim to either Brown or McRae for the senatorship since the State-righters were recognized when Davis secured a cabinet position.[102]

On April 4 Brown wrote an open letter to the people of the fourth district, explaining that it had been understood for some time that he would not be a candidate for reelection to Congress. He said nothing directly about running for the Senate, but implied that Barcus was willing, for, in retiring, he was "moved by no dislike of the public service, or disinclination to be useful, as far as possible, to my country." He again insisted that the policy of the country on "the unhappy conflicts" of the last two years was unalterably settled and that any discussion of them "will only keep alive an unnatural estrangement among party friends and thus promote the prosperity and power of a common foe." Therefore, no Democrat should be

[98] *The Mississippian,* March 4, 1853, quoting letter of F. L. Claiborne of Feb. 10, 1853. *Mississippi Free Trader,* March 9, 1853.

[99] *Natchez Courier,* July 1, 1853.

[100] MS. J. F. H. Claiborne Collection, Vol. B, No. 38, letter McRae to J. F. H. Claiborne, June 14, 1852.

[101] *Ibid.,* Vol. C, No. 78, letter Stanton to Claiborne, March 13, 1853.

[102] *Natchez Courier,* March 15, 1853.

nominated because he was a State-righter or denied recognition because he was a Union man.[103]

Two weeks later Brown announced that he would not undertake to control his friends in the use of his name. He would campaign for a Democratic legislature to choose a senator, would not "debate with any man of any party the obsolete issues of 1851; and least of all will I consent to enter the lists as a volunteer herald and defender of my own pretensions." The Democratic legislators must be pledged to vote for the candidate decided upon by a legislative party caucus. The Democratic party had plighted its faith in President Pierce, and thus its members had assumed "the high responsibility of giving him our votes. . . . Every party must have the control of its own affairs, and to secure this it must exact of its members obedience to its usages."[104] Thus, Brown endeavored to reestablish strict party discipline and harmony by the caucus methods adopted by the Democratic State Convention in 1843 upon the motion of Charles M. Price, editor of *The Mississippian*.[105]

The Whigs, of course, interpreted Brown's statement as an attempt to secure the senatorship for himself and so interpreted his appearance at Democratic county conventions, his address on May 4 at the Democratic State Convention, and the announcement of a barbecue in his honor.[106] The Democratic press continued to urge the claims of "this pioneer stripling,"[107] but the Democratic State Convention refused to commit itself on the choice of a senator, insisting on decision by a legislative caucus. A resolution nominating Brown was presented but was withdrawn upon insistence that the only footing on which the party could be united, was that of silence on the senatorial question,[108] a position which Foote had advocated in 1843.[109] McRae was nominated for governor.

The Whig press and former Unionist press opened up a most bitter attack against the conduct of the Democratic State Convention. To the *Natchez Courier* it all appeared as a slick game of manipulation in behalf of the aristocratic Davis and the plebeian Brown. In an

[103] *The Mississippian*, April 15, 1853. *Southern Reveille*, April 20, 1853.

[104] *Southern Reveille*, May 18, 1853, quoting letter of Brown to Dr. S. F. R. Abbay, April 16, 1853.

[105] *Mississippi Free Trader*, March 10, 1843.

[106] *Hinds County Gazette*, April 21, 1853. *Natchez Courier*, April 19, 21, 1853.

[107] *The Mississippian*, April 22, 1853, quoting *Sentinel*. *The Mississippian*, May 6, 1853, quoting *Columbus Democrat*. *Woodville Republican*, April 26, 1853.

[108] *Southern Reveille*, Sept. 7, 1853.

[109] *Mississippi Free Trader*, Feb. 28, 1843.

editorial, "The political Chess Board," it charged that it was all pre-arranged that Davis should go into the Cabinet so that he might stand more prominently before the people, that Brown should give up his seat in the House and run for the seat Foote had given up in the Senate, and that McRae should be pensioned off with the governorship—all because of "hostility to Foote, and a careful eye to the future interests of Davis." Half a dozen State offices are given to Union Democrats so they will be willing to go into caucus for senator, where "the State rights men—the Brownites and Davisites—will have a numerical majority and can force Brown on a Union minority." [110]

Immediately after the end of the Democratic State Convention Brown started an aggressive campaign for the senatorship. He wrote to his principal lieutenant in southern Mississippi, J. F. H. Claiborne, for whom he had secured a federal timber agency, asking him to send papers and personal letters to party leaders in six southern counties and pointing out clearly his belief that the campaign centered in his contest with Foote, who refused to accept the decision of a Democratic caucus.[111] A week later Foote announced the appointments for his canvass and invited "all competing aspirants, *and especially Governor Albert Gallatin Brown* to courteous and free discussion of our conflicting claims." If they failed to appear he said that he would "take judgment by default final against each and all of them." At the same time Brown announced twenty-two different appointments [112] and a week later referred to Foote in a satirical and saucy vein for especially singling him out and for setting his own times and places of meeting without consultation.[113]

The campaign was made particularly difficult for Brown because of the general dissatisfaction in northern Mississippi. It was the old, typical story of complaint by the newest section of a State against dominance by older sections. Northern Mississippi was strongly Democratic from the first. In 1836, when the Chickasaw counties had just been admitted to representation, dishonest, underhand attempts were made to keep these counties from swinging the State Senate

---

[110] *Natchez Courier*, May 6, 1853. Also *Hinds County Gazette*, May 11, 1853.

[111] MS. Claiborne Collection, Vol. A, No. 77, Brown to Claiborne, May 6, 1853. Riley, in his article on *"Life of Col. J. F. H. Claiborne,"* implies that Claiborne took no active interest in politics after he settled in southern Mississippi. His correspondence testifies that he was quite active on Brown's behalf. *Publications of Mississippi Historical Society*, VII, 233.

[112] *The Mississippian*, May 13, 1853.

[113] *Ibid.*, May 20, 1853.

from Whig to Democratic control.[114] There was complaint in the rich Mississippi River counties that the newer counties had far too large an apportionment in proportion to their wealth—that soon "Old Adams will scarcely be heard in the Legislative Hall, and we must sink into a state of vassalage to the young and vigorous North." [115] Northern Mississippi likewise felt aggrieved. In 1849 there was much bitter feeling because the North did not get its share of State officers, and it felt that the Democratic State Convention was dominated by party managers and demagogues from central and southern Mississippi. Particularly were they dissatisfied because Jefferson Davis was chosen senator over the claims of Foote, and it was remarked with some truth that "Foote and Davis like each other about as well as a dog with hydrophobia likes water." [116]

So, in 1853, the nominations of men from the southern part of the State for the highest offices were received in northern Mississippi "with mingled feelings of sorrow, vexation, and disappointment." A fifth representative had been won because of the growth of the Chickasaw counties. The northern counties, therefore, felt that they should choose the congressman-at-large and should be consulted in the choice of a governor. McRae defeated W. H. Johnson, a Union Democrat from southern Mississippi, whom the northern delegates supported for governor. The northerners' choice for congressman-at-large fell upon Reuben Davis, also a Unionist, but the state convention chose William Barksdale of Lowndes County, who had been elected to the November, 1850, convention as a Unionist, but had voted with the State-righters. While Barksdale secured the votes of twenty-eight counties and Reuben Davis of twenty, yet the aggrieved northerners pointed out that the voting population of the Davis counties was over 3,500 more than that of the Barksdale counties and that only one county (DeSoto) in northern Mississippi voted against Davis.[117] Even the *Mississippi Free Trader* admitted that it was natural for Reuben Davis to feel deeply mortified and disappointed,[118] while the northern press dilated upon the "Jackson clique" and the conduct of the

[114] MS. Claiborne Collection, Vol. C, George W. Winchester to Quitman, Dec. 26, 1836.

[115] *Natchez Courier*, Feb. 3, 1846.

[116] *Ibid.*, July 4, 1849, Dec. 28, 1849. *Southron*, Oct. 26, 1849.

[117] *Southern Standard*, May 28, 1853, quoting *Pontotoc Sovereign* and *Monroe Democrat*.

[118] *Mississippi Free Trader*, July 16, 1853.

Democrats of southern Mississippi as "perhaps the most unparalled (*sic*) act of fraud now on the records of party proceedings." [119]

Thus, it was made to appear that the contest was to be waged on the issue of the desire of a State-rights clique to defeat the Unionists, Foote and Reuben Davis, and to prevent northern Mississippi from securing its full share in State politics. It was charged that Brown was at the center of the intrigue, that "Prince-Albert-Gallatin-would-be-U. S.-Senator-so-help-me-God-Brown knew as well, three weeks before the Convention, who would be the nominee, as three weeks later." [120]

Reuben Davis was thus again on the side opposing Brown as he was in 1839 when Brown defeated him for Congress, but the contest between Brown and Foote held the center of the political stage. The Brown press pointed out that Foote himself had demanded nomination for the Senate by a Democratic legislative caucus in 1845, while the Foote forces showed that Jefferson Davis had been elected with the aid of Whig votes in 1850 and that Foote also desired to be the senator of all Mississippi and not simply of one party. To this argument Brown continued to insist that a candidate who refused to submit to the discipline of a caucus was a disorganizer who would prefer his own temporary advancement even to the destruction of the principles of his party.[121]

It was now clear that the widely-advertised reunion and harmony of the two wings of the Democratic party were gone. The bitterness of 1851 had returned. The Whig press felt that the purpose of the Davis and Brown men was to hoodwink and cajole Union Democrats into affiliation with them and that "the Union Democrat who would now desert Gov. Foote would deserve himself to be deserted by his friends in the day of his greatest trial." [122] Brown insisted on standing on Pierce's Inaugural Address which fully accepted the compromise measures. Since Foote had consistently favored the compromise, while Brown was a late, unwilling submissionist, it was argued that Foote's antecedents were "in more strict conformity with the opinions of the President. . . . If supporters of Brown desire to be

[119] *Southern Standard,* May 28, 1853, quoting *Pontotoc Sovereign* and *Monroe Democrat.*

[120] *The Mississippian,* June 3, 1853, quoting *Aberdeen Independent.*

[121] *Port Gibson Reveille,* May 25, 1853; *Natchez Courier,* May 26, 1853; *Mississippi Free Trader,* June 14, 1853, quoting *Southern Sun* (Kosciusko).

[122] *Independent,* May 28, 1853, quoting *Port Gibson Herald.*

States Rights men—they must fall back on Quitman. If they desire to be Pierce democrats how can they otherwise than support Foote?"[123]

Brown continued his equivocal policy of refusing to seek to be *the* Democratic choice, even suggesting other possible candidates and insisting that he would humbly submit to King Caucus. *The Mississippian,* actually Brown's chief supporter, assumed a like attitude. Although it praised him highly when he declined to run for the House, it maintained a neutral attitude on the choice for senator, but insisted that the enemy, the Whigs, must no more be allowed to share in the choice than one would consult an enemy in choosing a lawyer or a general for an army.[124]

The opposition insisted that *The Mississippian* was the chief manipulator in Brown's behalf, and Brown was likened to the man who brought a handful of salt to a group of men eating turnips in the hope that he would be invited to eat some of their turnips.[125] More specifically, James Phelan, who was to become Brown's colleague in the Confederate Senate, charged that Brown and McRae held a midnight caucus with their adherents, many of whom were not delegates to the convention, in the office of *The Mississippian* in order to save from defeat the conspicuous State-rights candidates for senator, Brown, McRae, and William Barksdale. At that meeting it was decided that Brown was to be senator, McRae governor, and Barksdale congressman-at-large, thus trampling under foot the desire of northern Mississippi for Reuben Davis for congressman-at-large. At the convention "Governor Brown controlled every movement and into his hands was committed all power, and he rewarded treachery to Union and to Whig principles—made or unmade candidates—obeyed or disregarded public sentiment—just as the movement would serve to raise Brown and prostrate Foote!"[126]

Reuben Davis refused to accept the decision of the convention, campaigned against Barksdale, and attacked "the dictatorial and versatile conduct of A. G. Brown."[127] As a result of this "Chickasaw Rebellion" a special Democratic convention was called at Pon-

---

[123] *Independent,* June 11, 1853.

[124] *The Mississippian,* June 10, 1853.

[125] *Flag of the Union,* June 3, 1853.

[126] *Ibid.,* July 8, 1853, quoting from *Monroe Democrat. Independent,* June 11, July 16, 1853. *The Mississippian,* July 8, 1853. *Hinds County Gazette,* June 15, 29, 1853. *Natchez Courier,* June 18, 22, 23, 1853.

[127] *Southern Standard,* June 11, 1853, quoting from *Holly Springs Guard.*

totoc on July 4 to nominate a candidate for congressman-at-large. This convention nominated Reuben Davis and proposed changes in the convention system which would secure justice for northern Mississippi—that the State convention be held at a more central point, that the relative strength of the Democratic party in each county form the basis of representation, and "that no caucus or extra self-constituted assembly shall assemble during the sitting of the Convention, to consult with reference to its action; and that the meeting of any such body shall destroy the authority, and work a dissolution of the Convention." [128]

Attempts were made to get Brown and Foote to canvass together, and on June 24 Brown announced the conditions on which he would meet Foote: discussion must be confined strictly to the issue, ("Shall Democratic candidates for the United States Senate submit to the decision of a Legislative caucus of Democratic members?") and each party must abstain from discussion of the compromise measures or of his personal pretensions or claims to the Senate. Foote refused these terms and announced that he would take but little notice of Brown hereafter.[129] In his speeches Foote constantly proclaimed "the fierce and undying malignity of those who have been baffled in their scheme for the violent disruption of this noble confederacy." He insisted that his enemies demanded his profound degradation, delayed the election of a senator in order to mortify him, and that no sacrifice on his part could satisfy their appetite for vengeance "except such as might be marked with the political martyrdom of myself and of every faithful and beloved friend that I have in the State." [130]

However, when Brown spoke at Carrolton on July 4 a number of Foote's friends asked him to come also. Foote agreed and attacked Brown's desertion of his party in 1835 when he supported Plummer against Walker, the regular nominee for the Senate, but more particularly for his actions in 1850 and 1851 when "he regularly disbanded the democratic party by having given up even the ancient name." When Brown, in reply, supported Pierce's inaugural Foote followed the obvious course of quoting from Brown's speeches denouncing the constitutionality of the compromise measures.[131] The two rivals met again at Greensboro, where Brown showed his keen political

---

[128] *The Mississippian,* July 22, 1853.
[129] *Flag of the Union,* June 24, 1853.
[130] *The Mississippian,* July 1, 1853.
[131] *Flag of the Union,* July 15, 1853.

acumen by his attempt to get Foote to admit—what the Democratic press had been hammering upon—that he sought to divide the Democratic ranks and form a coalition of the Unionist minority of Democrats and the whole body of the Whig party. He put this question to Foote: "Are you in favor of the unity of the party, do you wish and desire to see the two wings of the Democratic party united for the purpose of opposing their common enemies, the Whigs?" When Foote evaded this question Brown repeated it and declared if Foote would answer "Yes," he could restore harmony within the Democratic party. More than that, Brown promised that he would refuse to be a candidate before the legislature and would give his written pledge that he would not accept the election if offered to him. When Foote still refused to answer "Yes," it was natural that the Democratic press concluded that he was placed "in the ranks of the now organized Whig party. . . . If he be the Senator, he will be the pet and exponent of Mississippi Whiggery." Brown had won a great tactical victory, since he knew that there was no chance for the Whigs to defeat a united Democratic party. He insisted that friends and foes in 1851 should and ought to support Pierce and that Foote would be supported by nine tenths of the Whigs and repudiated by a like number of Democrats if he refused to repudiate Whig support.[132]

During July and August Brown stumped through southern and eastern Mississippi and was received with the usual enthusiasm of this section for him. Wiley P. Harris, who was running for Brown's seat in Congress, reported that Foote was making no impression. Harris gave up his own speaking appointments because "the people are interested in the senatorial contest only and in the conduct of that Brown fills the measure of public expectation completely." He expressed anxiety about only two counties, Green and Perry.[133] During September and October Brown concentrated his canvass on territory which was new to him—the populous, dissatisfied northern Mississippi. The way was made more easy by James Phelan's acceptance of the denials of both Brown and McRae that they had conspired to

[132] *Southern Reveille,* July 19, 1853. *Sentinel,* July 23, 1853, also same viewpoint in *Flag of the Union,* June 24, 1853, quoting *Southern Argus* (Houston). *Woodville Republican,* June 21, 1853. *Southern Reveille,* June 1, Aug. 3, 1853. *The Mississippian,* July 29, 1853.

[133] MS. J. F. H. Claiborne Collection, Vol. B, letter W. P. Harris to J. F. H. Claiborne, Aug. 27, 1853. Rowland, *Jefferson Davis,* II, 231-232, letter F. L. Claiborne to Jefferson Davis, June 8, 1853. F. L. Claiborne felt that it was indispensable for Harris to carry the fourth district in order to save Brown.

make way for each other.[134] However, the Whig press did not lessen its attack against "this extinguished gentleman . . . Ex-Governor A. G. (All Gas) Brown," and insisted that he could not win where genuine patriotism had a hold.[135] During the last month Brown made thirty-one addresses in northern Mississippi,[136] but he did not forget the rest of the State. He wrote to J. F. H. Claiborne from Monroe County that he would carry the legislature by a very close vote, if at all, and urged Claiborne to look after and keep right his own county of Hancock, and also Perry and Green, about which Harris had expressed doubts.[137]

In the last few days before election the leading Whig paper in northern Mississippi asked frantically, "Shall the Jackson Clique Rule" and believed that Brown in the Senate would unite with fire-eaters in both houses to seek to repeal the compromise measures. "Repeal these measures and you sever asunder the bonds of Union. Shall it be?" [138] However, these appeals did not suffice to counteract the pleas of Brown to support the regular Democratic state organization and to uphold the national Democratic administration, for the regular Democrats won a majority in both branches of the State legislature. After the result was known Foote, in an open letter "To the People of Mississippi," withdrew his candidacy for the Senate. But he did not neglect to take a final fling at his opponents. He pointed out that two years before he had a majority of twenty-six members of the legislature pledged to reelect him to the Senate. When the State Senate insisted on postponing the election for a full two-year period "in order that, through the instrumentality of expedients to which I feel sure no truly high minded statesman has ever yet lent even his temporary sanction, my defeat might be at last accomplished and unmerited discredit be thus cast upon those sacred principles for which I have so long and zealously contended." [139]

But the elimination of Foote did not mean by any means that Brown now had clear sailing ahead. The year 1853 marks the end of the schism between Union and State-rights Democrats in the cap-

[134] *The Mississippian,* Aug. 19, 1853.

[135] *Independent,* Sept. 17, 1853, also quoting from *Hinds Gazette; Flag of the Union,* Sept. 23, 1853.

[136] *The Mississippian,* Sept. 23, 1853.

[137] MS. J. F. H. Claiborne Collection, Vol. A, No. 79, letter Brown to Claiborne, Oct. 16, 1853.

[138] *Independent,* Oct. 29, 1853.

[139] *Flag of the Union,* Nov. 25, 1853.

ture of the Democratic organization by the latter wing. The under-lying cause of this victory is accurately defined by Wiley P. Harris. In 1851 the State-righters disclaimed secession as an immediate aim, but upheld the ultimate right of secession, while "the Union party went too far the other way, and lost its influence. They condemned secession as revolution, . . . (and consequently that resistance which went beyond resolutions and remonstrances would be treason). . . . The Union Democratic leaders were soon shelved. . . . It was im-possible for a Union party denouncing secession to live in Missis-sippi." [140] This year marks also the beginning of the bitter personal rivalry between Jefferson Davis and Brown, the two leaders of the reunited party, a rivalry which becomes more and more acute in the following years up to the outbreak of the War of Southern Nationalism.

In June, 1853, the Vicksburg *Sentinel,* the Democratic organ of Davis' home county, declared that it was the universal wish of the party that Jefferson Davis should be the next senator.[141] After the famous speech of Davis at Philadelphia on July 18, in which he fol-lowed Calhoun in urging federal aid for a transcontinental railroad from Memphis to California,[142] the *Sentinel* pointed out the deep in-terest which the people of Mississippi had in a Pacific railroad. It felt that he could aid this project best in the Senate, where he could "do more in forwarding that grand work than any other man in the nation." [143] On August 20, as a result of constant appeals from its subscribers that Davis alone could win for the State-righters in northern Mississippi, it placed his name at the top of its editorial column and titled its editorial, "Col. Davis and the Pacific Railroad-Right to Defend State Rights and the Pacific Road." [144] A few days later the *Sentinel* felt it necessary to assert that "in bringing Col. Davis' name forward, . . . we are influenced by no desire to defeat Gov. Brown. . . . We believe Gov. Brown to be a very strong man before the people but we believe Messrs. Davis and Brown are still stronger." [145] The *Southern Standard* of Columbus also urged Davis for senator. The opposition interpreted these moves for Davis as tricks to help to secure a majority of votes for the fire-eaters by appealing to the great prestige of Davis, for "they know he wouldn't leave his present

[140] Wiley P. Harris, *Autobiographical Sketch*, p. 37.
[141] *Natchez Courier,* June 19, 1853, quoting *Sentinel.*
[142] Dodd, *Jefferson Davis,* pp. 143–144.
[143] *Sentinel,* Aug. 13, 1853.
[144] *Ibid.,* Aug. 20, 1853.
[145] *Ibid.,* Aug. 23, 31, 1853.

position for the Senatorship—(he is Secretary of War and President de facto so far as Southern influence extends)." Others felt that Davis might choose to run, in which case, Brown would probably be taken into the Cabinet. Still others rejoiced that Brown was now "among the dead men, abandoned by all." [146]

That Brown had not campaigned with purely unselfish motives to uphold King Caucus and the Democratic party was clearly shown by his reaction to the Davis supporters in two strictly private letters to J. F. H. Claiborne which throw much light upon his true motives and character. In the first letter he expressed the belief that there would probably be a Democratic majority of thirty on the joint ballot for senator, but he wanted his able friends to be on the alert, and asked Claiborne to write one or two articles in the New Orleans press as he had done in 1851. Brown then urged his own cause with vigor. In 1851 he alone had carried his district for the State-righters, yet in 1853 his best friends said he was rushing on to certain defeat with Foote in the field, with northern Mississippi in rebellion, and the party torn by faction. "The enemy tauntingly said, *'You were never beaten but Waterloo is just ahead.'* I made 115 speeches, traveled 3,200 miles, and spent 1200$ (*sic*). The cold & heat, dust & mud, sunshine & rain, were alike encountered and for six long and tedious months I literally gave no rest to the soles of my feet— Our victory is more complete than our most sanguine friends dared to hope for." He would not have a friend of his say anything against Jefferson Davis, but "there is some difference between sitting on an easy chair at Washington—getting his 8,000 a year, and drinking champagne, and riding through the pine woods with the heat at 90°—paying three prices *often* for miserable fever, and drinking *rot gut*." [147] If a laborer is worthy of his hire, "between Davis & myself no man can doubt who should have the reward." On the same day he received a letter from Claiborne and sent off a second letter in the same vein, but showing that he was almost frantic in his frenzy to be elected senator. After he alone had carried his district in 1851

[146] *Southern Reveille,* July 19, 1853, Aug. 17, 24, 1853. *Natchez Courier,* July 31, 1853. *Hinds County Gazette,* Aug. 3, 31, Oct. 5, 1853.

[147] Buck, "The Poor Whites in the Ante-bellum South," pp. 53–54, gives an instructive picture of the political advantages of drinking "the red-eye . . . with every Tom, Dick, and Harry" in the piney-woods area. On the other hand, McCutchen, "The Political Career of Albert Gallatin Brown," p. 181, quotes the *Paulding Eastern Clarion* of Feb. 5, 1859, to show that "Brown had a discriminating taste for champagne and could entertain ambassadors as well as constituents."

"by almost superhuman exertions," making his district the rallying point of the whole State, to discard him "will be to degrade me in the estimation of all the world. . . . I have done the work and it will be a monstrous outrage to deny me the rewards of a victory." He had taken the field in the late campaign "under the most appaling (*sic*) circumstances. My friends were alarmed for my *personal* safety. . . . I have borne the Democratic cross and now the Jews cry 'crucify him'— If my friends will speak out as they ought I will not be *crucified*—Pilate may be on the judgment seat but he will not condemn if the multitude speak against it." If the Democrats had been defeated the odium would have been on him, not on Davis. "We are victors. Ought I or Davis to have the honor—." [148]

Personal friends, especially C. S. Tarpley of Jackson, his chief political adviser in Mississippi, urged Davis to run for the Senate. Tarpley informed Davis of the *sub-rosa* agreement between Brown and McRae and wrote concerning Brown, "I consider him as having out managed himself and without anything like a reasonable hope of success. . . . One thing has given your friends here some trouble. The democratic party of Missi[ssippi] almost without a division are anxious that you should be elected to the Senate next Winter." [149] In September Davis wrote to McRae, implying that he had been the administration candidate for the Senate before his nomination as governor. Although Davis gave no hint that he would allow his name to be considered for the Senate, he fully appreciated the significance of the contest in his State. "No election within my recollection has been more important than the approaching one. The administration will need at least as many true friends as it will have. Our state character is at stake— Surely the fruit we have gathered by the disorganization of 1851 is sufficiently bitter to teach all the necessity for organization and the value of party allegiance." [150] After the Democrats had won the elections Davis informed Stephen Cocke that he would accept the senatorship if elected by the legislature. He already had told Pierce and Brown that he was willing to leave the Cabinet as "the President has need of a confidential friend in the Senate. . . . It is doubtful whether I could be more useful in the Cabinet than in the

[148] MSS. J. F. H. Claiborne Collection, Vol. A, No. 80, No. 81, letters Brown to Claiborne, Nov. 15, 1853.

[149] Rowland, *Jefferson Davis*, II, 212–213, letter C. S. Tarpley to Davis from Jackson, May 6, 1853, p. 209, letter Madison McAfee to Davis from Lexington, April 20, 1853.

[150] *Ibid.*, pp. 264–265, letter Davis to McRae, Sept. 17, 1853.

Senate as a supporter of the administration in full communion with the Executive Dept. . . . It is the mortification at being beaten by such a man as Foote and by such shallow artifices as were used which have made the result of 1851 galling, anything which would remove the barb would answer all the end I ever sought." [151]

During December four Democratic papers continued to urge the election of Davis. The *Yazoo Democrat* denied the claim of Brown's friends that he was mainly responsible for the Democratic victory and declared that the applause of a grateful people ought to be ample reward for Brown's services. However, if Davis refused to accept the election, it admitted that "none would be more acceptable to the people than Gov. Brown." [152] The East, as usual supported Brown, and its leading paper, *The Paulding Clarion,* resented the aggressive attitude of the Vicksburg *Sentinel* in supporting Davis and in asserting that Brown nearly destroyed the prospects of the party in the early part of the campaign by allowing the belief to get abroad that he engaged in intrigue in order to get McRae out of the way and by refusing to meet Foote.[153]

Quitman was also suggested because he had been "the principal sufferer by the former triumph of Footeism and now should be elevated by its downfall." B. F. Dill wrote to Quitman confidentially that he believed Brown would have a large plurality in caucus on the first ballot, but that he would lose thereafter. He was convinced that the Brown vote would be swung to Quitman rather than to Davis. He continued, "I have seen a letter from Gov. Brown (private and confidential) in which he pretty distinctly takes ground that Col. Davis ought not to expect the place, and that he is so confident of the injustice and indelicacy of Col. Davis running that he does not believe he will consent to be a candidate." [154] Since this letter is in the Claiborne Collection, it is most probable that the letter of Brown referred to is the one he sent to J. F. H. Claiborne. In any case, it is clear that party leaders were aware of the growing estrangement between Brown and Davis and that, if Brown could not be elected, it was felt that Brown would try to prevent Davis from securing the senatorship. Although some opposed Quitman because he refused to

[151] *Ibid.,* pp. 336–337, letter Davis to Stephen Cocke, Dec. 19, 1853.
[152] *Southern Standard,* Dec. 3, 1853, mentioning *Sentinel* and *Southern Argus* also for Davis. *Yazoo Democrat,* Dec. 28, 1853. *Sentinel,* Dec. 31, 1853.
[153] *Flag of the Union,* Dec. 30, 1853.
[154] MS. J. F. H. Claiborne Collection, Vol. A, No. 30, letter Dill to Quitman, Dec. 14, 1853.

support Pierce,[155] the powerful *Mississippi Free Trader* and others supported Quitman, who alone of the State-rights leaders had not received recognition since the defeat in 1851. It rejected the plea of Brown that the senator should be chosen to support *any* national administration, for State-rights principles demanded that a senator must be chosen by a sovereign State "as a sovereign chooses his ambassador." [156] All of this pleased the *Natchez Courier,* for it pointed out that it was logical for the secession press to favor Quitman, who had stood consistently for his radical ideas: "Others may be better party men. Davis is a greater Machiavelian, and Brown a greater demagogue, but Quitman is their superior in manliness, honor and candor." [157]

On January 6 the Democratic caucus met. Excitement ran high between the Davis and Brown men, each claiming the nomination by a vote or two. Two Union Democrats from northern Mississippi were denied the right to vote because they would not pledge themselves to support the caucus nominee. Brown won the nomination [158] and the next day was elected on the first ballot by the legislature with a clear majority of eighteen, the Union Democrats who entered the caucus voting for him. Brown carried not only the poorer counties in his own fourth district, but the majority of the counties in northern Mississippi, while the Whigs, represented from the more wealthy counties of western and north central Mississippi, split their votes between Foote and Sharkey.[159]

The *Natchez Courier* attributed Brown's victory to "his peculiar

[155] *Southern Reveille,* Dec. 7, 1853.

[156] *Mississippi Free Trader,* Dec. 20, 27, 1853.

[157] *Natchez Courier,* Dec. 24, 1853.

[158] McCutchen, p. 161, quoting *Natchez Courier* of Jan. 13, 1854, states that Brown got 38 votes in the caucus and Davis, 36.

[159] *Hinds County Gazette,* Jan. 25, 1854. Rowland, *Encyclopedia of Mississippi History Comprising Sketches of Counties, Towns, Events, Institutions, and Persons,* II, 424. Maps of taxable slave population, 1853, and number of slaves (taxable) per free white poll, 1853, based on official sheet of assessment of persons and personal property in Mississippi, 1853. Brown received seventy-six votes, Foote, twenty-two, Sharkey, seven, and there were a few scattering votes. In his congressional district Brown won both House and Senate votes in thirteen counties and even made inroads into the four wealthy river counties—the only counties in his district which had over 10,000 taxable slaves and over ten taxable slaves per free white poll. (He carried both House and Senate in Jefferson, the Senate in Claiborne, and the House in Wilkinson. In the wealthiest alone—Adams—he failed to win support.) Brown won votes in every one of the twenty-eight counties in the State with less than five taxable slaves per free white poll. (He won the votes of both House and Senate in seventeen of these counties, the House vote alone in seven, the Senate vote alone in three, and a minority of the House vote in the remaining county.)

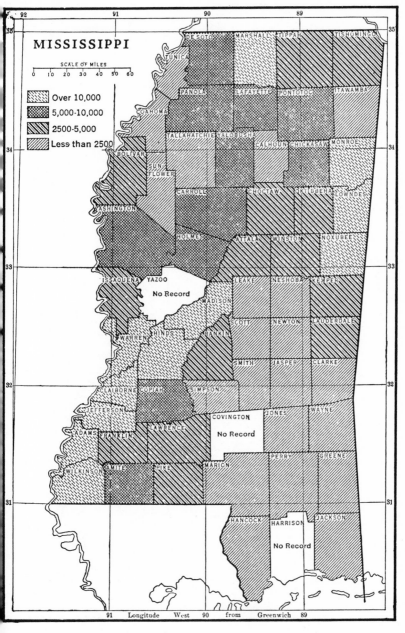

MAP 12. TAXABLE SLAVE POPULATION, 1853

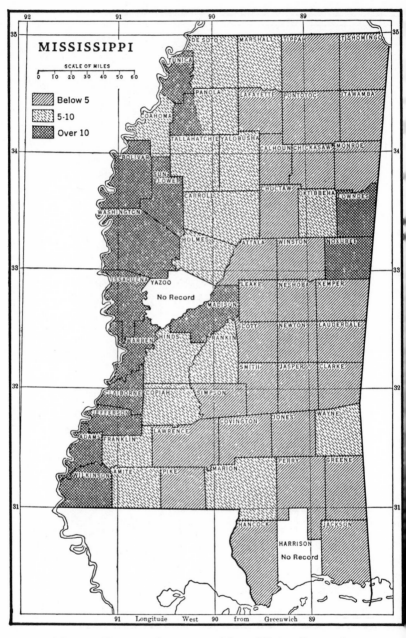

MAP 13. TAXABLE SLAVES PER MALE WHITE POLL, 1853

powers of management, his acquaintance with human nature, his perfect willingness to pull the wires for his own benefit and his knowledge of the art of pulling them, and his entire freedom from any reluctance to allow pride of consistency to stand in the way of future elevation." It claimed that Foote would have beaten Brown two to one if the election had been held in July when northern Mississippi was in open revolt, but Brown managed the canvass with the most adroit skill by paying meticulous care to small points and, by not appearing as a candidate, allaying the distrust and jealousy of Davis' friends. Although not one of the ablest, he was credited with being "one of the most adroit managers and the most lucky politicians the State has ever boasted." [160]

The result was interpreted as a signal triumph for the national administration, but more particularly as an "endorsement of the course pursued by the members of Congress from this State who opposed the enactment of the compromise measures of 1850 . . . as a full, complete, and well-matured popular verdict in favor of the course of our members to Congress who contended for an equality of rights for the South in the great struggle of 1850." [161] The State-righters by retreating had revenged the defeat of 1850. Could they keep control and dominate the current without backing water when the slavery issues again arose as the absorbing national issues during the next six years?

[160] *Natchez Courier,* Jan. 25, 1854.

[161] *Yazoo Democrat,* Jan. 18, 1854. As a symbol of this victory, the *Flag of the Union,* created from the *Southron* to combat the State-righters, went out of existence at this time, leaving the *Natchez Courier* the one outstanding opposition paper. (*Sentinel,* Feb. 18, 1854.)

CHAPTER V

RADICAL SOUTHERN NATIONALIST LEADER, 1854–1858

Senator Brown left Mobile for Washington on January 18, 1854,[1] and took his seat on January 26, nearly two months after the session had started.[2] He found Congress again absorbed by the slavery issue— this time with the Kansas-Nebraska bill. On February 24, a month after he took his seat, Brown spoke on this bill. Although he was inclined to think that slavery would not be introduced into these territories, he rejoiced that it annulled or repealed by implication the Missouri Compromise which had stood on the statute book, "a blot upon its justice, and a mockery of the Constitution which it violated." But he did not think the bill recognized the principle of squatter sovereignty, for, he asserted, "if I did, I would withhold from the bill the sanction of my vote. I utterly deny and repudiate this whole doctrine of squatter sovereignty." He no longer believed, as he did in 1850, that Cass favored this doctrine, but was now very complimentary to him. Cass used better arguments, he believed, than any living statesman to prove that Congress had no power to exclude slavery from the territories. Brown continued, presaging the line of argument which Lincoln used against Douglas' Freeport doctrine: "If Congress does not itself possess this power, it cannot confer it on another. Congress cannot give what it has not got. Congress cannot reverse the whole order of nature, and make the creature greater than the creator," for the people of a territory, "have no existence as a political organization but by our act. . . . Then they have not that higher degree of sovereignty which entitles them to say what shall, and what shall not be property in a territory, inhabited by them, and belonging to the states of this Union." Brown, however, was not entirely sure of his own interpretation of the bill and expressed a willingness to allow the constitutionality of the Missouri Compromise "to go before the Supreme Court, free from the influence of a congressional pre-judgment. I

[1] *The Mississippian*, Feb. 3, 1854.
[2] Cluskey, *Albert G. Brown*, p. 17. *Cong. Globe*, 33rd Cong., 1st sess., p. 247.

will abide the result, though it be against me." [3] A month later he suspected the bogie of squatter sovereignty in Douglas' amendment "to leave the people thereof [i. e. of the territories] perfectly free to form and regulate their domestic institutions in their own way," and admitted that in voting for this amendment "I stood on the outer verge of the precipice. One hair's breadth further, I felt, would put me overboard." [4] To the very last he sought unsuccessfully to have a clause inserted which would specifically declare the Missouri Compromise, which he considered "an insult to the whole southern people," inoperative and void.[5]

In this speech of February 24 Brown explained with greater clarity and force than ever before his justification of the institution of slavery. "Sir, I have no fellowship with that sickly sentimentality that speaks of slavery as a great moral evil. Slavery is of divine origin, a blessing to both master and slave." Indeed, it creates a higher morality in the South because it equalizes all men as it does nowhere else—Negroes are not men within the meaning of the Declaration of Independence. "The wives and daughters of our mechanics and the laboring men stand not an inch lower in the social scale than the wives and daughters of our governors, secretaries, and judges" because the slaves do the menial work. It would take longer to find a *white* bootblack or chambermaid in Mississippi than it took Captain Cook to sail around the world. As for the Negroes, who thus equalize the whites by relieving them from toil, God, in his providence, brought them from cannibalism and barbarism to "these happy shores, where, under the benign influences of our laws, they may learn morality and Christianity." [6]

This high-sounding bombast about the Negroes placing all white men in the South on the same social level was contradicted by the status of the very classes upon whose support Brown had risen to prominence. In his own congressional district there were nine counties which had a total population of less than 5,000 in 1850 which had a taxable slave population of less than 2,500 in 1853. A large minority,

[3] Cluskey, pp. 329–343, Feb. 24, 1854. *Cong. Globe,* 33rd Cong., 1st sess., appendix, 228–232.

[4] Cluskey, pp. 415–417, March 20, 1854. *Cong. Globe,* 33rd Cong., 1st sess., pp. 690–691.

[5] Cluskey, pp. 373–375, May 25, 1854. *Cong. Globe,* 33rd Cong., 1st sess., appendix, 782.

[6] Cluskey, pp. 329–343, Feb. 24, 1854. *Cong. Globe,* 33rd Cong., 1st sess., appendix 228–232.

if not a majority of these farmers had to do their own menial work. It is doubtful whether they ever blacked their boots; surely they had no chambermaids. In such unreasoned, sweeping generalities as Brown made above, he showed most clearly what a dangerous leader he was in a time of crisis.

The Mississippian favored the Kansas-Nebraska bill and spoke in the highest terms of Brown's speech of February 24,[7] but the *Natchez Courier,* also opposing squatter sovereignty, was acute enough to see that the bill did allow the people of a territory to decide for or against slavery *before* they drew up a State constitution. It opposed the bill and felt that Brown, in defending it, was "a strong man feeling bound to do for party what he would willingly have avoided." [8]

Although Brown had canvassed and had been elected as a strict party man, in harmony with the national administration, he very soon began to lose faith in Pierce. In a private letter to Claiborne he admitted that there was much bitterness among Democrats, that many spoke slightingly of Pierce and showed a manifest want of high admiration for both the President and his Cabinet. He himself greatly regretted this, but confessed that he was afraid that Pierce would fail because "the administration has no great national scheme on which to rest its claims for confidence and admiration. The credit for the most important measure before Congress, the Kansas-Nebraska bill, was appropriated by Douglas, who stood outside the administration." [9] A month later Brown expressed himself on the administration to Claiborne again with greater vigor. The administration "has not vitality enough in both houses of Congress to lift it above the sneers and scoffs and ridicule of the veriest dolt that chooses to assail it." His main indictment was his fear that war would not be declared against Spain over the *Black Warrior* affair. If the men in power are too weak to strike for glory, i. e., for Cuba, "the whole country will be ready to write *to let* on the doors of the White House." [10]

So far Brown's criticism was expressed in confidential private letters. He soon found occasion to differ publicly with the administration. On March 2 he spoke in favor of the bill sponsored by the reformer, Dorothea Dix (for which he had voted in the House) to give 10,000,-

[7] *The Mississippian,* March 24, 1854.
[8] *Natchez Courier,* March 30, 1854.
[9] MS. J. F. H. Claiborne Collection, Vol. A, No. 82, letter Brown to Claiborne, March 1, 1854.
[10] *Ibid.,* No. 83, April 4, 1854.

000 acres to the States for the benefit of the indigent insane. Although he admitted that the government did not have the power to make appropriations from the treasury for internal improvements, the authority to dispose of the public lands was more unlimited. And since lands had been granted to the sane, he argued "how much more wise and humane must it be to give it to the insane?" This bill passed both houses by large majorities but was vetoed by President Pierce. Although the President considered the vote on the vetoed measure a test of party loyalty, Brown refused to change his position, but joined with three other Democratic senators in a futile attempt to override the veto [11] and sought to refute the arguments of the veto message. Brown, like Davis on the issue of national aid to a transcontinental railroad, was departing from the strict-constructionist school with respect to internal improvements. Brown denied that there was danger of the States becoming dependent upon Congress to protect their poor, blind, and lame any more than they were dependent on the national government for education when lands were appropriated for that purpose. Such a grant, he claimed, was entirely a matter of expediency. While countering the arguments of the President, he was careful to express a great personal respect for him which he did not feel and even to declare himself "very far from finding any fault with him for having sent in this veto," for the President, as well as Congress, was free to judge the expediency of the grant.[12] It is clear that Brown was eager to guard himself from the accusation of being an anti-administration man. That, he knew, would be disastrous with the all-powerful Davis in the Cabinet. Indeed, he admitted he was greatly concerned about the reception of this speech in Mississippi—as well he might be, for Davis had spoken against the bill in both 1850 and 1851.[13]

Brown's fear that the Democratic press would follow its habit of "simply reechoing the sentiments of the President" [14] was realized for the Democratic press unanimously supported the President. *The Mississippian*, "having fought many a hard battle by his side, and always beheld his plume waving where the fight was thickest and

[11] Nichols, Franklin Pierce, pp. 348–350.

[12] Cluskey, pp. 344–351, March 2, 7, 1854; pp. 353–367, May 17, 1854. *Cong. Globe*, 33rd Cong., 1st sess., pp. 517–519; 560–561. appendix, 642–645.

[13] Rowland, *Jefferson Davis*, I, 557, Sept. 26, 1850; II, 17, Feb. 11, 1851.

[14] MS. J. F. H. Claiborne Collection, Vol. A, No. 84, letter Brown to Claiborne, May 17, 1854.

hottest," found it hard to differ from Brown, as did other Democratic papers.[15] The *Yazoo Democrat* held that "federalism, in its boldest strides towards centralization, has never maintained positions more completely subversive of the rights of the States" than that of Brown in claiming that Congress could do as it pleased in granting lands with conditions imposed on the States.[16]

The Whig press took occasion to praise Brown's action, declaring that it illustrated his consistency in upholding the poor man's interests and rights. The *Natchez Courier* expressed surprise at the criticism of Brown in the Democratic press,[17] and Brown himself was much concerned. In a letter to William N. Whitehurst, collector of customs at Natchez, he threatened to attack his assailants. "As God is my judge," he swore, "I am only restrained by my devotion to the best interests of the Democratic party. . . . I will not submit to every injustice & outrage." [18]

As intimated before, Brown was very impatient because Cuba was not secured. Over a year before in the House he had frankly expressed his own aim in seeking the Pearl of the Antilles— "If I go for the acquisition of Cuba, or for any other territory in the South, let it be distinctly understood now, and through all time, that I go for it because I want an outlet for slavery . . . We want it, we cannot do without it, and we mean to have it. . . . I am willing and anxious that all the world should know that I want it." Just as the Northern and the border States sent their slaves farther South when they became profitless or troublesome, so the South, where the Negro population would be doubled in another generation, needed an outlet farther South. Brown's jingoism was so patent that he caused much laughter when he made it clear that land, i. e., Cuban land, must be secured in preference to any other satisfaction from Spain in a war which he was only too eager to see break out over the *Black Warrior* affair.[19]

In the late winter and spring of 1854 Quitman was busy preparing

[15] *The Mississippian,* June 9, 23, 1854. *Sentinel,* June 17, 1854. *The Mississippian* took especial pleasure in praising Brown's speech favoring a graduated homestead bill a few months later because it disagreed with him at this time. (*The Mississippian,* Sept. 13, 1854 on July 20, 1854 speech.) Cluskey, pp. 378–380. *Cong. Globe,* 33rd Cong., 1st sess., appendix, 1101–1104; 1119–1121.

[16] *Yazoo Democrat,* June 7, 1854.

[17] *Natchez Courier,* May 16, 1854, quoting from *Vicksburg Whig;* June 24, 1854.

[18] MS. William N. Whitehurst Papers, Vol. N, No. 9, letter Brown to Whitehurst, July 1, 1854.

[19] Cluskey, pp. 321–329, Jan. 3, 1853. *Cong. Globe,* 32nd Cong., 2nd sess., pp. 193–195.

another filibustering expedition to Cuba. Quitman, like Brown, had lost confidence in the administration, which he claimed catered alternately to fire-eater and free-soiler, State-righter and centralist, all of whom were "good democrats in the opinion of Peirce (sic) & Davis." Quitman looked forward eagerly to the end of compromise and the early formation of clear-cut slavery and anti-slavery parties.[20] He corresponded with J. F. H. Claiborne (very active at this time in gerrymandering the new congressional districts) [21] and other Democratic politicians. Hundreds of letters were written to him from all sections of the country by those eager to accompany him to Cuba. Agents were sent out to secure recruits and active recruiting was carried on in Jackson where muster rolls were drawn up,[22] while the leading Democratic papers in the State supported his plans.[23]

It was most important for the filibusterers to gauge accurately the possibility that the administration might declare war against Spain— a possibility which Quitman thought quite remote.[24] If war should not be declared, it was necessary to secure an understanding that the administration would not interfere to prevent the filibusterers from organizing and setting sail for Cuba. Senator John Slidell of Louisiana, the chief spokesman of the filibusterers in Washington, introduced a bill in the Senate to have the neutrality laws suspended, but failed to secure its passage.[25] On May 30 President Pierce consulted six leaders on the advisability of issuing a proclamation against any violation of our neutrality laws. The conferees were equally divided. Slidell voted against such a proclamation, while Jefferson Davis voted for it. The next day, to the utter chagrin of the direct-action men, the proclamation was issued.[26] F. C. Jones of *The Mississippian* wrote to Quitman that this caused great surprise and regret, for "the desire

[20] MS. John A. Quitman Papers, 1854, letter Quitman to B. F. Dill, Feb. 9, 1854.
[21] MS. J. F. H. Claiborne Collection, Vol. C, No. 28, letter O. R. Singleton to Claiborne, July 19, 1854.
[22] MSS. John A. Quitman Papers, 1854, passim, especially letters J. F. H. Claiborne to Quitman, March 17, 1854; W. M. Estelle of Jackson to Quitman, May 25, 1854.
[23] John S. Everett, "John A. Quitman's Connection with the Cuban Filibusters," citing *The Mississippian, Mississippi Free Trader, Sentinel, Woodville Republican,* and *Oxford Star.*
[24] MS. John A. Quitman Papers, 1854, letter Claiborne to Quitman, March 17, 1854.
[25] Dodd, *Jefferson Davis*, pp. 139–140.
[26] MS. John A. Quitman Papers, 1854, letter G. W. Whitman to Quitman, July 13, 1854. James D. Richardson, *The Messages and Papers of the Presidents, 1789–1897*, V, 272.

that Cuba should be acquired as a Southern conquest, is almost unanimous among Southern men in this part of the State" where about fifty young men had enrolled to follow Quitman.[27]

Although Brown was cognizant of the schemes of Quitman and was impressed with Slidell as "a bold independent man, and as far above a mean or little thing as the stars are above the clods of the field," [28] there is no evidence that he was one of the active conspirators. He preferred to confine his activities to the strictly political sphere and to inform Claiborne of the administration's activity or rather inactivity about Cuba. To Claiborne he expressed again his growing antagonism to Pierce— "My confidence is giving way. The honest truth is the President wants *backbone*. The great opportunity to get Cuba is at hand, but nothing is done. If he was a Whig I should like to express my opinion of some of his acts," especially his appointment of Northern officers in Kansas which displeased his Southern friends.[29]

But more significant was the growing antagonism between Brown and Jefferson Davis, who dominated the administration.[30] Pierce himself sensed this feeling and informed Brown, as Brown expressed it, "of what I had not thought before, that Col. Davis did not want the position of Senator." [31] But this explanation did not improve relations between the two Mississippians. Whether or not Brown was jealous of the powerful influence Davis wielded, his growing distrust of the administration's policies was sufficient to cause him to write confidentially to Claiborne in May: "My relations with the Sec. of War are *dubious,* not hostile and not decidedly friendly. We passed twice without speaking but this *probably* grew out of a mistake. I understand we are to speak the next time we meet." The mistake was a matter of social punctilio which could hardly have arisen between cordial

27 MS. John A. Quitman Papers, 1854, letter Jones to Quitman, June 10, 1854.

28 MS. J. F. H. Claiborne Collection, Vol. A, No. 83, letter Brown to Claiborne, April 4, 1854.

29 *Ibid.,* No. 85, June 29, 1854.

30 This antagonism between Brown and Davis during the 1850s has never been emphasized in a published work. None of the recent lives of Jefferson Davis make any mention of it. Indeed, Tate, Schaff, and Gordon make no reference whatever to Brown in their works. Cutting (p. 78) mentions him only once, as appointing Davis to the Senate in 1847, and Winston writes only three passing sentences (pp. 105, 126, 128) about Brown, who is called "an outspoken secessionist" and "an original secessionist." Eckenrode mentions Brown four times, pp. 37, 86, 95, 113, but each time his name is only one in a group of names. (See the bibliography for the names and dates of these works on Jefferson Davis.)

31 MS. J. F. H. Claiborne Collection, Vol. A, No. 82, March 1, 1854.

friends. Brown had not spoken because he did not know that Davis had left his card after Brown arrived in Washington, and Davis did not speak because Brown had not returned his call.[32] In any case, this incident shows that, although Brown had ably supported Davis throughout the crisis years of 1850 and 1851, Davis, now exerting the principal influence in the administration, did not consult Brown or take him into his confidence. In all probability Brown strongly resented this ostracism, and it in turn helped to increase his antagonism to the administration. During the latter part of the summer Slidell and Brown were together a good deal at White Sulphur Springs, Virginia, the famous watering-place and "meeting ground for politicians from every quarter of the South," and Slidell wrote that Brown had given him much insight into the character of Davis and "has related several things that have very much qualified the high opinion I once entertained of him." [33]

There is negative evidence which indicates that this ostracism was not only political but was also extended to social relations and that it continued throughout the entire period when Brown was a senator in Washington and a confederate senator in Richmond. The author has examined carefully the works of Mrs. Jefferson Davis, Mrs. Clement C. Clay, Mrs. Mary Boykin Chesnut, Mrs. Burton Harrison, Mrs. D. Giraud (Louise Wigfall) Wright, Mrs. Roger A. Pryor, Mrs. Judith W. B. McGuire, Mrs. Sallie A. Brock Putnam, Mrs. Dunbar Rowland, and Thomas Cooper DeLeon,[34] which describe the aristocratic social life of Washington during the 1850s, and of Richmond during the war. Southern women dominated this brilliant society as their husbands controlled politics, but only one reference in all these works [35] makes any mention of the Browns in social life in either capitol. Although the author is fully aware of the pitfalls which meet one in interpreting negative evidence, nevertheless, he believes that it indicates that Brown was shunned because he led a poor white nonslaveholding and small-slaveholding constituency and that it was a major factor in causing Brown's growing bitterness towards the aristocratic Jefferson Davis.

In the November elections the Democrats lost seats in Congress to the Know-nothings. Brown privately expressed no regrets, but

[32] *Ibid.*, No. 84, May 17, 1854.

[33] *Ibid.*, Vol. C, No. 41, letter Slidell to Claiborne, Sept. 11, 1854. Phillips, *Life and Labor in the Old South*, pp. 365–366.

[34] The titles of these works appear in the bibliography.

[35] Mrs. Clement C. Clay, *A Belle of the Fifties*, pp. 139–140.

thought the result quite justified. He denounced the appointment to a foreign post of a German, Francis Grund, whom he considered "by nature a brute, education a knave, . . . scoundrelism personified. . . . As if to defy public sentiment he selects the moment when there is the greatest outcry against foreigners to appoint the meanest and dirtyest of them all to a foreign court. Does anyone marvel that the party is broken down?" [36]

In the meantime Quitman was not deterred by Pierce's proclamation of May 31, 1854; he only became more wary. Each accomplice agreed to pay $50 to an agent and received Cuban bonds for $150, to go at his own cost to the nearest seaport when requested, and to preserve entire secrecy. As Quitman explained to a correspondent, "the plan of operations is framed to avoid a breach of the neutrality law. As we cannot organize a military expedition within our territory, we cannot appoint nor engage to appoint officers until out of the territory." [37] Mike Walsh, Quitman's agent in Washington, wrote to Quitman, "General Davis is not only a bitter, but an unmanly opponent of yours—so much so indeed, that the shamelessly transparent injustice of his comments, amply reveals and more than neutralizes the virulence of his malice. He would doubtless be delighted at an opportunity to thwart you in anything calculated to place your fame beyond the reach of envious, would-be rivals." Walsh reported that he had to be very cautious in his plans to raise $5,000 in Washington, but that Davis was "gloriously in the dark on the subject, and exceedingly likely to remain so." [38] In February, 1855, Quitman himself came to Washington in the interests of Cuba. Brown attempted to have the neutrality laws repealed so that Quitman could work in the open, but, like Slidell, he failed. [39]

Brown had succeeded in keeping his dissatisfaction with the administration from the public and so was enthusiastically received upon his return to Mississippi—Clarke County Democrats going so far as to suggest him for the presidency. [40] In campaigning for the State elections this year he had to face new issues. The opposition had changed from

[36] MS. J. F. H. Claiborne Collection, Vol. A, No. 86, letter Brown to Claiborne, Dec. 17, 1854.

[37] MS. Quitman Papers, 1854, letter Quitman to L. Nowell Walker, Aug. 24, 1854. Copy in Quitman's handwriting.

[38] *Ibid.*, 1855, letter Walsh to Quitman, Jan. 25, 1855.

[39] *Ibid.*, letter James S. Piper to Quitman, March 5, 1855.

[40] *The Mississippian*, April 17, 1855. *Sentinel*, April 25, 1855. *Natchez Courier*, May 3, 1855.

Whig or Unionist to Know-nothing. Before expressing himself publicly he outlined to Claiborne the tactics which he thought it best to employ. The administration, he believed, had broken down in the North; the national party was no longer united and victorious,—"we are going down, the Know-nothings are rising." Yet with prudent management he thought the State could be carried. This would require a change in tactics; the bold, defiant tone of the press did not befit a defeated party. "A little more oil and honey, and a little less gall and worm-wood would be nearer my idea. . . . I would by mild persuasion get the public mind set against Know-nothingism and then bear down on it with all the power we could command." [41] It is obvious that the new issues did not excite such an intense interest in the fire-eater of 1850 as did the slavery problems.

Brown's previous attitude towards foreigners and Catholics had not been in accord with the prejudices of the Know-nothings. In April, 1852, in defending Andrew Johnson's homestead bill in the House, he held that the power of Congress to dispose of the public lands was as unlimited as the power to declare war. He explained his pride in being a squatter's son and in defending squatter's rights. This power over the public lands should be freely used, even if 500,000 to 1,000,-000 foreigners came to the United States every year. "Heaven made this mighty continent," he declared, "not for our benefit alone, but for the use and benefit of all mankind. . . . It is the gift of God, and we have no right to withhold it from his people." If there is any objection to foreigners congregating in the towns, they should be given lands in the West. His liberalism was particularly marked when it was argued that these immigrants were opposed to slavery, for he replied, "If slavery is to be defended by excluding those from abroad who have prejudices against it, its doom is fixed, and the sooner the fiat for its extinction goes forth, the better." Slavery must be defended on high moral principles, not by the weight of the numbers of its advocates. To the objection that large numbers of foreigners were Catholics, he asserted, "It is no part of my Protestant faith to fear the Catholics." [42]

[41] MS. J. F. H. Claiborne Collection, Vol. A, No. 88, letter Brown to Claiborne, March 29, 1855.

[42] Cluskey, pp. 304–315, April 28, 1852. *Cong. Globe,* 32nd Cong., 1st sess., appendix, pp. 510–514. Fred A. Shannon, "The Homestead Act and the Labor Surplus," American Historical Review, July, 1936, quoted from this speech of Brown as typical of the demand of agrarian agitators in the South, "that the homeless, destitute, and downtrodden . . . be given the opportunity to start life anew on the public domain." American Historical Review, XLI, 641–642.

On April 12, 1855 Brown wrote a public letter from his home at Newtown, Hinds County, against the Know-nothings. He was opposed to all secret political organizations, which became particularly dangerous when they sought to take away the State's right to determine whether or not foreigners should vote. He objected to a change in the naturalization laws, and yet (he now bestows the oil and honey about which he wrote to Claiborne) he will vote for a change if the people wish, for, "it is my business on a question of public policy, to follow rather than to lead public sentiment." He would not call the Know-nothings fanatical or intolerant, for had he not spoken and voted against allowing foreigners to vote in the territories of Kansas and Nebraska, and refused to participate in honoring Kossuth, that intermeddler in our affairs? [43]

Brown's equivocal attitude was considered a shrewd move by the opposition press. The *Natchez Courier* discerned Brown's motives when it asserted, "The truth is Gov. Brown does not like to denounce it [Knownothingism] root and branch, until he knows how the dear people are likely to view it." [44] But the opposition press did not yet discern Brown's own explanation of his letter. He explained to Claiborne that he had not written about the *origin* of the Know-nothings, for that would not be proper in a public statement: "The Democratic party is so deplorably headed at Washington that no one should wonder at its members straying off. . . . My opinion from the beginning has been that the blunders of the Adm. was [*sic*] the prolific source of these singular demonstrations." The only chance of restoring public confidence was for Pierce to move boldly to secure Cuba, but that this would be done, he writes, "for myself I have not faith as a grain of mustard seed." [45]

Furthermore, the antagonism between Brown and Davis continued. There was a certain aristocratic aloofness and conscious dignity about Davis which rubbed many the wrong way. It was sometimes charged that he did not recognize the intelligence of his audience, that "it seems hardly proper that a speaker should assume that he is *great Jupiter* and his audience pigmies." [46] Brown resented this attitude and, in doing so, clearly showed his intense jealousy of his principal

[43] *Cong. Globe,* 32nd Cong., 1st sess., p. 161, Jan. 2, 1850; pp. 376–378, July 10, 1854; pp. 394–403; 33rd Cong., 1st sess., appendix pp. 765–766; 1662, 1668.

[44] *Natchez Courier,* May 9, 1855.

[45] MS. J. F. H. Claiborne Collection, Vol. A, No. 88, letter Brown to Claiborne, April 27, 1855.

[46] *Port Gibson Herald,* July 18, 1851.

rival for control of the Democratic machine in Mississippi. On May 19 he reported to Claiborne that his relations with Davis were no better. He was not certain whom he would support for the other senatorship from Mississippi, but "it is certain that it will not be Col. Davis." He believed Davis should be challenged on his views on Knownothingism: "This thing of allowing him to stand back as too important a character to be brought forward except on his own nod is a humbug that has been played often enough." [47] Brown's jealousy is more clearly illustrated by his report of the Democratic State Convention. Davis, warned against the dissatisfaction of Brown,[48] directed affairs in person and everything was managed as he wished. Brown complained that he was not allowed to see the resolutions and was not invited to speak under favorable circumstances. Brown refused to speak, "not wishing to seem dissatisfied with what had been done and determining in my own mind not to allow my enemies to hear me under circumstances (purposely arranged by themselves) to show me off to disadvantage—I need hardly add that every possible opportunity was given Davis to make an impression— He made it. Whether for good or evil time will tell." Davis thus controlled the situation, while Brown did not dare to attack him, but resolved to keep out of the canvass and to make only occasional addresses. Quitman, Brown claimed, had been treated even worse than he. Quitman also declined to address the convention, but, always more daring and straightforward than Brown, he attacked the course of the administration from the outside.[49] Brown, however, did not succeed in hiding his disaffection. The *Natchez Courier* reported an address made by Brown at Gallatin as an "exceedingly funny attempt to compound praise and censure of the Administration," itemized his ledger account of debit and credit, and concluded that he was "damning with faint praise . . . blowing hot and cold in one breath . . . and stabbing genteelly." [50]

Events, however, drew Brown into an active canvass. On June 25, William A. Stone, a leading politician in Brown's old district (now the fifth, under the reapportionment) urged Quitman to run for Con-

[47] MS. J. F. H. Claiborne Collection, Vol. A, No. 89, letter Brown to Claiborne, May 19, 1855.
[48] Rowland, *Jefferson Davis*, II, 359, letter James W. Williams to Davis, May 30, 1854; 549, 551, letter H. J. Harris to Davis, Nov. 10 and 13, 1855.
[49] MS. J. F. H. Claiborne Collection, Vol. A, No. 90, letter Brown to Claiborne, June 7, 1855.
[50] *Natchez Courier*, June 7, 12, 22, 23, 1855.

gress. Quitman did not answer, so he wrote again. Stone had just seen Brown, who had recently been through the eastern counties, and wrote, "he [Brown] authorises me to say that there is a general desire that you should be in Congress from this district, and furthermore *'that no man in the district would be more acceptable to him and his friends than you would.'*" He added significantly that there was much feeling against Davis among Brown's friends, "the effect of which will greatly add to your prospects for the Senate of U. States." This appeal brought a prompt reply in which Quitman indicated his willingness to run as "a States Rights democrat of the strictest school. I have no connection or affinity with any other party." [51]

Hiram Cassidy, a devoted follower of Brown, and later representative from his district, in writing to J. F. H. Claiborne showed clearly that the leading politicians were thoroughly aware of the friction between Brown and Davis. He reported that there was a concerted movement to give Brown the cold shoulder as he was "specially deserving the frowns of the Secretary of War." The plan, he claimed, was to strike down every active friend of Brown "as preparatory to the main attack on him. . . . I consider him in a more critical position now politically than at any former period." Brown, he actually observed, could hope for success only in the Democratic party to which he was thoroughly committed, and yet such a victory must accrue to his enemies in the administration, especially to "the elevation of one man [Davis] that so abuses the name of Democracy." And if Brown sulked, the Democrats would lose. Cassidy therefore proposed that "some man Brown favors be the nominee of the Convention and let him be saved." [52]

That man was Quitman. As a result of the efforts of Brown, Cassidy, and Claiborne, whose proxies "were right on the question and helped to intimidate opposition," [53] Quitman was nominated by acclamation on July 23 when his letter to William Stone was read. As the *Natchez Courier* pointed out, the leaders of the district realized that it was hopeless to carry it with a genuine Pierce candidate and that they had to look beyond their ranks to the radicals to find a candidate.[54] Al-

[51] MSS. Quitman Papers, 1855, letter Stone to Quitman, June 25, 1855; July 15, 1855, letter Quitman to Stone, July 19, 1855. (Copy in Quitman's handwriting, many changes and corrections.)

[52] MS. J. F. H. Claiborne Collection, Vol. A, No. 27, letter Cassidy to Claiborne, July 17, 1855.

[53] *Ibid.*, No. 28, Aug. 20, 1855.

[54] *Natchez Courier*, July 28, 1855.

though Quitman had resigned his commission as commander-in-chief of the Cuban Junta on May 29,[55] the day after his nomination, he showed that his mind was still centered on securing Cuba. All party contests, and even other vital slavery issues sank into insignificance in his mind when compared with the acquisition of Cuba. "Our future destiny," he wrote, "perhaps the improvt [sic] or destinan [sic] of man on earth, may be dependent on it." He reiterated his lack of faith in the administration and indicated his ambition to be in the Senate. However, he accepted the nomination for the lower house for the time being.[56] A few days later in a confidential letter he made clear his plan of campaign. Under no circumstances would he expressly or by implication endorse the whole course of the administration,[57] for he wrote: "in doing so I would disappoint the expectations of those who nominated me, and would assuredly be defeated as I would deserve to be." However, he would treat the administration with respect, would avoid abuse and denunciation, and wherever possible would support it—a concession which was greatly appreciated by more practical politicians.[58]

The opposition press was quick to point out the incongruity of the Democratic press in linking the names of Brown or Quitman with that of Davis.[59] Brown, of course, was much pleased with the nomination of Quitman, for it meant the continued dominance of his own radicalism in his old stamping ground of eastern and southern Mississippi. He boasted to Claiborne that Quitman could not have been nominated without his support and rejoiced that "the nomination is wormwood and gall to Davis & his friends," although they would be forced to support Quitman. "They hate me, and they hate Quitman— and their hope is that Quitman will become my rival—that we will quarrel and Davis be made the gainer." Brown gave up all idea of remaining out of the canvass and expressed eagerness that his friends should canvass in the seaside counties where his enemies would rejoice in the downfall of Quitman, for he would be active in other quarters and would "labor with as much zeal as if I were myself a

[55] Everett. Rowland, *Encyclopaedia of Mississippi History,* II, 491.

[56] MSS. Quitman Papers, 1855, letters Quitman to B. F. Dill, July 24, 1855; Quitman to Committee, July 27, 1855.

[57] Thus, he refused to sign the prospectus for a new newspaper which favored the administration. (MS. Quitman Papers, 1855, letter Quitman to W. D. Roy, Aug. 21, 1855.)

[58] *Ibid.,* letters Quitman to W. S. Wilson, July 31, 1855; Wilson to Quitman, Aug. 5, 1855.

[59] *Natchez Courier,* Aug. 1, 1855; Aug. 3, 1855, quoting *Vicksburg Whig.*

candidate, and success mainly depended (as it has always done) on my own efforts." He did not expect to get publicity for his activity because he was sure that "it is a part of the policy of the Davis press to say as little about me as possible." [60]

Brown and other leaders in the State were quite puzzled by the growth of the Know-nothings whose policies would exclude many of the best foreigners such as Soulé, who had been recalled from Spain by the administration.[61] Brown sought to combat the new party by asserting its Yankee origin and abolition tendencies, even giving the impression that Giles Hillyer, the able editor of the *Natchez Courier* and now the Know-nothing candidate of the fifth district, was an abolitionist,[62] but Brown's charge that Hillyer had expressed anti-slavery sentiments in the *Natchez Courier* in 1849 was easily answered by showing that he did not become editor until April, 1850. Both Brown and Hillyer indulged in petty personalities which were discreditable to both men.[63] During the last month of the canvass Brown spoke at a score of places, making a second tour of his district, often in company with John J. McRae who was a candidate for re-election as governor. McRae, like Brown, expressed the greatest confidence in the ability of J. F. H. Claiborne to manage the seashore counties.[64]

The election proved to be a big victory for the Democrats. They carried all offices except that of congressman for the third congressional district whose new boundaries had been fought by the Democratic politicians.[65] After the November elections, as two years before, interest centered in the senatorial contest. Jacob Thompson, the candidate of northern Mississippi, showed the same petty jealousy of Davis which Brown had evinced.[66] When Brown got to Washington in December he found another honor suggested for Davis. He thought he discovered an intrigue by Davis to buy up leading papers in Louisi-

[60] MS. J. F. H. Claiborne Collection, Vol. A, No. 91, letter Brown to Claiborne, Aug. 14, 1855; No. 92, Sept. 11, 1855.

[61] *Ibid.*, No. 28, letters Cassidy to Claiborne, Aug. 20, 1855; Vol. B, W. P. Harris to Claiborne, Aug. 30, 1855; A, No. 92, Brown to Claiborne, Sept. 11, 1855.

[62] *Mississippi Free Trader*, Sept. 18, 1855. *Natchez Courier*, Oct. 23, 1855.

[63] *Natchez Courier*, Aug. 30, Oct. 10, Nov. 2, 3, 20, 1855.

[64] *The Mississippian*, Sept. 26, 1855. MS. J. F. H. Claiborne Collection, Vol. B, No. 45, letter McRae to Claiborne, Sept. 30, 1855.

[65] MS. J. F. H. Claiborne Collection, Vol. B, No. 46, letter McRae to Claiborne, Nov. 15, 1855.

[66] *Ibid.*, Vol. C (no number) and Vol. C, No. 21, letters Thompson to Claiborne, Aug. 23 and Nov. 17, 1855.

ana, Mississippi, and Alabama in order to support Dallas for President and Davis for Vice-President. "I am fully confirmed in my opinion that an attempt is being made to control public sentiment in Mississippi through the agency of a purchased & prostituted press," he wrote. Fearing the action of the Mississippi Democratic State Convention in favor of Davis or of a second term for Pierce, he strongly opposed the making of any nominations.[67] While the fear that Davis would become Vice-President did not materialize, the fear of Thompson was realized. Davis, now definitely seeking the senatorship,[68] although opposed by Brown's friends, succeeded after a number of tie ballots in the legislative caucus, but, as Dodd observes, "it was by no means such a victory as he and his friends could have desired." [69]

Brown quickly sized up the political situation and foresaw the coming bitter contests: "all the issues are dead except abolitionism, and Knownothingism is the deadest of them all." [70] He was no longer willing to see Kansas become a free territory. Indeed, on his way to Washington he had already indicated the extreme measures he favored in order to secure Kansas for the slavery interest. In a letter to Ethelbert Barksdale, editor of *The Mississippian,* he insisted that "Southern people owe it to their own safety to use all the means in their power to introduce slavery into Kansas, and protect it after it gets there." Individual, voluntary subscriptions such as Colonel Buford suggested were too slow. Every slaveholder should contribute in proportion to his interest. The legislature should quickly levy a tax of $1 a head on slaves. Thus $325,000 could be collected, 300 slaves bought by the State, and 300 emigrants sent with them to Kansas. Slavery thus backed by the sovereignty of the State would be placed on a solid and certain basis in Kansas. "In short," he explained, "my proposition is for our State to colonize 300 slaves, and appoint 300 of her young men to defend them with ballots, and if necessary, with bullets! . . . If all slave states will follow the example, in twelve months we shall have a slave colony in Kansas that all the Abolitionists in the Union could not expel [sic]." [71] This scheme was received most enthusiastically by *The Mississippian,* and a Copiah County

[67] *Ibid.,* Vol. A, No. 93 and No. 94, letters Brown to Claiborne, Dec. 10, 19, 1855.
[68] Rowland, *Jefferson Davis,* II, 585, letter Davis to S. Cocke, Jan. 6, 1856; 605, letter William McWillie to Davis, Feb. 18, 1856.
[69] Dodd, *Jefferson Davis,* p. 153. MS. Quitman Papers, 1856, letters Reuben Davis to Quitman, Jan. 12, 1856; Edward Pickett to Quitman, Feb. 7, 1856.
[70] MS. J. F. H. Claiborne Collection, Vol. A, No. 93, letter Brown to Claiborne, Dec. 10, 1855.
[71] *The Mississippian,* Dec. 11, 1855, quoting Brown's letter of Nov. 24, 1855.

meeting, although specifically recognizing the wrong in sending special voters into a territory to influence the adoption of a constitution, declared, "when our rights were threatened by imminent and immediate danger, we could do no better than to act on the principle of fighting the devil with fire." [72]

As was to be expected in this new crisis over slavery issues, Brown and Quitman cooperated whole-heartedly upon suggestions from Claiborne to control the patronage in southern Mississippi: to secure appointments to collectorships of customs, to have post-offices discontinued if it would not "offend those of our party who get their letters & papers at these offices," to establish new post-offices and post masters "for the interest of our party and of the community generally" and to get a new post route agent who would be most expedient from a political point of view, for "he would supply our friends with papers & documents, and render more service than fifty other men." [73] At the same time Brown showed great reluctance to seek favors from the Secretary of War for the removal of a light-house keeper or for appointments to West Point and complained, "my influence with Col. Davis amounts litterally [sic] to less than nothing." [74] When Claiborne failed for a year to get some Know-nothing officeholders removed, he wrote to Quitman, "They denounce you—they denounce Brown—the only man they speak kindly of is Col. Davis, and they seem to think that they cannot be removed without his consent." [75] Under these circumstances Brown eagerly came forward to defend Quitman's claim to have been the first to place the American flag in Mexico City [76] and felt it necessary constantly to keep mended his political fences in Mississippi.

The slavery issues were fast darkening the political horizon again, and Brown felt that the election of Banks as speaker of the House was disastrous in its consequences, that it was a blow to the South,

[72] The Mississippian, Dec. 11, 21, 1855. Hinds County Gazette, Dec. 19, 1855.

[73] MS. J. F. H. Claiborne Collection, Vol. A, No. 93, 94, 95, letters Brown to Claiborne, Dec. 10, 19, 1855, Feb. 4, 1856. MS. Quitman Papers, 1856, letters R. Eager to Quitman, Jan. 13, 1856; Quitman to Claiborne, Jan. 26, 1856; Brown to Quitman, Feb. 15, 1856; Claiborne to Quitman, Feb. 19, April 12, Dec. 12, 1856; F. R. Witter to Quitman, March 5, 1856.

[74] MS. J. F. H. Claiborne Collection, Vol. A, No. 98, letter Brown to ———, May 3, 1856.

[75] MS. Quitman Papers, 1856, letter Claiborne to Quitman, Dec. 12, 1856.

[76] Cluskey, pp. 418–421, Jan. 7, 1856. Cong. Globe, 34th Cong., 1st sess., pp. 163–164.

and that it reopened the sectional contest. The spirit of the Northerners who elected Banks he considered "the most vindictive and devilish ever manifested by men living under the same government. They pursue their objects with a fiendish delight and increasing pertinacity. . . . It seems to me that the Union of our fathers is hopelessly lost." [77] Still refusing to attribute squatter-sovereignty doctrines to Douglas, he favored him for the Democratic nomination.[78] He would, however, be satisfied with Buchanan. As to Pierce, he was "sick, tired, disgusted with the *wishy-washing, shilly-shally milk & cider filling in and filling out* of which the country has had a surfeit under Franklin Pierce." And yet he would sustain Pierce if he were nominated, although it would try his fidelity to his party to an extent he had never known. He would take Pierce, he vividly explained, like the Dutchman took heaven, "mit a d—n tight squeeze." The next President, in his view, must have an eternal scowl on his brow, like Mars, and say by his expression, "Be quiet or I'll hang you up like dogs." [79]

However strongly Brown might express himself about Pierce and Davis in private, he held himself in check in public. He had never dared openly to antagonize a Democratic administration in an election year. And yet, in March he showed his dissatisfaction openly to the extent of joining with six Democratic senators to force Pierce to get Forney, the editor of the *Washington Union,* to withdraw his candidacy for printer of the Senate.[80] Although he admitted that his relations with Pierce were such that he could not be considered as representing him in the Senate,[81] he defended him whenever he saw a favorable opportunity to do so. He upheld the President's constitutional

[77] MS. J. F. H. Claiborne Collection, Vol. A, No. 95, letter Brown to Claiborne, Feb. 4, 1856.

[78] Brown had shown his close political and personal friendship for Douglas over a year before. On September 8, 1854, he asked Douglas to use his influence to secure a position for his brother-in-law, James R. Young, in the surveyor-general's office in Kansas or in Nebraska. More significant was Brown's comment about the mob scene in Chicago the week before when Douglas was howled down by the Knownothings: "I have but one opinion of your reception at Chicago, and it is that it was disgraceful to your opponents and highly honorable to you. If your *friends* failed to make you President in 1852, your enemies will succeed in making you the first man in the Republic in 1856." [Douglas MS., letter Brown to Douglas, Sept. 8, 1854 (U. of Chicago, 1854 wrapper). Milton, *The Eve of Conflict: Stephen A. Douglas and the Needless War,* p. 177, quotes the last sentence of this letter.]

[79] MS. J. F. H. Claiborne Collection, Vol. A, No. 96, letter Brown to ——, Feb. 14, 1856.

[80] Nichols, pp. 454-455.

[81] Cluskey, p. 412, Jan. 2, 1856.

power to dismiss naval officers at discretion and denied the right of Congress to demand his reasons.[82] In two long and heated anti-British speeches, which were praised by the opposition press in Mississippi, he lauded the actions of Pierce and of Marcy as gentlemanly and forbearing in protesting against the violations of our neutrality during the progress of the Crimean War.[83] He aided the favorite scheme of Davis for a southern transcontinental railroad by introducing a bill to grant 40,000,000 acres to a private company which would give $500,000 security for completing 100 miles in eighteen months.[84] In order to keep in line with traditional Southern Democracy he still opposed internal improvements in principle—but demanded a full share of such improvements for his own State; he vigorously contested the expediency and constitutionality of the construction of the proposed transcontinental road by the government as a *public* work.[85]

Brown's attitude towards the administration was much improved by its policy towards the most important issue of the time—the status of Kansas. He felt there was no such weakness displayed as towards Cuba during the two preceding years, but that every encouragement was being given to the slavery element which controlled the territorial government. On April 28, 1856, Brown presented his views on the Kansas enabling act in an extended address in the Senate.[86] He had unfeigned satisfaction that Douglas, his choice for the presidency,[87] had introduced this bill, for he "deals justice to the South with a liberal hand" while he "deducts not one jot nor tittle from the equal rights of the North." This enabling act, Brown felt, clearly repudiated the doctrine of sovereignty in squatters, i. e., in a territory. Congress, the trustee or representative of the United States, can no more confer on its creature, the territorial legislature, the power to exclude slavery

---

[82] Cluskey, pp. 403–415.

[83] *Ibid.*, pp. 423–450, March 11 and 13, 1856. *Cong. Globe,* 34th Cong., 1st sess., p. 634, 647; appendix, pp. 234–242. *Hinds County Gazette,* May 7, 1856, quoting favorably from *Vicksburg Whig. Mississippi Free Trader,* April 9, 1856, quoting from *Sunny South.*

[84] *Mississippi Free Trader,* March 25, 1856.

[85] *Natchez Courier,* Feb. 19, 1857, quoting letter of Brown to *The Mississippian.* Cluskey, pp. 470–475, May 6 and July 30, 1856 in Senate. *Cong. Globe.,* 34th Cong., 1st sess., 1118–1120, 1835.

[86] Cluskey, pp. 455–464. *Cong. Globe,* 34th Cong., 1st sess., p. 1041; appendix, pp. 433–435.

[87] MS. J. F. H. Claiborne Collection, Vol. A, No. 97, letter Brown to Claiborne, April 1, 1856. George N. Sanders wrote to John Forney on March 10, 1856 that Brown and Quitman were making an effort to have Douglas "play a desperate game for the Southern vote."—Milton, p. 219, n. 37, quoting Buchanan MSS.

than it can exclude foreign or domestic goods. A stream (territorial legislature) can not rise higher than its source (Congress). A territory can regulate the use of slave property to protect public morals or safety, but does not have the sovereign power to destroy this property. If sovereignty were in a territory, then it could contract alliances and make treaties with foreign States, and it were a mockery to send a governor to rule them, judges to expound their laws, marshals to arrest, and district attorneys to prosecute them, "and finally, to require these sovereigns to send up their own laws for your sanction, and then, by your disapproval to render them null!" He admired Pierce's views on Kansas in his annual message as "marked by a boldness and originality of thought and a frankness of expression." He believed Cass, towards whom he showed such deference in the years after he was Democratic nominee in 1848, was now thoroughly committed to squatter sovereignty and provoked the Senate to laughter at his expense.[88]

Brown's suggestion that the legislature impose a tax in order to buy Negroes to send to Kansas was not carried out, but subscriptions were then taken at many meetings to aid southern emigration into Kansas. Brown, convinced that an enabling act would be passed as soon as Kansas had population to entitle her to one representative, sent $1 for each slave he owned to the editor of *The Mississippian,* and offered to double, triple, or quadruple his subscription if necessary, "so that when the day of trial comes we may not be overpowered and fall an easy prey to the enemies of our institution and disturbers of our domestic peace." He felt that the aggressive Emigrant Aid Society of the North should be met on its own grounds.[89] Thoroughly convinced that the North was on the aggressive, he considered the attack of Preston Brooks on Sumner as a proper answer to Sumner's philippic. He sought to condone the outrage and insisted that there was no added insult because it occurred in the Senate Chamber, since the Senate was not in session.[90]

Brown managed to keep within the good graces of the party chiefs and was considered sufficiently "regular" to be appointed a member of the committee to notify Buchanan of his nomination. At the inter-

[88] Cluskey, pp. 455–467, April 28, May 12, 1856. *Cong. Globe,* 34th Cong., 1st sess., pp. 1041, 1190; appendix, 433–435, 520–521.

[89] *Hinds County Gazette,* May 21, 1856. *Mississippi Free Trader,* May 27, 1856, quoting Brown's letter to *The Mississippian* of April 28, 1856.

[90] Cluskey, pp. 502–505, June 16, 1856. *Cong. Globe,* 34th Cong., 1st sess., pp. 1415–1416.

view Buchanan expressed his eagerness to settle the slavery question "and then add Cuba to the Union." Brown was entirely satisfied with him and wrote, "Could there be a more noble ambition? In my judgment, he is as worthy of Southern confidence and Southern votes as ever Mr. Calhoun was." [91] Four years before he had compared Pierce to Calhoun in like terms, but he was to be as antagonistic to the Buchanan administration as he had been to that of Pierce.

Brown was thoroughly aroused by the growth of Republicanism and by the nomination of Fremont. Although there was no question of the vote of Mississippi, he warned his constituents of the danger of the election of Fremont and asked whether the South should submit to a president and a party "breathing undying hostility to our progress, our safety, and our domestic peace, and buoyed up by the breath of a devilish fanaticism that would tear the Union from its moorings and trample the constitution under foot." If submission be made, the South should take "without murmuring that subordinate position which our masters assign us." [92] Thus was Brown again prepared to raise the cry of 1850 for Southern rights and to foreshadow that of 1860 for Southern nationalism.

Congress remained in session during the summer of 1856 while civil war raged in bleeding Kansas following the sack of Lawrence and the massacre at Pottawatomie Creek in May. Complaints poured into Congress against acts of the territorial legislature elected on March 30, 1855, by a minority of the population but controlled by the pro-slavery forces through the illegal interference at the polls of "border ruffians" from Missouri. [93] Brown maintained that it would be flagrantly unjust for a prejudiced Congress to pass on the constitutionality or advisability of obnoxious acts of the territorial legislature. These decisions should be left to the Supreme Court. If the legislature was a usurpation and a tyranny, then all its laws should be annulled. Brown saw no evidence that unauthorized persons were making the laws of Kansas. He admitted that there had been the inevitable irregularities such as one found in any newly-settled land, but he failed to draw the same conclusion he had made about the irregularities he saw in California in 1850. Now he held that Congress had no more right to in-

[91] Foote, *The War of the Rebellion,* p. 221. Horace Greeley, *The American Conflict,* I, 277–278. John Bassett Moore, *The Works of James Buchanan,* X, 81–85, June 16, 1856.
[92] *Mississippi Free Trader,* Sept. 9, 1856, quoting letter of Aug. 17, 1856 to D. B. Clayton. *Hinds County Gazette,* Oct. 1, 1856.
[93] James Ford Rhodes, *History of the United States, 1850–1909,* II, 81–84.

terfere in the legislative acts of Kansas than it did in those of Massachusetts or of Vermont, which have the right to pass outrageous laws if they wish. He rebuked Cass for defending the right of Congressional review at the same time that he pled so loudly for the right of the territories to govern themselves. If Congress was going to allow only those laws which it favored, it would be better for Congress to say in the first place, "Here are our notions of what laws you ought to have; take them and be content." [94]

Brown's fears were not allayed after the election of Buchanan. In a long speech on "The Slavery Question" on December 22 he reviewed the speedy growth of the sectional Republican party from a little, despised band to a power which had triumphed in twelve Northern States and had lost in the four remaining States "by a vote so close as to make our victory over it almost a defeat." He refused to accept the denials of Seward and Hale that they sought to assail slavery in the Southern States; he had constantly taught his people to prepare for the hour "when the whole northern freesoil phalanx [would be] turned loose in one mighty assault upon slavery in the States." He was sure that his direful predictions of the fearful increase of abolition sentiment were fully justified. The South, entirely on the defensive, must not yield one inch, "for it is better to die defending the door-sill than admit the enemy and then see the hearth-stone bathed in blood."

Brown now directed his attack directly upon Seward, quoting from his speeches to show how he encouraged the abolition of slavery. Whether Seward did or did not favor abolition in the *States,* he led his followers to believe he did. The Constitution sanctions slavery, the Bible tolerates it, God has ordained it, and yet he talked about a higher law! Seward made the most insidious attack, Brown claimed, by charging that the 350,000 slaveholders are a small, privileged class. "If he [Seward] expects, by appeals like these, to turn the hearts of the non-slaveholders of the South against slavery, he will miss his aim. They may have no pecuniary interest in slavery, but they have a social interest at stake that is worth more to them than all the wealth of all the Indies." The non-slaveholders know that if the slaves were freed the propertied men would depart after a class struggle, the whites in large numbers would leave the South, and in a few years the blacks would outnumber the whites four or five to one. Brown, who owed his political career to the radicalism of the poor

[94] Cluskey, pp. 467–470, Aug. 26, 1856. *Cong. Globe,* 34th Cong., 1st sess., pp. 32–33.

whites of the piney-woods of southern and eastern Mississippi, could point to his own experience when he declared that he would even prefer an army of non-slaveholders to an army of slaveholders to defend the institutions of the South.

Brown next turned upon Henry Wilson and quoted his statement to Wendell Phillips that the policy of the abolitionist anti-slavery party "will yet be impressed upon the country." When Wilson denied that he favored Phillips' extreme views on abolition in the States, Brown replied that he was "certainly the most unfortunate man that ever took up a pen to express an idea." He forced Wilson to hedge and repeatedly drew the laughter of the Senate at his expense. Brown admitted that slavery was a frightful outrage on humanity when seen through *Uncle Tom's Cabin,* the *Liberator,* or one of Wilson's speeches, but asserted that practically all who know anything of slavery by experience believed it the normal condition of the Negro race. Furthermore, the liberty of the Negro would not have been so restricted, education forbidden, and manumission denied to thousands, had it not been for the "impertinent intermeddling of himself [Wilson] and his friends with matters that did not concern them."

All the South ever asked was to be let alone. Very few Southerners, he asserted, expected Kansas to become a slave State when the Kansas-Nebraska bill passed. It was only when the North sought to colonize Kansas with a vagrant population that "the Mississippians were inflamed to madness by their conduct . . . rose en masse, and swore, by the God that made them, these things should not be." Brown reiterated his pledge to stand by decisions of the Supreme Court to settle the slavery question on a firm and lasting basis. Knowing the Southern complexion of that court, it is not surprising that he should thus prophesy the result: "We mean to rout the Abolitionists and bury Black Republicanism so low that the sound of Gabriel's trumpet will not reach it in the day of judgment!" He ended this speech by a warning to settle the issues fairly, or "there will be but one alternative left us, and that an appeal to the God of battles. May Heaven, in its mercy, avert such a calamity!" [95]

This fiery address was hailed in Mississippi as one of the best if not the very best Brown ever delivered. Two pamphlet editions were printed and broadcast in the State, and it was widely printed in the

[95] Cluskey, pp. 475–501, Dec. 22, 1856. *Cong. Globe,* 34th Cong., 3rd sess., appendix, pp. 92–99.

Southern press and commented on.[96] This speech appealed to all parties; his opposition to the clause in the proposed State constitution of Minnesota which allowed aliens to vote (following upon a like attitude on the Kansas-Nebraska bill) won for him Know-nothing support. The House had allowed aliens to vote, but the Senate struck out the provision, twenty-seven to twenty-four, the Whigs, Know-nothings, and the Southern Democrats uniting to defeat it. When this vote was reconsidered Brown warned that it would shake the Democratic party to its foundations by creating 500,000 Know-nothing votes. The Republicans, eager for the foreign vote, were all in favor of the provision. "I know not," Brown declared, "whether we are here more under the influence of foreigners or Black Republicanism."

It was a notable day for Brown when the *Natchez Courier,* admitting its long bitter hostility to him, was pleased to confess "that but few men have risen more rapidly in public estimation, and on a firmer basis than that gentleman. Few there are, who have within the last three or four years improved more in grasp of mind, comprehensiveness of intellect, and range of thought." It knew him as a formidable, successful, adroit politician. Now, "he is rapidly uniting to that character the more noble and lofty one of an American Statesman." The *Vicksburg Whig* and the *Hinds County Gazette* (Whig) joined the *Natchez Courier* in this praise, and the Davis organ, the Vicksburg *Sentinel,* rejoiced that he could increase his prestige by adopting one of the fundamental doctrines of the Know-nothings. When *The Mississippian* was unkind enough to say that this praise was "extracted from reluctant lips," the *Natchez Courier* retorted, "They were voluntarily uttered, and with extreme pleasure." [97]

Upon his return to Mississippi after the adjournment of Congress, a signal mark of popular favor was shown to Brown when a banquet was given in his honor by the citizens of Jackson irrespective of party. The invitation, signed, among others, by Chief Justice W. L. Sharkey, a Whig, and John D. Freeman, his Unionist opponent, asserted that his public and private life commanded the respect and confidence of his opponents. One hundred and twenty-five attended the banquet which included a large number of the leading citizens of Vicksburg. The opposition press outdid itself in praising the services of Brown to the

[96] *Hinds County Gazette,* Jan. 28, 1857. *Mississippi Free Trader,* Feb. 10, 1857.

[97] *Natchez Courier,* Mar. 25, 31, April 7, 1857, referring to Vicksburg *Sentinel,* also referring to *The Mississippian* and *Vicksburg Whig. Hinds County Gazette,* Jan. 28, May 13, 1857.

State, and Giles Hillyer hailed "the era of political kindness in the South."[98] The fact was that all organized opposition to the Democratic party was fast crumbling away. The leading opposition paper predicted that in ten years at least the Southern branch of the Democratic party would accept the Know-nothing principles because of the added power the incoming horde of immigrants gave to the anti-slavery movement.[99]

But where party strife is dead, faction within a party abounds. During 1857 the cleavage between the two party chiefs, Davis and Brown, became more marked than ever. At the beginning of the year Brown wrote to his confidant, J. F. H. Claiborne: "It is hardly possible for Davis and myself to be friends— The man does not breathe who shall treat me as Davis treats his friends who are in position. No man shall play the 'big man me and little man you' all the time with me." They were on speaking terms, but Brown had "no disposition to have with him any more intimate relations."[100]

The day after Brown accepted the invitation to the banquet in his honor in Jackson he wrote to Claiborne that he hoped the Democrats of Vicksburg and Jackson would be more just to him in the future, but he urged Claiborne to do all in his power to prevent any one hostile to him from being nominated for governor as this would endanger his reelection to the Senate. Remembering the furor in northern Mississippi over the nomination of McRae in 1853, he was convinced that the nominee must come from that section. "Any fair man who will do me justice will suit me,"[101] he wrote, typically self-centered when his own political fortunes were concerned. His mind was absorbed by the fear of Davis. A month later his friends in the North favored Robert S. Grier who had voted for Davis for the Senate in 1854, but for Thompson and against Davis in 1856. Brown thus considered himself quite liberal in supporting Grier and wrote, "We shall see if Davis is as much so. I am glad to escape any suspicion of opposing men be-

[98] *Mississippi Free Trader,* April 22, 1857, quoting invitation and acceptance by Brown. MS. Quitman Papers, 1857, Committee to Quitman, April 13, 1857. *Natchez Courier,* May 2, 1857, quoting *Vicksburg Whig. Natchez Courier,* May 5, 1857, quoting *New Orleans Bulletin.*

[99] *Natchez Courier,* March 31, 1857.

[100] MS. J. F. H. Claiborne Collection, Vol. A, No. 100, letter Brown to Claiborne, Jan. 4, 1857. McCutchen, "Political Career of Albert Gallatin Brown," p. 159, suggests the social distinction which separated Brown and Davis when he states that many Whigs lined up behind Davis, "who was a gentleman and one of their sort."

[101] *Ibid.,* No. 101, April 5, 1857.

cause they happened to prefer Davis to myself." [102] A few days later he secured the appointment of one of Davis's friends as marshal of the southern district because he "did not want it supposed that Davis' friends were excluded— There is policy in peace as well as in war." Now that Davis was out of the cabinet the new administration was consulting Brown about all appointments in his State, and he used this favor to the full extent to keep up his fences.[103]

This under-cover antagonism between Davis and Brown was brought into the open when the Davis forces were dubbed "The Third Party" by the *Hinds County Gazette*.[104] Although only suspected within the last few months, this paper claimed that the foundations of this party were laid immediately after the senatorial election of 1854. Meetings which lauded Buchanan, Pierce and his Cabinet, but omitted all reference to Brown and the senatorial election, "that laud Col. Davis as something more than human—as a very God here on earth in disguise," who frown on all who do not worship the Dictator and "think that the Sage of Briarfield is not the greatest of all living men! This is the third party." It charged that "the great Mogul" was determined that Brown must be destroyed and that "all his machinery is secretly at work for the accomplishment of that object." [105]

Brown felt keenly the danger to his political future in this contest with the powerful Davis and snatched eagerly at the indication of favor shown by a Democratic meeting of Davis' own county in complimenting both Brown and Davis. "Is it a holding out of the olive branch?" Brown asked Claiborne. "I hope so, for God knows I never wanted to quarrel with Davis or his friends." But in the same letter Brown expressed his fear that C. S. Tarpley, who successfully conducted Davis' campaign for the Senate in 1855–1856, would be chosen governor.[106]

[102] *Ibid.*, No. 102, May 4, 1857.

[103] *Ibid.*, No. 103, 104, May 13, 30, 1857.

[104] A generation ago William Garrott Brown recognized the existence of three parties in the South—although he would have called the party of Brown, rather than that of Davis, the Third Party, since by "extreme state rights men" he included extreme southern nationalists. "Politically, the people of the Cotton states were divided into three parties. There were, indeed, few who did not call themselves either Whigs or Democrats, but the extreme state rights men, though they usually cooperated with the Democrats, repeatedly asserted themselves in such a way as to present the aspect of a third party."—Brown, *The Lower South in American History*, p. 122.

[105] *Hinds County Gazette*, April 27; May 20, also quoting *Vicksburg Whig*, June 3, 1857.

[106] MS. J. F. H. Claiborne Collection, Vol. A, No. 104, letter Brown to Claiborne, May 30, 1857.

William McWillie of Madison, a central county, was nominated in June, so the northerners, having failed to secure the governorship, sought to win the Senate seat for former governor Joseph Matthews, W. S. Featherston, or W. S. Barry, in order to prevent the re-election of Brown. Brown was thus forced as in 1853 to center his campaign in northern Mississippi.[107] Brown succeeded in centering attention on the contest in Kansas. The decision of Robert J. Walker, the new governor and former senator from Mississippi, to interpret his instructions as to eligibility for electors favorably to the free-soilers enraged the South. Brown, who had been so friendly towards Buchanan, now asserted that he would be a traitor to the best interests of the South if he retained Walker and declared emphatically that he would not vote to ratify his nomination if he was not removed before Congress met.[108]

Brown's old district renominated Quitman without difficulty and recommended Brown unanimously for the Senate as the best man to check the rapidly increasing power of the Black Republicans in the Senate and to stay the tide of abolitionism. The convention further declared that Kansas should come into the Union as a slave State and condemned "any attempt on the part of the present Governor to force upon the territory a Free Soil constitution." [109]

While Brown, sure of the support of the South and East, was bitterly assailing Walker, many felt that Davis was not so much a Southern-rights Democrat as a national Democrat who would support the administration through thick and thin, even to the extent of attempting to reconcile the people to a Buchanan-Walker free-soil policy in Kansas. The *Natchez Courier* and *Hinds County Gazette*

[107] *Natchez Courier*, May 14, 1857, quoting *Paulding Clarion*, June 25, 1857. MS. William N. Whitehurst Papers, Vol. N, No. 9, letter F. L. Claiborne to Whitehurst, July 24, 1857.

[108] *Natchez Courier*, July 24, 1857, quoting *Yazoo Sun* on Brown's speech at Yazoo; July 31, 1857. *Mississippi Free Trader*, Sept. 4, 1857. So great was the indignation against Walker that Davis had joined with Brown in denouncing Walker's "treachery" at a mass meeting in the State capitol. Henry Foote had been vigorously defending the President against Southern politicians who charged "the President with the basest ingratitude to the Southern States and people, to whose support they asserted him to have chiefly owed his elevation." The day after Davis and Brown spoke, Foote defended Walker and Buchanan so ably that the large audience adopted resolutions supporting the administration. (Foote, *Casket of Reminiscences*, pp. 114–116. George Fort Milton, *The Eve of Conflict: Stephen A. Douglas and the Needless War*, p. 267.)

[109] Claiborne, Quitman, II, 250. *Mississippi Free Trader*, July 28, 1857.

were convinced that Davis' main object in the canvass was to defeat Brown. At Hernando, Davis eulogized Pierce, defended his veto of the indigent insane bill, and then turned to denounce Brown as a man who voted with the enemy, and yet "he still returns to our powerful camp, to share in the issue of the rations which still belongs to Democracy as a majority to distribute." [110]

Brown, however, was quite satisfied with his canvass in northern Mississippi and felt confident of election if the sentiment of the people would be respected by the legislature.[111] And his confidence was justified. Brown received 68 of the 80 votes in the Democratic caucus and 111 of the 115 votes cast by the legislature. It was the most brilliant triumph of his career and was hailed enthusiastically by the *National Intelligencer,* the party organ in Washington.[112] Mississippi had placed the stamp of approval upon her radical leader and had thereby encouraged him to go to further extremes in order to vindicate the rights of the South.

Although Robert J. Walker resigned his office as governor of Kansas, other causes of complaint against the administration were not lacking when Brown returned to Washington. William Walker, after having seized control of the Nicaraguan government a second time, had been arrested by Commodore Paulding. Brown criticized Buchanan for not condemning Paulding for the illegal seizure of Walker and justified Walker by the same arguments which Quitman used in defending his projected expedition to Cuba in 1853–1854. True, Brown argued, the men and materials for the expedition came from the United States, but, since the expedition was not actually organized within the territory of the United States, there was nothing illegal in it. Furthermore, Walker himself could not violate our neutrality laws because he had voluntarily expatriated himself—

[110] *Hinds County Gazette,* July 29, Sept. 16, 23, 1857. *Natchez Courier,* Sept. 12, 1857.

[111] MS. William N. Whitehurst Papers, Vol. N, No. 9, letter Brown to Whitehurst, Sept. 16, 1857.

[112] MS. J. F. H. Claiborne Collection, Vol. A, No. 105, letter Brown to Claiborne, Nov. 16, 1857. *Hinds County Gazette,* Nov. 18, Dec. 9, 1857 and *Mississippi Free Trader,* Dec. 4, 1857, both quoting *National Intelligencer* of Nov. 14, 1857. Map of House and Senate votes for senator, based on *Journal of the Senate of Mississippi,* 1857, pp. 54–55. There was only one Senate vote against Brown, representing the wealthy river cotton counties of Bolivar, Washington, Issaquena, and Yazoo. The three House votes against Brown came from the river counties of Coahoma and Hinds, and from Neshoba in the east. Brown secured every vote in both House and Senate from his former congressional district.

a right which Buchanan was struggling to have recognized by the international community. Paulding, in violating the territorial integrity of Nicaragua, disgraced his epaulets "which ought to have been torn from his shoulders." When Doolittle of Wisconsin proposed to present a medal to Paulding, Brown renewed his attack and held that his action would have warranted a vote of censure against the Secretary of the Navy or against the President himself if it had been ordered by the government.[113]

Disappointed by the failure of the scheme for Southern expansion in Nicaragua, Brown sought to delay the admission of the new free State of Minnesota and to aid the entrance of Kansas under the proslavery Lecompton Constitution. In both cases he opposed Douglas and showed again (as in his relations with Cass and Pierce, and soon with Buchanan) that it was impossible for him to continue in harmony with the Northern leaders of his party. Minnesota, he said, had violated the enabling act in allowing aliens to vote. If Kansas was now to be excluded because of irregularities in the forming of her constitution, then let Republicans show their good faith by excluding Minnesota and there would be peace all over the country. When Brown forced from Douglas the significant concession that neither an enabling act nor the submission of the State constitution to the people was always essential, he insisted that Douglas should cease to complain that Kansas did not present herself properly because her whole constitution was not submitted to the people to be received or rejected. Although Brown admitted that Minnesota could admit to the vote anyone she pleased after she was within the Union, he continued to oppose the acceptance of her present constitution which gave the vote to aliens and mixed-breed Indians, breechless savages who would don the garb of civilization only for the purpose of voting. He opposed the recognition of her two senators and objected to granting her three representatives before a new census could be taken.[114]

Before the vote was known on the Lecompton Constitution of Kansas, with or without the further introduction of slavery, Brown suspected that the free-soilers would refrain from voting, but he an-

---

[113] Cluskey, pp. 508–514, Jan. 7, 1858. *Cong. Globe,* 35th Cong., 1st sess., pp. 218–219; 360–363; 515–520, Jan. 21, 1858. Davis also felt that Walker should not have been seized, but, unlike Brown, he had no sympathy with the Walker expedition. Rowland, *Jefferson Davis,* III, 130–131, Jan. 7, 1858.

[114] Cluskey, pp. 528–535, Feb. 1, March 25, 1858; pp. 570–575, Feb. 25, March 29, April 7, 1858. *Cong. Globe,* 35th Cong., 1st sess., pp. 500–504, 867–878, 1325, 1410–1411, 1514–1515. Allan Johnson, *Stephen A. Douglas: A Study in American Politics,* p. 340.

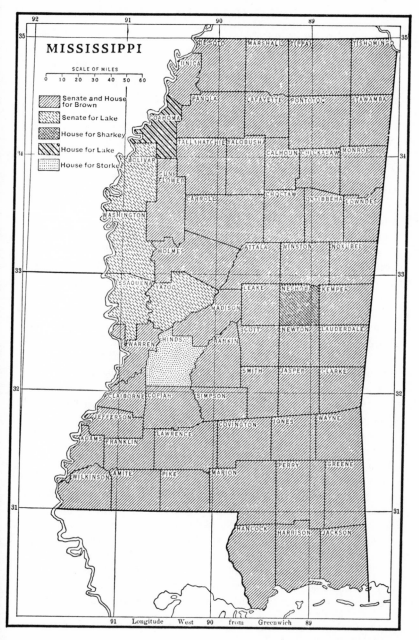

MAP 14. ELECTIONS IN STATE LEGISLATURE FOR SENATOR, NOVEMBER, 1857

nounced that he would abide by the result.[115] After the vote was known he ardently urged the admission of Kansas under this constitution. In a long address on February 3 and 4, 1858, he charged the free-soilers with bad faith for resorting to technicalities and special pleading to defeat the will of the people. While the South allowed new Northern States to be admitted, the greatest objections had been raised over the admission of Arkansas, Florida, Texas, and now of Kansas. Sectional parties were forming and his own party was in imminent danger of dissolution. "When all the North is pulling in one direction," he prophesied, "and all the South in a contrary direction, that the Union must be drawn asunder is as certain as that the sun rose this morning and will go down tonight." He admitted that he had no hope of influencing Republican votes, but said that his speech was addressed to the South for home consumption. Those who claimed to be the best friends of the Union passed the Compromise of 1850 which he abhorred from the beginning and had now been proved an utter failure. The Compromise of 1854 he accepted reluctantly. Republican senators showed bad faith by helping to organize the Emigrant Aid Society which brought the spirit of rebellion into Kansas. This spirit continued after a constitutional convention was assembled and a State constitution drawn up.

Although Douglas had been the first choice of Brown for the Democratic nomination in 1856, Brown now completely broke from Douglas politically as he had from the other Northern leaders of his party. Since Douglas, "who has stood by us from the beginning of the controversy," admitted that it was not necessary to submit this constitution to the people, why should he oppose accepting it because a majority of voters refused to go to the polls? Whose fault, Brown demanded, was that? Could Congress, or the territorial legislature, force the people to vote? Only a Vermonter like Douglas could think of such a Yankee trick to overturn an election whenever defeat was feared by abstaining from voting. Douglas now violated his own principle of non-intervention, he claimed. The people are to regulate their domestic affairs in their own way, yet Congress interposes its authority "at every step—tell them what they shall and what they shall not do; that they must submit this clause of the constitution and that they need not submit others; or that they must submit the whole constitution, or that they shall not submit any part of it!" Brown ad-

[115] Cluskey, p. 536, Dec. 23, 1857. *Hinds County Gazette,* Feb. 3, 1858. *Cong. Globe,* 35th Cong., 1st sess., p. 165.

mitted the right of Congress to look behind the returns if there was palpable fraud, but again directly contradicted his own attitude when the admission of California was at stake when he asserted, "I think they [Congressmen] should proceed behind the presentation of the constitution with exceeding caution, and never to the point of inquiring into the validity of an election." Brown challenged Douglas to deny his charge that "at last the broad fact stands out staring the world in the face, that the constitution is to be rejected because it tolerates slavery." Douglas, of course, denied this, for he pointed out that he had denounced the constitution as a fraud before the vote was taken because it gave the people no opportunity to express themselves for or against the existence of slavery in Kansas. Brown countered that the free-soilers in Kansas were in open rebellion and had no cause to complain. And yet, if Douglas' doctrine of popular sovereignty was to control, then there could be no objection to Dorr, representing the majority, to seize the government of Rhode Island; to Brigham Young, acting like a sovereign in Utah and expelling federal judges; or to "Lane and his Topeka followers . . . undertaking to control Kansas, law or no law."

Brown returned to the charge against Douglas that his Southern friends were justified in believing that slavery had something to do with resistance even on his part. Douglas has fallen from grace, has voluntarily walked out of the Democratic party into the ranks of the Republicans. By doing this he has endangered the very existence of the Union, which hundreds of thousands even now believe to be rocking beneath our feet. He, more than any one else, can calm the public mind—"whether he thinks so or not, he is the very life and soul of this agitation. The senator from Illinois gives life; he gives vitality; he gives energy; he lends the aid of his mighty genius and his powerful will. . . . If ruin come upon the country he more than any other and all other men, will be to blame for it. . . . If desolation shall spread her mantle over this our glorious country—let not the senator ask who is the author of all this, lest expiring Liberty, with a death-rattle in her throat, shall answer to him, as Nathan answered David, 'Thou art the man!' " [116]

On the same day that Brown so realistically recognized the power of the Little Giant and the probable consequences of the sectional bitterness, Henry Wilson of Massachusetts quoted from Brown's oft-

[116] Cluskey, pp. 536–570, Feb. 3, 4, 1858. *Cong. Globe,* 35th Cong., 1st sess., pp. 548–553, 570–574. Johnson, p. 341. Milton, p. 289.

criticized speech of January 30, 1850, to show that its tone and sentiment looked "to the triumph of a sectional southern policy, to the
expansion of slavery, or to the ultimate overthrow of the government
of this country." [117] Brown, as usual, maintained that it was delivered calmly and deliberately as a Union speech, but took occasion to
reaffirm his creed: "I put the rights of the states above the Union, I
put the sovereignty of the States above the Union; I put the liberty of
this people under the Constitution above the Union. . . . The rights
of my state, the rights of my oppressed section, are worth more to
me than the Union. I have said so before, here and at home. I say so
now, and, if that is to be disunion, let it be so." [118] Here was a clear-
cut expression of Southern nationalism, for it was evident that he was
more concerned with "the rights of my oppressed section" than with
merely the rights of his own State.

The Kansas territorial elections in October, 1857, had resulted in
free-soil control of both branches, and it was obvious that Kansas
could not be won for slavery. Upon the rejection of the Lecompton
Constitution by the House of Representatives the compromise English bill was introduced which submitted the whole constitution to the
voters for acceptance or rejection. Again Brown refused to follow
Douglas. Brown decided to vote for the bill as a peace measure, but
he had no enthusiasm for it because it represented the hopelessness
of the Southerners in ever winning Kansas. "I have been so accustomed to vote for things that I do not precisely like," the disillusioned senator observed, "that I have no great trouble in bringing
my mind to the conclusion that I ought to vote for this." [119]

Oregon also came up for Statehood during this session. Brown
had opposed its admission as a free-soil territory because he wanted
to use it as a bargaining point to secure concessions for territory
south of 42°. Now he opposed its entry as a State for an even more
flimsy reason. He found that many Republicans opposed its admission because it excluded free Negroes and declared that it was none
of his business to help to multiply free States which were against his

[117] Henry Wilson, in his *Rise and Fall of the Slave Power in America* quotes
from Brown's speeches a number of times in order to illustrate the extreme pro-
slavery argument (II, 224, 391, 578–581, 612, 627, 659–663) and the growth of
Southern nationalism (III, 25).

[118] Cluskey, pp. 506–507, March 20, 1858. *Cong. Globe,* 35th Cong., 1st sess.,
appendix p. 167.

[119] Cluskey, pp. 576–580, April 29, 1858. *Cong. Globe,* 35th Cong., 1st sess., appendix, pp. 1871–1872.

interest and that of the South. He took occasion to emphasize what he considered the hypocrisy of the North—often expressed in the sweeping generalization, "The North loves the negro race, but hates the individual." In a humorous vein he offered to divide the few thousand free Negroes in Mississippi between Wilson and Seward, but felt sure that they would refuse them. "I have always known that they were anxious to make negroes free, and when they were free, I have understood they were very anxious to get clear of them." Take them handcuffed to the Kentucky shore, advertise them for sale, and the Ohio abolitionists will steal them and spirit them away, but send them without shackles to Ohio, and "they will not have them on any account. [Laughter.] What mockery is all this sympathy with the negro . . . and yet northern gentlemen will no more allow him to go into their states than they would allow a pestilence to come in if they could prevent it." They would force Oregon to take free Negroes but will not take them themselves. "I am not going to beg you to take another free state," he concluded in good humor. "If you ask it, and ask it genteelly and cleverly, I think we shall let you have it; but we will not beg you to take it." [120]

While Brown was opposing the admission of the Northern States of Minnesota, Kansas, and Oregon, and urging that the navy, as our main arm of defense, be more than doubled,[121] the leading paper in the western part of Brown's old district, the *Mississippi Free Trader,* began urging Brown for the presidency, taking its cue from a Democratic paper in Salem, Massachusetts.[122] The leading piney-woods paper, the *Paulding Clarion,* followed suit, characteristically supporting his claims to be "the great champion of the preemption law which secured homes to thousands of poor families in the South and West" and which earned him the title "the squatter's son alias the people's friend." [123] The *Monticello Journal* in the central part of his old district, the *Argus* of Gallatin, his old home town, and the *Pontotoc Examiner* all expressed preference for Brown, while his old opponent, the *Natchez Courier,* looked on favorably.[124] Brown, still ably aided by the powerful influence of J. F. H. Claiborne, was without a rival

[120] *Ibid.,* pp. 581–582, May 5, 1858. *Cong. Globe,* 35th Cong., 1st sess., p. 1969.
[121] Cluskey, pp. 582–584, June 7, 1858. *Cong. Globe,* 35th Cong., 1st sess., p. 2742.
[122] *Mississippi Free Trader,* May 6, 1858, quoting *Union Democrat,* Salem, Mass. of April 22, 1858; Aug. 6, 9, 1858.
[123] *Ibid.,* June 19, 1858, quoting *Paulding Clarion.*
[124] *Natchez Courier,* July 8, 1858.

in southern and eastern Mississippi. McRae, now running for Congress, was backed by Brown. It was true, as a correspondent noted, that "that fact is almost omnipotent in this district." [125]

Brown returned to Mississippi and felt so sure of popular support that he made a more radical and unrestrained speech than he had ever delivered at a barbecue in his honor on September 11 at Hazlehurst, Copiah County. He pictured the results of squatter sovereignty in Utah, where it was necessary to send an army to put down rebellion, but more particularly in Kansas, where "Jim Lane and his robber gang . . . set all law, order, and decency in defiance, and in the name of popular sovereignty murdered the people, pillaged their houses, and drove their defenceless families into the wilderness, or without the limits of the territory." Brown insisted that every requirement of the law and of the constitution had been complied with in the formation of the Lecompton Constitution and still felt that Douglas was influenced in his opposition because it was a pro-slavery constitution. But this was no time, he believed, to criticize Douglas who was engaged in his great contest with Lincoln. Douglas "is a giant in intellect, a giant in will, a giant in eloquence, a giant in everything that makes up the characteristics of a great man, and I hope he may thrash Abolition Lincoln out of his boots. . . .[126] God forbid that I should discard a great man like Douglas, who differs from me on one point, and take a small man like Lincoln, who agrees with me in nothing." Quitman and only one other Southerner voted against the compromise English bill. In thus standing out against all compromise, Quitman "showed a moral heroism worthy of a Spartan . . . a heroism before which the sublime history written by him on the walls of Mexico might pale and hide its face." And now Brown vowed that he also was through with all compromise in order to save

[125] MSS. William N. Whitehurst Papers, Vol. N, No. 9, letters H. S. Van Eaton to Whitehurst, Aug. 18, 1858; J. F. H. Claiborne to Whitehurst, July 29, 1858.

[126] Milton, p. 347, quotes this statement to illustrate the continuing influence of Douglas over Brown. Brown was "joyous and enthusiastic" after Douglas' victory and loaned his personal frank for circulating Douglas' speeches in the South. (Milton, p. 355, quoting letter of Winslow S. Pierce, Nov. 9, 1858. Stephen A. Douglas MSS., letters of Daniel McCook, Nov. 7, 1858, and W. M. Lowe, Nov. 18, 1858.) J. F. H. Claiborne wrote from Bay St. Louis, Mississippi, a highly complimentary letter to Douglas in which he congratulated him "on the great victory you have won *for us all*. My sympathies & confidence have been with you all the time *at Washington*, & in Illinois, as my friend Senator Brown, will tell you." He declared that Douglas' recent speech at Chicago "embodies my political creed & the creed of the masses, north & south, as I hope to *believe. In hoc signo vincit.*"— Douglas MSS., letter of Dec. 5, 1858.

the Union. He admitted frankly that he had feared he would not be sustained if he had taken a more extreme position like Quitman, for he knew "how utterly powerless a representative becomes, and especially on those sectional issues, the instant he is not sustained by his people."

It is significant that Brown, in his great anxiety to have the approval of his constituents, felt that he was playing safe in criticizing the administration. Buchanan, he admitted, was sound on the Kansas issue and would not urge her admittance until her population warranted one representative, but he was easily scared "with hobgoblin stories about breaking up the Democratic party in 1860 and the election of an Abolitionist, and the final downfall of the Union, and all that, and then right away he does something wrong." Thus, Buchanan upheld William Walker in Nicaragua at first but then deserted him. He was quite frank in explaining the direct interest of Southerners "in planting a slave-holding state in Nicaragua. We are so, because slavery must go South, if it goes at all. If Walker had been allowed to succeed, he would have planted such a state, and the Southern States would have populated it." He was not concerned now with the minor arguments about neutrality laws which he presented in the Senate. He had opposed the Cass-Irissari treaty because he feared Nicaragua would then be controlled by Northerners.

He warmed up on his aggressive expansionist views. His audience may think it strange, he asserted, that he should talk about taking possession of a part of Central America when it belonged to some one else. "Yes, it belonged to some one else, just as this country once belonged to the Choctaws. When we wanted this country we came and took it. If we want Central America or any part of it, I would go and take that." If the population was willing to live under our good government, well and good, if not, "they might go somewhere else." He admitted that sentiments like these would set him down by many as "a regular fire-eating filibuster," but in extenuation he pointed to the stately mansions which now replace the wigwams and the railroads which take the place of the war path. True, we have treaties with the Central American states, but so we had with the Indian tribes, but they were mere scraps of paper, "all fudge and fustian, signifying nothing" when the white man came to spread civilization. So, "if we want Central America, the cheapest, easiest, and quickest way to get it is to go and take it, and if France and England interfere, read the Monroe Doctrine to them." Cuba, Tamaulipas, Potosi, and one or two other Mexican states must also be secured, "and I want them all for the same reason—for the planting or spreading of slavery. . . . I would spread the blessings of slavery, like the religion of our Divine Master, to the uttermost ends of the earth, and rebellious and wicked as the Yankees have been, I would even extend it to them. . . . I would preach it to them, as I would preach the gospel. They are a stiff-necked and rebellious race, and I have little hope that they will receive the blessing, and I would therefore prepare for its spread to other more favored lands." If there ever was an aggressive slavocracy, surely Brown could qualify as a prominent member.[127]

But when he dealt with the rising problem of the reopening of the African slave trade he set aside all this jingoistic bombast. True, the wealthy planters might secure cheaper labor with more slaves, but then the poorer farmers, upon whom Brown had always relied for support, would be pushed out and would leave the State, thus diminishing the chances for acquiring more slave territory. More slaves without more land he considered quite impracticable. He would make an honest effort to secure more territory, "and if we failed, I would go out of the Union and try it there. I speak plainly. I would make a refusal to acquire territory because it was to be slave territory, a cause for disunion, just as I would make the refusal to admit a new state because it was to be a slave state, a cause for disunion." After more land was secured, then would be the time to open the African slave trade and remove the insulting law of 1808 which implied that the trade was inherently wrong.

While the more conservative Davis still clung to the hope that the difficulties between the sections could be settled satisfactorily so that it would not become necessary for Mississippi to secede,[128] Brown showed clearly in this speech that he had given up hope for a reconciliation between the sections. Like Lincoln, he accepted a "house-divided-against-itself" doctrine. "In twenty years," he told his audience, "I have not changed my opinion as to the great fact, that you

[127] French Ensor Chadwick, *Causes of the Civil War*, p. 107, quotes these jingoistic statements to show why it was impossible to secure Cuba by treaty. Northern senators were repelled by such statements as these. Clearly, Brown was defeating his own purpose of securing foreign territory for the slavery interests. Virginius Dabney, in *Liberalism in the South*, p. 113, refers to Brown's extreme views concerning the blessings of slavery as "equally fantastic" as the "unpardonable absurdity" of Angelina Grimké, who said she had never seen a happy slave.

[128] Rowland, *Jefferson Davis*, III, 343, Davis' address to Mississippi legislature, Nov. 16, 1858.

must give up the Union, or give up slavery. . . . The sentiment of hostility to the South and its institutions, is widening and deepening at the North every day. . . . It is madness to suppose that this tide is ever to roll back. Today, Seward, the great arch spirit of Abolitionism, marshals his hosts. . . . The day of battle cannot much longer be delayed." When that day came, Brown resolved that he would stand, where he had always stood, on the side of slavery and the South. He had been raised in almost superstitious reverence for the Union, "but," he continued, "if the Union is to be converted into a masked battery for assailing my property and my domestic peace, I will destroy it if I can, and if this cannot be done by a direct assault, I would resort to sapping and mining. This is plain talk." It was indeed! Brown was stirring up revolutionary passions as effectively as a Marat or a Desmoulins in 1789. To prove further that he had returned again to the radicalism of 1850, he quoted from his January 30, 1850, and Ellwood Springs speeches, and not to condone and minimize their more extreme statements as he constantly had done since 1851, but to emphasize them, and he assured the journalists present that this time he would not write a single letter of explanation of his speech if he was quoted correctly.

Very soon all must "stand in the breach as one man determined to do or die in defence of our common heritage. . . . I would now, as in 1850, give Cromwell's advice to his army: 'Pray to the Lord, but keep your powder dry.' " Obviously, Brown now felt sure of his ground and did not fear that public sentiment in his own State or events in other Southern States would force him to retreat as he was forced to do so painfully in 1851. The day when he would fight a Wilcox for calling him a disunionist was gone. He was now the acknowledged radical leader of his State and felt sure of his ground. He had even lost faith in his party. Northern Democrats had sacrificed Pierce and had abandoned Buchanan, and he had no confidence that a Democrat, if elected in 1860, would be sustained. He took notice of those who were urging his own name for the presidency, but keenly observed, "I am not deceived as to my true position. No man entertaining the sentiments I have expressed today, can be elected President of the United States. . . . I am ambitious but my ambition does not lead me towards the presidency. That is the road to apostasy." Whenever the South gives up the Northern Democracy and decides to act alone, "I will stand for her, if she can find no son more worthy of her confidence. But I will never consent to compromise my principles or flatter Free-Soilers for their votes. When it comes to that, I stand out." [129]

This speech was immediately interpreted as a bid to win support against the more conservative Davis who was making conciliatory speeches throughout the North. Indeed, it was felt that the extremist views of this speech were partly due to Brown's belief that Davis was compromising his principles in order to "flatter Free-Soilers for their votes," a belief quite unfair to Davis. Dubbed as "the most ultra made in any of the Southern States since the canvass of 1851," it was considered "a bold stroke for the leadership of the disunionists. . . . As Davis goes North, Brown comes South. . . . If Davis should penetrate further into Maine, we shall probably hear of Brown bathing in the crater of a volcano" as the prince of fire-eaters. The *New York Herald,* the Buchanan organ which favored the speedy admission of Kansas, roundly criticized Brown's extreme views and called forth from the *Mississippi Free Trader* the sneer that it would be a sacrifice of respect and judgment beyond the bathos of degradation to follow such a man as James Gordon Bennett, the editor of the *New York Herald.*[130]

When Seward delivered his famous "irrepressible conflict" speech at Rochester a month after Brown's Hazlehurst address, Brown's accusation that Seward sought to destroy slavery in the Southern States was felt to be substantiated and his statement, "It is madness to suppose that this tide is ever to roll back," vindicated.[131] If the policies of either of these radical leaders, Seward or Brown, could not be moderated, it was only too evident that the country had arrived at the eve of secession if not of civil war.

[129] Cluskey, pp. 588–599, Sept. 11, 1858. The eager activity of Brown in nursing his constituency is shown by the fact that he sent 18,000 franked public documents during 1858, while Davis sent only 5,000. Indeed, only one Southern senator sent more than Brown. Hinton R. Helper, *The Impending Crisis of the South: How to Meet It,* p. 431.

[130] *Natchez Courier,* Sept. 17, 1858, also quoting *Vicksburg Whig;* Oct. 5, 1858, quoting *New York Herald. Mississippi Free Trader,* Oct. 25, 1858, criticizing *New York Herald.* Davis recognized and regretted the opposition of Southern extremists to his Northern tour: "That tour convinced me that the field of useful labor is now among the people and that temperate, true men could effect much by giving to the opposite section the views held by the other. The difference is less than I had supposed."—Rowland, *Jefferson Davis,* III, 498, letter Davis to Franklin Pierce, Jan. 17, 1859. The contrast between this statesmanlike utterance and the speeches of Brown is typical of the wide difference of viewpoint which separated these Mississippi leaders.

[131] *Mississippi Free Trader,* Nov. 18, 1858.

CHAPTER VI

The Eve of State Secession and the Establishment of a Southern Nation, 1859–1861

Brown returned to Washington to find the administration resolved to crush Douglas. The party caucus removed him from the chairmanship of the powerful committee on territories. Brown, astute politician that he was, warned that this action might have the same effect as the rejection of Van Buren's nomination as minister to England and land Douglas in the presidency.[1] In spite of Brown's vigorous disclaimer of any presidential ambitions, two more Mississippi papers declared for him, while the *Mississippi Free Trader* and the *Eastern Clarion* continued actively to agitate in his favor. It was admitted that the ultra sentiments of his Hazlehurst speech caused many tried men in the North to fear his influence, but that "all straightout—State Rights Democrats in that section, like him all the better for that speech." Only one more Northern paper could be shown to favor Brown, and it was far nearer the truth, as Brown himself recognized, that "instead of courting Northern support, he has actually thrown it off by his devotion to his own State and section." [2]

In the short session of Congress, Brown, foreseeing the break up of the Union, moved back towards his earlier State-rights views. The friction with Davis increased. When Davis urged the Pacific railroad bill, Brown, although formerly favoring it, opposed it on the ground that the federal government could not appropriate funds unless the military necessity was direct and absolute. "I deny your right as much to construct an unnecessary road in a territory," he asserted, "as I deny it to construct a road in the states. . . . I never expect to see this Government take the first step toward the construction of such a work as this. . . . Leave your Pacific railroad alone, leave

---

[1] *Natchez Courier*, Dec. 29, 1858.

[2] *Mississippi Free Trader*, Sept. 18, 25, Oct. 11, 1858, noting support of *Vicksburg True Southron* and *New Hampshire Democratic Standard*. *Paulding Eastern Clarion*, Nov. 13, 1858, noting support of *Corinth Cross City*; Feb. 5, 1859.

it to individual enterprise; let capital commence the road where it pleases to commence it, and construct it in its own way and noiselessly and much more rapidly than by your interference, it will go on, and go on to completion." [3] In direct encounter over a difference of opinion on some District of Columbia legislation, both Davis and Brown showed an unfriendly and irritated attitude towards each other.[4]

Brown initiated an historic debate on February 23, when his extreme slavery views and his bitter struggle with Davis forced him to court an open political break with his warm personal friend, Stephen A. Douglas. Because of its far-reaching and tragic consequences this debate was a major link in the chain of events which finally led to the War of Southern Nationalism and was, as Theodore Clarke Smith has said, "the event of greatest significance during the session" of Congress.[5]

The Kansas issue, which was the occasion for the debate, took on a new phase at the beginning of 1859. Brown, still opposing the admission of Kansas as a State until its population should equal the federal ratio, maintained that it was the duty of Congress to provide adequate protection to slavery in Kansas. The Dred Scott decision upheld the view that slaves were property which a territorial legislature could not abolish by unfriendly legislation. Congress, Brown insisted, was derelict in its duty if it refused the protection which the legislature would not give—"The Constitution, as expounded by the Supreme Court, awards it. We demand it; and we mean to have it. What I and my people ask is action: positive, unqualified action. . . . Douglas' doctrine of nonintervention does not mean that the South can have no remedy when its rights are violated. If Congress, by mere force of numbers, denies rights guaranteed by the constitu-

[3] Allen Marshall Kline, "The Attitude of Congress toward the Pacific Railway, 1856–1862," *Annual Report of the American Historical Association, 1910*, p. 191. *Eastern Clarion*, Feb. 5, 1859, quoting correspondence from Washington. Cluskey, *Albert G. Brown*, pp. 599–601, Jan. 20, 1859.

[4] Rowland, *Jefferson Davis*, III, 527, 535, Feb. 5, 7, 1859. When Brown denied that Georgetown had protested against a bill to construct a railway along Pennsylvania Avenue, Davis replied, "A protest has been sent to Congress. My colleague has the same chance [of finding it out] as the rest of us." Brown emphasized his opposition to any railway along Pennsylvania Avenue with the words, "I say [so] today, as I said before, and I hope my colleague will take note of it." As Brown had voted for the consideration of a railway bill, Davis replied, "I do not misunderstand the argument of my colleague; but I did not see, nor do I see now, how to match that argument with his vote."

[5] Theodore Clarke Smith, *Parties and Slavery*, p. 242.

tion," Brown declared that his "mind will be forced irresistably [*sic*] to the conclusion that the Constitution is a failure, and the Union a despotism. . . . Then, sir, I am prepared to retire from the concern." When asked how he would retire, he responded, "We shall not sneak out of the concern; but, throwing our banner to the breeze, we will march out like men, leaving such a trace behind as that our enemies may pursue us if they have the courage to do so." Even a wild beast would fly from some one who was making war on him. The assertion by Republicans that they were not attacking slavery in the States was quite insincere, for they all fell into line behind Seward, their great Napoleon, and his irrepressible conflict theory. Wade demanded to know from Brown, "the Napoleon of that side," whether Congress was not bound to protect slavery in the States if it was obliged to do so in the territories. Brown's answer was a direct attack upon Douglas, a thorough-going repudiation of squatter sovereignty,[6] and a reassertion of State sovereignty. The territorial legislature had no more power than to regulate so "that the master shall not permit the slave to endanger the public safety or corrupt the public morals" while the States were free to do as they pleased with slavery. The only obligation of Congress to the States was to guarantee that fugitive slaves should be surrendered.[7] "I understand from the Senator from Illinois that when I make that appeal he will deny it. . . . I want in the next presidential election, that we shall know where we are, what we are and where we stand. If we agree let us stand together like honest men. If we disagree, let us separate like honest men."

Douglas, in reply to Brown, stated that he admired his frankness and candor, but argued that Congress had never enacted a criminal code for any organized territory in order to protect property and that an exception should not now be made to protect slave property. He

---

[6] After Brown got back to Mississippi he admitted that he had acquiesced in these doctrines in 1856, because "they had just then, contrary to the expectations of their friends, began [*sic*] to work in our favor. I did not think it the most appropriate time in the world to abandon them." *Eastern Clarion*, April 27, 1859, quoting letter of Brown to William H. McCardle, editor of *Vicksburg True Southron*, April 14, 1859. Andrew C. McLaughlin, in *A Constitutional History of the United States*, pp. 549, 587, refers to Brown's views on the inability of a territorial legislature to exclude slavery and the duty of Congress to protect slavery in Kansas as typical of Southern sentiment. He presents the viewpoint of Davis on the latter issue, but does not distinguish it from that of Brown.

[7] Cluskey, pp. 604–614, Feb. 23, 1859. *Cong. Globe*, 35th Cong., 2nd sess., pp. 1241–1251.

did not believe that the Democrats could ever carry a single State of the North on such a platform. When Davis, "upon whom more than any other Southerner the mantle of Calhoun had fallen," rose to denounce Douglas, it was the signal for the definite and final breach between Douglas and the Southern Democrats. And Douglas, on his part, recognized, and even encouraged the conflict with the Southern faction after February 23. The stage was fully set for the inevitable disunion of the Democratic party at Charleston in 1860.[8]

Now, as in 1850, Brown was calculating the value of the Union. "We who come from the planting States get nothing from this Government but postal facilities. . . . We know nothing of this Government but to feel its power of taxation, except through the post office." And even that one service was very poor in Mississippi because the distances between post-offices were so great. He did not think that the post-office department should be self-supporting and opposed the cataloguing of offices which did not pay half their expenses for he feared this would result in the discontinuance of more offices in sparsely settled communities.[9]

While urging aggressive action by Congress to protect slavery in Kansas, he sought to get through a bill to open negotiations to secure Cuba. He did not mince his words, but frankly spoke out, "I want to advertise to all the world that we mean to have it. . . . I am willing to pay for it, or I am willing to fight for it." [10] His views on Cuba were given national prominence when he addressed Tammany Hall in New York a few days after the adjournment of Congress.[11] He had been invited to address Tammany once before, in 1854, but declined because he feared his views on slavery in the territories would be out of harmony with those of his hosts.[12] But now, apparently, he did not care, having given up hope of winning over the Northern Democracy. He spoke as he had done at Hazlehurst; the burden of his message was that Cuba must be secured in order to extend the slavery interest either by purchase, conquest, or filibuster. Before this Irish organization, however, he was more pronounced in his expres-

[8] Johnson, *Stephen A. Douglas*, pp. 397–403. Louis Howland, *Stephen A. Douglas*, pp. 332–333. Milton, *Stephen A. Douglas*, pp. 366, 367.

[9] *Cong. Globe*, 35th Cong., 2nd sess., II, pp. 1451, 1454. Smith, pp. 242–244.

[10] *Cong. Globe*, 35th Cong., 2nd. sess., II, pp. 1352, 1357–1358, 1363.

[11] Douglas had been invited, but declined. The engraved invitation of March 8, 1859 to speak on "The Acquisition of Cuba," on March 14 at Tammany Hall in Douglas MSS., University of Chicago.

[12] *The Mississippian*, April 7, 1854.

sions against England. England might be offended by the acquisition
of Cuba, but that should make no difference, because "England, the
bloody old bruiser has gone slashing round the world insulting everybody, fighting everybody, and plundering everybody. I tell you
now, by conquest, or through the agency of filibusters, two years will
not elapse before Cuba will be in the embrace of America." He appealed to the abolitionists whether slavery was not infinitely worse in
Cuba than it was in the Southern States, and whether this condition
would not be improved if we secured Cuba. He further suggested
that each member of his audience "would be better off if he had a
negro to wait upon him." [13]

The Northern reactions to Brown were in marked contrast to those
towards Davis after his tour of the previous summer. As the *New
Orleans Delta* observed, the "stout and plainspoken Southerner . . .
has given great offense to all sides and shades of opinion at the
North" which were "mightily outraged by these candid expressions
of the adventurous Mississippian." [14] The *New York Tribune* declared that Brown "defiled a platform Augean, not merely by plain
and unmistakable and broad filthiness, but by avowals and inuendoes
only morally base." The acme of morality of Senator Brown was
that we should steal Cuba in order to keep others from stealing it.
Other New York journals commented in like vein. The *Washington
Union* was more restrained, but objected that Brown's foundations
were not broad enough for any national action on the subject of
Cuba. These criticisms were hailed as an excellent advertisement by
Brown's friends who felt that "a more candid and out-spoken enunciation of views and sentiments has never been made by any of our
public men." As after his Hazlehurst speech, the contrast was made
between the radicalism of Brown and the conservatism of Davis, who,
the *New Orleans Delta* claimed, "last summer barely escaped political
annihilation in Mississippi under the high commendation of Northern
journals." [15]

The *Eastern Clarion* and the *Mississippi Free Trader* kept up their
ardent advocacy of Brown for president, and they made much of the
support of the *Democratic Standard* of Concord, New Hampshire,
which urged the South to "put forward her representative man for

[13] *Mississippi Free Trader*, March 30, 1859.
[14] *Eastern Clarion*, March 30, 1859, quoting *New Orleans Delta, New York
Courier, Enquirer, Times,* and *Journal of Commerce,* and the *Washington Union.*
[15] *Ibid.*

the next Presidency, and let that man be Albert Gallatin Brown of Mississippi." [16] Before Congress adjourned the Democratic Convention of Clark County declared for Brown,[17] and the convention of Lawrence County did the same on May 16.[18] At the latter meeting at Monticello, the county seat, Brown spoke on the "Probable Issues in the Presidential Contest of 1860." He was fully aware that the existence of the government itself might depend on their determination because they would "touch every interest, every passion, and every prejudice in the whole country."

Three issues stood out preeminently in Brown's mind. The first was the old, leading phase of the slavery question, i. e., slavery in the territories. On this issue Brown largely repeated the views he had expressed in Congress, particularly in his speech of February 23. Since, by the Dred Scott decision, Congress could not prohibit slavery in a territory, surely its creature, the territorial legislature, could not do so. Just as no State can protect citizens from piracy on the high seas, so no State could defend its rights in the territories. This duty devolved upon Congress in both cases. Just as Congress declared war on the Barbary states and sent an army to punish the Mormons who pillaged emigrant trains, so Congress ought to and must protect slavery in Kansas against both hostile legislation and in default of adequate legislation. If the South, he declared, "consents to be thus hood-winked she deserves to be enslaved" and it would be treason for her to uphold the national Democratic party if the Northern wing deserted to the Douglas forces.

The second issue was that of territorial expansion, which he believed involved "bringing practically for the first time, the Monroe doctrine under the supervision of the American people." On this issue he went even further than in his Tammany Hall speech. A month before, at Gallatin, he had condemned the government for "its persecuting and uncalled for vigilance in the frustration of the plans of private enterprises [such as the proposed Quitman expedition], adopted for the good of the South." Now he urged the repeal of "our odious neutrality laws." He was not in the least startled by the old fogy outcries against filibusters, for "whenever patriotic work had to be done, some one had to take responsibility." He favored immedi-

[16] *Eastern Clarion,* March 9, April 27, May 11, 1859. *Mississippi Free Trader,* May 7, 12, 1859. *The Mississippian,* May 13, 1859, quoting *Democratic Standard.*

[17] *Eastern Clarion,* Mar. 9, 1859, reporting Democratic county convention of Feb. 28.

[18] *The Mississippian,* June 10, 1859.

ate expansion in Cuba and parts of Mexico, "and sooner or later over the whole of Mexico; and as for Jamaica, Hayti and Porto Rico, they would by and by come along with Cuba." The Clayton-Bulwer treaty must be set aside so that we may look constantly to the ultimate incorporation of the Central American states into the Union or into a Southern Confederacy. He would tell England, France, or any other power that "we are the master power on this continent, and we expect to absorb the whole of it. . . . As for your possessions, keep them until we want them, and then we will give you notice to quit." Surely, there was no lack of vision in the imperial schemes of this champion of aggressive slavocracy!

The third issue was the renewed agitation for the opening of the African slave trade. The Democratic meeting in Gallatin at which Brown spoke resolved that this trade should be opened [19] and the Southern Commercial Convention at Vicksburg, which met a few days before his Monticello speech, took similar action by an overwhelming majority and organized the African Labor Supply Association.[20] Again, as in his Hazlehurst speech of the previous September, Brown took a very moderate attitude. A few minutes earlier he did not seem to care what happened to the national Democratic party, but now he urged the impracticability of the reopening of the slave trade because of the opposition of Northern Democracy. Disunion would come soon enough and would be terrible enough, he declared, without adding this issue to the grievances of the South. The repeal of the anti-slave trade laws must wait for some future day—even the law of 1820 which declared the trade to be piracy. However, he did point out that the domestic slave trade was legal. He reprobated the liberal policy of Buchanan in providing $45,000 for feeding, cloth-

---

[19] *Ibid.*, May 3, 6, 1859, quoting *Gallatin Mirror*.

[20] *Ibid.*, May 13, 17, 1859. This convention at Vicksburg was the last of fourteen Southern commercial conventions. At first, as the name implied, these conventions were economic in nature, but the year before, at Montgomery, under the leadership of Yancey, "the rabid politicians were to assume control of the convention and to convert it into a completely political debating society." This last meeting at Vicksburg "was the final battleground of what was now an oral conflict between secessionists and Unionists of the South." Radical pro-slavery resolutions were introduced at the request of Governor McRae of Mississippi which were opposed by the former Mississippi senators, Walker Brooke and Foote. Although a motion in favor of secession if a Republican President were elected was tabled, the motion urging the repeal of all federal laws prohibiting the foreign slave trade was passed, forty-four to nineteen. There is no evidence that Brown took an active interest in any of these commercial conventions. Herbert Wender, *Southern Commercial Conventions, 1837–1859*, pp. 207–234.

ing, and educating the wild Africans seized on the *Echo,* while he vetoed the agricultural colleges bill on the ground that "Congress had no power to give the states wild lands to aid them in instructing native children in the great art of Agriculture." The best interests of the Africans would be served if white masters would clothe, feed, and instruct them in the arts of civilized life, but this policy would be detrimental to the poorer whites because it would lead to overproduction of cotton and to lower prices. This meeting passed resolutions in favor of Brown for President, for Congressional protection of slavery, but only by a bare majority for the repeal of the prohibition of the foreign slave trade.[21]

The Mississippian received this address lukewarmly. It felt that Brown's criticism of Buchanan was too severe, but its main objection was to his remarks about the inexpediency of reopening the foreign slave trade. It maintained that the principle of free trade should hold for slaves as well as for other forms of property. The prohibition was a form of paternalism utterly repugnant to Democratic principles. It raised the question, "Are the people of the South competent to decide for themselves what supply of slaves they need, or shall the government, under the control of an unfriendly majority, decide for them?" It believed that Brown's economic reasoning was also fallacious. Planters would buy no more slaves than they would need; the prices of slaves would be lessened to such an extent that the profits on capital invested would be greater even if the price of cotton should fall. New lands would be brought under cultivation, thus adding to the aggregate wealth, just as intensive cultivation and the invention of the cotton gin had done. Thus, between 1825 and 1859, although the price of cotton per pound was halved, the total crop had increased in size seven times and the export had increased five times in value. It made a strong plea for more scientific farming, particularly for a rotation of crops and an increased labor supply. "Purged of its vices, Providence, not man, has made this trade a powerful element of moral, social, and industrial progress in climates adapted to the negro constitution. . . . It is not piracy to civilize and Christianize heathen Africans, as has been done in the Southern States." All the Negroes in Africa, it claimed, would hardly overstock the South and the territories, but, when that was done, Mexico and Central America would be open to enable the South to restore

[21] *The Mississippian,* June 10, 14, 1859.

the balance with the North "and to protect themselves either in or out of the Union."

However, the leading party organ did agree with Brown that the issue should not be made a test question before the party and commended a number of other leading Democratic papers which took the same position.[22] All recognized how difficult it would be to hold together the national Democracy as a result of the older slavery issues upon which the southern branch of the party was united.

A month after Brown's Monticello address he was the honored guest at an immense barbecue at Terry, a mile from his estate in Hinds County. In a lengthy speech Brown returned to the slave trade issue. Again his argument was typical of agricultural southern and eastern Mississippi. In a democracy law and order depend on sparsely settled communities; they "reigned supreme in the thinly settled rural districts, while our crowded cities were often given up to riot and bloodshed." If the slave trade were reopened, Negroes would be so cheap that people would buy beyond their ability to pay and race riots might devastate like the Mississippi floods. As an alternative for southern Mississippi he urged that a railroad be constructed from Canton and Jackson to the Mississippi sea-shore harbor at Ship Island so that New Orleans would not get the bulk of the traffic as at present. This all-Mississippi outlet for the produce of central and southern Mississippi, he believed, was "worth more to us than all we should ever make out of reopening the African slave trade, or half a dozen such issues." *The Mississippian* countered to this speech also, assuring its readers that those able to buy slaves would have good sense and competency to regulate their own interests in using them to develop the majority of lands yet uncultivated in the Southern States.[23]

On July 5, 1859 the Democratic State Convention followed the radical leadership of *The Mississippian* in resolving unanimously that Mississippi would regard the election of a Black Republican "as a declaration of hostility, and will hold herself in readiness, to cooperate with her sister states of the South, in whatever measures they may deem necessary for the maintenance of their rights of co-equal members of the Confederacy," and declared that the acquisition of Cuba was a commercial and political necessity. The Buchanan administra-

[22] *Ibid.*, June 14, 17, 1859. *Natchez Courier*, May 28, 1859.
[23] *The Mississippian*, May 20, June 21, 28, July 8, 1859.

tion was only faintly praised, being endorsed "in the main." *The Mississippian* lauded the convention for taking no action on the African slave trade, but remarked, "We have never in all our experience of journalism, seen any cause grow so rapidly upon public favor as this. And why? Because it is founded upon truth, justice and wisdom—and had grown out of the necessities of a people who are struggling for their political existence against overwhelming odds." [24] The address of Jefferson Davis, the conservative leader of the party, was fully reported in the press. He hoped the United States would acquire tropical territory, but denounced filibustering as a method of acquisition. As a representative of the large planting class, he was more favorable to the reopening of the African slave trade than Brown, but his most popular appeal for the necessity of disunion in case of the election of a Republican "was hailed by the Convention with universal and prolonged acclamation." [25]

The views of the Democratic party represented those of an overwhelming majority of the people of Mississippi. This was well illustrated when, a week later, the "opposition" State convention met, but made no nominations and drew up no platform. The old organizations, Whigs, Unionists, and Know-nothings had gone by the board, leaving only a corporal's guard without a name to form a State central committee and to urge the formation of county organizations. This weakness was amply proved when J. J. Pettus, the Democratic candidate for governor, defeated the Opposition candidate by over three to one.[26]

Brown continued his agitation against the North, now quarreling with a New York Democratic journal, now urging the expansion of Southern higher education so that Southern youth would not be sent to Northern institutions. *The Mississippian* applauded and eagerly calculated the value of the Union, going so far as to assert, in answer to an editorial heading, "Can the South Prosper under a Separate Government?" that "it would be easy to show that, while a dissolu-

[24] *The Mississippian*, July 8, 1859. Foote, p. 256. A month later (Aug. 9) *The Mississippian* quoted the current prices of the Richmond slave market, asserting that "none but the most favored of our people *can afford* to buy slaves at the above ruinously high figures" and demanded whether it was not preferable "to buy slaves from Africa at from $200 to $300 a piece than to buy from Virginia at from $1,150 to $1,500?"

[25] Rowland, *Jefferson Davis*, IV, 63, 69–70, 80–81, July 6, 1859. *The Mississippian*, July 26, 1859.

[26] *The Mississippian*, July 12, 1859. *Natchez Courier*, July 25, Nov. 15, 1859.

tion of the Union would be fraught with certain ruin to the Northern States, it would tend to elevate and give increased security to the South." [27]

There were important reverberations during the summer from the famous debate with Douglas which Brown had initiated on February 23. Douglas had experienced a heavy demand in the South for reprints of his answer to Brown and to Davis.[28] The pamphlet of the debate which Douglas issued contained an appendix which gave quotations from previous statements of Brown, Davis, and Quitman in favor of popular sovereignty. The effect of this pamphlet was so favorable to Douglas that the rumor gained currency that Brown had arranged the debate of February 23 so that Douglas could win a personal triumph.[29] Brown wrote a long letter to Douglas on September 10 [30] in order to clarify his position. He denied that the debate was arranged "to give you an opportunity of explaining your position. There was positively no arrangement—nothing akin to it." His sole purpose in starting the debate, Brown continued, was to make clear to the Southern people "that most, if indeed, not all the northern Democratic Senators agreed with you, and while some of them were quite willing to see the denunciations against you in the South go on, they were very reluctant to take issue with us, & against you before a Northern audience." Brown stated that he did not expect or deserve an answer to his speech from Douglas, but rather he "did desire, and do still desire that other northern candidates for the presidency in the Senate, and out of it shall commit themselves upon the record on the issue between us—I think the game of hide and whoop has been played long enough."

Brown restated his own position and believed that it was self-evident that it must be accepted if there was to be harmony within

[27] *The Mississippian,* Aug. 9, 1859, quoting letter of Brown to editor of *New York Daily News;* Aug. 5, 1859, quoting *Yazoo Democrat* on Brown's address on Southern education at Madison College, Aug. 12, 1859, Feb. 21, 1860.

[28] The letter of W. L. Spinks, the editor of a pro-Douglas newspaper of Meridian, in eastern Mississippi, is an interesting illustration of this demand. Spinks had declared for the policy of non-intervention. "We are going and even now are having a war on this question in the South. . . . It is charged up to me now that I am a 'Douglas-man'—an epithet of peculiar heinousness in the eyes of many southern politicians."—Douglas MSS., letter Spinks to Douglas, Aug. 31, 1859.

[29] Milton, pp. 378, 379.

[30] Douglas MSS., letter Brown to Douglas, Terry, Hinds County, Mississippi, Sept. 10, 1859. The author consulted the original letter. Milton uses it extensively, quoting from it on pp. 366 n. 48, 371, 379 n. 30, 389.

the nation. "Any assumption direct or implied that the law-giver may in any manner discriminate against slave property is insulting to us as equals and is virtually saying to us that while we are expected to bear the burthens of government equally with our neighbors we are not to expect equal benefits & protection under the Government." Then followed the astounding assertion: "Much as I love the South, if she ever consents to take this or any other unequal position in the confederacy I turn my back upon her forever." Radicalism could go no further! It went even beyond the separatism of Southern nationalism to the separatism of individual anarchism.

Brown, nevertheless, stated categorically that the demands of the Ultras at Charleston for the full protection of slave property in the territories and on the high seas would be the demands of the South, "and failing to get it she will retire from the convention." [31] And if Congress also refused to grant these demands "we will as we ought, resist the Government and throw off its authority. We have been faithful to the Demo^t party and loyal to the Government. But we are prepared to abandon the one & sacrifice the other sooner than surrender our equal rights under the Confederacy."

In spite of the irreconcilable differences between the views of Brown and Douglas which this forceful letter made crystal-clear, Brown retained his respect for and his personal admiration of Douglas. Brown congratulated Douglas for his notable article in the September, 1859, number of *Harper's Magazine,* in which he derived the doctrine of popular sovereignty from the founding fathers: "I think you have made the best of a bad cause." Brown made it clear that he did not think that "you are more against us than other Northern statesmen. I say to you as I have said to others, that I would as soon trust you as any of them. None of you are willing to give us that full measure of justice which is our due under the constitution, and I hope we shall all be d**ned together if we consent to take less." He ended this letter on a distinctly personal note: "With sentiment[s] of cordial personal friendship and with the highest regard for you politically in all things save *niggers,* I am as heretofore Very truly and sincerely Your friend & obst A. G. Brown."

Before leaving for Washington Brown addressed a joint meeting

[31] Daniel P. Rhodes, the father of the noted historian, James Ford Rhodes, fully recognized that Brown's attitude would be fatal to party unity when he wrote that Ohio should keep voting for Douglas "even after Brown shall have blown the party to flinders."—Milton, p. 377, quoting letter of July 15, 1859 in Martin F. Douglas MSS.

of the State legislature on November 7. He went right to the heart of the issue by stating at the very beginning that he dismissed as beyond the pale of reason all Northerners who were not Democrats, and as in his letter to Douglas, he sought to point out "as clearly and succintly [sic] as possible the points of difference between the Northern and Southern Democracy" and the course the South should pursue to secure their constitutional rights in the Union or out of it. It was clear that now, even on the eve of a presidential year, all party loyalty as such was secondary to the all-absorbing sectional strife. Brown was more thoroughly aroused than in 1850—partly because of 1850—and asserted, "In twenty-four years of political life I have not seen so many signs of danger as at the present." The South had been loyal to the federal government, doing its full share to fill its coffers and to fight its battles, but now, "if it turn against us, [the South] will tear down its colossal pillars and scatter them to the four winds of Heaven." The President, most of his cabinet, and his Northern supporters admit the equal and just right of Southerners to take their slaves into the territories and that they are entitled to protection after they get there, but if this protection is not given, they will not urge Congress to pass further laws, but will leave this protection to the courts, unaided by statute laws. Buchanan raised his eyes in holy horror at both Seward and Douglas, "stands by, smiles graciously and says 'For shame, gentlemen, how can you act so!' but, though panoplied in power, he does nothing to prevent the outrage." Northern politicians generally presented the South with a sugarcoated pill which was, nevertheless, "just as nauseating in its effects as naked tartar-emetic. No, the president falls . . . immeasurably short of doing us justice. To refer to the courts for our remedy is nothing short of downright mockery. And it is not a whit less insulting to our intelligence when done by the President than when done by Judge Douglas. . . . I abhor Douglas' Squatter Sovereignty —and I await with great patience and little hope the *expose* which we are to have from the President at the opening of Congress." He was not very hopeful as to the results at the Charleston convention. "Perhaps," he ended pessimistically, "I am not because I feel a certain sort of presentiment that things will be managed to our prejudice." [32]

The *Mississippi Free Trader* and the *Eastern Clarion* had continued to urge Brown for President, and the *Ripley Advertiser* and

[32] *The Mississippian,* Nov. 16, 1859.

the *Southern Reveille* were added to the list.[33] In June, 1859, the
Democrats of Lauderdale County resolved for either Davis or Brown
for President, and in November, Democratic conventions in Lawrence and in Harrison Counties instructed their delegates to the Democratic State Convention to vote for Brown as the nominee.[34] There
is no evidence that Brown encouraged this propaganda in his behalf. On the contrary, on November 27, just before leaving for Washington, he wrote to some of his ardent backers in Jackson, Livingston
Mims and J. J. Smiley, that Mississippi, in taking the lead for great
principles, should not turn to the secondary and hazardous question
of nominations. "For myself, I would rather see my State the mother
of one sound theory than of ten Presidents." To show that he was
sincere concerning his own position, he concluded, "If, therefore,
any friend of mine should present my name to the approaching State
Convention, I authorize and request you, as my neighbors, friends,
and immediate representatives to withdraw it promptly." At the state
convention, Mims carried out this request when Brown was nominated; [35] as a result, the more moderate and more nationally-minded
Davis won over Brown by a five to one majority.[36] Both the Natchez
papers regretted the result. The *Natchez Courier* called Brown "both
in head and heart . . . vastly superior to Davis . . . less selfish, and
less of the mere partizan," while the *Mississippi Free Trader* announced that it would continue to keep Brown's name at the head
of the paper "until the fulminations of Charleston go forth as political Gospel." Yet even the *Mississippi Free Trader* recognized that
Brown would have a more appropriate position in the Southern Confederacy which it foresaw than in the national government.[37]

[33] *Mississippi Free Trader*, Oct. 7, 1859. *Eastern Clarion*, Aug. 3, 1859, noting
support of *Ripley Advertiser*. *The Mississippian*, Oct. 11, 1859, noting support of
Southern Reveille.

[34] *The Mississippian*, June 28; Dec. 2, 3, 1859.

[35] *Ibid.*, Jan. 18, 1860, quoting letters of Brown, Nov. 27, 1859, and of Mims to
editor, Jan. 16, 1860.

[36] *Ibid.*, Dec. 13, 1859, gives vote seventy-five to thirteen. *Natchez Courier*, Dec.
20, 1859, gives vote seventy-five to fifteen.

[37] *Natchez Courier*, Dec. 20, 1859. *Mississippi Free Trader*, Dec. 20, 1859. John
Savage wrote thirty-four short biographies of *Our Living Representative Men*
"who have been prominently suggested for the Presidential succession in 1861,"
p. iii. Brown was one of the thirteen who came from States which seceded,
pp. 78-89. This recognition, however, does not imply that Brown was seriously
considered for the presidency beyond Mississippi. David Bartlett, in his twenty-
one sketches of *Presidential Candidates*, does not include Brown. Milton is probably incorrect in stating, p. 374, that Brown had "nursed a boomlet of his own."
The evidence does not indicate that Brown encouraged his own candidacy, although

There was nothing to alleviate the tension between the sections when Congress met in December, for the entire country was stirred by John Brown's raid and by the endorsement by Northern Congressmen of the arguments of Helper's *Impending Crisis of the South* against the slavery system. On December 7 Brown said he accepted the statements of Northern senators that they had had no previous knowledge of the raid, but he censured them for not rebuking and repudiating the political and religious meetings which lauded John Brown as a martyr. If a raid had originated in Virginia or in South Carolina and had sought to seize Springfield, overturn the New England governments, and force slavery on the North, then Northern senators would have expected Southern senators to rebuke any indication of sympathy with the movement. Now Northern senators, Brown was convinced, owed it to themselves to check the view almost universally held in the South that the sympathy expressed for John Brown was a reflection of Northern sentiment. Brown was convinced that the sympathy was not expressed for John Brown, as such, heroic as they claimed him to be. No, "he came to levy war upon a slave State, to murder slaveholders, because they were slaveholders. It is for that and that alone, that sympathy has been elicited." The silence of senators, "their silence under extraordinary circumstances, under a most extraordinary state of facts, does excite my suspicion, that after all they do sympathize with forays into the slave States for the purpose of overthrowing their institutions." If these senators are afraid they will lose the votes of abolitionists if they condemn the raid, then John Brown "was less guilty than the great men who prompted him to his misconduct. The irrepressible conflict could end nowhere else." [38]

The next day Brown engaged in a spirited argument with Senator Wilson of Massachusetts on the relative tolerance of the two sections. Wilson insisted that a meeting which favored the opening of the African slave trade could be held without any disturbance in his home town of Natick, but sarcastically remarked that it was difficult for Southern senators to understand this tolerance since they came from a section where freedom of speech on some political, moral, and social subjects was not tolerated. Brown responded that Wilson

---

Davis, in writing deprecatingly that Brown's opposition to Douglas was Brown's chief asset, may have thought so. Milton, referring to Davis' letter of May 17, 1859, in C. C. Clay MSS.

[38] *Cong. Globe*, 36th Cong., 1st sess., I, 33–34.

would kick him out if he would teach his servants to rebel against Wilson's family; so when Northerners come to teach slaves to disobey the legal authority of the master, "we kick them out of the door, and, if we have the further power, we will hang them up like dógs." Wilson answered that Brown did not present a fair case and asked whether men who believed like Washington or Jefferson on the slavery question could travel safely through the South quietly and temperately expressing their views. To this both Brown and Davis responded in the affirmative, but Brown qualified his statement by "any sentiments that you have a right to entertain." He made clear immediately afterwards that he would not tolerate any one who went to Mississippi to urge the election of Seward on the basis of an irrepressible conflict. "No such doctrine would be allowed to be taught there, because our safety, our domestic quietude, our peace, the peace of our hearths, depends upon the repression of such doctrines with us." [39]

The increasing tension between the sections is also illustrated by the action of the Mississippi legislature. Two laws showed the growing fear of race riots as a result of Northern propaganda. The first bill forbade free Negroes or mulattoes to reside in the State without the special license of the legislature after July 1, 1860. Any seized after this date could be sold into slavery for life. The second bill restricted masters in permitting their slaves to go at large and to hire themselves out. [40] Although the State treasury was empty, and the legislature neglected to appropriate funds for paying the Planters' bank bonds, recently urged by both Governor McWillie and by ex-Governor Brown, a bill for spending $150,000 for arms passed the legislature almost unanimously on December 14. *The Mississippian* described this last law as "one of a series of measures designed to place the State in an attitude of defense, if she should be required to oppose physical resistance to the aggressions of the antislavery organization," while the *Natchez Courier,* still daring to resist the rising storm of secession sentiment, dubbed the bill "a piece of gasconade and humbug." [41]

[39] *Cong. Globe,* 36th Cong., 1st sess., p. 64.
[40] *Natchez Courier,* Dec. 15, 1859. These bills should not be construed to illustrate the charge that Mississippi Negroes were treated with peculiar severity. Charles S. Sydnor has shown that "the negro as a slave had a longer life in comparison with his white master than he has as a free man in comparison with the white people of Mississippi today." "Life Span of Mississippi Slaves," *American Historical Review,* XXXV, 566–574.
[41] *Ibid.,* Dec. 20, 1859. *The Mississippian,* Dec. 15, 1859.

Brown, continuing his attack in the Senate, condemned Seward and sixty-eight representatives—including John Sherman, the Republican candidate for speaker—for indorsing the *Impending Crisis* which urged the boycott of slaveholders in order to force the abolition of slavery and interpreted it as further evidence that the Republicans sought to abolish slavery in the States as promptly as possible.[42] Because the *Washington Constitution,* the administration organ, had bitterly attacked Brown's extreme doctrine of congressional protection of slavery in the territories, he returned to this subject, denying that he did "at any time, entertain or express an extreme sentiment upon any question!" When Senator Pugh of Ohio claimed that under the constitution slaves were property only under the laws of certain States, Brown insisted that this was true also of all the territories, but that slave property had never been protected like other property. "Whenever the Government fails," he concluded, observing that he was addressing empty Republican benches, "to protect me and my people in our lives, our liberties, and our property, upon the high seas or upon the land, it ought to be abolished. If that be treason, gentlemen, make the most of it." [43]

Brown criticized Buchanan's message to Congress, although he denied that he would attack him as some newspapers announced. He rebutted Buchanan's claim that the Supreme Court had made a final settlement of the slavery question in the territories by showing that there was continued agitation in the North. He insisted that the statement that slave property had never been disturbed in the territories, was untrue. To Buchanan's assertion that it would be time enough to legislate further when the rights of slave masters had been interfered with, he replied, "Congress is today, at this very hour, at this very instant, imperiously called upon to pass additional laws." The common law and the federal constitution define rights, but do not in themselves afford remedies for violations of these rights. "I reply with the utmost frankness that I want a code of laws which shall be adequate and sufficient for the protection of my property. If it pleases you to call it a slave code, why call it so. . . . I no more ask a slave code than you ask a horse code, or a cow code, or a dry-goods code." He admitted frankly that he was so tenacious on this point because "without such protection, there never will be another slave Territory; and without slave Territories you can never have slave States."

[42] *Cong. Globe,* 36th Cong., 1st sess., pp. 145–146.
[43] *Ibid.,* pp. 185–187.

Without more slave States, in time two-thirds of the States would be free, and then the Republicans could abolish slavery in the remaining States by constitutional amendment—a condition which the slave States would never tolerate within the Union.[44]

Although Brown had said that he was not attacking Buchanan, he could make no claim that he was not antagonistic to the administration when he bitterly denounced George W. Bowman, editor of the administration organ, the *Washington Constitution,* who was chosen printer of the Senate by the Democratic caucus. Brown charged Bowman with violating the act of 1852 which forbade the superintendent of public printing to be interested personally in the public printing, but it appears that his real motive for opposition to Bowman concerned Brown personally—Bowman had praised William C. Smedes, a leader of the opposition in Mississippi and had criticized Brown's radical address to the Mississippi legislature but had refused to print the speech.[45] This antagonism, of course, was very pleasing to the opposition press in Mississippi, particularly when Brown dared to bolt the party caucus and to make a long speech against Bowman.[46] For this bold action the antagonism between the Mississippi senators flared up again. Davis criticized Brown for the violent language he used over this little question, "the merest tempest in a teapot" and asserted that Brown, by his attitude, "but exemplifies the well-known fact that self-interest is apt to pervert our judgment, and passion is the worst of counselors." This sally led to a discussion between Davis and Brown as to the editorial attitude of the *Washington Constitution* towards the territorial question, which was largely that of the President's message. Davis claimed that its editorials were excellent during the last half year, but Brown insisted, "with all deference to my colleague," that "during the summer, when the elections were coming on, the *Constitution* was all wrong—advising wrong, doing wrong, perpetrating wrong," but that they only improved after the elections and that the editor wanted Southern votes to make him public printer.[47]

[44] *Cong. Globe,* 36th Cong., 1st sess., pp. 298–301, 470–471.

[45] *Washington Constitution,* Nov. 26, 1859. The editorial denounced Brown for not upholding the policies of Buchanan and of the Cincinnati platform, and declared that Brown's assertion that he favored Seward in preference to Buchanan was "an outrageous sentiment." Bowman rejected Brown's statement that there was no unity of sentiment between the North and the South, and insisted that the slavery question was settled.

[46] *Natchez Courier,* Jan. 3, 1860, quoting *Vicksburg Whig;* Jan. 31, 1860.

[47] *Cong. Globe,* 36th Cong., 1st sess., pp. 471–478.

Brown's next step in advance of his party was the introduction, on January 18, of two resolutions to the effect that it was the duty of both the territorial legislatures and of Congress to protect all types of property in the territories and that the committee on territories should insert these principles in all bills for establishing new territories and should apply them immediately in all the present territories.[48] Even the radical Mississippi legislature was more moderate than Brown. By the time these resolutions came up for discussion on March 6 the legislature had accepted almost unanimously five resolutions which did not fully meet Brown's extreme position. Four, dealing with the necessity of joint action by the Southern States if a Republican President should be elected and promising aid to Virginia if she should be attacked again, could be accepted by conservative Southern Democrats. The first resolution, however, fell short of Brown's resolutions in the Senate, in that, although it stated the duty of Congress to protect slavery in the territories, like Davis, it did not demand immediate legislation. Instead of the aggressive, positive tenor of Brown's resolutions, it was further weakened by being expressed in the negative: "The Federal Government . . . cannot, nor can any tribunal acting under its authority . . . justly withhold from the owners of slaves that adequate protection for their slave property, to which the owners of other kinds are entitled." [49]

The debates on Brown's resolutions showed clearly that his position, as in 1850, was an extreme one. But there was a great difference now. In the years after 1850, as we have seen, Brown climbed back on to the party band wagon. During 1860, however, with greater sincerity and depth of conviction, he carried his radical views to their logical conclusion and remained in front of his party until revolution made the radicalism of 1860 the conservatism of 1861.

Brown found slaves excluded from all territories except New Mexico and was sure they would be excluded from all future terri-

[48] *Ibid.*, p. 494. Senator Wilson of Massachusetts did not wait until these resolutions came up for formal discussion, but took the occasion, a week after their introduction, to address the Senate on "Democratic Leaders for Disunion." The *New York Tribune* published Wilson's speech as "Tribune Tracts No. 2" as anti-slavery campaign material.

[49] *The Mississippian,* Feb. 14, 1860. *Natchez Courier,* Feb. 18, 1860. There was only one dissenting vote to these resolutions in the Senate and four in the House. The editorial of *The Mississippian* on these resolutions shows how thoroughly conscious of the growing feeling of Southern nationality the leading journal in Mississippi had become. Instead of speaking of these resolutions as representing the demands of Mississippi, it constantly affirmed in passionate language that they spoke for "the Southern States" and for "Southern Institutions."

tories unless Congress interposed. When the Kansas-Nebraska bill was introduced he believed that slavery would not go to Kansas; now he answered the argument that the climate and soil of Kansas were unfitted for slavery by showing that Kansas was in the same latitude as the border slave States. Slave property was denied protection everywhere. Some claimed that an average of seventeen slaves were spirited to Canada every night. If these had been cattle, he was sure the non-slaveholding States would demand that the President notify the British government that "unless the stolen property was given up, non-intercourse would be declared, and if its colony persisted in receiving and concealing the stolen goods of American citizens, this Government would resent the outrage, even by the shedding of blood. My complaint goes unheeded; yours would be listened to." Senator Saulsbury of Delaware criticized Brown's resolutions as mere abstractions,[50] and even the fire-eating *The Mississippian,* although admitting that "no true Southern man will deny the correctness of the principles declared in this speech," nevertheless felt that the golden opportunity had been lost and that the adoption of a slave code at this late period "will be like locking the stable door after the exit of the stolen steed." [51]

Davis showed his ill-will towards Brown a number of times during this session. When Brown sought to repeal the law granting the franking privilege to certain private individuals, Davis did not try to conceal the disdain—almost bordering on contempt—which he felt towards his colleague: "There is a want of decency in repealing a law by which you have conferred a compliment upon an individual. I abstained from saying so . . . because I thought it was barely necessary to suggest it—that every one's own instinct would show that it was, in its very nature, low and offensive." [52]

This desultory sniping, which had been going on for years, finally broke out into open warfare between the Mississippi senators when Davis, on March 1, introduced and carried by a large majority in the Democratic caucus seven resolutions on the slavery issues. In the previous September Davis had written to Pierce, urging him to run

[50] *Cong. Globe,* 36th Cong., 1st sess., II, 1001–1006.

[51] *The Mississippian,* March 27, 1860. Robert Toombs felt that it was "the very foolishness of folly" to present resolutions on slavery since the Kansas act and the Dred Scott decision had removed the problem from Congress. He believed that hostility to Douglas was the sole motive of the resolutions. ("Robert Toombs to A. H. Stephens," Feb. 10, 1860, *Annual Report of American Historical Association, 1911,* vol. 2, p. 461.)

[52] Rowland, *Jefferson Davis,* IV, 194, 230, Feb. 15, April 12, 1860.

again for the presidency, and expressing his opposition to a congressional slave code for the territories.[53] Now the fifth resolution of Davis was directly opposite to the Brown resolutions of February 18, since it declared that there was no present necessity for Congress to act to protect slavery in the territories. A month later Brown defended his own resolutions. He denied that he was introducing new theories and pointed to a number of instances where Congress had nullified acts of territorial legislatures—particularly to one of 1834 which prevented discrimination against slave property in Florida territory. And yet, when he demanded no more, he complained: "Republicans call me a terrible extremist, and my Democratic friends give me the feeblest imaginable support. Oh, God! to what depths of infamy are we sinking in the South if we allow these things to pass." If Congress does not interpose at this precise point, it will never do so. The principles of his resolutions were only denied since squatter sovereignty became the vogue as a dodge from the Wilmot proviso.

Brown next turned to attack the Davis resolutions, which were to form the basis of the platform of the Southern Democrats at the critical Charleston convention. "I cannot allow myself to be humbugged in this way. There is nothing in these resolutions. . . . I would not give a snap of my finger for these resolutions. I utterly reject them; not in disrespect, of course, to the gentleman who offered them," he felt it necessary to add, "but because there is nothing in them." [54] Never before had Brown showed such independence in a presidential year. He failed to get a vote on his resolutions and two weeks later failed again to force a vote either on his own or on Davis' resolutions.[55] Since the Charleston convention was fast approaching, evasion was the order of the day. On May 7 Davis answered Brown's criticism of his fifth resolution. He was not seeking legislation, "but making great declarations on which legislation may be founded. . . . They will speak a restraining voice to the Territorial Legislatures." He declared that Brown was unfair in criticizing his resolutions harshly when he was absent because of illness. Davis insisted that his views were those of his constituency as approved by the State delegation at Charleston. Brown answered in a restrained manner, but instead of ending the quarrel with the party chief of his State, as

---

[53] *Ibid.,* p. 94, letter Davis to Pierce, Sept. 2, 1859.
[54] *Cong. Globe,* 36th Cong., 1st sess., pp. 1486–1488. Chadwick, *Causes of the Civil War,* p. 109.
[55] *Cong. Globe,* 36th Cong., 1st sess., pp. 1729–1730.

he had sought to do in 1856 when he was more careful of his political future, he moved that Davis' fifth resolution be struck out, and in its place a resolution be adopted that, since experience had shown that the common law could not give protection to slavery in territories which had passed unfriendly legislation, it was the duty of Congress "to interpose and pass such laws as will afford to slave property in the Territories that protection which is given to other kinds of property." [56]

On May 24 the fifth resolution of Davis was before the Senate. Brown again dubbed it as a mere abstraction, since it looked to no concrete legislation, and demanded, "if there is nothing upon which we are called to act, why has the public mind been lashed like an ocean tempest—tossed into a fury?" The Senate adjourned without action. The next day Brown offered his amendment to the fifth resolution. Davis responded, restraining his anger with difficulty, "Though the provocation is extreme, I shall waive all controversy with my colleague about it, and limit my remarks to a single sentence." Since his resolutions were not joint resolutions, they called for no bills. Therefore, he argued cogently, Brown's amendment, calling for action, could have no effect in a simple Senate resolution. "A general declaration of a principle, on which legislation may arise, may have some future value. The assertion of a particular special fact, by the Senate alone, would be a mere nullity." Iverson of Georgia, Clay of Alabama, and Mason of Virginia also spoke against Brown's amendment in moderate tones, but Wigfall of Texas was more caustic because he felt that Brown's action would divide and distract the Democratic party and destroy the major purpose of the party to adopt principles which would reunite the party, North and South. Nine-tenths of the Democrats in the North, he claimed, favored the Davis resolutions and all in the South, and yet Brown brought forward resolutions which all Northern senators and a large majority of Southern senators will reject. Brown maintained his position, but admitted that he was left out by both elements in the party: by the Douglas men who were wrong in opposing any congressional action but concluded correctly from their premises, and by the Davis men, who were right in admitting that Congress can interfere in the territories, but concluded wrongly that no action should be taken. When the vote on Brown's amendment was taken, it was found that he was in a hopeless minority, only Johnson of Arkansas and Mallory of

[56] *Cong. Globe,* 36th Cong., 1st sess., III, 1941–1943.

Florida following Brown. But Brown stood his ground and uttered defiance, "We are three. We are a small band. That is as many as was required to save Sodom. I think the Republic is safe." Immediately afterwards Davis' fifth resolution passed with only two dissenting votes, Brown joining with many Republicans in refraining from voting.[57]

Brown's ultra position won high praise from the leading opposition paper, the *Natchez Courier,* not because it loved Brown, but because it hated Davis more. It ridiculed Southern senators who advocated the principle of protection for not insisting on its exercise in caucus. Brown was frank and above-board; Davis was academic and an impractical trifler, an anti-Douglas trimmer. "For ourselves," the editor wrote, "bitterly as we have opposed Albert G. Brown, we tender to him a tribute of an opponent's admiration for his manly course. Among the faithless, faithful only he." His open hospitality and kindliness to friend and foe alike in Washington were considered a great contrast to any one of the other Mississippi representatives in Congress [58]—praise that was quickly acknowledged by Brown's leading apologist, the *Mississippi Free Trader,* which dubbed Davis' fifth resolution "an ignis fatuus—a Will o' the Wisp" and maintained that "Mississippi demands something substantial." [59] The *Natchez Courier* further denounced the platform of the bolters from the Charleston convention as a shameful compromise because it took the Davis position that protection must be given if necessary, "the jesuitical reservation being made, that it is never to be necessary." [60]

Brown's extreme position was also used as a vantage ground to attack conservative Southern Democracy by Senator Hale, Republican, of New Hampshire, who declared there was something heroic in Brown's attitude. "He stands in noble contrast to these theorists who are propounding general sentiments." He mentioned Brown by name,

[57] *Ibid.,* pp. 2324–2325, 2347–2350. Senator Henry Wilson saw clearly the difference in attitude between the two Mississippi senators. In later years he wrote that Davis took a more advanced position than Douglas. "But, more wary and politic, he contented himself rather with the enunciation of general principles than by demanding immediate legislation. . . . Mr. Brown, seemingly emulous of his colleague, and anxious to rival him in the championship of the slaveholding cause was more extreme in his opinions and extravagant in his demands. And his actions corresponded with his sentiments."—Wilson, *Rise and Fall of the Slave Power in America,* II, 657–660.

[58] *Natchez Courier,* March 14, 1860, also referring to *Vicksburg Whig;* May 12, 23, June 12, 1860.

[59] *Mississippi Free Trader,* May 24, June 15, 1860.

[60] *Natchez Courier,* May 23, 1860.

and humorously explained, "If I say the distinguished Senator from Mississippi, nobody would know which I meant." He insisted that Brown was right in demanding that the Davis resolutions be followed through to legislative action if they were presented in earnest and were anything more than a political almanac to be used in the presidential election.[61] Even the *Washington Constitution* which had so denounced his radical demands for congressional action in December, 1859, now, after the Democratic split at Charleston, declared that it was convinced that Brown was right "and that we owe him this tribute to this superior foresight. . . . He must have had a vision of the minority platform, and of the action of the delegations of his own and seven of her sister States" who bolted the convention.[62]

But all was not harmonious among the Democrats of Mississippi. After the Charleston convention there was complaint against the bolters' platform, and a test between the Davis and the Brown forces was anticipated at the Democratic State Convention which met at Jackson on May 30. At that convention the delegates to the Charleston convention were unanimously endorsed. The conflict arose over a resolution to instruct these delegates to defer final action at the Richmond convention until after the assembling of the Baltimore convention which the Mississippi delegates were to attend. This resolution gave no specific instructions as to the policies they were to follow. They were simply asked to pursue "such a course in reference to the two Conventions, as may in their discretion be best calculated to secure the unity and harmony of the Democratic party." Wiley P. Harris, an ardent supporter of Brown, presented a substitute motion which bound the delegates by specific instructions to "adopt a platform of principles which will give the requisite guarantees of adequate protection to the rights of the citizens of the Slaveholding States

[61] *Cong. Globe*, 36th Cong., 1st sess., pp. 2348–2359.

[62] *The Mississippian*, May 25, 1860, correspondence of May 19, 1860 from Washington. *Mississippi Free Trader*, May 12, June 8, 1860, quoting *Washington Constitution*. At the Charleston convention all the seven votes of the fourteen Mississippi delegates were cast against the minority report which was adopted, 165 to 138, and all fourteen left the convention with the other Southern delegates after reading a protest which the *Mississippi Free Trader* declared "breathes the purest spirit of National and Southern Patriotism. It is the outburst of brave and chivalrous gentlemen—the true representatives of a brave and chivalrous people." Ethelbert Barksdale, Mississippi's representative on the platform committee reported that "perfect harmony characterized the deliberations of the Mississippi delegation. There was no creeping Douglasite among them. Nor was there any one whose position was at all equivocal."—*Mississippi Free Trader*, May 17, 1860. *The Mississippian*, May 8, 1860.

in the Territories." They were only to proceed to Baltimore, "if, in their judgment, it shall appear expedient, and to act therein under the instructions heretofore given."

The original motion sought another attempt to reunite the Democratic party; the substitute motion looked to the inevitable struggle between the Southern States represented at Richmond and the Northern States. Harris feared a compromise at Baltimore and "wanted the Richmond Convention to be a substantial thing, and not a mere shadow of the Baltimore Convention." This substitute motion was carried by fifty-one to thirty-six. This vote foreshadowed the returns of the presidential election half a year later. In the southern half of the State where Breckinridge support was strongest, all except four counties which voted favored the Harris resolutions, while the northern half, from which came the Douglas strength, was almost evenly divided—eleven counties voting for the Harris resolution, ten against it, and three were tied.

However, neither of these resolutions was finally adopted. Since at least the appearance of a united front was deemed essential in the crisis, the Harris resolution was reconsidered, and a compromise resolution to instruct the delegates to defer final action at Richmond until *after* the adjournment of the Baltimore convention and to give the Mississippi delegates plenary powers was unanimously adopted.

This compromise resolution was recognized as a victory for the Davis wing of the party over what the *Natchez Courier* called the "honest, radical wing of the party, who are after a practical enforcement of the principle the first mentioned wing hint at in bated breath." [63] Despite the statements of Brown and the actions of the Democratic State Convention, the *Monticello Southern Journal* and the *Mississippi Free Trader* continued to favor Brown for the presidency in the early part of 1860.[64] Only on June 28, after the nomination of Breckinridge, did the *Mississippi Free Trader* cease to advocate Brown for President. For this shift "from Senator Brown's manly and decided, even if ultra, position . . . to Senator Davis' milk-and-water platform, which it had before condemned," the *Natchez Courier* charged the *Mississippi Free Trader* with gross inconsistency.[65]

[63] *Natchez Courier*, May 19, June 6, 1860. *The Mississippian*, June 1, 1860. See map on Vote on Harris Resolution.

[64] *Mississippi Free Trader*, April 21, 1860, also citing *Southern Journal;* June 13, 1860.

[65] *Mississippi Free Trader*, June 28, 1860. *Natchez Courier*, July 28, 1860.

In this last Congress before the War of Southern Nationalism, Brown urged measures which would increase the influence of the States. He sought the cession to the States of all public lands unsold after four years after the lowest prices had been offered. He opposed the granting of freeholds to settlers as they would be given a privilege which the settlers of Mississippi did not have, but he favored the reestablishment of the credit system which had been abolished in 1820. Those born with silver spoons in their mouths may demand quick payments, but Brown could not, for, he explained, "I came from among the poor. I was one of them; born to no fortune but poverty, I struggled through the earlier years of my life for a living." He again objected to curtailing local postal services when special privileges were given to overland routes and to ocean lines.[66] He was no longer embarrassed by his opposition to the reopening of the African slave trade, for the State legislature declined to force the issue with the federal government by deciding not to repeal the State law against the introduction of slaves from Africa.[67] Brown, however, continued to oppose the use of national funds to aid and educate Africans who had been rescued from slave ships. "All this talk about its being an act of inhumanity to take them back to the precise place from which we are told they were ruthlessly torn, is humbug," he insisted. He was unwilling, however, to support them out of the national treasury one hour after they got to the coast of Africa.[68]

During the spring of 1860 the leading opposition press, when not praising Brown for bolting from the Davis regulars, urged a Union convention "to make another effort to overthrow the sectional, disunion faction which now controls Mississippi. . . . Surely our friends do not wish our proud State, the first to roll back the tide of disunionism in '51, to falter now." It felt that the success of either the Republicans or the Democrats would lead to disunion. This opposition group was finally given a name when it rallied to support the Constitutional Union candidates, Bell and Everett.[69]

After Congress adjourned Brown spent the month of July at Cape May, N. J. (where he delivered an Independence Day address) and

[66] Cong. Globe, 36th Cong., 1st sess., II, 1320, 1552–1553; IV, 3249–3250.

[67] Natchez Courier, Feb. 3, 1860.

[68] Cong. Globe, 36th Cong., 1st sess., III, 2307. Pierce Butler, Judah P. Benjamin, p. 196.

[69] Mississippi Free Trader, April 18, 1860, quoting Vicksburg Whig. Natchez Courier, April 25, July 3, 1860.

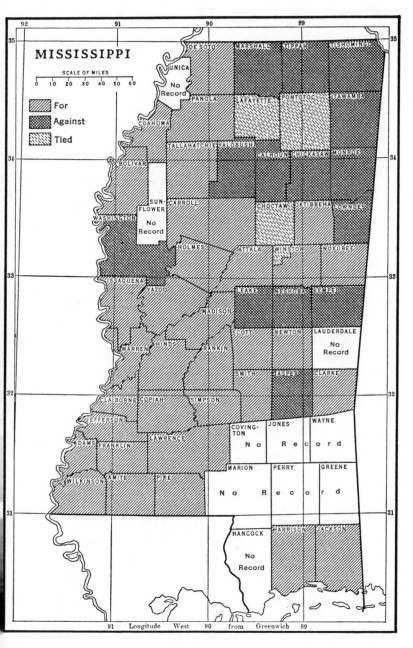

MAP 15. VOTE ON HARRIS RESOLUTION AT DEMOCRATIC STATE CONVENTION, MAY 31, 1860

at White Sulphur Springs, Virginia.[70] Rumors flew thick and fast about the position Brown took in the presidential contest. From Richmond, Memphis, and Cincinnati came the news that Brown was not satisfied with Breckinridge's letter of acceptance, that he saw no difference between Breckinridge and Douglas, and would remain neutral during the contest.[71] From New Orleans and Aberdeen it was reported that he would favor Douglas in protest against the abstract Breckinridge platform.[72] From Washington it was stated that he would support Breckinridge although it was recognized that his ultra position made this difficult.[73]

Brown finally set these rumors at rest by two letters to *The Mississippian*. In the first letter he objected to the second plank of the Breckinridge platform which asserted "that it is the duty of the Federal Government in all its departments to protect, *when necessary,* the rights of persons and property in the Territories and wherever else its Constitutional authority extends." Brown would have made this more explicit by inserting the words "slaves included" after the word "property" and the words "on the high seas" after the word "Territories." His main objection, however, was to the words "when necessary" which implied the Davis position that protection was not necessary now. He further objected to Breckinridge's statement in his letter of acceptance, "The friends of Constitutional equality do not and never did demand a Congressional slave code nor any other 'code,' in regard to property in the Territories." General Lane, he complained, used much the same language. "Neither," Brown continued, "give [*sic*] the assurance that the whole power of the Government in all its departments is to be used, as soon as we get control of it, to protect our slave property in the same way . . . that other property is protected. Without such assurance, I cannot as an honest man say 'I am satisfied.'" In spite of these objections, he made it clear that he would vote for Breckinridge, for he considered these objections "as dust in the balance when weighed against the formidable array which rise up against Lincoln, Bell, and Douglas." In his second letter he repeated his complaints against Breckinridge

[70] *The Mississippian*, July 13, 1860.

[71] *Natchez Courier*, July 19, 1860, quoting *Richmond Dispatch;* July 26, 31, 1860, quoting *Memphis Appeal* and *Cincinnati Enquirer*.

[72] *Ibid.*, July 27, 31, 1860, quoting *New Orleans True Delta;* July 18, 1860, quoting *Vicksburg Whig*.

[73] *Mississippi Free Trader*, July 31, 1860, quoting *Washington Constitution*. *Natchez Courier*, Aug. 1, 1860, quoting *Washington Star*.

and Lane, asserting truly that "this much may have been inferred by any one who has done me the honor to observe my course in the Senate." He expressed his opinion that Lincoln would be elected, and that his election would be the overt act which would require secession.[74]

In the middle of August Brown returned to Mississippi and spoke at a number of Breckinridge rallies. In northern Mississippi, where Douglas was strongest, he convinced his audience that he would not favor Douglas.[75] At Hazlehurst he termed Lincoln "a bold, fanatical and determined man, and of considerable ability," and announced his willingness to support either Douglas or Bell if he thought either could defeat Lincoln.[76] He was now on his old fifth district stumping ground, still called "Brown's District," where five of the fourteen newspapers were neutral, two for Bell, and only half for Breckinridge.[77] Under these conditions his luke-warm, half-hearted praise of Breckinridge was very displeasing to the Breckinridge men. Already Brown's letters had been variously interpreted as "an admirable campaign document for the Bell men" and as notice to Breckinridge to retire in favor of Douglas so as not to distract the party and ruin the country by holding on when there was no possible hope of succeeding. And now the *Natchez Courier* reported that Brown's Hazlehurst speech had convinced a number of people that it was right to drop Breckinridge and to support Bell.[78]

The address which attracted most comment was given at a barbecue in his honor at Crystal Springs, Copiah County. He had spoken at the same spot twenty-five years before, when he was a candidate for the legislature. He urged the people of the region to trust him

[74] *The Mississippian,* Aug. 14, 1860, quoting Brown's letters of July 14 and Aug. 2, 1860 from White Sulphur Springs, Virginia. *Mississippi Free Trader* Aug. 28, 1860. In a letter to Whitehurst on Sept. 9 his predictions of the returns by States failed only with respect to California and Maryland, and partially to Delaware, whose vote was divided. (MS. William N. Whitehurst Papers, Vol. N, No. 9.)

[75] *The Mississippian,* Aug. 21, 1860, reporting rally at Corinth. Milton is probably correct in stating that "Brown . . . considered him [Douglas] as great a man as America had ever produced," p. 478. However, Brown not only opposed the principles of Douglas, but realized that his victory would dislodge the Southern Nationalists from power.

[76] *Natchez Courier,* Sept. 4, 1860, quoting *Raymond Gazette* and *Gallatin Mirror.*

[77] *Mississippi Free Trader,* Aug. 11, 1860.

[78] *Natchez Courier,* Aug. 22, 29, 1860, quoting *New York Daily News;* Sept. 6, 1860.

now as they had done for twenty-five years. As one of their sentinels, he came to give a gloomy report. "The storm gathers thick and fast; and in a little while it will burst over our heads and in our very midst. I warn you to rise, put your house in order, and prepare to meet the shock." Changing the figure, he saw the three parties opposed to Lincoln like three brothers quarreling over their father's estate, "and while they quarrel the incendiary comes, torch in hand, and consumes the whole in one general conflagration." Again changing his metaphor, he warned that it would be too late when "the black wave of the black sea of Abolition sweeps us all into the common vortex of irrecoverable ruin."

Brown next characterized three of the candidates for the presidency. He had known Lincoln when he was in Congress and now very fairly recognized that "he has strong native intellect without much of what college people call learning. He has made man his study, and he has mastered his subject." Brown could hardly be expected to be as fair to him when he considered his views on slavery, but it is nevertheless a major tragedy that Brown, in common with only too many Southerners, should have considered him as fanatical as William Lloyd Garrison. He dubbed Douglas "intrepid and dashing—full of talents and full of ambition." Although Brown had no sympathy for him in this contest, he felt that it was unjust to call him a renegade, apostate, and traitor to his party. Breckinridge was young and ardent, enthusiastic and talented, but he qualified his praise— "If he has a fault as a statesman, it is in being too cautious. Prudence is a virtue, but too much of it is a fault."

Brown next discussed the platforms. He failed to point out that both the Republican platform and Lincoln, while opposed to the existence of slavery in the territories, did not seek to abolish slavery within any State. In a time of crisis it was but natural that Brown should not take the platform at its face value, but should interpret it as "based on the single idea of hostility to slavery . . . to keep up a fanatical and never ending war on the South" and that Lincoln's far-seeing vision of the house divided against itself should be interpreted erroneously as representing his immediate policy after election. He had omitted to characterize Bell, and for the Union party platform he had only ridicule as an "innocent looking little infant."

The four parties grew out of different interpretations of the Constitution. He was not surprised that this should be true, for the framers themselves did not agree on many points, just as thoroughly conscientious men differed about the interpretation of the Bible. For himself, he stood by the Breckinridge interpretation, but again he qualified— "not because it is entirely right but because it is nearer right than any other. . . . I support Mr. Breckinridge himself because he is partly right while the other candidates are totally wrong." Breckinridge alone recognized the duty of Congress to afford protection to slave property, but had no concrete suggestions and was opposed to a slave code. Brown, declaring it made no difference whether the terms "slave code" or "code" were used, demanded congressional laws, "because I know that slave property never has been and never will be adequately protected anywhere without them. . . . As my love of justice has prevented me from joining in the cry of treason and apostasy against Mr. Douglas, so my love of principle rising above all other considerations impells [sic] me to say even to so good a friend as Mr. Breckinridge, 'I differ with you.'"

Brown reiterated his belief that Lincoln would be elected. He expected no overt acts of violence against the South after the election. Instead, Brown claimed, Lincoln "will row you gently as sucking doves. In words he will be plausible. . . . No restive steed was ever more kindly patted on the neck than Lincoln will pat the South. But once he is fairly in the saddle and has a little used you to the abolition curb, he will fling the rowels to your sides and ride you with fearful rapidity down the deep declivity to your own ruin." But long before he is secure in the saddle the South must win guarantees for the safety of its institutions, failing which "they should proceed at once to the formation of an independent government with a view to a speedy and permanent separation from the North." [79]

The Mississippian received this speech very coldly. It hoped the Democrats of Mississippi would not be turned aside by the somewhat anomalous position of this former staunch party man. As the feeling against Douglas was most bitter because it was felt that he had broken up the party, Brown's tolerant attitude towards him was considered "really sickening to a Southern stomach and . . . does not comport with a very high standard of Southern Simon Pureism after all," and Brown was reminded that Benedict Arnold also was intrepid and dashing. His objections to the Breckinridge platform were judged puerile. The editor, Ethelbert Barksdale, a leader of the Davis faction who headed the Mississippi delegation at the Charleston convention and was a strong adherent of the Davis resolutions on the platform

[79] *The Mississippian,* Sept. 7, 11, 1860.

committee,[80] claimed that not a single delegate held that the platform did not meet the issue, not even "Yancy [*sic*], with all his alleged ultraism" or "the South Carolina State Rights men, with all their punctiliousness about matters of principle." *The Mississippian* printed approvingly probably the most cogent criticism of Brown's position, given by L. Q. C. Lamar, then a member of the national House of Representatives, in answer to the question why the Senate refused to concur in Brown's resolutions. He pointed out that the anti-slavery laws of Kansas under the Dred Scott decision were null and void and that therefore every judicial officer and justice of the peace must protect the rights of slaveholders. "Now, there was no evidence before the Senate to show that these officers had been recreant to their duty in a single instance, and it was wrong to presume them impotent and dishonest before their fidelity to the Constitution had been tested." [81]

Even more significant of the isolation in which Brown had placed himself was the attitude of Brown's leading apologist, the *Mississippi Free Trader*. It started out by lauding him for defeating men of better scholarship and more mature experience because he was a tactician of the first order who even resembled Chatham "in the boldness of his ideas, in his knowledge of human nature, and in urging his points with untiring energy." No State had his superior in practical talent and statesmanship, for "he was intended by nature for a leader, and long experience has made him an adept in the art of guiding men." And yet, despite this fulsome praise, it recognized, like the orthodox *Mississippian,* that his present position was anomalous. It considered that his objections to the party platform were flimsy and his friendly attitude towards Douglas quite uncalled for, and concluded that "it would have been good policy for the Senator, entertaining his present opinions, to have remained quiet and let others uphold our standard in the contest." [82] The *Natchez Courier,* as usual, rejoiced in this criticism by the two leading Democratic journals and again praised Brown for his radical realism in struggling "after the substance and not the shadow." [83] The star of Davis

[80] Rowland, *Jefferson Davis,* IV, 196, letter Barksdale to Davis, Feb. 20, 1860.

[81] *The Mississippian,* Sept. 11, 25, 1860, from *Hernando People's Press.* The Davis resolutions were in accord with the Alabama platform drawn up by Yancey. The Mississippi delegates seceded from the Charleston Convention when this platform was not accepted (Dwight Lowell Dumond, *The Secession Movement: 1860-1861,* p. 35).

[82] *Mississippi Free Trader,* Sept. 18, 1860.

[83] *Natchez Courier,* Sept. 19, 1860.

was decidedly in the ascendant, and both *The Mississippian* and the *Mississippi Free Trader* hailed his speeches in glowing terms.[84]

But towards the end of September Brown was on good orthodox ground again and won unstinted praise from the Democratic press when he wrote a long letter to six men of Carrolton answering the question which Helper's book had raised, "What interest have non-slaveholders in the South in the question of slavery?" [85] First, Brown pointed out, the non-slaveholder had a moneyed interest in slavery. The slaveholder creates the markets, builds the railroads and provides the most profitable means of selling the productions of the soil, while the non-slaveholding farmers get the benefits with very little cost. The slaveholder is the most profitable employer of the mechanic, buys the most goods from the merchant, pays the most fees to the lawyer. Brown sought to answer the argument that non-slaveholders would get better wages if there were no slaves by showing that slavery is the handmaid of free labor. The Northern capitalist hires white labor at the lowest cost, but turns his wage-slave loose when he is no longer profitable "to shift for himself or it may be to starve or beg or steal." Slaveholders, on the other hand, protect their hands in whose future they have a direct interest so that they can be sold at the highest price. Thus, Brown argued, the slaveholder "creates and keeps up markets for the sale of his productions or the productions of his slaves' labor and into these markets the non-slaveholder enters and sells on equal and often on better terms."

To the Northern charge that slavery degrades labor in the South [86] Brown gave an answer directly opposite to the one he gave to the

---

[84] *The Mississippian,* Oct. 2, 1860. *Mississippi Free Trader,* Oct. 3, 1860.

[85] The nearest Brown had approached this question was in his flimsy argument about the slaves equalizing all white men because they relieved white men from all menial work, but he had never discussed directly the problem presented by this very important question. This omission may seem strange, especially because his strength lay with small slaveholders and non-slaveholders. However, his very silence was the more significant, for it showed that Brown took it for granted that non-slaveholders *did* have a large interest in the slavery system. They had proved it by constantly supporting such a radical pro-slavery man as Brown.

[86] Helper had argued that "in the South, unfortunately, no kind of labor is either free or respectable." White labor "is treated as if he were a loathsome beast, and shunned with disdain . . . himself a slave, he is accounted as nobody, and would be deemed intolerably presumptuous, if he dared to open his lips in the presence of an arrogant knight of the whip and the lash." The great influence of Helper's book forced slaveholding politicians to answer the charge that they "have hoodwinked you [i. e., the non-slaveholders], trifled with you, and used you as mere tools for the consummation of their wicked designs." (Helper, *The Impending Crisis of the South,* pp. 40, 98–99.)

same question from small slaveholders a year earlier. Then he had said that slavery made all white men equal because it relieved them from manual labor, thus doing away with all class distinctions among the whites. Now to non-slaveholders he maintained that "the master and the slave work continually in the same field, at the same bench or the same forge, and each maintains his own position in society." Indeed, he considered it a gross slander to say that a white man loses caste because he works with a slave.

Brown felt himself on firmer ground when arguing for the social interest of non-slaveholders in slavery. The pecuniary interest "is a dross, when compared with that other, higher, loftier and holier interest." No sane man will pretend for a moment that the two races can live together in peace when both are free. Abolition would make another Haiti of the South, in which the rich would seek security and flee, while the poor would remain and have to bear the fury of a race war in which millions of Negroes would steal, murder, insist on being treated as equals to the whites, and on inter-marriage with the whites. Therefore, since it is impossible to send the 4,000,000 Negroes back to Africa, slavery must be maintained. But then, peculiarly enough, he returned to the argument that the Negro provides perfect social equality because there are no white menials. He gloried in the fact that the non-slaveholder and the members of his family are excluded from such work as carriage driver, waiter, or chambermaid. If the Negroes were all exported, such jobs would have to be done by poor white men as in the North, who lose caste as do the Negroes in the South. "I fancy his Southern blood would boil like a seething cauldron. . . . How would he like to see his sons and daughters become waiters and chambermaids in public hotels, to be ordered as we order our slaves?"

Brown ended his appeal by urging the seriousness of the present fearful conflict in which the hosts, North and South, were fully arrayed. There could be no middle ground. "Slavery must be defended or it will be abolished. . . . Paltering with the question is treason. The South expects, and presently she will imperiously demand, an open undisguised defense of her rights, or absence from her soil. The hour has come. 'He who dallies is in danger and he who doubts is damned.' " [87]

On October 11 Brown spoke at New Orleans. He urged special State conventions and the recall of all representatives from Wash-

[87] *The Mississippian*, Oct. 9, 12, 1860. *Mississippi Free Trader*, Oct. 18, 1860.

ington if Lincoln were elected. As to whether a civil war would result, and the North attack the South, he cried, "But let them come:
never did the British at New Orleans have a bloodier job with General Jackson than would these Yankees have with us. . . . What is
to be done? Some say, 'Wait'; others reply, 'I won't wait—I will
resist.' " [88]

The Bell forces, led by the *Natchez Courier* and over a dozen other
papers, constantly decried the disunion tendencies of the Democrats
as the Unionists had done in 1851. The *Natchez Courier* demanded
to know why those who, like Brown, were sure Lincoln would be
elected and favored disunion after election, stood by Breckinridge,
whom they admitted could not win. It asked the question, "Is it because they *desire* the election of an Abolitionist so that confusion,
anarchy and exasperation may be made to rage, in order that immediate or ultimate dissolution may be consummated? . . . Now, how
much more manly and patriotic would it be for these misguided,
passion-blinded Southern leaders to seek to *preserve,* instead of to
destroy the Union. . . . As it is, we believe their labor will be lost,
and that the Union, with every constitutional guarantee respected,
will live long after the disorganizers shall be number (*sic*) among
the things that were." [89]

This Unionist appeal won 25,000 votes for Bell, the largest opposition vote cast since the Unionist-Whig party had won in the
contest of 1851. As in 1851, the Unionists secured their largest votes
in the conservative, large-plantation counties along the Mississippi
and Yazoo Rivers. But this time the State-righters polled 40,000
votes for Breckinridge. They carried every county in eastern and
southern Mississippi, although Bell secured large minorities in the
south-central counties. Douglas won his largest votes in northern
Mississippi, but Breckinridge or Bell had majorities in each of these
counties. In Brown's stronghold, the poorest counties in the State
in southern Mississippi, Breckinridge secured his largest majorities.
Again it was shown that those who had the least property in slaves
were the most ardent and aggressive supporters of the slavery system.[90]

Three days after the election of Lincoln *The Mississippian* headed
its editorial columns with the slogans, "All Hail!—The Deed is Done

[88] *Mississippi Free Trader,* Oct. 17, 1860, quoting *New Orleans True Delta.*
[89] *Natchez Courier,* Sept. 11, 26, Oct. 31, 1860.
[90] See map based on MS. Secretary of State Archives, Mississippi, Series F,
No. 85.

—Disunion the Remedy—There is Danger in Delay" and looked forward to the establishment of a Southern Confederacy.[91] And now, with secession everywhere in the air, Brown's party had caught up to his radical position. Brown, who had constantly threatened secession, was now in his element. He was the first speaker at a monster meeting in Jackson. He was in favor of hanging the Southern banner on the outer parapet "and writing Resistance on every square inch. . . . If it should cost us the Union, our fortunes, our lives, let them go—better do it then [sic] submit to a disgrace so deep and damning." The submissionist, he was sure, was the worst enemy of the South.[92] A few days later he expressed the same sentiments at Vicksburg. The Mississippian quoted and heartily endorsed Brown's fire-eating New Orleans utterance above quoted. The Mississippi Free Trader declared, "We have . . . never seen the man who could swallow too big a fire coal for us—the bigger the better at such a time as this." In a long editorial, this paper now repented of its objections to Brown's Crystal Springs speech. The editor explained that the critique of Brown's ultra position "was not written by us, nor did it express our views." The editor had heard the speech and declared it quite consistent with Brown's career as a staunch, consistent, and uncompromising Democrat. It called attention to Brown's Senate resolutions of last spring with an "I-told-you-so" attitude. Events, it was assured, had proved Brown's contention that the South did demand immediate protection for slavery in the territories even though the party organization turned it down. "What he demanded and insists on, the South now demands. But the South has waited, when Brown was opposed to the delay. We have now got where the great Quitman always stood, and where Brown would some time since have had us stand. The people will vindicate him, for he has scarcely had fair play in the late Presidential canvass. Mississippi has no truer son, the South no better friend—we know of no purer, more consistent, reliable, determined, wise-judging, far-seeing politician and statesman, than Albert Gallatin Brown." [93]

After the election, the Natchez Courier still dared to oppose secession. It taunted the senators and representatives for not resigning and for continuing to draw their salaries from this "accursed government." It accused the secessionist leaders of taking advantage of

[91] *The Mississippian,* Nov. 9, 1860.
[92] *Ibid.,* Nov. 16, 1860.
[93] *Ibid., Mississippi Free Trader,* Nov. 19, 23, 1860.

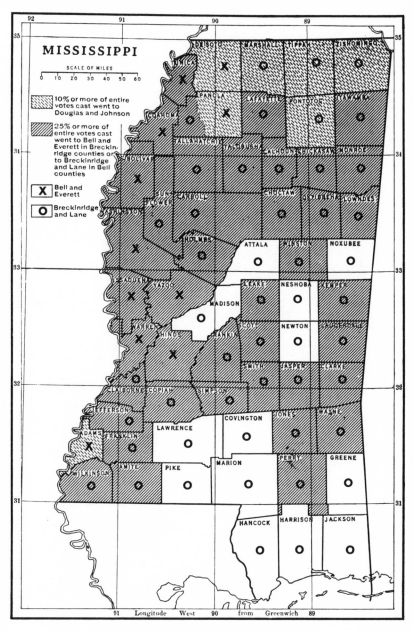

MAP 16. ELECTIONS FOR PRESIDENT, 1860

popular exasperation to hasten unduly the necessary steps leading to secession. It charged that these leaders were afraid of the sober second thought of the masses, and so, having planned and plotted secession for months, they chose to precipitate them into revolution while passions were aroused, and so drive them, like sheep before wolves, over the precipice. But the position of the leading Unionist organ was not the same as that of 1851. Events had driven both parties to more extreme positions. While the Democrats were taking active measures for immediate secession, the *Natchez Courier* was forced to take the more vague and indefinite attitude which the State-righters had assumed in 1851. It insisted, as the State-righters had done in 1851, that the issue was not secession or submission, since no one favored submission. Its side of the true issue, as it saw it, might have been taken in toto from the State-rights platform of 1851—"Resistance within the Union; Southern cooperative action for redress; a Union of the South to secure our rights in the Union if possible, or out of it, as the last resort . . . on the one hand—and separate State secession, with an utter abandonment of every right we now possess on the other." [94]

Brown attended the short session of Congress, knowing full well that it would be his last. On the third day he announced that he would not enter into debate, for, since Mississippi "has assumed her own attitude, and will, in her own way, and in her own good time, vindicate her position, silence, I feel, best becomes me." But he did not keep his resolve. He immediately asked Hale if he thought war would result if the South did not yield to the election of Lincoln. When Hale answered in the affirmative, Brown assured him that the South would not start it. All the South asked was to be allowed to depart in peace. To submit would be "the deepest degradation that a free people ever submitted to. We cannot. Calmly, quietly, with all the dignity which I can command, I say to you, we will not submit to it." [95]

This session of Congress brought out even more clearly the divergent viewpoints of Davis and Brown. A month before Davis had written to Robert Barnwell Rhett, Jr., urging South Carolina to delay action. "If South Carolina should first secede, and she alone should take action, the position of Mississippi would not probably be changed by that fact. . . . My opinion is, therefore, as it has

---

[94] *Natchez Courier,* Nov. 21, Dec. 1, 1860.
[95] *Cong. Globe,* 36th Cong., 2nd sess., I, 10.

been, in favor of seeking to bring those (planting) States into co-operation before asking for a popular decision upon a new policy and relation to the nations of the earth." [96] As Dodd observes, this letter is "not that of a revolutionist filled with the fires of innovation. . . . This was not the language the South loved to hear in 1860; in 1850 it might have been welcome. . . . The truth is that Davis did not desire to see the South secede except in last resort." [97] Brown, although favoring immediate secession, as a Southern nationalist, had voted with Davis and L. Q. C. Lamar at a conference of Mississippi senators and congressmen called by Governor Pettus at Jackson on November 22 to oppose secession by separate State action, but they all joined in favor of this action when they were out-voted by the four other members of the conference.[98] But Brown and Davis did not continue to agree on the method of procedure in the crisis. On December 8 at a caucus of Southern senators, Brown and Slidell were most eager for immediate secession, but Davis was among the group which favored further attempts at conciliation. Two days later, when the committee of thirteen was proposed by Senator Powell, Davis expressed his willingness to wait and see whether any evidence of kind feelings would develop in the North. "If you submit to them [the Southerners] that evidence, I feel confident that, with the evidence that aggression is henceforth to cease, will terminate all the measures for defense." [99] Despite this conciliatory attitude, he refused to serve on the Committee of Thirteen when it was appointed on December 20.[100]

Brown, as usual, expressed himself more strongly; he had no time for conciliation. He refused to vote for the Powell resolution "because it would be an intimation—darkly given, it is true, but yet an intimation—to my State which is moving, that there is a hope of reconciliation. I do not believe there is any such hope. . . . I see . . . no ray of light. . . . Gentlemen talk about making appeals. I make no appeals, because I will not appeal where I know my appeal is to

[96] Rowland, *Jefferson Davis*, IV, 541–543, letter Davis to R. B. Rhett, Jr., Nov. 10, 1860.

[97] Dodd, *Jefferson Davis*, pp. 190–191.

[98] Edward Mayes, *Lucius Q. C. Lamar*, pp. 86–87. Wirt Armistead Cate, *Lucius Q. C. Lamar: Secession and Reunion*, pp. 75–76. This conference was discussed by a number of the participants in the *Jackson Clarion* of May 8, June 5 and 12, 1878.

[99] *Cong Globe*, 36th Cong., 2nd sess., pp. 28–30. Horace Greeley, *The American Conflict*, I, 373.

[100] *Cong. Globe*, 36th Cong., 2nd sess., p. 158.

be rejected." To this fatalistic statement Pugh of Ohio asked the cogent question, "Will you pretend that the southern people are capable of free government hereafter if they cannot now commune with their northern brethren upon fair and honorable terms of adjustment? . . . We stultify ourselves, all of us, in saying that we cannot hear, cannot discuss, and cannot compromise the controversy, with which we are threatened." [101]

The grim logic of Brown's radical position was recognized in Mississippi after the election of Lincoln. Now it was recognized in the Senate. On December 11 Wigfall of Texas, who had so severely criticized Brown's resolutions on May 24, declared that the Southerners demanded protection for slavery by federal legislation in the District of Columbia, in the forts, navy-yards, on board merchant vessels, and in the territories. Douglas answered that he was "utterly mistaken in supposing that that is the cause of complaint . . . because a majority of this Senate, the Senator included, voted under oath this very year, that that is not the cause." When Wigfall demanded, "show it," Douglas pointed out that Brown's amendment to Davis' fifth resolution, which demanded that which Wigfall now insisted upon, was voted down. The Senate voted, continued Douglas, "that there was no such cause existing, that no such outrage had occurred as to create a necessity for legislation by this Government, and consequently they would not enact it." Wigfall denied this "flatly and unqualifiedly," but Douglas returned to the charge that the Senate almost unanimously voted against the necessity of congressional intervention. If it was necessary, as Wigfall now claimed, "that only shows," Douglas insisted, "that those gentlemen were all recreant to the cause of the South in not bringing it in; and when they never have brought in the bill, certainly they are not going to dissolve the Union because I was not in favor of it." [102]

In the Senate, Brown kept his resolve to refrain from extended discussion until December 27, when he introduced a section at the end of the bill establishing the territory of Arizuma. This added section extended to Arizuma the Act of 1859 of the New Mexican legislature, providing for the protection of slaves, and that "it shall not be repealed during the territorial existence of said Territory." In arguing for this amendment, he declared that the Southern people had $4,-000,000,000 locked up in slave property, for "their real property, their stock, their household goods, and all that belongs to them, are dependent upon the security of that kind of property." He asserted that the Republican party insisted that this vast amount of property must be outlawed and voluntarily abandoned "so far as the action of this Federal Government is concerned. . . . That is the stern proposition which you submit to us." Turning to the historical argument, he showed how colonial laws of Massachusetts, the New England Confederation, and the treaties of 1783 and of 1814 with England recognized slavery, and asked, "Are you wiser and better and purer than your ancestors? . . . All we ask of you is to live up to the faith of the Pilgrim Fathers; to do what your ancestors did." There can be no peace unless slave property is fully recognized; "Standing in this great presence, and in the higher presence of Almighty God, I tell you today that if this is insisted on the Union cannot last ninety days." Returning to his amendment, he justified congressional action in order to prevent the judges whom Lincoln would appoint from declaring that there was no such thing as slave property in Arizuma.[103]

A week before this the people of Mississippi had voted for the members of a State convention called by the legislature. The issue was no longer that of unionism or of Southern nationalism as in 1850. Mississippi had now fully caught up with the more extreme position of South Carolina in 1850–1851. The controversy no longer contained an alternative of remaining within the Union; it was a question of separate State secession or of cooperation with the other Southern States to form a Southern nation. Brown's old section of eastern Mississippi was particularly zealous for separate State action, almost no cooperationists appearing.[104] Again the *Mississippi Free Trader* announced its preference for Brown for president—but this time of a Southern Confederacy, a preference also urged by the *Brookhaven Advertiser* and by the *Ripley Advertiser*.[105]

The people of Mississippi chose an overwhelming majority of separate secessionists to the convention, only three rich counties (Adams, Warren, and Tishomingo) giving majorities for coopera-

[103] *Cong. Globe,* 36th Cong., 2nd sess., pp. 195, 201–203.

[104] *Mississippi Free Trader,* Dec. 21, 1860, quoting *Paulding Eastern Clarion.* There remained, of course, many Unionists, as Chadwick, *Causes of the Civil War,* p. 146, says, "In Mississippi there was yet a strong Union sentiment, but all gave way before the impulse of the aggressive action of the leaders," and he quotes a correspondent in the *National Intelligencer,* as writing that "those who move at all move in obedience to the voice of the extreme leaders."

[105] *Ibid.,* Dec. 22, 1860, Jan. 18, 1861.

tion, although many other counties were closely contested.[106] At the end of the year the *Mississippi Free Trader* reported that a panicky fear had seized the State. Many banks and mercantile houses suspended business. "There is doubt and distrust among the commercial community. Agriculturalists are cramped, or their drafts are not met by their factors and merchants. The mechanic finds employment scarce, and the laborer knows not whether the morrow is to be one of work and pay, or idleness. . . . Creditor and debtor alike will wear long faces" on January 1. "It is peculiarly fitting then that Humiliation, Fasting and Prayer should characterize the last day of the last month of the year, Gov. Pettus has wisely sat apart as a day when man should ask Heaven counsel and assistance." [107]

Twelve Southern senators, including both Brown and Davis, took the initiative on January 5 in urging each Southern State to secede "as soon as may be," to call a convention at Montgomery, Alabama, in order to form a Southern Confederacy, and to be instructed by their states whether or not they should remain in Congress until March 4 for the purpose of defeating "the hostile legislation that is threatened against the seceding States." [108] Two days later Brown telegraphed to D. B. Wright, a member of the State convention at Jackson, "Hope is dead. Secede at once. Today is the darkest yet. Telegraph the ordinance. Pay here. . . ." [109]

The economic depression, however, did not affect the determination of the people of Mississippi to follow the leadership of South Carolina and of the Mississippi senators, for the advocates of immediate and independent action were complete masters of the State convention, and on Wednesday, January 9, 1861, the convention voted, eighty-four to fifteen, to secede from the Union. The convention appointed Brown and Davis, together with the Mississippi congressmen, members of the Congress of the proposed Southern Confederacy.[110] Even the *Natchez Courier's* "Union-at-any-price song" was now "old and weak, and its echoes are faint and scarcely, if at

---

[106] *Mississippi Free Trader,* Dec. 25, 1860, Jan. 9, 1861. *Natchez Courier,* Jan. 3, 1861.

[107] *Mississippi Free Trader,* Dec. 29, 1860.

[108] *Official Records of the Union and Confederate Armies in the War of the Rebellion,* letter Senator D. L. Yulee of Florida to Joseph Finegan, inclosing resolutions. Series I, Vol. I, pp. 443–444. Hereafter cited as *O. R., Army.*

[109] *O. R., Army.* Series I, Vol. LII, Part 2, p. 3.

[110] Mayes, *Lucius Q. C. Lamar,* p. 94. Cate, p. 82. Thomas H. Woods, "The Mississippi Secession Convention of 1861," *Publications of the Mississippi Historical Society,* VI, 93.

all, heard," and, a few days later, the cooperationist delegates signed the Ordinance of Secession.[111]

The senatorial "conspirators" [112] decided that they would not remain in the Senate in order to obstruct legislation. The day after the ordinance was passed Senators Brown and Davis and Representatives Singleton and McRae showed their eagerness to leave Congress by sending the following telegram to W. S. Barry, the president of the Mississippi convention: "Dispatch received. Is it intended we shall withdraw immediately or shall we wait for the official ordinance?" [113]

Five days after the Ordinance of Secession was passed Brown made his farewell speech in the Senate, a week before that of Davis, who was sick at the time. In a calm, dignified manner, he explained that he could no longer take an active part in either speaking or voting because his State, together with Alabama and Florida, had taken definite steps to withdraw from the Union. He did not take the time to justify the action of his State, as did Davis, nor did he express in felicitous language hopes that the two nations would exist side by side in peace and harmony. Even in the hour of separation Brown was true to his uncompromising radicalism, spurning honeyed words of conciliation.[114]

In *The Day of the Confederacy,* Stephenson named six leaders in the State of Mississippi during the ante-bellum period—Davis, Thompson, Quitman, Foote, Walker, and Prentiss—all of whom were born out of the State. He then admirably stated the development of a feeling of Southern nationalism in these words:

"In 1861 the State was but forty-four years old, younger than its most illustrious sons. How could they think of it as an entity existing in itself, antedating not only themselves, but their traditions, circumscribing them with its all-embracing, indisputable reality? These men spoke the language of state rights. [Prentiss and Foote must be excepted from this statement.] It is true that in politics, combating the North, they used the political philos-

111 *Mississippi Free Trader,* Jan. 10, 12, 15, 1861.

112 Chadwick, pp. 242–243, 245, argued for the use of this term. He claimed that the senators intended to keep the actions of their cabal a secret. There can be no question, however, that they violated their oaths of office to support and to defend the Constitution.

113 *O. R., Army.* Series I, Vol. LII, Part 2, p. 4.

114 *Cong. Globe,* 36th Cong., 2nd sess., pp. 352, 487. James W. Garner, *Reconstruction in Mississippi,* p. 6.

ophy taught them by South Carolina. But it was a mental weapon in political debate; it was not for them an emotional fact. . . . The people themselves were overwhelmingly Southern. . . . Consequently the new community presented a composite picture of the whole South, and like all composite pictures it emphasized only the factors common to all its parts. What all the South had in common, what made a man a Southerner in the general sense— in distinction from a Northerner on the one hand, or a Virginian, Carolinian, Georgian, on the other—could have been observed with clearness in Mississippi, just before the war, as nowhere else. . . . What may be called the sense of Southern nationality as opposed to the sense of state rights, strictly speaking, distinguished this brilliant young community of the Southwest." [115]

Certainly Brown should be added to this list of eminent antebellum Mississippians. No one so well represented the viewpoint of the poorer people in the State who were, moreover, those most eager to defend the social and economic institutions which were most peculiar to the South. These poor whites had become a more definite and distinctive class during the 1850s. Agitators like Brown had inflamed their triple prejudices against the large slaveholders, against the Negroes, but most of all, against the North. Even though the slavery system actually worked to the growing economic and social disadvantage of the poor whites, Helper had been unable to arouse them against the privileged planters. This was, truly, "the chief paradox of the Southern social system." [116] Leaders of Southern na-

---

[115] Stephenson, *The Day of the Confederacy*, pp. 30–31. It is not without significance, also, that all these men served in Congress. As Chadwick, pp. 345–346, has well pointed out, Southern congressmen directed Southern sentiment to a much greater degree than Northern congressmen influenced the opinions of the North. In the North anti-slavery sentiment was "nourished by societies, by a voluminous literature, and by the then potent lecture system."

[116] Cole, *The Irrepressible Conflict, 1850–1865*, p. 38. Buck, "The Poor White in the Ante-bellum South," p. 41. Hart, *Slavery and Abolition*, p. 76, calls this paradox "one of the perplexing things in human history," and Chadwick, pp. 23–25, 34, after emphasizing the "severe mental servitude" of the six million non-slaveholding whites, making up three fourths of the white population of the South, states that it is "one of the extraordinary facts of history" that they should "have fought stubbornly for four years to fasten more completely bonds which restricted them to every inferiority of life." In the chapter on "The Poor White" in his work, *The Southern South*, p. 40, Hart gives the "good sound, logical reason for fighting what was apparently the quarrel of their planter neighbor. A white man was always a white man, and as long as slavery endured, the poorest and most ignorant of the white race could always feel that he had something to look down upon, that he belonged to the lords of the soil. In the war he was blindly and unconsciously fighting for the caste of white men and could not be brought to realize that slavery helped to keep him where he was, without education for his children, without opportunities for employment." In Mississippi by 1860 there was great disparity in the distribution of wealth between the average white of the black belt "on the fertile bottom-

tionalism like Brown had, indeed, found it necessary to argue in favor of the advantages of slavery to the non-slaveholders, and they had succeeded so well as to invalidate the sweeping statement of Rev. John H. Aughey of northern Mississippi that "the poor whites have no love for the institution of slavery. They regard it as the instrument of inflicting upon them many wrongs, and depriving them of many rights." [117] Aughey claimed that the poor whites "dare not express their sentiments to the slaveholders, who hold them completely under their power." Rather, fire-eaters like Brown so played upon their prejudices against the Negroes that they accepted the slavery system. Aughey presented the arguments of Brown in a speech at Iuka Springs in order to show how he tried to reconcile the wretched, degraded poor whites to the slavery system. If the slaves were liberated but remained in the South, the rich would have enough money to leave the South, while "the poor whites would be compelled to remain amongst the negroes, who would steal their property, and destroy their lives." If, on the other hand, the Negroes were removed from the South, the rich would take the poor whites for slaves, in their stead, and reduce them to the condition of the Irish and Dutch in the North, whose condition he represented to be one of cruel bondage. Aughey admitted that this clever argument, combining powerful emotions against both the Negroes and the North, "had some effect upon his auditors. . . . Labour is considered so degrading that any argument, based upon making labour compulsory on their part, has its weight." [118]

Cole has correctly informed us that "this concern over maintaining the allegiance of the yeomanry is in many ways the key to the success of the Southern movement of the fifties." DeBow feared the "tendency at present to consolidate in fewer and fewer hands the entire control of labor," and felt that the reopening of the African slave trade would raise the economic and social status of the poor whites. As we have seen, the Vicksburg commercial convention in 1859 gave its unqualified endorsement to this movement, but Southern leaders remained divided as to its merits.[119]

The greatest boon to the Southern fire-eaters, however, was not

---

lands of the Mississippi River and its tributaries" and "the average inhabitant of East Mississippi by ten to fifteen times."—Buck, p. 42.

[117] John Hill Aughey, *The Iron Furnace: or Slavery and Secession*, p. 229.

[118] *Ibid.*, pp. 229–230.

[119] Cole, *The Irrepressible Conflict, 1850–1865*, pp. 74–75.

economic arguments, but the overt act of John Brown's raid. The non-slaveholder "saw his home and hearth threatened as well as the wives and children of the gentry. His leaders had always warned him of the menace of Negro equality; here was the climax of that menace. No wonder that he was often more zealous for the South than the planter himself." [120] No better opportunity could have been afforded the extremists to convince both the privileged and the underprivileged that the South, as a minority section, had been forced on the defensive in order to maintain its peculiar institution, while they could point out that the South was not endangering any Northern institution. Conciliation with the North became almost impossible as extremists such as Brown gained a greater influence and "were held in far higher respect at home and greater awe in the councils at Washington" than the abolitionists in the North.[121] Conservative leaders, Northern and Southern, realizing that the attitude of the Southern extremists was a direct threat to the perpetuity of the Union, had tried to restrain and to placate them, but to no avail. The Southern leaders had been dominant in Washington, and they bitterly resented the entrance into Congress of a group of radical anti-slavery men as determined as the Southern fire-eaters, whom they met "with equal spirit, if not with equal eloquence." [122]

As John Brown's raid was effective in convincing the South that its varied economic groups had a common concern in the stability of the slavery system and that the South was fundamentally a unit economically, so the presidential campaign of 1860 and the victory of a President who represented a party which was entirely sectional served to unify the South politically. The consciousness of common and distinctive economic and social interests was so keen that this resultant political unity no longer represented a unity based on loyalty to the now divided Democratic party or to the fetish of State rights, but a unity based on allegiance to a Southern nation.

For a generation writers have been effectively stressing the Southern movement not so much as a negative secession motivated by protest against the North, but as a positive economic, social, and political force within the South itself, which finally grew into a consciousness of national solidarity.[123] The supreme tragedy of this

[120] *Ibid.,* p. 78.
[121] Smith, p. 10.
[122] *Ibid.,* pp. 50–53.
[123] Many preceding references exemplify this approach, which is represented by such expressions as "a separate national consciousness, . . . a real national

movement was that "slavery drove the South into opposition to the broad, liberal movement of the age." The South was almost untouched by the multitude of reform movements which were seething in the North and in Europe.[124] The South was culturally backward and "had little of a creative nature to contribute to science, scholarship, letters and the arts. More and more it lived to itself, closed in by tradition and by loyalty to a social institution which it alone in all the civilized world maintained and defended. The widening breach between the sections thus reached beyond political acerbities into the very substance of life itself."[125]

And Albert Gallatin Brown excellently epitomized in his own person, while constantly serving in an elective military, legislative, executive, or judicial office for a generation, the distinctive spirit of this Southern movement in Mississippi as it developed from frontier nationalism in the 1830s into State-rights dogmatism in the 1840s, and finally into Southern nationalism in the 1850s.

---

consciousness, . . . a sectional patriotism" in Smith, pp. 286, 293; "Southern nationalization, . . . a nation whose corner-stone was negro slavery, . . . a nationality of its own, . . . a feudalistic nationalization" in Chadwick, pp. 3, 10, 14, 16; "Southern nationalism" in Buck, p. 49; and "national independence" in Cole, *The Irrepressible Conflict, 1850–1865*, p. 78.

[124] Chadwick, p. 14; Smith, pp. 286, 291; Buck, p. 49.

[125] Cole, *The Irrepressible Conflict, 1850–1865*, p. 242.

CHAPTER VII

Captain and Senator During the War of Southern Nationalism, 1861–1865

And now, upon the outbreak of war, Brown at last had an opportunity to put his policy of Southern action into practice. He was not slow in grasping this opportunity. When 8,000 troops were called for by the State, he organized a company of 105 infantrymen known as Brown's Rebels, which was mustered into the State's service as Company H of the Eighteenth Regiment on April 29. On June 7 this regiment, led by General J. L. Alcorn, enlisted for one year for service under the Confederate States of America. Three days later the regiment set out for the theater of war in Virginia and arrived at Camp Walker near Manassas on June 18. There the regiment was brigaded with the Seventeenth Mississippi and the Fifth South Carolina under General David R. Jones.[1] Brown's company acquitted itself well in the ensuing engagements about Bull Run. The brigade, stationed on the extreme right, met the first attack of the Union forces on July 18. Three days later, in support of General Ewell's attack on Centerville, while advancing up Rocky Run, "in attempting a charge over ground with unexpected difficulties under a murderous artillery fire, the Eighteenth was compelled to retire with the exception of Company H." After these engagements the regiment marched to Leesburg, where it lost heavily in the battle of Ball's Bluff in October, and Brown was cited for bravery.[2]

But Brown was again transferred to the political field. Early in May he had been urged as a candidate for the Confederate Senate. He was praised for accepting a captaincy, "a position so much below his reputation," and doubt was expressed that he would be allowed

[1] Rowland, *Official and Statistical Register of the State of Mississippi*, pp. 478–484. *Eastern Clarion*, May 3, 1861. *O. R., Army*, Series IV, Vol. II, pp. 919, 932.

[2] Rowland, *Official and Statistical Register of the State of Mississippi*, pp. 478–484. *Richmond Whig*, Nov. 6, 1861. *O. R., Army*, Series I, Vol. II, pp. 537–541, reports of Col. W. S. Featherston of the 17th Mississippi Regiment, Brig. Gen. David R. Jones and Col. E. R. Burt of the 18th Mississippi Regiment. Series I, Vol. V, pp. 365–366, report of Lieut.-Col. Thomas M. Griffin.

to serve out the full term of his enlistment.[3] Soon after the engagement at Ball's Bluff twenty of his fellow-officers from Mississippi in Virginia urged Brown to run for the Senate in the first permanent Congress, "giving as a reason that he can be of more service in the Senate than on foot in the field." In reply Brown expressed his passionate devotion to the cause of the Confederacy in words which ring true: "When I took up arms in defense of the South, it was to illustrate, by example, the heartfelt sincerity with which I had for many years urged our people to strike for equality in the Union, or independence out of it. I cannot now, camped as we are in sight of the enemy, consent to lay down those arms except it be to render my bleeding country more efficient service somewhere else. Arms, as you all know, is not my profession, and if I bear them it is from necessity and not from choice. That I have not sought a higher command than a Captaincy has been because my early training, habits of thought, and pursuits in life have not been such as to qualify me for such command. Unskilled as I am in the arts of war, I have felt at liberty to do no more than risk my own life in the pending conflict. I shrank instinctively at the beginning, and ever since, from the responsibility of risking the lives of others.—In camp near Leesburg." The *Richmond Whig* praised the patriotism of Brown in a leading editorial entitled "A Noble Example" and noted the contrast "with those possessed of not one tenth the knowledge and qualifications of Governor Brown, who seek field offices, and obtain them too, in many instances, not on the score of merit, but on account of party services." [4]

Brown did not resign his captaincy in order to conduct a campaign,[5] but he was elected and took his seat in the Senate on February 18, 1862.[6] Three days after Senator Brown took his seat he was appointed a member of the Senate committee on arrangements for the inauguration and won a four year term in the draw, while Judge

---

[3] *Mississippi Free Trader*, May 1, 1861. *Eastern Clarion*, May 3, 1861.

[4] *Richmond Whig*, Nov. 15, 1861.

[5] *The Mississippian*, April 27, 1863.

[6] *Journal of the Congress of Confederate States, 1861–1865*, II, p. 5. (Hereafter cited as *Journal*.) *O. R., Army.* Series IV, Vol. III, p. 1187. Brown's position as commander of Company H was soon taken by his eldest son, Robert Young Brown, who had graduated from Georgetown University in 1860. He was studying law at the University of Virginia when the war broke out, but joined his father's company. In June, 1864, Robert Y. Brown was promoted to major of the Sixth Cavalry. *Hinds County Gazette*, July 23, 1862. Rowland, *Official and Statistical Register of the State of Mississippi*, pp. 478–484.

James S. Phelan, the other senator from Mississippi, drew for two years. Upon the organization of the Senate, Brown became chairman of the Committee of Naval Affairs, and a member of the Committee on Territories.[7]

As Brown had been a radical Southern nationalist before the war, a sectionalist rather than a strict State-righter, so during the war he favored those aggressive measures which he felt would aid the Confederacy as a whole and was not as jealous of the reserved rights of the States as the school led by Governors Vance of North Carolina and Joseph E. Brown of Georgia. He had already expressed his belief that all pre-war party politics should be adjourned and that there should be no discrimination against former Whigs. He wrote to a friend in Jackson, Mississippi, from Leesburg that the war had marked out for all a common destiny— "Under such circumstances, it is a duty so clear as to make elucidation needless, that all past differences should be laid aside, not in theory but in fact, and that the most cordial brotherhood should be habitually cherished and practised. This cannot be, if the old and dominant States rights party does not make a fair division of honors with their former opponents and present allies." The *Richmond Whig* praised the "noble-hearted Mississippian" who scorned the selfish motto "that they who made the revolution are alone entitled to the offices and honors which are bestowed in conducting it," and urged the public to "visit with indignant reprobation all who acted on a different policy." [8]

The evidence relating to Brown as a senator of the Confederacy is not as complete as we could desire because of the lack of contemporary information from his own State, and, as in all periods of his career, because of the absence of his personal correspondence which could give us a wealth of material to help us to interpret his inner motives. Nevertheless, his fundamental attitude will be made quite evident as we proceed with an analysis of his position in the Senate.

As chairman of the Committee of Naval Affairs, Brown immediately introduced measures to increase the efficiency of the navy. He worked harmoniously with Mallory, the Secretary of the Navy, and with B. J. Sage of Louisiana, the apostle of the volunteer navy. After the Monitor had proved the effectiveness of ironclads, he furthered the policy of Mallory of contracting for ironclads in Eu-

[7] *Journal*, II, pp. 12, 13, 19, 20. *Richmond Enquirer*, Feb. 22, 1862.
[8] *Richmond Whig*, Nov. 15, 1861.

rope.[9] Brown opposed the creation of a joint committee "to investigate the management of the Navy Department under its present head" and vigorously defended the judgment of President Davis. "The President," he insisted, "is not an idiot. If the charges made against the Secretary were well founded, the President would not retain him in office. The President is cognizant of all the facts, and he knows that the denunciations of the Secretary are unfounded." When it was evident that the joint resolution would pass, Brown sought in vain by an amendment to have all charges preferred in writing, "and a copy of each and every [one] of such charges shall be furnished to the Secretary before the investigation commences." [10]

In spite of the growing effectiveness of the Federal blockade and the consequent withdrawal of Southern naval activity into more and more narrow limits, Brown continued to seek to maintain as efficient a volunteer service as possible by urging reorganization, and later on, the conscription of seamen, the construction and equipment of further vessels abroad, and by engaging skilled mechanics in foreign countries under assurances of liberal pay, constant employment, and exemption from military duty.[11] And at the end of 1864, when the naval committee was instructed to inquire into the advisability of suspending appropriations for war vessels and of limiting naval operations, Brown brought forth a resolution "that it would be unwise, at this time, to suspend the appropriations of the Navy Department within narrower limits than they are at present." [12]

Brown urged strict governmental regulation and control of cotton. He introduced the second Senate bill recorded during this Congress —a bill to provide a $20 prohibitory war tax on each bale of cotton produced after an exemption of three bales for the head of each family and one extra bale for each hand actually employed in cultivating and gathering the crop.[13] A week later this former strict constructionist took the next step in accepting the doctrine of war powers by

[9] *Journal*, II, pp. 85, 93, 157, 168. *Richmond Enquirer*, Mar. 11, 1862. Letters in *Official Records of the Union and Confederate Navies*, Series II, Vol. II, pp. 172, 405, 406, 408, illustrate the friendly relations between Brown and Mallory, letters Mallory to Brown, Mar. 21, 1862, Apr. 20, 21, 1863; E. M. Tidball of Navy Dept. to Brown, Apr. 21, 22, 1863. William Morrison Robinson, Jr., *The Confederate Privateers*, pp. 319, 327.

[10] Journal, II, p. 243. *Southern Historical Society Papers*, XLV, pp. 260, 262.

[11] *Journal*, III, pp. 31, 38, 104, 141; IV, p. 295. *Richmond Whig*, March 9, 1863. *O. R., Navy*, Series II, Vol. II, pp. 172, 405, 406, 408.

[12] *Journal*, IV, p. 373.

[13] *Southern Historical Society Papers*, XLIV, p. 43.

introducing favorably resolutions of planters which urged the government "to adopt measures for the purchase of the entire crops of cotton and tobacco now on hand throughout the Confederacy, in order to prevent their appropriation by the enemy." [14] But Brown presently advanced further than the advocacy of prohibitory taxation and government ownership. On March 12 he moved the consideration of the House resolution recommending that planters refrain from cultivating cotton and tobacco and to raise provisions instead. When this resolution failed, Brown, anticipating the collectivistic principle of the Agricultural Adjustment Act of 1933, introduced a bill to limit the production of cotton during the current year. The bill made it unlawful for any head of a family to produce more than three bales of cotton and one more bale for each hand. A forty dollar fine was imposed for every additional bale. This was too much for those senators who remembered and retained their strict constructionist views of earlier days. Wigfall of Texas claimed that the bill was unconstitutional because it created a crime—a power reserved to the States. Barnwell of South Carolina called the bill monstrous: "there was no warrant in all history for a government to assume the right to punish innocent men." Brown answered that the punishment did not involve the creation of a crime, but was a simple forfeiture like the punishment of perjury for false statements. Brown clearly expressed the doctrine—so repugnant to him during his early career— that implied or incidental powers were necessary to the effective conduct of the central government. When a man committed an act which conflicted with the interests of his country, Brown insisted that he must be made to answer for it. "The Constitution, it was true, conveyed no direct authority for it. The Constitution gave no direct authority for the issue of treasury notes. It was a matter of incident." If the destruction of property, the burning of houses, and the cutting of forests were necessary incidents in waging war, "why," he demanded, "could not a prohibition to raise cotton be recognized too?" He was firmly convinced that two great defensive operations were needed, "first, to burn all the cotton that we have, and second, to raise no more until we had formed a market for it." [15]

[14] *Journal*, II, p. 30.

[15] *Southern Historical Society Papers*, XLIV, pp. 147–148. *Richmond Enquirer*, Mar. 13, 1862. *Richmond Whig*, Mar. 14, 1862. A year later Brown used his influence to secure permission for a Mr. Smylin of Richmond to export any amount of cotton from ports in Confederate possession. (J. F. H. Claiborne MSS., Library of Congress, Vol. III, letter Brown to J. J. Smylin, March 28, 1863.)

Three days later Senator Benjamin Hill of Georgia added his voice in protest against the prohibition of the production of cotton because "this would involve a destruction of slavery, the very thing our enemies most desire," and, since Congress had only delegated powers, "none but the sovereignty of the States could interfere."

Senator Hunter of Virginia also protested that the central government had no right whatever to limit cotton production in the States. The States themselves would hardly dare to do this, "much less the delegated power of the Confederacy. If he believed that Congress would pass any such act, or the Government possess any such power, he would pronounce it a most notorious despotism, worse even than that from which the people of the South had just escaped." [16] The Senate was not yet prepared to take Brown's advanced nationalistic and collectivistic position, for the bill to prohibit cotton production failed, and the recommendation to planters, simply advising them not to plant cotton, passed only by a vote of ten to eight.[17]

On other issues Brown also showed his disposition to interpret the constitution flexibly. When Orr of South Carolina objected that the Senate did not have the power to originate a bill to repeal the import duty of May 21, 1861, Brown voted with a minority of six that it did against a majority of seventeen.[18] Brown, however, remained fearful of the undue encroachment of power by the judicial department of the government. He was in a minority of eighteen to three in voting that the bill to organize a Supreme Court be postponed indefinitely.[19] He voted with the majority to have the salaries of the judges reduced from $7,000 to $5,500, but failed to win his motion that their salaries be further reduced to $4,500.[20] On the final vote he supported the minority against the establishment of the court.[21] Brown further showed his fear of the judiciary when he voted that the Claims Court could render no judgment for over $10,000 until Congress made a special appropriation and that the court should transmit all cases, decisions, and opinions to Congress at the beginning of each month.[22]

[16] Edward A. Pollard, *Life of Jefferson Davis*, p. 215.

[17] *Southern Historical Society Papers*, XLIV, pp. 160, 178. *Journal*, II, pp. 57, 67. *Richmond Enquirer*, Mar. 17, 1862.

[18] *Journal*, II, p. 96.

[19] *Ibid.*, III, p. 32.

[20] Late in the war we find him voting with a small minority against increasing a judicial salary. (*Ibid.*, IV, p. 323.)

[21] *Ibid.*, III, pp. 36, 177.

[22] *Ibid.*, III, pp. 194–195.

Brown was a leader in insisting that the war be prosecuted with the utmost vigor. His consistent attitude throughout the war is illustrated by his reaction to a resolution of Clark of Missouri that the war be prosecuted until the enemy was driven from every foot of soil in each and every one of the Confederate States and that no proposition of peace be entertained which contemplated, however remotely, the relinquishment of any portion of any State. Brown had no objection to this resolution, and yet he regretted that it had been introduced because "it gave currency to an idea which was nowhere seriously entertained. He had never heard it whispered—no such design was ever dreamed of by Congress, or by anyone in authority." [23]

Throughout the war Brown was extremely solicitous that all ablebodied men, particularly those in the civil service, should be required to serve in the army. On April 3, 1862, he introduced a bill "to secure greater efficiency in the clerical force of the various Executive Departments." It provided for a board of one clerk from each department for examining candidates so that appointments might be based on merit, and that a preference should be given to ex-soldiers. His anger flared up at the abuses which had developed under the spoils system. "Let merit be acknowledged, and the pets turned out to graze." He denounced young men who offered to work for nothing in order to avoid fighting as "wretched cowards! Miserable miscreants! If I had been Secretary I should have kicked them from my door, or employed someone to do it for me." [24] A week later he returned to the attack: "Young, strong men, pets of the heads of departments, who walked the streets like antelopes, and whose precious bodies were not to be exposed to Yankee bullets, were feeding on government pap whilst wounded soldiers . . . were in a state of positive want. It was a burning shame; and yet, when he introduced a bill to cure the evil, he was met with a pooh! pooh! as if the matter did not deserve patriotic consideration and action." [25]

Brown continued his attack upon the clerks in the fall when he opposed an increase in salaries. While the soldiers in the field endured hardships "these clerks were quartered in snug apartments and employing their time in drawing up petitions for an increase in pay,

[23] *Southern Historical Society Papers*, XLIV, pp. 62, 64. *Richmond Enquirer*, Feb. 28, 1862.

[24] *Southern Historical Society Papers*, XLV, pp. 62–65. *Journal*, II, p. 121.

[25] *Southern Historical Society Papers*, XLV, p. 111.

and consequent increase of comforts and luxuries." He proposed that they live in the country where it was cheaper, or better yet, join the army. He complained that he could not get disabled soldiers into the departments and that his letters of recommmendation went unanswered. Semmes, in answering Brown, justified the salary increase because of the great rise in the cost of living, insisted that many disabled were employed as clerks and that the force was too small to answer all correspondence. In spite of Brown's protests the bill passed, and Brown failed to secure its reconsideration.[26]

Brown was not only concerned with civilian clerks capable of serving in the field; on September 12 he introduced and had passed a resolution instructing the Committee of Military Affairs to inquire whether commissioned officers were employed as clerks in the departments and especially in the quartermaster and commissary offices in Richmond, "whether they are paid as clerks or commissioned officers, or both; and whether the duties performed by such commissioned officers, as clerks, may not be as well performed by persons taken from civil life, and at less cost to the Government." [27]

The issue of conscription probably differentiated nationalists [28] from State-righters more clearly than any other. The *Richmond Dispatch* in bold realistic language expressed very well the position which Brown and Davis took on this issue: "We are told, for instance, that it abrogates 'State-rights.' If the Yankees overrun and subjugate us, they will leave us no rights at all, either State or personal." If there was to be a despotism, it considered that one of our own would be better than a despotism imposed by the Yankees. This was no time to talk of rights and privileges. "If we do not beat these Yankees, we shall soon have not the vestige of a right, not the shadow of a privilege, left us. We must adopt the means to do this, let them be what they may, even to the appointing of a dictator with absolute power. . . . It is vain to talk about liberty and law in such circumstances. In war there is neither liberty nor law. . . . We must make a tempo-

[26] *Richmond Enquirer,* Oct. 13, 14, 1862.

[27] *Journal,* II, p. 276.

[28] The term "nationalists" is used in the sense in which the *Richmond Whig* drew the distinction between nationalists and State-righters: "We are sorry to see the word 'national' sometimes used with reference to Confederate affairs. This Confederation is not a nation but a league of nations—and we think it would be better when we come to readjust affairs . . . to substitute for Confederate States, The Allied Nations or The Allied Republics."—Quoted in *Richmond Enquirer,* Aug. 15, 1862.

rary surrender of our privileges, that they may be permanently secured." [29]

Although Brown did not vote on the bill, recommended by President Davis on March 28, 1862 and passed on April 11, which conscripted those between the ages of eighteen and thirty-five, on September 4 he voted to amend this bill in order to extend the age of conscription to forty-five.[30] Brown not only favored conscription, he opposed the exemption of large classes of the population. Thus, he could imagine no better proposition by which "the whole army would melt away like snows beneath the rays of an ardent sun" than the one to exempt all mechanics. Brown continued to describe in vivid colors the dire results which he claimed would follow. Every man who owned a few stones and ground out a peck of meal in half a day would claim to be a miller; "every man who could put a squirrel skin in a sardine box and cover it with a piece of bark, would claim to be a tanner. Every doctor who could kill his patients and dabble in medicine; every fellow who might undertake to expound the writings of St. Paul; every cobbler who could drive a peg and mutilate a piece of shoe-leather, all would claim, and by this law, be exempt! We would have more millers, more tanners, shoe-makers, and candidates for preaching, than we ever had before. He had no language to express his utter and intense opposition to the bill. If Abraham Lincoln were here and had the privilege of introducing a proposition to effect the ruin and complete disorganization of the Confederate army, he would introduce this bill." [31]

Brown aimed to reach the thousands of persons who were trying to avoid the conscription law on various pretexts by taking the right of decision away from the enrolling officers. He sought to eliminate exemptions by changing the conscription bill from "all persons liable to military duty" to include all persons between the required ages. Brown would enroll all foreigners and allow them to prove exemption afterwards, and he objected to the practice of exempting former soldiers whose enlistment period had expired.[32]

Brown also complained against abuses in introducing substitutes into the army. Some, he claimed on August 20, were Yankee spies,

[29] *Richmond Dispatch,* Apr. 4, 1862.
[30] *Journal,* II, pp. 153-154, 261.
[31] *Richmond Enquirer,* Sept. 4, 1862.
[32] *Southern Historical Society Papers,* XLV, p. 264.

while 3,000 were deserters from the army of Virginia who thus robbed those who hired them of $300,000. Many started to follow an exempted vocation in order to avoid military service. "It was cruel, almost murderous," declared Brown, "on the part of the Government to allow such abuses to go on, permitting thousands of strong men to stay at home, when their services were needed and should be had, and while we might have our little Spartan bands cut to pieces, liberty lost, and our country conquered and ruined." [33] A few days later he complained that there were abuses in every executive department and that "this Congress had a right to correct them, and ought to go to work firmly and vigorously to put them down." [34]

Brown continued his vigorous opposition to exemptions as the bill approached a final vote. On September 16 and 17 only four senators followed him in opposing the exemption of ministers of the gospel, and only three voted with him to strike out the exemption of "all presidents and teachers of colleges, academies, schools and theological seminaries, who have been regularly employed as such for two years previous to the passage of this act." "If everybody is to be exempted," he declared, "we might as well disband the army." In both these cases seventeen senators voted for exemption for these groups.[35] The only groups he was willing to exempt without substitutes were those engaged in the construction of "ships, gunboats, engines, and sails, or other articles necessary for the public defence under contracts with the Secretary of the Navy." The only exemptions with substitutes Brown favored were planters who had over fifty slaves so that these larger slaveholders would have "the power to protect the public interest by keeping their slaves in subjection; and at the same time gave the same opportunity to the poor artisan

[33] *Richmond Enquirer,* Aug. 21, 1862.

[34] *Ibid.,* Aug. 26, 1862. Brown's dissatisfaction with conditions in Richmond was not limited to the executive departments. He was very bitter against "Gen. Winder's Provost-Marshal and his Plug Ugly alien policemen" because of their high-handed actions under martial law. (John B. Jones, *A Rebel War Clerk's Diary of the Confederate States Capital,* Aug. 23, 24, 1862, I, p. 150.) Brown, nevertheless, apparently had influence with Gen. Winder, for two months later, Brown and W. W. Boyce, a member of Congress, secured the release from Libby prison of William Chase Barney, who had been accused of giving important information to the Federal army at the second battle of Bull Run. (*O. R., Army.* Series II, Vol. IV, letters A. G. Brown and W. W. Boyce to Gen. Winder, Oct. 4, 1862, W. C. Barney to Winder, Oct. 13, 1862, pp. 908, 916.)

[35] *Journal,* II, pp. 287–288, 291–292. *Richmond Enquirer,* Sept. 17, 1862. Albert Burton Moore, *Conscription and Conflict in the Confederacy,* pp. 25, 34.

to protect his own and advance the public interest by following his pursuit." [36]

When the exemption bill finally passed Brown declared it "would result in taking more men out of the army than it would put in," [37] and the *Richmond Dispatch,* in an editorial on "Congress and the Conscription Law," denounced the delay in its passage and declared that "many intelligent persons are so disgusted with the course of Congress upon the Conscription law that they begin to lose faith in the usefulness of representative bodies, especially in such a period as the present." [38]

When Brown returned to Mississippi after the legislative session of 1862, large sections of the northern and western parts of the State were under Union control. From the capital Brown issued an impassioned appeal on November 18 "To the Conscript Fathers—An Appeal to the Old Men of Mississippi." This was a plea to old men exempt from conscription and from militia duty to tender their services without pay "for the purpose of driving back the ruthless invaders who now pollute our soil." Companies were asked to report to Brown at his estate at Terry or to Col. J. E. Stuart at Jackson. "Fellow citizens," Brown continued, "a powerful, haughty foe, distinguished for all the heathenish brutality of savage war, and every vice of civilized life—confident in their numbers and their superior military appointments for warfare, now threaten the desecration of your firesides, the spoilation [*sic*] of your property. . . . The rapacity and depredation which have marked the march of their armies in Tennessee and Arkansas, indicates to us what we may expect in case of their success in overrunning our State. They say that they have handled Tennessee and Arkansas *with gloves,* but when they get into *Mississippi,* they will handle us *without gloves.* Let every man who is afraid our State will be overrun, and is able to fight, shoulder his arms to prevent it, and we will, by God's help, drive them back. A. G. Brown." [39] Brown was highly commended for this appeal—"one in which we feel assured his whole heart and soul is engaged. . . . Gov. Brown is not likely to make a callous or silly proposition in regard to a question so momentous. . . . This is the first appeal which has been made to the

[36] *Southern Historical Society Papers,* XLV, p. 271. *Richmond Enquirer,* Aug. 30, Sept. 18, 1862.

[37] *Richmond Enquirer,* Sept. 24, 1862.

[38] *Richmond Dispatch,* Sept. 26, 1862.

[39] *Natchez Courier,* Nov. 26, 1862. *Richmond Enquirer,* Dec. 1, 1862.

aged for succor in this great revolution, and we look with confidence for an unhesitating response." Fathers and those who had substitutes were urged to enlist for self-preservation in "Senator Brown's Brigade" to save their wives and daughters.[40]

Brown's appeal to the aged, as well as his unwavering advocacy of universal conscription and opposition to exemptions during 1862 are all the more remarkable when we consider the disheartening evidences of disaffection and of desertions in Mississippi presented in the works of Miss Tatum and Miss Lonn.[41] Miss Tatum points out that the Peace Society was probably organized after the conscription act was passed, that the Unionists were particularly active in the northeastern counties, and "when the exemption clauses became known, a great protest arose from all parts of the state." The belief gained credence that it was "a rich man's war but a poor man's fight." Senator James Phelan of Mississippi wrote to President Davis on December 9, 1862, that no law had ever met with more universal odium than that exempting slave owners. "Its influence upon the poor is most calamitous. . . . It has aroused a spirit of rebellion. . . . It seems as if nine tenths of the youngsters of the land whose relatives are conspicuous in society, wealthy, or influential, obtain some safe perch where they can doze with their heads under their wings." [42]

The high quality of Brown's loyalty to the Southern nation is thrown into even greater relief when we turn to the large amount of disloyalty in the poor southern and eastern counties which had supported Brown in political office for thirty years. In Jones, Jasper, Harrison, Jackson, and Hancock Counties "there were many who refused to give any support to the confederacy," and many volunteers deserted. First lieutenant Jasper Collins refused "to fight for the rich who were at home having a good time," and Captain Knight organized a "Jones County Confederacy" with himself as President.[43]

Upon his return to Richmond in January, 1863, Brown renewed his efforts to release more men for service in the field. He secured an amendment to a bill concerning the clerical forces in the Treasury Department that preference should be given to men who were not

---

[40] *Natchez Courier*, Nov. 26, Dec. 6, 11, and Dec. 4, 1862, quoting *Quitman Advertiser* of Nov. 28, 1862.

[41] Georgia Lee Tatum, *Disloyalty in the Confederacy*, pp. 88–97. Ella Lonn, *Desertion During the Civil War*, pp. 14, 62, 71.

[42] Lonn and Tatum, quoting *O. R., Army*. Series I, Vol. XVII, Part II, pp. 790–792.

[43] Tatum, pp. 97–98.

liable to military duty and to women whose relatives were in the army in all future appointments. His resolution was passed which requested the Secretary of War to inform the Senate whether army officers doing clerical work in Richmond received fuel and forage for horses, and whether they got their horses and clothing at cost and clerical salaries in addition to those of officers in the field.[44]

Brown continued to oppose exemptions. On February 17 he voted against exempting "those heretofore discharged on account of bodily or mental incapacity" and against the provision that "persons exempted shall not be again liable to be enrolled." In his zeal to purge the civil service of slackers he introduced a radical amendment requiring all executive officers who had clerks in the executive departments "who are liable to military duty to cause such persons to be enrolled at once as conscripts, and then proceed as rapidly as possible to have their places filled by competent persons who are not liable to military duty."

Senator Sparrow of Louisiana, chairman of the Committee of Military Affairs, opposed this provision on the ground that it would disrupt the administration, and that it would violate article two, section two, of the constitution which provided that civil officers could only be removed for incapacity. Brown brushed aside the constitutional objection by the statement that Congress had as much right to prescribe the qualifications for civil officers as it had to determine those of surgeons in the army. The departmental pets were not secure from legislation. If these clerks were enrolled at once as conscripts and put into the service as soon as practicable, Brown claimed that from 30,000 to 50,000 would be added to the ranks, and men over thirty-five could take their places. "If the country knew the extent of the abuses in the employment of these young and able-bodied men in the civil departments, there would come up to Congress a demand which the Senate could not resist." [45] Sparrow, wishing to emphasize how extreme he considered Brown's position, asked if the Senator from Mississippi thought that members of Congress could be conscripted. Brown was not cowed, but answered, "Yes, they ought to be conscripted." Sparrow replied that the whole State and Confederate governments

[44] *Journal*, III, pp. 38, 40, Jan. 28, 29, 1863.
[45] Brown's prejudice against the clerks applied also to the heads of bureaus. In April he opposed making them brigadier-generals. He declared that he would vote to confirm brigadier-generals for the army, "but the Senate should not set about conferring rank upon office . . . the carpet-knights of the bureaus knew no more of battle than a spinster."—*Richmond Examiner*, Apr. 18, 1863.

could then be over-turned at the will of enrolling officers. Brown's amendment failed by a vote of twelve to nine.[46]

The next day Brown's variant of the above motion which provided that exemption should be refused to "all clerks in the offices of the Confederate and State governments authorized by law" failed, as did also the denial of exemption to "every minister of religion authorized to preach according to the rules of his sect," even to include ministers of pacifist sects such as Quakers, Dunkards, and Nazarites. A few days later Brown also failed to have struck out exemption for "all physicians who now are and have been for the last five years in the actual practice of their profession." [47]

Brown had a direct clash with the *Richmond Enquirer* because of his attempt to exclude newspaper reporters from exemption. On September 16, 1862, he had attacked them when he declared that "he knew of some papers which had thirty or forty editors, and he doubted not that some of the papers in this city had at least half a dozen. If everybody is to be exempted, we might as well disband the army." He even voted against exempting one editor for each paper.[48] On February 23, 1863, Yancey had carried amendments to exempt engineers and mailing clerks of newspapers, but when he sought to include reporters, Brown objected vigorously. He thought sometimes that the Senate would act wisely in dealing with exemptions, "but suddenly it would seem to become perfectly wild. The exemption bill of the last session actually stunk in the nostrils of the people, and now it was proposed to reenact one of its odious features. A newspaper was a private enterprise conducted for individual interest and emolument, and there was no reason why its employers should be exempted any more than the clerks of any merchant." Yancey replied that the press must be guarded as one of the estates of the government, as it was an immense public utility. Brown countered with a most intemperate tirade against the reporters of Congressional proceedings. "The country was not enlightened by the reports now made of the proceedings of Congress. He was not to be overawed by the attacks of newspapers here or elsewhere." He claimed that the reports from the Senate "published in the daily papers of this city were disgraceful. A man hardly knew his own speech. If the proposition was to improve the character of

[46] *Journal*, III, p. 75; vote on bill, Apr. 16, 1863, p. 299. *Richmond Enquirer*, Feb. 14, 18, 1863.

[47] *Journal*, III, pp. 78, 93, 100, Feb. 18, 23, 25, 1863. *Richmond Enquirer*, Feb. 19, 1863.

[48] *Richmond Enquirer*, Sept. 17, 1862.

the reporting, he might have listened to it. But to ask the Senate to exempt reporters that they might get up such reports as were now made, was preposterous." Senator Hill of Georgia answered sensibly that the scarcity of paper, forcing the papers to limit their size to one sheet, compelled them to give very brief reports of Congressional proceedings.[49]

As a result of the above discussion, Mr. Stedman, the reporter for the *Richmond Enquirer,* after his formal report of the Senate proceedings, placed in brackets a bitter arraignment of Brown, although he did not mention him by name. Stedman charged that Brown's "chief business on the floor is, apparently, to collect material for his next political campaign." Certain dignitaries, like April-fool packages "are found to be nothing but trash when the newspaper envelop is taken from them." Brown did not think the press "had any more claims for consideration than a grocery."

The next day Brown objected to the article as "a scurrilous attack on himself." The issue of the *Richmond Enquirer* published a long article defending the departmental clerks whom Brown had so often assailed. The following day the *Richmond Enquirer* published this note : " 'Reporter' takes occasion to say to the Senate, that he meant no disrespect whatever to the honorable body by his reply to the uncalled for attack on the reporters." The *Richmond Enquirer* showed also that it wished to drop the issue by refusing to publish a letter by "Fair Play" defending the departmental clerks.

Senator Wigfall, however, refused to drop the incident and forced a consideration of the status of the press. He criticized the reporter for publishing "his own views of that Senator's opinions, and also of his private and public character" without presenting fully the remarks of Brown. The reporters, he insisted, had no *right* to seats on the floor of the Senate, but were there only by the courtesy of the Senate. He moved and carried a motion that a committee of three examine the conduct of the reporter.[50]

The Wigfall committee reported on March 11. It declared that reporters were only allowed in the Senate as a matter of privilege, not of right, and that vituperation and abuse of members could not be allowed. It recommended that the reporter of the *Richmond Enquirer* be expelled and that the presiding officer might withdraw any reporter without giving any reasons for his action. Brown moved that the res-

[49] *Richmond Examiner,* Feb. 24, 1863.
[50] *Richmond Enquirer,* Feb. 24, 25, 26, 27, 1863. *Richmond Whig,* Feb. 26, 1863.

olutions be laid on the table and explained that "perhaps it would be too harsh a proceeding to expel the reporter who did a very foolish thing. He had no personal feeling in the matter. If he had considered it a personal grievance he would have sought personal redress. He closed his remarks by moving to strike out both resolutions."

However, the Senators were not willing to drop the incident. Senator Phelan of Mississippi read an editorial in the *Richmond Enquirer* of March 12 on "The Confederate Senate and Our Reporter" in which the offending reporter was defended on the principle of the freedom of the press. It asked what fell with the expulsion of the reporter and answered, "Not the newspaper that employs him, but the right of the people to learn what their servants are doing. Not the liberty of the Press, but the dignity of the Senate, falls in this contest." The reporter corrected and made readable the speeches in the Senate "night after night, and day after day," as a result of which it claimed "many of the members have been . . . saved the mortification of a ridiculous expose." The editor took upon himself the responsibility for ordering the reporter to make the offending statement so that "it might attract the attention of Senator Brown." The peculiar animus against Brown was further shown by the editor in claiming that the reporter was the "equal [of Brown] in intelligence, in social standing, in prive [*sic*] character, in everything except the abnormal and temporary position of Senator."

This editorial stirred Wigfall to present a substitute motion "that no reporter of the *Richmond Enquirer* shall be admitted to a seat on the floor of the Senate." Yancey, ever vigilant in defense of the rights of the States and of individuals, opposed any action against the reporter because the statement in brackets was not a part of the report of the Senate proceedings and, therefore, did not violate the privileges of the Senate since the reporter was writing as a private citizen who had the right to criticize the Senate. If the Senate objected to this, it "savored of an infringement of the liberty of the press." After a further discussion, Wigfall withdrew his substitute motion, but Phelan renewed it. Although this motion to exclude every reporter of the *Richmond Enquirer* failed, eight to twelve, the original motion passed with only Senators Yancey and Clark voting against it.

Although the *Richmond Enquirer* did not report the proceedings of the Senate during the remainder of the session, it refused to retract its position. In a leading editorial on March 13 on "Reporting for

the Senate" and in another editorial on the following day it denied
making any attack on the dignity of the Senate, but at the same time
declared that the army had absorbed the men who could best maintain
the dignity of the Senate. "We employed the two best stenographers—
indeed, the only qualified Reporters that can now be employed in the
Confederacy. . . . We shall not forfeit our self-respect, however
much the Senate may choose to compromise its own. . . . The history of legislative assemblies presents no parallel to the scene of
childish temper that was exhibited. . . . While a coordinate branch
of the Legislature is displaying a most laudable anxiety for the des-
patch of business the Confederate States Senate is wasting many hours
of valuable time in a silly exhibition of temper and spleen over one of
the employees of this paper." It believed that the senators were angry
because their speeches were not published—not one of Brown's had
been given in extenso. "Having been overrun with solicitations for a
hearing through the columns of the *Enquirer* which our necessities
forbid, the first chance to *pay us back* that Senators have found, they
used."

There were reverberations of this incident in other papers. The
South Carolina Watchman facetiously suggested that Brown's wrath
might have been caused by "some over-honest or less able reporter
giving his speeches true to life—and when he read over his own vapid
remarks so truthfully reported, became indignant, and hence his hostility to the press," but insisted that "both the army and the people
must have the news!" The *Richmond Dispatch* also expressed the extreme jealousy of the southern press for its freedom. "Nothing can
be more absurd and disgusting than the lordly contempt consciously
affected by some politicians for the newspaper press." In England it
is a power hardly second to the throne, and here it is "the life and
breath of this Revolution. . . . Ten thousand such politicians as
undertake to denounce this powerful organ of public sentiment could
not accomplish as much for the public interest as a single press." Politicians may ruin the country, but not till they muzzle the press.[51]

Upon his return to Mississippi, Brown entered into the acrimonious
dispute about the allocation of troops. On June 10 he signed a joint
letter with Governor Pettus, Wiley P. Harris, Ethelbert Barksdale,

---

[51] *Richmond Enquirer,* Mar. 12, 13, 14, 1863. *Richmond Examiner,* Mar. 7,
quoting *South Carolina Watchman,* Mar. 13, 1863. *Richmond Whig,* Mar. 12, 13,
1863. *Richmond Dispatch,* Mar. 14, 1863.

and D. F. Kenner, to President Davis, urging him to send 30,000 additional troops to relieve Vicksburg.[52] They warned Davis that "the failure to re-enforce to this extent certainly involves the loss of the entire Mississippi Valley." They agreed with General Joseph E. Johnston, commander of the Department of the West, that the administration should decide the issue. "We respectfully submit that Vicksburg and the country dependent upon it should be held at every sacrifice, and that you order the requested number of troops to be sent forward with that view. It is unnecessary to say that time is all important and that the decision should be promptly made." [53] Ten days later Davis answered caustically. We catch a glimpse of his tragic distrust of Johnston in his statement that the military authorities should know that the withdrawal of 30,000 troops would involve "the dismemberment, through the center, of the Confederacy east of the Mississippi River. . . . Your dispatch is discouraging, as indicating no reliance on efforts to be made with the forces on the spot, but as suggesting that there is no time to be lost, when much time would be necessary to carry out your proposition were it practicable."

The battle of Gettysburg was an even more grievous blow to Brown than the capitulation of Vicksburg, because his elder son, Robert Young Brown, was captured, and "his naturally delicate constitution was greatly impaired" by a long imprisonment. Brown wrote to Robert Ould, the chief Confederate officer for the exchange of prisoners, but Ould was unsuccessful for months in his efforts to secure any exchange of prisoners. He wrote to James A. Seddon, Secretary of War: "I sympathize with Governor Brown and his most excellent wife in their affliction, and I am sure when he is acquainted with all the facts, he will not only acquit this office of all blame, but will be satisfied that everything which honor and a proper regard for the interests of the Confederacy would permit has been done to secure the release of his son." [54]

[52] O. R., Army. Series I, Vol. LII, Part 2, pp. 493–494, 498.

[53] The extremely difficult position of Johnston with relation to both Bragg and Pemberton is clearly discussed by Major Donald Bridgman Sanger, in "Some Problems Facing Joseph E. Johnston in the Spring of 1863" in *Essays in Honor of William E. Dodd,* pp. 257–290. Johnston had urged reenforcements for Vicksburg from the trans-Mississippi area before this joint letter of June 10 to Davis, p. 272. During May, when Grant marched through Mississippi and seized Jackson, hurried efforts were made to secure reenforcements, and "all the pent-up wrath against Pemberton in Mississippi burst forth," particularly because of his failure to cooperate with Johnston, p. 281.

[54] O. R., Army. Series II, Vol. VI, p. 331, letter Ould to Seddon, Sept. 30, 1863. *Clarion,* Oct. 25, 1866.

Brown did not take the oath of allegiance to the United States in August, 1863, as Garner asserts in his *Reconstruction in Mississippi*.[55] On the contrary, instead of allowing the disasters of Gettysburg and Vicksburg to cause him to give up hope, Brown returned to the next session of the Confederate Congress and introduced nine resolutions which took a more advanced Southern nationalistic position than he had ever taken before. These resolutions called upon Congress, with the least practicable delay, to enact laws to carry the resolutions into effect. The first four resolutions summarized Brown's views on military service. His fundamental position was stated in the first resolution which demanded a law "to declare every white person residing in the Confederate States, and capable of bearing arms, to be in the military service of the country." The second and third resolutions provided for carrying out this far-reaching result by repealing "all laws authorizing substitutes or granting exemptions" and by requiring all aliens to take arms or to leave the country within sixty days. The fundamental assumption being that all white men were in the military service, the fourth resolution made provision "to detail from those in the military service such only as are absolutely needed in civil pursuits, having reference in making such details to competency alone." [56]

The next four resolutions proposed radical financial measures: the levying of "a direct tax . . . on every kind of property, according to its value in Confederate notes, including the notes themselves"; the making of "Confederate notes a legal tender in payment of debts after the expiration of six months"; and the prohibition of the buying and selling of gold and silver coin, notes of United States banks, and United States treasury notes. Brown recognized that these resolutions went far beyond the letter of the Confederate constitution, for the ninth resolution declared "these laws war measures and . . . those who violate them amenable to the military courts alone." [57]

[55] Garner, *Reconstruction in Mississippi*, p. 53. Miss Tatum repeats this error, classifying Brown with "other unionists." pp. 13, 100-101. She is also incorrect in stating that Brown was one of the "old-time Whigs" who had opposed secession, p. 13.

[56] At the end of the last session of Congress the *Richmond Examiner*, April 20, 1863, denounced those who wanted to change the exemption and conscription laws as demagogues who had their eyes focused on the coming elections. The consistent agitation of Brown shows how far from the truth had been the *Examiner's* statement that "there is not a man in either house of Congress who does not know in his heart that it is beyond the power of Congress to make a better one [i.e., exemption law]."

[57] *Journal*, III, p. 455, Dec. 10, 1863. It was an irony of fate that Brown should deliver a eulogy on the death of Yancey between the presentation and the defense

Two weeks later Brown defended his nine resolutions in a two-hour speech. He insisted that radical measures were necessary to meet an extreme crisis. "We were engaged in war for our independence with a powerful nation, and if we were to succeed it was only by the united effort of our whole people. We had failed hitherto; and the country had been brought into its present imperilled condition by the thinness of our ranks alone. We had had all along just troops enough in the field to gain victory, but never enough to secure its fruits. If, in the very beginning of the war, we had had a levy en masse, our independence would have been now achieved."

Every white male capable of bearing arms should be conscripted. No reference should be made to age or occupation, but the only question should be, "Is he capable of bearing arms?" If the whole military power had been used at Manassas, the war would have ended soon— certainly Chickamauga would have ended the war. Instead of a general conscription, the first year was wasted because only handfuls were in the army, the second year brought no result because only those between eighteen and thirty–five were conscripted, and exemptions and substitutes were permitted. As a result, "we stand today with an army too weak to reap when the harvest is ready for the sickle. . . . He would include the President, Members of Congress, and Governors of States in this call." The central question now was whether the Confederacy was to stand or fall. All recriminations between the branches of the government must cease, for "we must determine to stand together in the common defense, or fall together in one common grave." His sense of realism led him to brush aside all constitutional objections by making an acute distinction between peace-time and war-time powers. "He had this settled conviction that when the States conceded the war-making power to the control of government, they gave every incidental power to make the main power effective. The framers of the Constitution were fully vindicated from the absurdity of getting us into a war and then trammeling us so that we could not conduct it successfully. . . . Talk not of 'invading the rights of the States.' . . . Better invade the rights of a State by calling out all the arms-bearing citizens, than dispute over constitutional quibbles whilst the Yankee army wrests the whole State from your possession." Brown thanked the House of Representatives for voting to repeal the substitute law, for

of these resolutions, for they showed conclusively that Brown had moved to the opposite pole from the particularistic State-rights doctrines of Yancey. (*Richmond Enquirer*, Dec. 16, 1863.)

all exemption and substitute laws should be repealed. He agreed cordially with Seddon, the Secretary of War, that the government had not made a binding contract to exempt those who had employed substitutes. He sought to answer the objection that there would not be enough men left to provide food for the army if there was a levy en masse by claiming that hundreds of thousands would still be left for the production of food after all the able-bodied had been taken.

Brown justified his third resolution to conscript aliens on the grounds that they "were eating up our substance and producing nothing," and that nineteen twentieths of them were engaged in contraband trade with the enemy. He considered it absurd that the alternative of taking arms or leaving the country in sixty days would give offense to foreign nations.

The greatest need after strengthening the army was to improve the currency. He opposed the issuance of notes without interest or of bonds with interest as proposed by the secretary of the treasury. Brown would prohibit all traffic in gold and in silver and would tax treasury notes 25 percent and declare them to be a legal tender. In advocating the latter policy Brown was clearly in an advanced position. Secretary Memminger had opposed action in 1862, and the House had rejected a bill which would have made treasury notes legal tender in secret session in January, 1863. In February, 1864, bills of Senators Phelan and Orr were tabled. The second permanent Congress which started in May, 1864, did not even discuss the question of legal tender.

However, when Brown defended legal tender legislation in December, 1863, he was strengthened by petitions of the Mississippi legislature of August 2, 1861, and of December 9, 1863, and by acts of August 6, 1861, and of November 26, 1863, which "authorized its State treasurer, tax collectors, and sheriffs to accept Confederate notes at their face value in payment of public dues." [58] Brown now admitted that his legal tender resolution and the legal tender bills of Senators Phelan and Orr might not be constitutional, but he defended them as absolutely necessary as war measures, justified by expediency. He even went to the extent of speaking as though the central government had residual powers when he argued that "there was no direct constitutional prohibition of such a legal tender law, except in so far as the State legislatures were concerned; the government had already made the notes a legal tender in dealing with the soldiers and its other

[58] John C. Schwab, *The Confederate States of America, 1861 1865: A Financial and Industrial History of the South During the Civil War*, pp. 90, 93–95, 99.

creditors; the rest of the community deserved to be treated in the same way; and finally, a legal tender law would increase the value of the notes." [59]

In concluding this lengthy address Brown insisted that the laws passed in pursuance of these resolutions must be regarded as war measures and that violations of them should be tried by military courts so that they could not be overthrown by the civil judges in some States. "We can't get along in the struggle much longer without resorting to strong measures. . . . Unless Congress was prepared to adopt such laws as these the country would be brought to the eve of destruction." In that case, when the spirits of the martyrs of the war hover over Richmond, and "demand to know the author of all this mischief, he, for one, at least, meant to say, 'I did not do it, shake not thy gory locks at me.'" The endangered condition of the country demanded the passage of these laws. "A high sense of duty to his country had impelled him to give his views fully on these subjects. He was confident that if Congress did its duty, and made every man in the country do his, filled up the thinned ranks of our armies, and passed wise laws to feed the soldiers in the field and their families at home, that our cause would triumph." [60]

Brown did not insist that his resolutions should be brought to a vote, but his votes on bills during this session showed that the Senate considered his remedies too radical, just as the Southern members of the Senate of the United States in the crisis of 1860 thought Brown's resolutions on the slavery issues (on which he did demand a test vote) too extreme. The press joined with Brown's colleagues in considering his resolutions too extreme. The *Richmond Dispatch* a few days after Brown presented his resolutions, after pointing to the opposition of other papers, declared that "it is impossible to conceive a madder project than to make soldiers of the entire population." The remedy for the present distress was to get the deserters back "instead of driving a motley crowd of weak-backed and rheumatic gray-heads and immature boys into the army." A month later the *Richmond Dispatch* claimed that the press was united against a levy en masse and continued its own opposition: "It is a confession of weakness not war-

[59] John C. Schwab, *The Confederate States of America, 1861–1865: A Financial and Industrial History of the South During the Civil War*, p. 94, Dec. 24, 1863. On February 16, 1864, Brown voted for a bill, which failed, "to make coupons of certain six per cent bonds a legal tender in payment of all debts." *Journal*, III, p. 765.

[60] *Richmond Examiner*, Dec. 25, 1863. *Richmond Enquirer*, Dec. 28, 1863. *Richmond Whig*, Dec. 25, 1863.

ranted by the circumstances of the case, calculated to create distrust in the minds of our own people of the extent of our resources, and has already given new encouragement to the hopes of our enemies." To take immature boys from sixteen to eighteen would be tantamount to destroying the seed corn; to take men over forty-five would only invite disease and death. Skill and prudence were required to husband the resources of the South. "What we want to see in Congress is coolness, combined with energy; and in the army, vigilance and discipline, united with courage." The *Richmond Dispatch* complained again after the Senate had passed the exemption bill because only the printers and one editor on each paper were exempted. It claimed that not over 100 would be added to the army by this provision. "Is it worth while, for such an addition, to strike down what all free nations have considered the 'Palladium of Liberty'?" Turning again to the threat of a levy en masse, it argued that "the Yankees will hail it with delight as the last resort of desperation and despair, and will cry out to their population that they have only to hold out a little longer, for the Southern Confederacy is already playing and will soon lose its last card." [61]

The *Richmond Whig* was even more critical of Brown's suggestions than the *Richmond Dispatch*. It opposed a general conscription as unconstitutional and felt that such a proposal and the abolition of substitutes were counsels of despair and of fear. An editorial on "Congressional Panics" claimed that Congress was subject to seizures of panicky fear since the early part of 1862 when "a blow was then struck at the vitals of our constitutional liberty. Let us hope that Congress, now laboring under similar panic may not repeat the blow which may prove fatal to our cause." In an editorial on January 8, 1864, on "A Hell on Earth," by which was meant subjugation by the North, it definitely charged Brown with spreading a spirit of defeatism by the desperate measures which he proposed. It did not know "whether the late legislation in Congress and such speeches as that of Senator Brown, or the lugubrious vaticinations of the newspapers, have occasioned the greater depression among the people and the more joyous exaltation of the enemy." The *Richmond Whig* claimed that Brown failed to stress the basic need of an adequate food supply. It did not believe Brown's contention that enough white men would be left on the farms, but insisted that agriculture would be crippled and that Negro labor could not support itself. Indeed, it held that a general conscription law would not increase the forces because it would take

[61] *Richmond Dispatch*, Dec. 14, 1863, Jan. 15, Feb. 1, 1864.

ten times the present number to detect deserters and to enroll the new conscripts. The way out was to allow fewer exemptions, but not of "the picket guard of liberty, the conductors of the Press," for that course would lead to despotism.[62]

During this session of the Senate Brown continued to favor the most drastic measures. He voted against the payment of compensation to those who secured substitutes and against the exemption of those who had furnished substitutes.[63] Thus far the Senate was now willing to go, but only two followed Brown in voting to abolish maximum and minimum age limits for service in the army and to conscript "all capable of bearing arms," and only five voted with him to refuse to exempt the conscientious objector to warfare "on account of religious opinions, and who has paid the tax levied to relieve him from that service." Brown, indeed, voted against the conscription bill as a whole because these exemptions were still allowed.[64]

Brown continued to seek to rid the executive departments of men liable to military duty. On January 2, 1864, he was particularly caustic and bitter towards the government clerks when he opposed a bill granting them increased salaries. "These clerks had been organized into a sort of Home Guard, which ought to be called a worthless guard. . . . He would not give a bauble for the military services of men who slept on comfortable beds, ate three meals a day, and did about three hours writing out of the twenty-four." Once every three or four months, he continued, they feared a Yankee advance, "and forthwith became very valiant, to the great excitement of the women and children and amusement of the negroes." [65] The day before, as a guest at the New Year's festivities at the Mississippi hospital, after expressing his confidence of ultimate victory, he had assumed the same bitter tone. "Congress," he said, "intended to catch these valiant carpet knights, who tripped about in kid boots to the tuneful sounds— if not of the lute—of the piano. . . . Congress wanted to fill up the army, and it meant to do it." [66]

When Brown was again unable to prevent the passage of a bill allowing increased pay to civil officers in the departments, on January

[62] *Richmond Whig,* Dec. 28, 1863, Jan. 4, 6, 8, 1864.

[63] Only Johnson of Georgia and Orr of South Carolina voted against this provision. (*Richmond Examiner,* Dec. 31, 1863.)

[64] *Journal,* III, pp. 498–499, 547, 582, Dec. 20, 1863, Jan. 9, 16, 1864. *Richmond Examiner,* Dec. 29, 1863.

[65] *Richmond Examiner,* Jan. 4, 1864.

[66] *Richmond Enquirer,* Jan. 5, 1864.

12 he proposed and won a proviso which denied these salary increases to those liable to perform military duty and able to bear arms. Jones, in stating this action in his *Rebel War Clerk's Diary,* does not comment, but he had already expressed his disfavor of Brown for his antagonism to government clerks when Brown had opposed an increase of salaries in October, 1862, because his letters applying for clerkships for his friends were unanswered.[67]

It was certain that Brown would stir up opposition because of his obsession against the government clerks. The *Richmond Whig* came to their defense. It called Brown's amendment an "obnoxious feature" because it would have starved out able-bodied clerks. It pointed out that Brown had been "conspicuous, from the organization of the Government, in denouncing Departmental Clerks," and observed that "it is a source of sincere regret that a man of Senator Brown's patriotism and energy should waste so much time and labor in abusing a few unoffending clerks." It would have been more straightforward if Brown had proposed legally to deprive these honorable and worthy men of office, since their pittance was entirely inadequate. As it was, Brown's amendment was "a buncombe proviso, which defeats the very object aimed at." [68]

Brown also sought to prevent abuses in the army. He secured the passage of resolutions requesting the Committee on Military Affairs to report further legislation to prevent officers "from detailing able-bodied men from the Army to collect the tax in kind and perform other light duties which may as well be performed by aged citizens and disabled soldiers as by men capable of bearing arms," and, in May, to report further legislation for retiring or dismissing officers unfit for action, absent in time of battle, or for over three months.[69]

Brown's growing consciousness of the desperate emergency was forcing him to accept the necessity of more and more centralized control of the government. On December 28, 1863, he argued that the writ of habeas corpus should be suspended. "The country should not be lost because of the opinion of every petty judge, authorized to issue a habeas corpus, giving different decisions in Virginia, Tennessee, Alabama, and Mississippi. To get uniformity Congress should pass a law declaring this law to be for the regulation and discipline of the army and by that means, as to this measure, suspend the writ of habeas corpus.

---

[67] Jones, II, p. 128, Jan. 13, 1864; I, p. 169, Oct. 13, 1862.
[68] *Richmond Whig,* Jan. 14, 1864.
[69] *Journal,* III, pp. 552, 577–578, Jan. 12, 16, 1864; IV, pp. 68–69, May 21, 1864.

Congress, there was no doubt, could suspend the habeas corpus as to particular measures, having authority to pass it generally. It would be bad to have it said, after we were in our graves, that our liberty had been lost whilst we were struggling over petty constitutional questions." After Henry of Tennessee also opposed delay, Johnson of Arkansas, with a more easy-going optimism, attacked these views as too extreme for the occasion, as they assumed that the Confederacy would fail if they were not adopted. "Really," he asserted, "the manner in which gentlemen had been talking was calculated to alarm one." [70]

Brown voted to suspend the writ in February, 1864, and also for the final habeas corpus act passed by the Confederacy in the following April.[71] This position Brown maintained even after Governor Clark of Mississippi opposed it and after the Mississippi legislature passed resolutions against suspension. On May 13, shortly after the opening of the first session of the second permanent Congress,[72] Brown presented these resolutions explaining that heretofore he had conformed to the instructions of the legislature from a sense of duty, to what had appeared to be the wishes of the people of his State, but regretted that on this occasion his sense of duty required him to take a different course. In ordinary times, he explained, he would resign if he could not conform, and even now, if he believed that these resolutions expressed the will of the people of Mississippi, he would without a moments' hesitation, lay his commission at their feet. However, there had been no public discussion of the issue and the people, he believed, did not know the facts. The suspension of the writ of habeas corpus, he admitted, was objectionable, but imperative necessity demanded it. The *Richmond Whig* thus paraphrased Brown's explanation: "Nothing but the most terrible necessity had induced him to give that vote, and whilst that necessity exists, he would do nothing to shirk his share of responsibility for the measure. . . . Let us first establish the fact that we have States before we quarrel about the 'rights of the States.' Let it be established that Kentucky, Missouri, and his own beloved

[70] *Richmond Examiner*, Dec. 29, 1863.

[71] *Journal*, III, p. 712; IV, pp. 387, 721, 723. This latter act lasted until August 1 and was not renewed because of the bitter opposition which believed, like the *Richmond Whig*, that the act was "unnecessary, unwise—a dangerous precedent for this country, and a misrepresentation to others of the actual state of things here."—*Richmond Whig*, May 25, 1864.

[72] *Journal of the Senate of Mississippi, Special Session, March–April, 1864*, p. 65. At the opening of this Congress Brown was defeated by Senator Hunter of Virginia for President *pro tem*, sixteen to three. (*Richmond Examiner*, May 3, 1864. *O. R., Army*. Series IV, Vol. III, p. 1189.)

Mississippi, are States, and his life for it, liberty would be maintained within their limits."

Brown was also critical of the resolutions of the legislature which sought relief from taxation, and declared, "among the most amazing things which this war has developed, is the fact that whilst the people of Mississippi, in common with those of the other States, have freely gone to or given their sons to the army, they are disposed to cripple the earnest efforts of their Government to feed and clothe their sons," and complained of their "rights" when their corn and bacon were taken as taxes in kind.[73]

Since Brown believed so deeply in the need for a strong central government, he recognized clearly the necessity for executive and legislative cooperation in the new nation. The attitude of Brown towards Davis is therefore instructive, particularly when we consider the growing bitterness between these Mississippi leaders in the decade before the war. Unfortunately, there is no direct or indirect reference to the attitude of Davis towards Brown in the Davis correspondence.[74] Although Brown was not outstanding as a Davis supporter as Ethelbert Barksdale, editor of *The Mississippian,* was in the House,[75] he did not join the ranks of the Davis detractors, which was made up mostly of State-rights men.[76] Brown was too loyal to his nation to allow the jealous personalities of pre-war days between him and Davis to continue.

There is sufficient evidence to show that Brown was not a "regular"

---

[73] Schwab, p. 189. *Journal,* IV, p. 34. *Richmond Whig,* May 14, 1864.

[74] Rowland, ed., *Jefferson Davis,* Vols. V and VI.

[75] Jones, I, p. 290; II, p. 133, April 12, 1863, Jan. 21, 1864. There is an interesting account of a visit of Brown and Barksdale to the army near Fredericksburg. They were serenaded by the brass band of the thirteenth Mississippi regiment, and both addressed "an immense crowd of soldiers." We are told that "the sentiments . . . were received with frequent and prolonged cheers. The occasion was a perfect jubilee to the soldiers, and their patriotic demonstrations highly encouraging to all present, and must have been especially so to the honorable gentlemen, who have manifested such interest in the comfort and efficiency of the army." Unfortunately, we learn nothing further of the personal relations of these two Mississippians. (*Richmond Whig,* April 30, 1863, quoting correspondence from Fredericksburg, April 27, 1863, signed "Y.")

[76] Such as Oldham of Texas, Haynes and Simms of Kentucky, Johnson, Toombs, and Joseph E. Brown of Georgia, and Wigfall of Texas. Owsley says of the first four: "They were so strongly attached to the idea of state sovereignty that rather than give up their theory they preferred to see the whole Confederacy go down in defeat."—Percy Scott Flippin, *Hershel V. Johnson of Georgia: State Rights Unionist,* pp. 243, 257. Frank L. Owsley, *State Rights in the Confederacy,* p. 228; Jones, II, p. 412, Feb. 7, 1865, in re Haynes and Wigfall.

pro-Davis man. He opposed some important military appointments and joined the clamor in January, 1865, to have Lee appointed General-in-Chief of all the armies. Brown became uneasy at the growing power of Davis. Thus, on April 9, 1863, he was in a minority in opposing an amendment which would require the President, rather than the Secretary of War, to furnish information with respect to the troops beyond the Mississippi River, and he declared that he "was opposed to any further accumulation of power in the hands of the President. In seventy years under the old Government, the President had not accumulated as much power as our President had accumulated in two years." In cases such as the one under consideration he felt that it would be better to *demand* information from department heads who were responsible to Congress, although on another occasion he had made it clear that he did not favor a member of the cabinet on the floor of Congress having "the privilege of discussing any measures appertaining to his Department." [77]

In order to prevent his being aligned with the anti-Davis men Brown was careful to say that "he would as soon trust the present incumbent as any man in or out of the Confederacy. It was the official, not the man, with whom he had to deal." [78] Again, in the heated controversy which the Senate had with Davis as to who was legally quartermaster-general, A. C. Myers or A. R. Lawton, Brown voted on January 26, 1864 with the Senate majority for Myers. However, it is not probable that he put the importance on the event which the bitterly anti-Davis *Richmond Whig* did when it called the report of the Judiciary committee "among the noblest and most able protests against Executive encroachments that was ever penned. . . . The dream of a dictatorship, if ever indulged, has been effectually dispelled." [79]

In a number of instances Brown voted to pass measures over the President's veto. One of these bills, sponsored by Brown as chairman of the Naval Affairs committee, illustrates more the extreme jealousy of Davis for his own executive prerogatives than the recalcitrance of Congress. It provided that each representative and senator should recommend an additional midshipman for the navy, and the President should appoint ten. When Davis returned this bill "in no spirit of unwillingness to receive the advice and recommendations of members

[77] *Journal*, III, p. 153, II, p. 217, III, p. 549, IV, pp. 489, 687, 710; II, pp. 328–329, 415, 471–473; IV, pp. 453–454, 456–457.
[78] *Richmond Examiner*, April 11, 1863.
[79] *Richmond Whig*, Jan. 27, 30, 1864.

of Congress, which are recognized to be entitled to special consideration, but from a sense of duty to constitutional obligations," Brown
thought the President misconstrued the whole bill. In his opinion
the President entered into a lengthy argument to prove what nobody
under Heaven ever asserted. The President made a very good argument if the case was such a one as he represented. His opinion, however,
had not changed in the least, and he was prepared to vote for the bill.
Brown moved and carried the passage of the bill over the veto, only
three upholding the veto. When the House sustained the veto, Brown
met the technical objections of Davis by reporting and securing a new
bill which provided that the midshipmen should be appointed by the
Secretary of the Navy upon the certification of residence by representatives and senators.[80]

On the other hand, we find Brown defending most of the important
policies and appointments of Davis. In his defense of the Davis administration before the Georgia legislature on December 11, 1862,
Benjamin Hill, the leading champion of Davis in the Senate, named as
the first issue against Davis "that the Navy Department has not done
its duty." Brown, like Hill, denied this charge. He had upheld the
contested appointment of Mallory and, as we have seen, stood by him
during the war.[81] Brown defended another cabinet member under fire
when he supported the appointment of Judah P. Benjamin, who was
probably the most intimate adviser of Davis, when a motion to re-
consider was brought up, and later he opposed a resolution of censure.
Brown further showed his confidence in the judgment of Davis when
he declared his willingness to have many officers "receive their commissions from the President without nomination to and confirmation
by the Senate," and on the crucial test of the writ of habeas corpus
he declared in May, 1864, that "he would stand by the President in
his heroic efforts to drive back the invaders, and would not mock him
by saying that he had confidence in his patriotism but none in his
recommendations." [82]

[80] *Richmond Enquirer*, Jan. 26, 1865. *Richmond Dispatch*, Jan. 26, 28, 1865.

[81] Haywood J. Pearce, Jr., *Benjamin Hill: Secession and Reconstruction*, p. 69.

[82] *Richmond Whig*, May 14, 1864. Negative evidence that Brown was not a
member of the anti-Davis faction is provided by Edward A. Pollard, the editor
of the *Richmond Examiner*, and one of the most bitter enemies of Davis. Pollard
would hardly have missed the opportunity to strengthen his case against Davis
by presenting the position of his fellow-Mississippian in the Senate if Brown could
have served such a purpose. Indeed, the only reference to Brown which Pollard
makes implies that Brown had confidence in Davis. Pollard called Brown's cotton
crop curtailment bill of March, 1862, "the ultima thule of despotism . . . an illus-

Although Brown voted to pass some measures over the President's veto, he could not be relied on by the bitter anti-Davis faction during the last session of Congress. Thus, on January 30, 1865, a few days after he succeeded in having the Senate pass his midshipman's bill over Davis' veto, he joined with three other Senators in a vain effort to sustain the veto of a bill which allowed newspapers to be sent free of postage to soldiers in the mails. In his *Diary,* Jones noted this vote as a test case between the Senate and Davis when he remarked, "Thus the breach widens. . . . Thus the war progresses between the executive and the legislative branches of the government." Brown did not join in widening this breach, and Jones could not say of Brown what he did say of Haynes and Wigfall a week later,—that they "denounced the President . . . as mediocre and malicious—and that his blunders had caused all our disasters." [83] Rather it is to be presumed that Brown would have joined his former colleague in the Confederate Senate, James S. Phelan, in defense of Davis against the attacks of Colonel Orr of the House, if he (Brown) had been present on March 5, 1865, at Columbus, Mississippi, where the legislature was then in session.[84] And finally, most of the criticisms of Davis' last unfortunate message to Congress of March 13 did not apply to Brown,[85] who all along had recognized the necessity for a loose construction of the constitution which would allow great increases in executive powers while the new nation was struggling for its very life.

The aggressive spirit of Brown was well illustrated in June, 1864, when he voted with the majority twice against the advisability of urging the President to open peace negotiations with the United States in the event "of signal success to our arms in the pending campaigns." [86] Brown most emphatically was not a defeatist. During the last session of the Congress, with defeat in the field imminent, Brown recommended ever more bold expedients in an attempt to save the desperate

---

tration of the rapid advance of despotic ideas in Richmond, that such a proposition should have been even entertained . . . the infamous bill." Certainly, Brown did not feel that the bill would lead to an executive despotism, while Pollard reported that "Mr. Hunter's denunciation of it and of the tendency it exhibited to despotic rule was conveniently omitted from the newspapers, while it smarted in the ears of Mr. Davis."—Pollard, p. 215.

[83] *Richmond Dispatch,* Jan. 30, 1865. Jones, II, pp. 403, 406, 412, Jan. 30, Feb. 1, 7, 1865.

[84] Frank A. Montgomery, *Reminiscences of a Mississippian,* pp. 229–230.

[85] *Richmond Dispatch,* Mar. 20, 1865. *Journal,* II, pp. 73–74, 437, IV, p. 553, Brown's support of Davis.

[86] *Journal,* IV, p. 211, June 10, 1864.

situation. His resolution was agreed to which requested the Committee on Finance to seek a more liberal or even a total exemption of property of soldiers' families from taxation, "and the deficiency thus created in the revenue supplied by an increased tax on the property of those who remained at home." [87]

Although Brown was eager for the impressment of all men and for increased taxation of property, he was bitterly opposed to the arbitrary powers which the military authorities used to seize property below the market price or to take it without authority to sign the vouchers for it. On November 17 Brown introduced a bill to prevent these illegal impressments and to punish lawlessness. The bill provided that officers who seized property when military necessity did not exist should be demoted to privates and be indicted for larceny. In defending the bill Brown pointed out the deplorable conditions which existed in his own State. "In the Department of Mississippi impressment had become but another name for robbery. Such things were done under the name of impressment as would make the blood curdle. The lawlessness complained of pervaded the department from the highest official to the lowest." He claimed that lawlessness increased in proportion to the distance from Richmond, "until when you reached the far off banks of the Mississippi you find no law at all.[88] He knew that whereof he did speak, and when the time came he would give the facts." When the bill was reported from the Judiciary Committee, Brown further showed his distrust of the army by opposing an amendment which would give the general commanding the army the power to judge the existence of military necessity. "He had seen something in his own country of what was called 'military necessity,' and he gave instances. He denied that the military officers should be required, on taking property, to give a receipt stating the circumstances under which it was taken. . . . He would vote against giving the power of making military necessity unless the punishment was attached for the abuse." [89]

Conditions to which Brown referred in his own State had become most deplorable. Mississippi, "with its pine-lands in the east and its marshy river counties in the northwest, was unquestionably one of the worst States" as a refuge for deserters.[90] A judge in 1864 described

[87] *Ibid.*, p. 331, Dec. 12, 1864.

[88] For earlier unfavorable conditions in southern and in eastern Mississippi, see p. 222.

[89] *Richmond Examiner*, Nov. 18, Dec. 8, 1864. Schwab, pp. 206-207.

[90] Lonn, pp. 62, 71.

the State as "almost a Sodom and Gomorrah. . . . I am no alarmist, but tremble in view of a just comprehension and full knowledge of the extent, depth, and magnitude of these evils." Ex-Senator James Phelan wrote Davis that Mississippi "literally swarms with deserters," and Secretary of War Seddon reported that "deserters and absentees from the army without leave abounded in Mississippi." [91] And southern Mississippi, upon which Brown had depended for support during his political career, was described as the "deserter's own country" and as "vastly rotten." A captain in Green County reported that "the whole southern and southeastern section of Mississippi is in a most deplorable condition, and unless succor is sent speedily the country is utterly ruined, and every loyal citizen will be driven from it." [92]

That Brown, in his sympathy for the sorry plight of soldiers' families and his denunciation of the abuses of impressment, was not following a policy of retrenchment was clearly illustrated by two radical resolutions which he presented in January and February, 1865. The first resolution requested the Committee on Military Affairs to inquire into the advisability of taking a census of all farms and plantations and to find out "whether the time has not come when it is encumbent on Congress to require every farmer and planter, under suitable penalties to be provided by law, to employ all his available land, stock, and labor in the production of supplies, and to make a full and fair report of such productions to the Government, to the end that each may be required to yield his fair proportion to the support of the common cause." [93] This resolution, collectivistic in the extreme, could not be defended by any specific article in the constitution and made clear the immeasurable distance which the exigencies of war had carried Brown and the majority of his colleagues who voted for it away from the principles of localism and State-rights upon which the Confederate Constitution was founded.

Brown's second resolution was far more radical. It raised the vexed problem of securing Negro slaves for reinforcing the army of Lee which had been under discussion since the previous autumn. President

[91] Tatum, p. 103, quoting *O. R., Army.* Series IV, Vol. III, pp. 688–690, 707, 710.

[92] Lonn, pp. 71–72, quoting *O. R., Army.* Series I, Vol. XXXII, Part 3, p. 711. The map of Deserter Country in the South, opposite the title page of Miss Lonn's work, clearly illustrates this situation in the counties of Copiah, Rankin, Simpson, Smith, Covington, Jones, Perry, and Green in south-central Mississippi and in the three seacoast counties of Hancock, Harrison, and Jackson. At least 1,000 deserters were believed to be living in the last three counties. (*O. R., Army.* Series I, Vol. LII, Part 2, p. 493.)

[93] *Journal,* IV, p. 425, Jan. 4, 1865.

Davis had urged that they be used as teamsters and as laborers on the fortifications. This proposal was received favorably, and on December 12 a bill passed the Senate which provided that all free Negroes between the ages of eighteen and fifty were liable for labor with the army and that 50,000 slaves should be impressed to work on fortifications.[94] But the proposal that Negro slaves should be used as soldiers raised a storm of opposition.[95] The *Richmond Dispatch* in early November declared such action would be "totally unconstitutional" because it would involve granting them their freedom, which the South had always insisted was a State function. "We give up the whole question when we adopt this measure. Whatever *we* may be fighting for, the *Yankees* are fighting for 'the nigger,' that is, to abolitionize the South." It would be as foolish as the Numantians who burned themselves and their city rather than submit to the enemy. Furthermore, it insisted that there was no need for such an extreme measure. "If we are reduced to the same extremity, perhaps it will be well to make soldiers of our Negroes, for it seems to us that the one is about as much an act of desperation as the other." [96]

Jones, in his famous war clerk's diary, was more favorable to the proposal because he had a more realistic conception of the seriousness of the emergency. He criticized rich slave-owners who were unwilling to send their slaves into the army. "They have not yet awakened to a consciousness that there is danger of losing *all,* and of their [slaves] being made to fight against us. They do not even remove them beyond the reach of the enemy, and hundreds are daily lost, but still they slumber on. They abuse the government for its impressments, and yet repose in fancied security, holding the President responsible for the defense of the country, without sufficient men and adequate means." On January 1, 1865, Jones noted that "the proposition to organize an army of negroes gains friends: because the owners of the slaves are no longer willing to fight themselves, at least they are not as 'eager for the fray,' as they were in 1861 ; and the armies *must* be replenished, or else the slaves will certainly be lost." [97]

[94] *Richmond Dispatch,* Dec. 13, 1864.
[95] This had been a vexing problem during the Revolutionary War after the theater of war was transferred to the South. After 1779 the issue "became at once more pressing and more delicate." Henry and John Laurens urged Negro enlistments upon Washington and Congress, but the scheme failed. (Phillips, *American Negro Slavery,* p. 117.)
[96] *Richmond Dispatch,* Nov. 9, 1864.
[97] Jones, II, pp. 353–354, 372, Dec. 13, 1864, Jan. 1, 1865.

Brown also realized that only desperate measures could save the Confederacy, but there was no note of defeatism when he rejoiced in the resolutions of the Texas legislature which denied the right of a State to undertake peace negotiations and insisted that the war must continue until the independence of the Confederacy was recognized. These resolutions, "had the genuine ring of the true metal. Peace! Our people would spurn the peace that the Yankee was now ready to give us. We would have peace when we conquer it with the sword and cannon." Brown not only indicated by implication the answer he would have given to the federal peace commissioners, but on February 2 he spoke in favor of the House amendment which struck out the limitation of the number of Negroes for labor to 30,000 east of the Mississippi and to 10,000 west of the river. The next day Brown voted for this amendment which failed by one vote.[98]

A few days later Brown introduced his famous resolution. It requested the Committee on Military Affairs to report a bill with the least practicable delay to enlist into the army Negro soldiers, "not to exceed two hundred thousand, by voluntary enlistment, with the consent of their owners, or by conscription, as may be found necessary; and that the committee provide in said bill for the emancipation of said negroes in all cases where they prove loyal and true to the end of the war, and for the immediate payment, under proper restrictions, of their full present value to their owners." [99] A reversal in policy could hardly be more pronounced. The Brown who was the most ardent advocate of the institution of slavery in the federal Senate before the war, who had denied that the federal government had any right to interfere with slavery either in States or in territories, and was eager to secede if the federal government would not protect slavery in the territories, was now willing to free those slaves who would be called into the service of the Confederacy. He deplored the fact that some senators opposed his resolution now as premature, but announced that they would support such a bill when it became necessary in order to win independence. Brown insisted that it was necessary and was necessary now because the army could no longer be recruited from white men. "Now, if ever, was the time: we were in the very crisis of our fate. . . .

[98] *Richmond Examiner,* Jan. 31, 1865. *Richmond Dispatch,* Feb. 3, 4, 1865.
[99] *Journal,* IV, p. 526, Feb. 7, 1865. Jones, II, p. 413, Feb. 8, 1865. *Richmond Dispatch,* Feb. 8, 1865. Henry Harrison Simms, *Life of Robert M. T. Hunter,* p. 196.

The enemy employed negroes, and made them fight well. We might do the same." [100]

This position, as usual, was in advance of that of his fellow-senators, as only two others, Henry of Tennessee and Vest of Missouri, voted for this resolution when an open vote was taken.[101] The *Richmond Dispatch* rejoiced that this vote "put this vexed question at rest, at least for a time." [102] However, the situation was so desperate that the problem of enlisting Negro troops remained in the foreground. On February 10 a great mass meeting, "the largest and most enthusiastic meeting ever held in this city," celebrated the failure of the peace conference at Hampton Roads. At this meeting Senator Henry urged that 1,000,000 Negroes be conscripted and emancipated and declared that they would make as good soldiers as any in the world. Secretary Benjamin also insisted that the Negroes were needed in the army at once. Jones, who had said that "now the slaveowners must go in themselves, or all is lost" when Brown's resolution failed, reported that Benjamin's speech caused much excitement among the slave-owners and described the dilemma which faced them. "They must either fight themselves or let the slaves fight. Many would prefer submission to Lincoln; but that would not save their slaves! The Proclamation of Emancipation in the United States may yet free the South of Northern Domination." [103]

These three embarrassing questions could no more be kept out of Congress than they could be avoided in public discussion: (a) Should slaves be armed under any circumstances; (b) if armed, should they be emancipated; (c) if anything is done, should it be done by the Confederate or by the State governments. On the day the mass meeting was held Senator Oldham of Texas sought to remove the chief objections to Brown's resolution by making emancipation optional. No Negro slave would be received into the service "without the written consent of the owner, and under such regulations as may be prescribed by the Secretary of War to carry into effect this act." Section four provided that Congress did not seek to change "the social or political status of the slave population of the States," but "leave the same under the jurisdiction and control of the States to which it belongs." Three

[100] *Richmond Examiner,* Feb. 8, 1865. *Richmond Enquirer,* Feb. 9, 1865. Stephenson, "The Question of Arming the Slaves," *American Historical Review,* XVIII, 298.
[101] *Journal,* IV, p. 528. *Richmond Dispatch,* Feb. 9, 1865.
[102] *Richmond Dispatch,* Feb. 9, 1865.
[103] *Ibid.,* Feb. 10, 1865. *Jones,* II, p. 416, Feb. 10, 1865.

days later the Senate military affairs committee recommended this bill with a revised fourth section providing that the slaves should be paid for and manumitted by the War Department "if the consent of the State, in which the said slaves may be at the time, is given for their manumission." [104]

The issue was now clearly joined. The *Richmond Examiner* asserted that the public now favored the use of Negro troops as a result of the failure of the Hampton Roads conference and of the insistence of General Lee. This bitter anti-Davis paper, however, continued to feel that the President's suggestion of emancipation was unwise. It brought out clearly the tragic dilemma which faced the Confederacy in its last days. The suggestion of emancipation, it was justly said, contained and affirmed the whole doctrine of the abolitionists of the North, "because if emancipation be a 'reward' to negroes, then freedom is a better state for negroes than slavery. But in reply to this it was urged: *they* think it a boon and a blessing; they will deem it a reward and will give more zealous and faithful service in the hope of it. This implies that we, the white race, are no longer to judge for negroes, but leave them to judge for themselves; that we are not only to withdraw our care and guidance from them, but also to cheat them, by holding out to them as a blessing that which we know would prove a curse. This, therefore, is also abolition; and the worse [*sic*] sort of abolition, because it would be abandonment of the negro race in this country to misery and eventual extirpation; it is abolition not of negro slavery only, but of negroes also." The moral argument for slavery held that slavery was a blessing to the Negroes and was more advantageous for them than for their white masters. Now, if it was admitted that the Negroes had a greater stake in the country as freemen which would make them fight better and be happier, then the major justification of the slavery system was gone. The *Richmond Examiner* reiterated its belief that "here is abolitionism again: abolitionism pure and simple. Those who thus affirm either are abolitionists in their hearts, or else they can give no good reason why they are not." The *Richmond Enquirer* also insisted that public opinion favored the enlistment of Negroes and printed letters from soldiers to the same effect. An editorial declared, "rightly and properly managed, it will give most material strength to our armies, and, without doing the least injury to the institution of slavery, [will] effect much towards the independence of these States." [105]

[104] *Richmond Dispatch,* Feb. 11, 14, 1865.
[105] *Richmond Examiner,* Feb. 16, 1865. *Richmond Enquirer,* Feb. 18, 21, 1865.

On the other hand, the *Richmond Dispatch,* which had denounced so unsparingly the proposal to use Negro troops in November, 1864, now accepted the view that the Negroes must be used to fight the Negroes in the Northern armies, at the same time admitting that "this necessity is, of course, disagreeable, as is proved by the evident reluctance with which we have entered upon the discussion." Not only that, but the *Richmond Dispatch* was willing to face emancipation— "We should rather sacrifice them all, and make emancipation universal, than hazard the independence of the Confederate States. If we fail, we lose everything, property of every kind, and our own independence." It was necessary to give up part of the cargo in order to save the rest. Repudiating more clearly its earlier position, it declared "if anything is to be done, it must be done at once. If it had been done at the beginning of the session of Congress, the future would have been without a cloud." [106]

In the meantime, the Oldham revised "inevitable nigger" bill was being considered in secret sessions of the Senate, while Jones complained that Richmond was likely to fall without a battle, "and yet Congress has done nothing, and does nothing, but waste the precious time. I fear it is too late now!" He even criticized Brown for retarding legislation by motions to postpone while "the Senate listens to him, not knowing what to do. Hours now are worth weeks hereafter." The next day the Senate acted, but it was to pass a resolution by eleven votes to ten to postpone the bill indefinitely. Brown, of course, voted against the resolution to postpone, for he fully realized how desperate the plight of the Confederacy was, not only about Richmond, but in his own State, from which Governor Clarke had just telegraphed President Davis "that nothing keeps the negroes from going to the enemy but the fear of being put in the Federal army; and that if it be attempted to put them in ours, all will run away." [107]

Again the troublesome issue seemed to be settled. The *Richmond Dispatch* wrote on February 24, "in official circles, this is considered as disposing of the question of putting negro soldiers into our armies finally." But it could be no more avoided than after Brown's original resolution had been defeated on February 9. The day after the Senate bill was indefinitely postponed, on February 22, a House bill, sponsored by Ethelbert Barksdale, was considered in secret session, thus keeping

[106] *Richmond Dispatch,* Feb. 20, 21, 1865.
[107] *Journal,* IV, pp. 543, 585, Feb. 10, 21, 1865. *Richmond Dispatch,* Feb. 17, 18, 20, 22, 1865. Jones, II, p. 427, Feb. 20, 1865.

the issue alive. This bill gave the President the power to ask the owners for any number of slaves he thought wise, but section five provided that they were to remain slaves "except by consent of the owners, and of the States in which they may reside, and in pursuance of the laws thereof." [108]

And now the *Richmond Examiner*, like the *Richmond Dispatch*, was forced by the bitter compulsion of events to change its position. It admitted, as it had previously argued, that Lee's request for freed Negro troops was "directly opposite to all the sentiments and principles which have heretofore governed the Southern people" and that nothing but Lee's repeated demands "could induce, or rather coerce, this people and this army to consent to so essential an innovation. But still the question recurs—can we hope to fight successfully through a long war without using the black population?" A grim and bitter military necessity faced the nation. True, in his letter of February 18 to Ethelbert Barksdale of the House, Lee's earnestness in insisting that it would be neither just nor wise to require them to serve as slaves "raised the question as to whether he was what used to be called a 'good Southerner'; that is, whether he is thoroughly satisfied of the justice and beneficence of negro slavery as a sound, permanent basis of our national polity." [109] But the *Richmond Examiner* was forced to give up its basic principles, for it continued—"Yet all these considerations must also give way if it be true that, to save our country from Yankee conquest and domination, it is not only expedient but necessary to employ Negroes as soldiers. *He* is the good Southerner who will guaranty us against that shameful and dreadful doom . . . to put in abeyance political and social theories which in principle we cannot alter." Still holding these principles, the *Richmond Examiner* was bound to sympathize with the eleven Senators who voted against the Negro bill because they recognized that it was "the beginning of abolition." In opposing this, they upheld "the true Southern principle and the only righteous principle." Again the *Richmond Examiner* faced the crisis realistically—"but what then? What good will our principle do if the Yankees come in over us? Will there be any comfort in going down to perdition carrying our principle with us intact? The principle of

---

[108] *Richmond Dispatch*, Feb. 23, 24, Mar. 8, 1865.

[109] Lee, it should be noted, urged that the question of emancipation, "should be left, as far as possible, to the people and the States, which alone can legislate as the necessities of this particular service may require." (Stephenson, p. 301, letter Lee to Barksdale, Feb. 18, 1865.)

slavery is a sound one; but is it so dear to us that rather than give it up we would be slaves ourselves? . . . It may be under protest that we yield to this imperious necessity; but still we yield." [110]

The *Richmond Enquirer* was far more impatient with the Senate for deliberately and defiantly disregarding the earnest appeal of General Lee; "it has criminally jeopardized the liberties of these States, recklessly hazarded the success of our cause, and presumptuously set its own judgment or rather the judgment of thirteen men [in the first vote on Brown's original resolution] against the will of the people, the earnest appeal of Gen. Lee, and the request of the army." The *Richmond Enquirer,* believing that the public safety was now paramount to the laws, the constitution, and the legislature, went so far as to assert that "these States and this cause stands today in need of a Dictator—of a man who will take the power of the people, and use it for their preservation," and was willing to entrust this power to either Davis or to Lee.[111]

The *Richmond Dispatch* was equally caustic. "Should our independence be lost, we may console ourselves as we best can, amid the triumphs of universal emancipation, that we have perished, not by the superior prowess of the enemy, but by our own incurable prejudices and unconquerable obstinacy. . . . We feel entirely confident that if General Lee's statesmanlike counsels had been adopted a year ago, the future freedom of Southern white men would be no longer a question. And that is what we are fighting for. Our own freedom! All else is but as the small dust of the balance." [112]

While the press argued the issues of emancipation and independence, the Senate continued to discuss the House bill in secret sessions during the latter part of February and the early days of March. There was hope for the passage of the bill after the Virginia legislature passed a mandatory resolution requiring the Virginia senators, who had voted for postponement of the Senate bill, to reverse their vote on the House bill.[113] On March 7 the *Richmond Dispatch* noted that the bill was still being discussed in secret session, although attempts had been made to bring the bill into the open. It hazarded the opinion that "the majority of the Senate are believed to be opposed to the policy of arming the slaves, but the outside pressure in favor of it is so great as to

[110] *Richmond Examiner,* Feb. 25, 1865.

[111] *Richmond Enquirer,* Feb. 25, 1865.

[112] *Richmond Dispatch,* Feb. 27, Mar. 1, 1865.

[113] The Virginia legislature passed its own bill for enrolling slaves as soldiers, but did not provide for their emancipation. (Stephenson, p. 307.)

induce the belief that the bill will be passed." This latter prediction was correct, for the bill passed by nine to seven on March 8 after an amendment had been added that "not more than twenty-five per cent of the male slaves between the ages of eighteen and forty-five in any State could be called into the service." [114]

Senator Hunter of Virginia, whom Jones had denounced for defeating the previous bill in order to please the slave-owners, now voted for the bill because of the instructions of the legislature, but he explained that he was still opposed to the bill because "it gave up the principle on which we went to war, and would add no strength to our armies." The position of Hunter caused much comment in the press. The *Richmond Examiner* admitted that his reasoning was strong and could not be answered by argument. But the logic of events now took precedence over formal reasoning. "If he [Lee] will but beat back the Yankee invasion, the country will gladly forgive any shock given to its traditional policy or social system. Let us be free of our enemy, and let negro labour and the negro race find their level afterwards as best they may." The *Richmond Enquirer,* however, sought to refute Hunter's argument, but in order to do so it was forced to go back to the outmoded logic of the mediæval age. The whole feudal system, it claimed, refuted the contention that it was necessary to give a slave his freedom when he was made a soldier. The serfs owed service to their lord, and of the various required services, "military service was the ground, in fact, of serfdom. Just as the mediæval serf was bound to military service for his lord's protection, so the modern negro slave was bound in duty to his master and to the state for national defense, and no revolution in his status was necessary." This ingenious argument was logical, but the simple answer of the *Richmond Dispatch* to the question of the *New York Herald,* "What are we now fighting for, since the nigger has been turned into a soldier?", came nearer to the thoughts of those who were still determined to continue the struggle— "We are fighting to drive from our soil the most infamous race that God, in His wrath with mankind, ever permitted to cumber the earth. We are fighting to get rid of the Yankees! Surely, this is enough." [115]

The foregoing discussion of the Negro soldier during the days of the dying agonies of the Confederacy is important because it afforded

---

[114] *Journal,* IV, p. 670. *Richmond Dispatch,* Mar. 7, 8, 9, 1865.

[115] *Richmond Dispatch,* Mar. 8, 17, 1865. *Richmond Examiner,* Mar. 9, 1865. *Richmond Enquirer,* Mar. 13, 1865. Jones, II, pp. 431, 434, Feb. 24, 26, 1865.

the acid test of the two great principles of the South—Negro slavery and Southern nationalism. The Confederacy was fighting for both these principles which seemed to be inextricably and inevitably joined. No more tragic and bitter dilemma could have been presented than the necessity of choosing one or the other if both were not to be lost. The delay in facing this issue, the embarrassment of the press and of Congress when it was faced, the secret sessions and great difficulty in getting a bill passed, even when the bill recognized the principle of State rights, are quite natural and understandable.[116]

And this issue throws into bolder relief than any other the position of Brown. Throughout his career he had always been, as we have seen, a radical in dealing with both of these principles. But when it came to the ultimate test, this extreme fire-eating pro-slavery man did not hesitate a moment to throw in his lot with Southern nationalism. Slavery, after all, was an anachronism in the nineteenth century, while nationalism was the dominant political motif throughout the world. Albert Gallatin Brown and Abraham Lincoln, so fundamentally unlike in other respects, were both typical of their age in their devotion to this principle of nationalism. Each placed the existence of his nation above that of the existence or non-existence of slavery. But the stars in their courses were fighting against a nation which based its right of self-determination upon an inefficient and undemocratic social system based on slavery.

[116] Stephenson, pp. 301, 302, makes too much of a mystery out of the frightful dilemma which faced the Senate and the House: "Would that we had a satisfactory clew to the psychology of the Confederate Senate during these dreadful weeks, when the wave of fire which was Sherman's advance moved steadily toward Richmond! . . . To repeat, the dilatoriness of Congress is a psychological mystery yet to be solved."

CHAPTER VIII

In Retirement During Reconstruction

After the war Brown returned to his estate at Terry in Hinds County. He took occasional trips to Jackson, thirteen miles away, but as an unpardoned rebel, he was not active in politics for the first time since the beginning of his career, thirty-three years before.[1] He took no part in the transfer of the State government from Governor Clarke to Provisional-Governor Sharkey, nor in the State convention, the election of Governor B. G. Humphreys, or in the "Black Code" which the subsequent legislature adopted.[2] Indeed, during the period of presidential reconstruction we catch only fleeting glimpses of Brown. In December, 1865, the *Clarion* of Jackson, "Official Journal of the State," reported him "in good health and hopeful of the future." It hoped he would soon be pardoned by the President because, like thousands of late secessionists, "he earnestly desires to see the Union restored, and fraternal relations once more established between the different sections." [3]

---

[1] The Jackson *Mississippian* made no reference to Brown between July 13 and Oct. 30, 1865, although the campaign for the State convention was in progress. A reference on Oct. 31 merely mentioned his good health.

[2] Walter L. Fleming, *Documentary History of Reconstruction*, I, 281–290, reproduces these laws.

[3] *Clarion*, Dec. 6, 1865. The only record of Brown during the critical year, 1866, which marked the transition from presidential to congressional reconstruction, reports the death of his elder son, Robert Y. Brown, in New Orleans on October 15. We have seen that this young man had succeeded his father as captain of "Brown's Rebels." He had been in fourteen pitched battles and had been severely wounded twice. In July, 1863, he was captured at Gettysburg. After a long imprisonment, "during which his naturally delicate constitution was greatly impaired, he was exchanged." He returned to his father's home near Terry to recuperate with an indefinite furlough. He reentered the service in June, 1864, as major of the sixth Mississippi cavalry, and later was appointed a colonel by President Davis, serving under Lieutenant-General Forrest. After the war he finished his law course and practised in New Orleans until his promising career was cut short. He was buried in Greenlawn cemetery in Jackson. Very fittingly, the remaining members of "Brown's Rebels" met at Terry to pass resolutions of respect for the deceased and of consolation to his family and to agree to wear a badge of mourning for thirty days. (*Clarion*, Oct. 25, 1866.)

At the beginning of 1867 Brown resumed the practice of law in Jackson. Immediately thereafter, upon the passage of the Reconstruction Act by Congress, he exerted a larger influence on public opinion than he had done during the past two years. He was hailed grandiloquently as "a man who has filled every honorable office in the gift of the people of Mississippi, and was never found wanting in any of them, and who is as glorious a specimen of a gentleman as ever stood in the presence of Kings and Presidents." [4] He was invited to address the legislature, but declined the honor because "he has no anxiety to appear before the public." [5] However, a month and a half later Brown overcame his reticence and, in a letter published in the Jackson *Clarion,* gave full expression of his views on the reconstruction issues, so deeply agitating all Mississippians, then subjected to the military rule of General E. O. C. Ord. One is immediately struck by the mild tone and chastened spirit, by the modesty and the good taste of this letter. How unlike the fire-eating radical Southern nationalist of pre-war and of war days! He explained that he had not meddled in political affairs since the war and that he had "studiously avoided every act that might be construed into an attempt to interfere in matters with which a 'prescribed rebel' had nothing to do." Even now he hesitated to express himself and hoped to escape censure only on the ground that he was answering inquiries and not volunteering his opinions. "To those who think it most becoming men in my situation to keep quiet, I am free to say, 'that is very much my own opinion.' "

Although expressing such extreme reticence to write, he did not go to the extent of retracting any former position. He stated explicitly that the acts of secession were valid and that the States which passed them were wholly out of the Union even though they had been forced after the war to declare them void from the beginning. "We fought to maintain an independent and separate nationality which we had created. And when we ceased to fight and gave up our arms, we laid them at the feet of the conqueror. From that day to this we have ceased to have any political rights which the conqueror was bound to respect. We know we were out, and that on fair terms we are willing to go back. While I say this, I utterly deny that we committed any treason. A foreigner cannot commit treason, however he may offend against the laws and constitution of another country than his own in other re-

[4] *Ibid.,* May 7, 11, 1867. *Natchez Courier,* Jan. 18, 1867, quoting *National Star* of Jan. 12, 1867.
[5] *Natchez Courier,* Feb. 5, 1867.

spects." In these words Brown but followed to its logical conclusion his dominant philosophy of Southern nationalism. While there was a possibility of forming a Southern nation, and while that nation existed in fact, Brown was a radical, fervent adherent, and exerted himself to the utmost to maintain that nation. But now that that nation, as a political organization, had been abolished, he logically accepted the political theory of Thaddeus Stevens—a theory which, incidentally, was thoroughly illogical for any one like Stevens, who believed in an indissoluble union—that the Southern States had become "conquered provinces." True, Brown might have taken one step more and have argued that since the North had won the war, it proved that her major contention was true and that, therefore, no more "reconstruction" could be imposed by the federal government upon indissoluble Southern States than upon indissoluble Northern States. Although this view would have been the easier one to accept under the present conditions of galling military rule, Brown was not willing to admit that might made right, and he would have violated his fundamental belief in the Confederate States as a former de jure nation. On the other hand, it is worth noting that Brown's Southern nationalism was not as ardent as the nationalism of the Poles, who refused to acquiesce in the "abolition" of their nation.

Brown applied these principles to the immediate issues at hand. Although the conquered nation had no political rights, it did not mean that all other rights were lost. He insisted that the rules of international law must apply. The conqueror "is bound to treat us as he has treated other conquered people, and as other conquerors have their conquered in modern times. Whether he does so or not, *not we,* but God, and the civilized world must be the judges. It remains to be seen whether they will honor themselves by tempering mercy with power, or degrade themselves—not us—by a contrary course. *We have nothing to do but submit.*"

Brown even applied this hard doctrine to the radical congressional proposals of Negro suffrage and Negro education. He agreed with the universal belief of Southern whites that these measures were "unnecessarily harsh" and "extremely dangerous to the safety and best interest of the whole country," especially when these measures were linked with the proposals to disfranchise and to proscribe permanently a large portion of the most intelligent white population. But even of these outrageous measures he said, "you and I are not to be the judges." However, he did not hesitate to warn the radicals in Congress: "The men who have done this thing will remember when I fear it will be too late, that the interest of this country is intimately blended with their own—so intimately indeed, that it will be found impossible to inflict a permanent injury on one without seriously damaging the other." Now that the Southern nation was no more, Brown was the better able to think in terms of the interests of the entire country without hate or rancor. Personally, he took an entirely passive attitude: "I am, as you know, among the proscribed, but I am satisfied." He disclaimed any desire to vote or to hold office and asserted that he would not be personally concerned if his disabilities were continued, "and I beg my friends not to include me in their thoughts when they are considering what to do with this subject."

Brown next advised white men on the attitude they should take in the difficult days ahead when the Negroes were to be registered as voters under the supervision of the military authorities. "If the negro is to stay here, and it is desirable to have him do so, what is the duty of the *intelligent* white man towards him? Why, to educate him and admit him when sufficiently instructed to the right of voting and as rapidly as possible prepare him for a safe and rational enjoyment of that 'equality before the law' which as a free man he has the right to claim, and which we cannot long refuse to give." In any case, Brown felt that the South would be compelled to submit to all that Congress had done or might do, "and this being so, I would have our people do it as gracefully as possible, not indeed pretending they like it—that would be disgraceful—but without any murmurings or childish regrets." In conclusion, Brown urged every white man, who was not disqualified, to vote and to "do so calmly, with dignity and with a fixed purpose to save as much of liberty as can be rescued from the wreck of the 'lost cause.' " [6]

In this letter Brown definitely allied himself with a respectable minority of prominent politicians and editors, led by L. Q. C. Lamar, Judges Watson, Campbell, and Yerger, and Ethelbert Barksdale of the Jackson *Clarion,* who believed that a sullen inactivity on the part of the white population would only increase the prejudice and harsh measures of the radicals in Congress. As Garner expresses it, they believed that a cheerful acquiescence and acceptance of their present

[6] *Clarion,* Mar. 27, 1867, letter to Wm. H. Allen, H. Hitzheim, and others, Mar. 22, 1867. Garner, *Reconstruction in Mississippi,* pp. 154–155.

lot "could not make their situation any the worse, and it would perhaps be the means of securing concessions from the radicals in Congress." [7]

Brown's letter caused much comment and even received notice in the New York press.[8] Ethelbert Barksdale, the fire-eating radical editor of the Jackson *Mississippian* before the war and the chairman of the Mississippi delegation at the Charleston convention in 1860, now approved of Brown's conciliatory course. He hailed Brown as "one of the most experienced, faithful, able, and accepted of all the statesmen who have served the people of Mississippi. . . . There never was a time when the people were in greater need of counsel from sagacious minds than the present. The questions which they are called upon to decide require calm discussion and practical common sense views; not a rant and fury, nor impractical theories. . . . We need not ask Mississippians to listen to counsels of one whom they have so long held in such profound regard as Albert G. Brown." [9]

But all was not praise. The *Natchez Courier* which had favored submission to the compromise measures of 1850 and had been the leading unionist journal in the State up to the very eve of the war, now denounced Brown for favoring "abject submission. . . . How are the mighty fallen!" It hailed the "refreshing contrast to Ex-Gov. Brown's epistle" in "two noble and manly letters from John D. Freeman and D. Shelton of Jackson, who do not yet seem prepared to consent to the sacrifice of constitutional liberty" or to lend aid to any unholy offering up of the South to Northern malice.[10]

Brown did not confine himself to writing his opinions. He delivered addresses in favor of accepting the congressional reconstruction policy, and the hostile *Natchez Courier* reported that the citizens of Terry were preparing a dinner on July 4 "at which the Hon. Ex-Gov. Brown and other distinguished gentlemen of both colors, are to expatiate upon the beauties of Radical rule and the propriety of accepting the mild conditions proposed for our admission into the Glorious Union of our Fathers!" We do not know whether Brown spoke at this dinner with Negroes, but it is quite probable that he did, for the vice-president

[7] Garner, pp. 178–179.

[8] *Ibid.*, pp. 154–155, 179, citing *New York Herald*, Apr. 3, 1867, and *New York Times*, Aug. 22, 1867.

[9] *Clarion*, Mar. 27, 1867.

[10] *Natchez Courier*, Apr. 2, 3, 1867.

of the committee of arrangements, of which Brown was president, was Alf Johnson, a colored man.[11]

At a speech at Holly Springs Brown made it more clear how difficult it was for him to acquiesce in the congressional policy. He admitted that "it was a nauseating and odious dose, but it should be taken without 'grimaces' which could serve only to increase the pleasure of their enemies." He could not restrain his bitterness towards Thaddeus Stevens, whom he charged was "drunk with rage" and "wants to run his engine over us." Again he indicated the strategy which should be used when he said that Stevens would not "run over me. I will not be the little bull to try to butt the thing off. I would rather step aside and see him grit and gnash his teeth at his disappointment." [12]

At this time we get one of the very few glimpses into the financial status of Brown. He had been conspicious for his generosity during the war, but his estate must have been quite depleted after the war. For 1868 his tax was only $5.03. He possessed only fifteen cattle and one horse and is reported to have earned only $300 as a lawyer.[13] It is quite unfortunate that there is not sufficient data available to estimate the influence of his economic status upon his political views.

Brown was as much concerned at this time about the threatened pauperization of the poorer classes as a result of indiscreet aid provided by Congress as he was about the political oppression of his State. He expressed these economic views in a remarkable letter to Senator Zachariah Chandler of Michigan, one of the leading Radicals.[14] Brown marked the first part of the letter "Private." He hoped that "the events of the last few years have not so far disturbed our former personal relations as to render it improper for me to address you on a subject, as I regard it, of the greatest public concern." How familiar the following argument sounds today when we are so accustomed to federal relief and to boondoggling! "Certainly no such calamity can befall us now, as to have an already idle & ignorant multitude imbibe the impression that Congress is going to feed them at the public expense. . . . And if the freedmen and lazy whites once take hold on the idea

[11] *Ibid.,* June 18, 1867; June 19, 1867, quoting *Jackson Advertiser.*

[12] Ellis Paxson Oberholtzer, *A History of the United States Since the Civil War,* II, 11, quoting *New York Herald,* Sept. 3, 1867.

[13] MS. Mississippi State Archives, Auditor's Series, G, No. 217.

[14] Zachariah Chandler MSS., Library of Congress, Vol. IV, 1866–1870, letter Brown to Zachariah Chandler, Jan. 4, 1868.

that they can refuse to work and appeal successfully to Congress for support, work will stop and then we shall have starvation in its most hideous forms. It is against this state of things that I would have you guard." The greatest assistance Congress could give, he believed, was to repeal the cotton tax and to relieve industry from oppressive burdens in order to open afresh the fountains of industry and enterprise. "Then Congress may safely lock the door of the Treasury and say to our people, 'root little hog or die.' It is relief against oppressive taxation and not appropriations from the Treasury that we want. . . . The last will be, at best, a wet weather spring that will dry up in a little while and leave our people in a more famishing condition than if it had never existed." This "private" letter further stated that the accompanying public letter was so worded "as to leave it open to such use as you may think proper to make of it."

Brown opened his public letter with a statement of his previous policy to remain silent on political issues since the end of the war. The only time he made an exception to this policy, his advice "was not taken in this state in regard to the adoption of the Congressional plan of reconstruction." Nothing could induce him now to make suggestions, even privately, "but a firm conviction, which I deeply feel, that a great wrong, under a mistaken notion of philanthropy, is about to be consummated." This "great wrong" was the information, given to Congress by General Alvan C. Gillem and sanctioned by Commanding-General E. O. C. Ord, that there was large-scale destitution in Mississippi. Brown admitted that there was very great destitution as compared with the period of prosperity before the war and that the impoverished people of Mississippi could not adequately assist the sick, the aged, and the infirm in body and mind, and that Congressional aid for these groups would be welcome. "But that there is any such wide-spread and universal distress as will justify Congress in making large appropriations of money to establish depots of provisions I utterly deny. . . . I hope and pray that we may be spared the terrible infliction of having an already frightfully long list of able bodied idlers and slothful vagabonds still farther augmented by dociers from Congress." The hard times would only "continue to harden if Congress continues to feed able bodied paupers from the government crib. I affirm what no honest man ought to deny, that there is not a healthy man or woman of sound mind in Mississippi under sixty years of age, white or black, who cannot make an honest living by honest labor." Brown was apprehensive that there would be "an appalling addition to this already fearful amount" of idleness among both whites and blacks "if Congress inaugurates the policy of feeding the vagrants at the public expense." The people of Mississippi must be left under the wholesome conviction that Congress has not become a "universal almoner, and above all that it has no intention of encouraging idleness by helping those who are able to help themselves. A false step in this direction will give the finishing stroke to an already mangled system of labor, and another year Congress will have a million of sure enough paupers on its hands." Brown closed this statesmanlike letter by "beging [sic] pardon for obtruding these unsolicited, but well meant suggestions upon your attention."

The evident sincerity and deep conviction of this letter make it quite clear that Brown has outgrown and has risen above the demagogic tendencies of his active political career. He had been chastened by the hot fires of adversity and was willing that all should know that he would not yield to the easy temptation to cater to the poor white groups who had consistently supported him in political offices for a generation, or to the freedmen whose political interests he supported, by favoring a dole for those who could secure employment.

During 1867 and 1868 the reconstruction policies of Congress were forced upon Mississippi by the military authorities under Generals E. O. C. Ord, Irwin McDowell, and Alvan C. Gillem. General Ord often overruled the civil authorities by removals from office and by holding trials of cases in military commissions when the civil courts were open. He brought into existence the 'Black and Tan' Convention, which, "viewed from the standpoint of both its personnel and its policy, . . . deserves to be ranked as the most remarkable political assemblage ever convened in Mississippi." [15] This convention was composed of 100 delegates, apportioned so as to ensure a large majority for the Republicans. There were seventeen Negro members and only nineteen native whites known as conservatives. The convention met on January 7, 1868, with B. B. Eggleston, a carpetbagger from New York, as president, and Thad. P. Sears, a former federal soldier, as secretary. This convention met for 115 days at a cost of $250,000 with the major purpose of framing a new State constitution.

The radical constitution contained severe proscriptive provisions against former Confederates which debarred them from officeholding

---

[15] Garner, pp. 186–187. The vote on holding the convention was 69,739 to 6,277, but the favorable vote was less than half the 139,690 registered voters. (William Archibald Dunning, *Essays on the Civil War and Reconstruction*, p. 188.)

and from voting. As a result, it was rejected by the people on June 22 by a vote of 63,860 to 56,231, and Humphreys was reelected as governor over B. B. Eggleston by over 8,000 votes. Humphreys was not allowed to remain in office, for General McDowell had placed the incompetent Adelbert Ames in the governor's chair as provisional governor even before the result of the elections was known.[16]

The excesses of the radical Republicans and the sullen hatred of most of the native white population led many Republicans to see that reconstruction would prove to be a failure unless a change to a more liberal and tolerant policy were made. As a result, a conservative faction arose within the Republican ranks. Brown and Barksdale urged the Democrats not to antagonize the radical Republicans by bringing forth their own candidates for office, but to join forces with these conservative Republicans. In order to win their favor, Brown reiterated his belief that Congress had the right to dictate terms and stated that he felt that the whites should be willing to make the best of it. He was ready to "meet Congress on its own platform and shake hands." [17]

The first important action of this coalition was to prevent the imposition of the rejected constitution on the State by the radical Republicans. When a committee of sixteen radicals was sent to Congress to urge that the returns of seven counties be rejected, Brown and Judge Simrall led a group, backed by moderate Republicans, which went to Washington to counteract this move. Their mission was successful, for Grant, after two interviews, accepted the suggestions of Brown and Simrall "that the constitution should be submitted anew, with the privilege of a separate vote on the proscriptive features. This action was induced by assurances that the people would accept the constitution without difficulty if such a course should be adopted. Accordingly, Congress so enacted," and provided that a full State ticket should be voted on.

While in Washington, Brown and his associates received much aid and encouragement from Judge Louis Dent, brother-in-law of Grant,

[16] Garner, pp. 182–221. Claude G. Bowers, *The Tragic Era: The Revolution after Lincoln*, pp. 206, 215–216; Mayes, *Life of Lucius Q. C. Lamar*, p. 163. Dunning, p. 206.

[17] Garner, p. 179, citing Brown in *Clarion* of Jan. 6, 1869, and in *New York Tribune* of Feb. 11, 1869. The Congressional conditions became more severe when the law of February 6, 1869 provided that all officeholders should be removed who refused to take the iron-clad oath, and that military commanders should appoint their successors. (Dunning, p. 229.)

an adopted Mississippian and a Republican, who had arranged the second interview with Grant. They "remembered his labors in their behalf gratefully, and when the political forces began to gather Senator Brown, in an open letter, suggested Judge Dent as a man available to defeat the radicals." [18] Barksdale invited the appointment of "intelligent men of the African race . . . to the Convention, where they can make known the views and wishes of their people and participate in the framing of the platform and the election of the candidates." One hundred of the 320 delegates were Negroes.

The Democrats in this convention, hoping to elect a conservative Republican as Virginia had done, joined forces with conservative Republicans on September 8, 1869, in unanimously nominating Judge Louis Dent, as Brown had urged. The conciliatory tendencies of this convention were further illustrated by the nomination of Thomas Sinclair, a Negro, for Secretary of State and by the fact that only two of the nominees for State offices had been white citizens of Mississippi before the war.

The platform, in accepting the reconstruction acts and a policy of toleration, liberality, and forbearance and in opposing any discrimination against the Negroes, was also in accord with policies which Brown had urged in April in a letter to the Jackson *Clarion* and which had been endorsed by mass meetings throughout the State. This letter proposed the acceptance of the Fifteenth Amendment, sought to avoid partisan opposition to the Grant administration, to grant civil and political rights to the freedmen, and to show "hostility to men who had come to the state for the purpose of making mischief, and hearty good will to all who came in good faith to share the fortunes of the Southern people."

At the end of September the radical Republicans nominated James L. Alcorn for governor. Alcorn, a large property-holder and an able man, won the election by 76,186 to 38,097 for Dent, largely because the Dent candidacy was repudiated by President Grant and because some 20,000 white voters remained at home rather than vote for the radical Republicans or for the conservative Republicans when a Negro was on the ticket.[19] Furthermore, fully 15,000 white citizens were still

[18] Mayes, pp. 163–164. Garner, pp. 224–225.

[19] Two correspondents of J. F. H. Claiborne during the campaign expressed their distrust of the conservative movement, which both referred to as organized by "Brown, Barksdale & Co." They had no confidence in "secession Democrats, who are willing to *barter* the right of self-government for office." They predicted that Dent, "a dead *duck*," would be badly beaten because he brought no influence

disfranchised. Alcorn won all the twenty-eight counties which had a colored majority and fifteen with a white majority. Although it is claimed that nearly every prominent man in the State favored Dent, the conservative movement was overwhelmed, and Mississippi entered upon the darkest and most tragic years in her history. The only compensation for the conservatives consisted in the defeat of the proscriptive sections of the constitution by large majorities while the constitution was ratified almost unanimously.[20]

During the next four years Brown retired into obscurity, for the conservatives were drowned in the flood of extravagance and corruption which accompanied the radical Republican domination under Governors James L. Alcorn and R. C. Powers.

There is very little information about Brown during this dark period. We are glad to learn that his younger son, Joseph Albert Brown, was "the first honor man of the fourteen graduates of the law class" of the University of Mississippi and the valedictorian at commencement on June 27, 1870. In his address, he paid a tribute to Chancellor L. Q. C. Lamar, who resigned at that time.[21]

During these years Lamar took the same position as Albert Gallatin Brown. Lamar abstained from politics because he believed that a former secessionist could only stir up suspicion and distrust by advocating compromise measures. He wrote in 1870, "I have thought, and still think, that all such a one can do, or should do, is not to uphold or approve, but quietly to acquiesce in, the result of the wager of battle." [22] Like Brown, Lamar "had descended into the shades a sectionalist, he emerged a nationalist." And, again like Brown and Barksdale, Lamar believed that "we of the South must settle the question of negro suffrage in a spirit of true regard to the rights, demands, and interests of the negro race; that such an adjustment, fair and honorable, we would have to make even if it were not forced upon us by Federal intervention." [23]

We catch another glimpse of Brown during these years when he

---

from Grant and had none in the State. "We therefore don't want him." (J. F. H. Claiborne MSS., Vol. III, Library of Congress, letter C. B. Vent and L. C. Nowell to Claiborne, July 29, Aug. 5, 1869.)

[20] W. H. Hardy, "Recollections of Reconstruction in East and Southeast Mississippi," *Publications of the Mississippi Historical Society*, VIII, pp. 137–148. Garner, pp. 179, 224, 239, citing Brown's letter to *Clarion* of April 22, 1869. Bowers, pp. 278–279, 367–368.

[21] Mayes, p. 127, quoting from *Clarion*.

[22] *Ibid.*, pp. 121, 157–158.

[23] *Ibid.*, pp. 168, 180, quoting letter Lamar to T. J. Wharton, Dec. 25, 1873.

advocated the system of public school education for both races which was the most constructive achievement of the radical Republican regime in Mississippi. We have seen how valiantly, but unsuccessfully, Brown had fought for an effective common school system for white children when he was governor. Now he addressed an audience of Negroes in Copiah County and "declared emphatically in favor of educating the freedmen." [24]

But the darkest days of Reconstruction in Mississippi did not come until 1874 and 1875, when Adelbert Ames, elected overwhelmingly over Alcorn in 1873, was governor. The long-dreaded domination of the Negroes had come. As an illustration of this control in the State government, A. K. Davis, the lieutenant-governor, James Hill, the secretary of state, and T. W. Cordoza, the superintendent of public instruction, were all Negroes, the latter then under indictment for larceny in Brooklyn.[25] State taxes had never been so high, "having increased from one mill on the dollar in 1869 to fourteen in 1874," while State expenditures had increased from $463,219.71 to $1,319,-281.60.[26]

In Brown's county of Hinds, under Republican control, the county tax was 11.4 mills, making a total State and county tax of 25.4 mills. This taxation was so crushing that there were 4,972 on the delinquent tax list, although there were fewer than 6,000 voters.[27] By the summer of 1874 the white citizens of the county felt able to raise their heads against their oppressors. A taxpayers' league was formed at Raymond. Since the feeling of unrest and the determination to rebel against the Republican rule grew throughout the county, it was not difficult to organize clubs at every voting precinct. These citizens were in too desperate a plight to cater to the Republicans by forming a conservative Republican organization as they had done in 1868 and 1869. They now urged every white Democrat to join one of these clubs and to get a Negro to join. Brown led the Terry club. Although Brown was convinced that the Democrats should now act as Democrats, he strongly opposed the formation of parties on the basis of color.[28] He succeeded

[24] Garner, p. 357. Elise Timberlake, "Did the Reconstruction Regime Give Mississippi Her Public Schools?" *Publications of the Mississippi Historical Society*, XII, 87.

[25] Bowers, pp. 413–414. Garner, pp. 292–294.

[26] Garner, pp. 296, 320, cited from reports of State auditors.

[27] *Ibid.*, pp. 313–314.

[28] W. Calvin Wells, "Reconstruction in Hinds County" in *Publications of the Mississippi Historical Society*, IX, 92–94.

in causing the abandonment of a proposed "Color Line" association at Terry [29] and published his views in two communications in the *Clarion*,[30] which fully maintained the high level of his course since the end of the war, which, as Mayes said, was "marked by great conservatism, wisdom, and patriotism." [31]

The *Clarion* had already denounced the formation of a "White Man's Party" because it would go counter to its consistent policy that "the best way to settle sectional troubles was to comply with the terms of the government (which though harsh were more moderate than we had promised ourselves, if we failed to maintain our independence) and to recognize the Democratic principle that all men of whatever race, clime, or nationality, should be made equal before the law." [32]

Brown likewise had come to "a very pointed and conclusive conviction . . . that the idea of 'White Leagues' is all wrong, and must, if carried out, end in the most disastrous consequences to both races. . . . I am opposed to the white-line movement. I see nothing in it but increased mischief, and this notwithstanding the triumph of the white men in Vicksburg" in the municipal elections on August 4. Such an enlightened and statesmanlike viewpoint was most remarkable when we consider that Ames had effectively drawn the color line by supporting the former government of Vicksburg and the present government of Warren County—"as corrupt and incompetent a government as ever afflicted an Anglo-Saxon community," [33] and by constantly asking for the aid of Federal troops which were withheld until after the fatal Vicksburg riots in December.[34]

In spite of the most galling provocation and the existence of heated passions ever on the point of leading to serious riots, Brown was able to keep his temper and to strive for a rational solution of the issues. "There is but one thing for us to expect in communities where the negroes are largely in the ascendant if this movement becomes general among the whites," continued Brown, "and that is negro domination in its most galling and revolting form. . . . I am glad that our Vicksburg friends, since they felt constrained to make the issue, succeeded; and shall be rejoiced if they shall use their power so as to convince the negro that his rights are safe in the hands of honest Southern white

[29] *Clarion*, Sept. 3, 1874.
[30] Both communications appeared on Sept. 10, 1874.
[31] Mayes, p. 246.
[32] *Clarion*, Aug. 27, 1874.
[33] Garner, p. 328.
[34] Oberholtzer, III, 211–213. Bowers, pp. 448–452.

men. Give him full justice, and he may no longer lend a willing ear to those who are his worst enemies. . . . However brought about, the negro constitutionally now had equal political and civil rights with the white men. If White Leagues were formed with the purpose of withholding these rights, there would surely be formed Black Leagues in retaliation." Brown then raised this question, "Will, in such a contest, all the whites stand on our side, and all the blacks on the other?" With the scalawags in mind, he answered, "Not a bit of it. We have painful experience that a large number of whites from motives or reasons of their own, will take sides with blacks. What has been done, we have reason to suppose, may be done again. . . . These [sic] sort of combinations point to but one end, and that is a war of races. . . . There is a mutual dependence between the races which once recognized in good faith, must lead to happy results. But ignored, no man, not endowed with supernatural gifts, can pretend to tell the consequences."

Brown next sought to refute the claim of the White Leagues that the whites had constantly held out the hand of fellowship to the blacks. While admitting that "a vast majority of the whites have been sincere in their professions, . . . that there has been at all times a minority not willing to admit the negroes clearly defined and well understood Constitutional Rights, there can be no question." This noisy and mischievous minority have no right to intimidate the majority. Brown ended this letter, so moderate and conciliatory in tone in the midst of the flaming passions inevitable under such a tyranny, by a plea for continued cooperation with the Negro. "Whatever people may say, and however popular assemblages may resolve, I have an abiding confidence that the negro can yet be made to understand that his interests is [sic] identical with the *Southern* white man, and when he comes to understand that, he will think with the white men of the South, act with them, and *vote* with them." [35]

In a card to the *Clarion* which appeared in the same issue as the above letter which explained his general views towards White Leagues, Brown wrote about the local situation at Terry. He attributed the desire to form such associations to "some very youthful and enthusiastic gentlemen," but was convinced that the thinking men—"the men who have drawn their lessons from the bitter experience of the past, do not propose to run into any such folly. . . . And it may be that my young friends in the neighborhood have paused to consider whether it was not better to take the advice of one who lived before they were

[35] *Clarion,* Sept. 10, 1874, letter Brown to J. W. Watson. Mayes, p. 246.

born than to plunge ahead madly and finally bring up in a ditch from which nothing short of Omnipotence can extricate them." [36]

Brown, as an elder statesman, "Who never knew defeat, and has filled all the offices in our republican government, below that of President, which ambition could crave," thus hoped to check the impetuosity of youth by his sage advice. But when he turned to advise young men on the choice of a career, he showed clearly that the heartrending experiences of the war and of reconstruction had left him disillusioned and disheartened. In an illuminating communication entitled "Be a Farmer," he reveals himself. "Looking back over a long, and, I hope not unuseful life, I can say with a clear conscience, my greatest regret is that I ever made a political speech, or held an office. There is a fascination in office which beguiles men, but be assured, my young friends, it is the fascination of a serpent, or to change the figure, it is the ignis fatuus which coaxes you on to inevitable ruin. I speak of that which I do know. . . . After all my success as a public man, now when my head is blossoming for the grave, I feel that it would have been better for me, if I had followed the occupation of my father, and been a farmer." It is far better to be a blacksmith, a carpenter, or an artisan of any sort "than be a jack-legged lawyer, a quack doctor, counter-hopper, or worse still, a wretched seeker after office." But best of all, and most respectable, is the occupation of a farmer. Not dependent on wages, fees, or subscribers, "the honest industrious farmer is morally certain of a fair return for his labor, or at least is assured of sufficient food." Although this picture is far too rosy, it does imply that Brown was finding a satisfactory compensation on his estate for the wreck of his political career. His pessimism about the political future of his section is again evident in his final advice: "Allow me again to 'caution' my young friends against the beguiling influence of office and to advise them most earnestly to stick to mother Earth." [37]

Although Brown advised the youth to avoid a political career, and he expressed the greatest regret that he had ever made a political speech or held office, he could not, for himself, escape from politics during the stirring events of the "Revolution of 1875" in Mississippi. He was a delegate from Hinds County to the State tax-payers convention which met in Jackson on January 4, 1875. He was a member of the committee of resolutions which demanded a reduction of the crushing taxation and the introduction of economy in expenditures,

[36] *Clarion,* Sept. 10, 1874.
[37] *Ibid.,* Aug. 27, 1874.

and he was one of the three representatives from his congressional district on the committee which prepared the address of the convention to the people of the United States.[38]

By unanimous call, Brown was asked to address the convention, and he delivered a lengthy extemporaneous speech.[39] He first made clear his sympathy with the purpose of the convention. "I have felt as keenly as any of you the grinding, withering and blighting influence of enormous taxation. . . . To say that I am in full sympathy with you in this movement is only to say that all who suffer from a like cause must bear a portion of each other's woes." Admitting that it was easy to say that economy, retrenchment, and reform were necessary in every branch of State and county governments, he recognized the difficulty of accomplishing these objects because, "sad to utter it, there is a want of sympathy between the Governor and the Legislature on the one side, and the taxpayers on the other." This unnatural state of affairs would be a fruitful source of mischief as long as it existed. Labor was represented in the legislature, but not capital. As long as this condition resulted, both would languish. Both should be represented in the legislature, "and it should be the first and highest care of the Governor to administer his office [so] as to keep these two great interests in harmony."

Brown contrasted the present deplorable conditions with the time when he was in the State legislature and was governor. In the days of Prentiss, McNutt, and Quitman legislators came "through the cold of winter on mail coaches or horseback and received $4 per day for their services." In 1870 the compensation had been raised to $7 a day and later was fixed at $500 a year.[40] Since the standard of fitness and of qualifications had not been elevated, "I will be excused for saying that, in my humble judgment, a proper excuse for increasing the pay of Legislators does not exist." The moderation of Brown's language is quite evident. After all, the Republicans were still in control, so he asserted that he was "very far from attempting to disparage members of the present legislature," but he did feel the most sensitive legislators would allow him to say "that I like the quid pro quo, and if we pay more money, I want more brains."

[38] Rowland, *Encyclopaedia of Mississippi History,* II, 191. J. S. McNeily, "Climax and Collapse of Reconstruction in Mississippi, 1874-1876," *Publications of the Mississippi Historical Society,* XII, 337-338.

[39] *Clarion,* Jan. 7, 1875.

[40] Garner, p. 325.

Brown reminded his audience that in six days it would be thirty-one years since he stood at the same desk and was inducted into the governorship. He reviewed the course of his two terms, but felt it wise to leave the implied but quite obvious contrast with the present administration to his audience. The bitterness of the canvass for election ceased after the election of 1843 was over. Although there was an indebtedness of $614,000 on account of the use of auditor's warrants, he neither recommended increased taxation nor a refunding of the debt. Instead, he secured a rigid economy, relied on an increase in population and in wealth, insisted on a more exact accountability for tax gatherers and other officers, and more than all else, won the cordial support of taxpayers. "Without this last I could have done nothing and I could easily have lost it by simply repelling the advances of every political opponent."

Brown's indirect but obvious attack upon Governor Ames' personal extravagance was most telling. In 1844 the governor's mansion had just been finished, but very little furniture had been provided. "I shall never forget my first night in that house," Brown said. "My wife slept on a shuck mattress, without sheets, and rested her head on a carpet sack. It was a bitter cold night in January and she used woolen garments as a substitute for blankets." During his two terms no funds were appropriated for furniture. "I did not ask it, and would not [have] allowed it if it had been offered, until the state was out of debt." For the first quarter of his $3,000 salary he got less than half of its face value, while Ames received $6,000 a year and used the executive contingent fund for household expenses.[41]

Although large sums were lost to the State treasury by the failure of banks and by the resulting worthless bank notes in which taxes had been paid, yet the credit of the State began to revive when it was known that the governor, the legislature, and the people all favored redemption. At the end of the second year auditor's warrants were at par, at the end of the third year the treasury was paying coin on demand, and at the end of the fourth year, in 1848, there was $80,000 of gold and silver in the treasury, independent of the trust fund. When the treasurer, in consternation, reported that "the bottom of the Treasury had dropped out," the damage was no worse than the somewhat decayed wooden bottom of a heavy iron safe holding some

----

[41] Garner, p. 318. The inconveniences of Governor and Mrs. Brown in the executive mansion are also stated on page 32.

$200,000, dropping out. "The present Treasurer," Brown pointedly remarked, "is not likely to suffer alarm from that cause."

Brown next referred to his course during the Mexican War in order to criticize the recent calling of a special election which he considered unnecessary. In 1846, although the war caused great excitement and mass meetings in almost every part of the State urged the governor to call a special session of the legislature, Brown declined to do so because, in the emergency, he "preferred relying on the prompt and energetic action of a patriotic people, rather than on the slower process of legislative action," and because "in the then excited state of the public mind, it would not have been conducive to wise and dispassionate counsels, and would have involved an expense, most of it useless, of quite $100,000." After the Mississippi troops had been sent quickly into battle and had won immortal renown, "the people thanked me for keeping cool, when they themselves had been carried away by an all-pervading excitement." Brown again pointed to the present contrast with that time by asking timidly and deferentially the following question, "Without meaning to find fault in this presence, with what has been done recently, I may be pardoned for asking whether you do not think the late call for the legislature could have been avoided without serious detriment to the public interest?"

Brown had ended his thinly veiled criticisms of the corrupt Republican administration by references to his own governorship. In the remainder of his address he presented more clearly than ever before his constructive proposals for the future. He reverted to the disastrous consequences of the antagonism between capital, represented by the property-holding white Democrats, and labor, represented in the main by the Negro Republicans backed by their scalawag allies. "We might as well expect a man to perform efficient labor with one side paralyzed as to expect prosperity in a State where one half of the people live in perpetual discord with the other. There must be harmony or the whole body will perish sooner or later." Instead of seeking a way out by intimidating the Negroes by White Leagues, Brown demanded a thoroughgoing change of attitude towards the Negroes. "Was not most of our legislation after the war founded in error? The fundamental error in my poor judgment, was our failure or refusal to recognize the great fact that we had lost the fight and that there was nothing left for us to do but accept such terms as the conqueror might dictate. Our refusal has heaped upon us a multitude of woes and we have been forced to it practically at last." Everywhere in the South the outraged whites "lay down their arms and retire on the first appearance of Federal soldiers." However deplorable such conditions may be, "candor compels me to add, you have no power to change them."

Brown elaborated upon the new attitude he felt should be taken towards the Negroes. The right of the Negroes to vote and to hold office should not only be admitted in theory, but should be faithfully carried out in practice. "I do not at all hesitate to say that the negro has the same right to restrict or call in question, by intimidation or other unlawful means, the right of white men, that the white man has to restrict or call in question by the same agencies, the rights of black men." He denounced attempts to deceive the Negro. "If we seek the confidence of the negro we must deserve it. . . . We must not talk with two tongues, one dipped in oil and honey for the negro, and another in gall and wormwood when we are talking about him. You would never get the confidence of a white man in that way, and it is folly to try it on the negro." The only way to secure his confidence, Brown was convinced, was to treat him "in cold earnest without hesitation or mental reservation" as an equal in politics and to give him the same measure of justice in business dealings as to fellow whites. "Do not presume on his ignorance. Forget that his skin is black in your political and business dealings with him, and though it be in fact as dark as the raven's wing, treat him with as much justice as though it were as white as snow." Brown was convinced that the Negro would respond to this fair treatment and would learn at once "that his interest and your interest are identical. This being done, he will not only vote with you, but for you."

Brown assumed that the Negroes, if treated fairly, would follow white leadership rather than adopt independent policies of their own. He regarded it a great error to suppose that everything had been done which could be done to induce our colored friends to think and act right. Rather, the beam of Negro repression had to be removed from the eyes of white men before motes should be searched in the eyes of Negroes. Even if the Negroes should remain suspicious and should still appear to be a "stiff necked, rebellious people" after years of friendly effort on the part of the whites, "does all this furnish a sufficient reason," Brown asked, "for giving up the struggle and handing them all over, and with them the State, to hopeless ruin?" Brown felt so keenly the importance of the political education of the Negro that he compared it to the missionary enterprise. If the whites gave up the struggle, they would be as derelict in duty as a missionary in China who gave up his work in disgust because of the obstinacy of the natives. Brown hastened to say that he did not mean to compare the Negroes to the heathen, but did assert that the Negroes, when emancipated, "were almost as ignorant in politics as a Chinaman is of Christianity." It was not at all surprising that they were as slow in comprehending political problems as the heathen in understanding Christianity. "The wonder rather is, that they should have learned so much when we take into account that every appliance has been used to mystify their minds and excite their prejudices." Not only the radical Republicans were guilty of deluding the colored man; the radical Democrats were also culpable of abusing him. The two radical groups "abuse one another until they get tired and then they unite in abusing Conservatives."

Brown pointed out that, as a conservative, he had been roundly denounced ever since an address at Terry in 1867. After each utterance since then he had been severely criticized, "and I suppose I shall be abused for the speech I am now making. Well, be it so, my equanimity now, as in the past, remains undisturbed." He was morally certain that the only way to reestablish "honesty, fidelity, economy, and that general and glorious prosperity which prevailed everywhere in the good old days of which we were speaking" was for conservatives of both races and of all parties to unite for a common purpose to defeat the extremists on both sides.

Brown had expounded his political faith at length and turned to refute the natural suspicion that he was laying the foundation for a return to office by catering to the Negro vote. Brown spoke categorically and unambiguously. "Office has been the ruin of me. I want no more, and I will have no more of it; . . . there is not an office in the gift of the people that I would accept." The crowning ambition of his life was to contribute something before he died to see all classes in his state "living peacefully together, under a government of their own choice, pursuing their several avocations without molestation, and none to make them afraid. . . . This being done, I can draw my cloak around me, and lie down in death with the consoling hope that my life has not been in vain." [42]

It is unfortunate that we lack comment on this speech and can not estimate the effect which it produced. Brown's hope that both conservative Republicans and Democrats would unite as they had done in 1868 and in 1869 was not fulfilled, and Brown allied himself

[42] *Clarion,* Jan. 21, 1875.

with the Democrats who now had high hopes of driving out the corrupt Republican machine. Brown's enlightened and liberal attitude is well illustrated by his enthusiasm for L. Q. C. Lamar after his great and statesmanlike plea for conciliation in his eulogy of Sumner. On May 26 Brown sent a communication to the *Clarion* in praise of Lamar, and explained his purpose to Barksdale, the editor: "The inclosed brief article contains my real sentiments. I feel more inclined to express them, inasmuch as I did not at first fully approve of Lamar's speech over the dead Sumner. But, having witnessed its good effects, I recant. It is now, I think, on every account our policy to make him our *recognized* leader. We thereby, amongst many other advantages, get the benefit of his conservative statements so often and so boldly expressed. By making him our leader, we make these expressions our own, and thus disarm our Northern slanderers."

The article is a tribute to Lamar, but it also does honor to the broad vision to which Brown had attained when he wrote: "Nothing could have quickened the hearts of all true friends of constitutional liberty to a higher degree than the announcement that this peerless orator and incorruptible statesman intended to take the field in defense of genuine reform, in accordance with the most approved principles of conservatism. . . . To him more than to any living man are we indebted for that approach to harmony and good will between the late conflicting sections of this great Union, which all good citizens hail with such sincere delight. . . . The fraternal feeling thus rekindled has been growing in fervor and intensity ever since. . . . Who need be ashamed to follow such a leader, I care not what he may call himself? . . . In the greatness of his soul, standing amid the ruins of his State, he has said: 'My countrymen! let us know one another, and we will love one another.' . . . The friends of equality, genuine equality, and of constitutional liberty everywhere, and of all races, colors, and nationalities, will know whose banner they ought to follow." [43]

Lamar was one of the leaders in the campaign of 1875, which was

[43] Mayes, p. 248, quoting Brown's communication to the *Clarion*, May 26, 1875. Cate, *Lucius Q. C. Lamar*, p. 202. Brown had served Lamar in March, 1858, when he wrote a very flattering endorsement of Lamar for the Chair of Mental and Moral Philosophy at the University of Mississippi. Twenty years later in the Senate, on January 24, 1878, Lamar rhetorically described Brown on the eve of the war: "There was Albert G. Brown, from my own State, who never had an aspiration not in sympathy with the wants and feelings of his own people; who yet was never overawed by their prejudices or swerved from his convictions by their passions."—Mayes, pp. 76, 90, 717.

"the most exciting in the history of the state." [44] He was renominated by acclamation for congressman from the first district on July 22, and the Republicans did not nominate any one to oppose him.[45] He was the leading orator at the State Democratic Convention which met on August 3.[46]

Brown also took an active part in the campaign. Although General E. C. Walthall suggested to J. Z. George, the State chairman, that Brown be sent to Washington with two others to refute the charges of the Republicans,[47] Brown confined his activities to Hinds County. On August 18 a mass meeting of the Democratic precinct clubs of the county was held at Raymond. The Terry club members came in fancy shirts trimmed in red, led by Brown. The parade was described as "the greatest demonstration of the kind ever seen before or since at Raymond." Great enthusiasm prevailed and "quiet could scarcely be restored until ex-Gov. Albert Gallatin Brown, with his red shirt on, was introduced as chairman of the meeting." Brown is reported to have given "an enthusiastic address." [48]

With Brown taking such an active interest in politics, it was inevitable that he should be urged to seek office. The month before the Raymond meeting, the *Clarion,* the official Democratic organ, suggested him for congressman from his old sixth district, "where the people know him and love him, as a people never loved man before," and predicted grandiloquently that the people would "rally to his standard with a wild whoop and a loud hurrah which will carry the notes of victory on every passing breeze." [49] Brown, however, gave no encouragement to this suggestion and it was dropped. But after the Democrats had won the "Revolution of 1875" by securing a majority of over 30,000 votes in the November election, Brown was again pressed to run for office—this time for the Senate. He was depicted as a leader in the past campaign who gave tone and direction to the platform which advocated the conciliatory policy Brown had constantly urged. Brown, in staking his judgment, his reputation, and

[44] Garner, p. 372.

[45] Mayes, p. 248.

[46] Garner, p. 372.

[47] *Boutwell Report, Mississippi Election of 1875*, I, 383, telegram E. C. Walthall to J. Z. George, Grenada, Miss., Sept. 18, 1875, testimony of John A. Galbreath. Fleming, *Documentary History of Reconstruction*, II, 394–404, reproduces pertinent documents of "The Mississippi Revolution."

[48] W. Calvin Wells, "Reconstruction and its Destruction in Hinds County," *Publications of the Mississippi Historical Society*, IX, 92–94.

[49] *Clarion*, July 21, 1875.

his statesmanship upon the principle of "equal rights to all before the law," had been ten years in advance of his party. Now that his policies had been victorious, the politicians were asked not to forget "that it was the statesmanship and foresight of Albert Gallatin Brôwn who first conceived and advocated this line of policy upon which we advanced to victory." The *Clarion* seconded these suggestions. It felt that a chivalrous and ardent love for the lost cause had induced the people to discard Brown's views, but now they have fully realized their folly and have "at last, fully, emphatically, and in thunder tones endorsed his position." It contended that the spark which kindled the political camp-fires which burned in every valley and on every hill top during the recent canvass "was first struck in a grove near Terry, in 1867," that there was the first impetus which finally swept the radicals from power, "where was heard the voice of Albert Gallatin Brown urging the people to accept and abide by the Reconstruction measures." The great debt to Brown could not even be cancelled by sending him to the Senate, but now that his views had been adopted and endorsed, the *Clarion* urged the people to "acknowledge the great wrong we did him in the past and partially atone for it by placing him where his voice will again be heard in defence of our rights." [50]

When the *Clarion* continued to urge Brown to be a candidate for the Senate and published the resolutions of the Democratic-Conservative party of Terry to the same effect, Brown again reiterated the stand he took at the tax-payers' convention the year before. "I wish then to say explicitly, that I am not, have not been, and do not intend to be, a candidate for the Senate or for anything else." He assured his friends that he had been entirely sincere in his oft-repeated declarations "that my mind has been long since made up, never again to compete for any office." He was most grateful because he had never been denied any office for which he had run, he was now willing to serve in other ways, but he would ask for no office. [51]

And yet, in spite of the self-denying tone of Brown's refusal to run for any office, one suspects that he was shrewd enough to know that the policy of political equality of whites and blacks would be repudiated as soon as the whites had effectively secured the upper hand again and that he would be rejected if he ran for office. Two weeks after Brown refused to run, the extreme Radical-Republican Senator Morton read to the Senate a statement from the *Newton (Miss.)*

[50] *Clarion,* Nov. 24, Dec. 22, 1875.
[51] *Ibid.,* Jan. 5, 1876.

Democrat which represented the attitude of most of the white population of Mississippi towards the Negroes: "Mr. Potter and Ex-
Governor Brown, of Hinds, think the negro can be reasoned into
democracy, and they have been thinking so ever since the war; but
for our part we would as soon reason with a shoal of crocodiles or
a drove of Kentucky mules. And so might they, for all the convictions
they have produced in the counties of Hinds and Copiah." [52] The fact
is, Brown could not have been an active force in practical politics even
if he had desired to be. When the *Boutwell Report on the Mississippi
Election of 1875* was published in two large volumes of over 2,000
pages, it was found that none of the hundreds of telegrams which
Chairman George either sent or received during the course of the
campaign was sent to or received from Brown and that Brown was
not called upon to testify before the committee. [53]

Brown's enthusiastic advice to young men to be farmers undoubtedly
meant, as we have intimated before, that he himself was finding the
management of his estate at Chicama near Terry a compensation and
a recompense for the loss of his political career. Unfortunately there
are no satisfactory records of his private and family life which so
largely absorbed his interest. [54] Particularly fine was the sympathetic
friendship which Mr. and Mrs. Brown showed during the fatal illness of their close personal friend, Mr. John W. Burnett, and to the
family after his death. Mrs. Brown sent him strawberry wine and Mr.
Brown showed his anxiety for his health and the day after his death,
wrote a touching note to Mrs. Burnett: "It may seem strange to you
that I did not call this morning. I went to town for that purpose. Then
my heart failed me. The truth is, I cannot bear to be in the midst of
distress without the slightest chance to alleviate. That is all!" [55] A
month later Brown sent a long tribute to the memory of Mr. Burnett
to his three small children. This document of tender thoughtfulness

[52] *Boutwell Report, Mississippi Election of 1875*, II, Part IX, p. 163, documentary evidence, quoted from Senator Morton's speech of Jan. 19, 1876.

[53] *Ibid.*, passim.

[54] Miss Ruth Burnett of Terry has rescued this phase of his life from complete
oblivion by kindly and graciously providing the treasured correspondence of Mr.
and Mrs. Brown with the Burnett family. From one of the few available letters it
is clear that Brown experimented with domestic tea which he was very eager for
Mrs. Burnett to try, "and tell me *candidly* what you think of it. If it will do, I see
no reason why every lady in the country may not make her own *tea* while she is
cultivating a shrub that is equal in beauty to the *Capi-Japanium*." (Ruth Burnett
MSS., letter Brown to Mrs. Burnett, June 17, 1875.)

[55] *Ibid.*, letters Mrs. Brown to Mrs. Burnett, Jan. 7, 1876; Brown to Mrs.
Burnett, Jan. 7, 1876; Brown to Mrs. Burnett, Dec. 15 [*sic*, obviously Jan. 15], 1876.

to "My dear little Friends" shows a side of the character of Brown of which we have all too little evidence. Realizing that these children were too young to understand fully the loss they had sustained, he knew that they would treasure his tribute in later years. Brown traced Mr. Burnett's honorable ancestry on both his father's and mother's sides and explained, "I state these facts my dear little friends so that in after years you may be assured when reading these lines (if you ever should) that you have no occasion to be ashamed of your liniage [*sic*] on either side. Act well your parts then. All the honor his." Mr. Burnett had been well-to-do before the war, and Brown was happy to remind his children that John C. Breckinridge, a schoolmate of Burnett's, appreciated his fine qualities.[56]

We catch another glimpse of Brown's affectionate nature in a letter to his old personal and political friend, J. F. H. Claiborne, the historian of Mississippi. Brown desired his candid opinion on the subject-matter and the style of the speech of his second and now only living son, Joseph A. Brown on "The Material Prosperity of Our State." "I would not ask this," Brown explained, "but my dear friend, I do not know how far a father may trust his judgment as regards the productions of an only son." Brown also showed his solicitous love for his son by warning Claiborne in a postscript not to judge too harshly as his son was only twenty-six years old, and has had to compete with the powerful bar of Jackson. "He has therefore had little opportunity to brush up any literary accomplishments which he may have acquired at school." [57]

Although Brown continued to practise law in Jackson,[58] his chief role was that of the retired statesman and philosopher, giving helpful advice and retaining a large moral influence. When Thomas S. Gathright, the liberal State superintendent of schools, resigned to become the president of a college, he was very glad to receive the congratulations and the endorsement of Brown. Brown, one of the founders of the public school system of the State when he was governor, took this occasion to reaffirm his confidence in public education. He regretted the loss of Gathright because he had been looking forward hopefully "to that day when, under your guidance, our promise to give the people cheaper and better schools would develop into realized fact."

[56] Ruth Burnett MSS., letter Brown to Norris, Edna, and Golda Burnett, Feb. 24, 1876.

[57] MS. J. F. H. Claiborne Collection, Vol. A, No. 108, letter Brown to Claiborne, July —, 1876.

[58] *Jackson Times*, Feb. 2, 1877.

He regretted the frequent changes which retarded the growth of confidence and support of the public schools, "which must become the chief glory of the State when it once enters deeply into the public heart." Since those who attended free schools were usually the children of poor farmers, they could not be spared from the cotton fields for five consecutive months. He therefore suggested a winter session of three months and a two months' session during the slack summer season so that all could get a minimum of five months.[59]

Brown sought to refute the claim of *The Nation* that Southern landowners intimidated colored voters. While admitting that *The Nation* was an impartial and independent magazine, edited with marked ability, he believed that "it sees Southern society through a Northern lens." A few years before, under Radical Republican rule, Brown would certainly have admitted the charge of correspondents of *The Nation,* but he would not admit it in October, 1876, when the Democrats again controlled Mississippi and the presidential election was at hand. Brown claimed that Northern capitalists did intimidate their employees by the threat of discharge, but he insisted that Southern landowners, although they would be willing to coerce their Negro laborers, did not dare to do so because the demand for labor so far exceeded the supply that there were "almost united efforts to secure immigration" of laborers into the State. Therefore, Brown argued, landowners would not discharge laborers "for light and frivolous causes." The weakness in this argument lies in the very obvious fact that the control or prevention of the Negro vote was no light or frivolous cause, but a major concern of the white population in the years after 1875.[60] Now that the Democrats controlled the State again, Brown became more definitely a partisan and debated with Judge Stafford at a Republican political meeting at Terry. When Brown interrogated Stafford and Alcorn an acrimonious and heated discussion ensued which extended to the audience. Brown later regretted that bad blood had been stirred up.[61]

In spite of Brown's repeated statements, he was still urged to seek office. The leading Democratic paper in Jackson still regretted that he was permitted to remain in private life,[62] and in May, 1877, when

[59] *Clarion,* Aug. 2, 1876.
[60] *Ibid.,* Oct. 11, 1876.
[61] *Jackson Times,* Oct. 26, 1876. This paper, which advertised itself as "The Only Republican Daily Paper in Mississippi," had made no reference to Brown in any previous issue of 1876.
[62] *Clarion,* Aug. 2, 1876.

Brown wrote a letter to the *Brookhaven Comet,* declining to be a candidate for governor, the *Jackson Times,* the only daily Republican paper in the State, also expressed its regret.[63] Two months later, on the same day that the *Jackson Times* announced the disbanding of the Republican party organization in Mississippi, a leading editorial on "The Next Governor" named Brown as the best man to replace selfish politicians in office, to allay political excitement, and to satisfy "the longing of the popular heart for *peace.* . . . It would be a pleasant thing to see the venerable statesman of Mississippi, as Governor of the State, reposing in his old age, beneath the shades of the trees planted by himself in the public ground, around the Capitol and Executive Mansion while holding the office of Governor some forth [*sic*] years ago." The *Jackson Times* felt that the very fact that Brown was not and would not be a candidate was a reason why he should be elected. "It ought to be enough for the people to know that he will not refuse to serve them if it shall be their pleasure to elect him." [64]

This trial balloon was followed the next day by an invitation to those who favored Brown to "promptly and boldly express their feelings on the subject" and by the publication of two letters already expressing approval. "A Life-Long Democrat" from Hinds County had met with a unanimous response among his neighbors and "A Colored Voter" of Jackson, recognizing that it was best for the Negroes to abandon the Republican party in the State, believed that the Negroes would vote for Brown "with great unanimity if permitted to exercise the elective franchise without molestation." Since Brown was "generally esteemed as the ablest Democratic Statesman in the State," this writer felt it would be most appropriate for the men of both races and of both parties to unite on Brown for governor.[65]

The *Jackson Times* continued to stress in its editorials and correspondence the universal appeal to all classes which it believed Brown would make. It claimed that party affinities never warped his judgment because he was not geographically-minded in politics, that he should not be put forward as either a Democrat or as a Republican, but as a man of the people who should be chosen because of his moral worth and administrative ability. Assurance was given that

[63] *Jackson Times,* May 21, 1877.
[64] *Ibid.,* July 10, 1877.
[65] *Ibid.,* July 11, 1877.

his old county of Copiah "will vote for him overwhelmingly against any Bourbon who can be named" and that "the piney woods will blaze for Albert Gallatin Brown." A correspondent from the eastern part of the State particularly praised his ability as governor in raising the credit of the State from "worse than nothing" to a stable basis. He claimed that Brown was popular with all classes—"Democrats, Republicans, Carpet-baggers, Scallawags and niggers. . . . All my Democratic friends here will vote for him, and the Republicans in this neighborhood would rather have him than one of their own men." [66]

The picture of Brown which the *Jackson Times* was presenting was far too favorable. Indeed, the very fact that it was this erstwhile Republican paper which sponsored Brown would have assured his defeat. The suspicion was immediately aroused that the *Times* favored Brown as an independent candidate because he was considered "a strong man to run against the regular Democratic nominee," and this suspicion could not be allayed by stating that Brown was not a candidate and that there was no sense in having a party contest when there was only one party in the State. The *Jackson Times* hit back at the Democratic press which questioned its motive in bringing Brown forward and feigned to consider it a hopeful sign "that some of the Democratic whippers-in are very wroth at the mention of the ex-Governor's name. The *Vicksburg Herald* for instance, plays the blackguard, and the *Brookhaven Comet* plays the ———." These two papers accurately sized up the situation: the latter when it remarked caustically, "We don't know what Governor Brown has done to the *Times* to make that paper seek to damn him before the people of Mississippi"; the former when it asserted that Brown would never consent "to be used as an instrument to revive the dead Republican party." [67]

The effect of this advocacy of Brown by the *Jackson Times* is best illustrated by the attitude of the Jackson *Clarion,* which for years had pressed Brown to run for office. It recognized that it would be impossible for Brown, "the noblest Roman of them all," after rejecting all the invitations of his political friends to seek office, to allow his name to be used "to be the resurrection and the life of a broken down faction, which in imitation of the leper in India, contaminated beyond the hope of prolonging his miserable existence, has consigned

---

[66] *Ibid.,* July 12, 13, 14, 20, 1877.
[67] *Ibid.,* July 13, 16, 18, 1877, quoting *Memphis Avalanche, Vicksburg Herald,* and *Brookhaven Comet.*

itself to the grave to hide its loathsomeness from public view." Since Brown now was as sincerely devoted to the State and to all its people, white and black, as he was eight or four years ago when the Republicans elected governors, the *Clarion* wanted to know why the Republican managers did not support Brown then. They favored him now, the *Clarion* charged, because "they are in the mud now, and only want Hercules to assist in rolling them out." [68]

The *Jackson Times* had assuredly killed any chances Brown might have had with the Democrats. At the Democratic convention which met at Jackson on August 1 there were ten ballots cast for four candidates, but not a vote had been cast for Brown.[69] The *Jackson Times* immediately appeared in its true colors as a partisan journal by trying to draft Brown as an independent candidate and by its assertion that "the Republican party sleeps, it is not dead, and those who think it is deceive themselves." It claimed that a large majority of the people wished him nominated, that he could win 90,000 votes outside of his own party, and that Brown was "the most sagacious Southern statesman living." [70]

For a few days the *Jackson Times* continued to try to lure Brown out of his political seclusion. It claimed that he was ignored by wire-pullers who managed the Democratic convention because he was not a self-seeking politician. It published letters urging Brown, "that grand old statesman, the father of Mississippi Democracy," to run as an independent, and assurance was given "from a personal friend" that Brown, although not a formal candidate, would not refuse a nomination after it was given.[71]

But all this editorial activity was of no avail. On August 12 Brown wrote a letter to put a stop to the numerous inquiries which had been made to him personally. Again he declared, "I am not an Independent or any sort of candidate for Governor, or [for] anything else." The remainder of his letter helps us to understand why the *Jackson Times* had hoped to use him for the purpose of creating an effective opposition to the dominant Democrats, for Brown showed clearly that he was out of harmony with the party when he expressed his disapproval of the radical course which the party had pursued during the year and a half since it had returned to power. "Its acts

[68] *Clarion,* July 18, 1877. *Jackson Times,* July 19, quoting *Clarion.*
[69] *Jackson Times,* Aug. 2, 1877.
[70] *Ibid.,* Aug. 4, 1877.
[71] *Ibid.,* Aug. 8, 10, 11, 1877.

of omission and commission do not afford assurance to my mind that we are to reap those rich rewards that were so lavishly promised us in 1875, and again in 1876." In a spirit of disillusionment he recalled his constant warnings to the party ever since 1867—warnings which were not heeded and only led to denunciation of himself. "I feel a moral conviction," he said, "that the Democratic party is hurrying on to its own overthrow" in the near future. "If I pointed to where the danger lies," he continued bitterly, "I should be again covered with obloquy, and again at the end of another eight or ten years, if I should live so long, hear people lament the folly of not having taken my advice in time and in the next [sic] award the credit of its paternity to other people. . . . About all that is left me is to do my own thinking and my own voting. . . . I am just as confident that I am right now, as I now am that I was right in 1867. I decline giving the reasons for the faith that is in me." [72]

In this letter Brown appears in a very unfavorable light. It is the letter of a disappointed and disillusioned old man. Brown may have been sincere in his disinclination to run for any office, but he was undoubtedly jealous of the political influence which he had lost and embittered by his thwarted ambition for power.

This letter called forth widespread comment. The *Jackson Times* asserted that it had scarcely hoped the conservative element could free itself now, but regretted that Brown refused to give the reasons for his disappointment with the conduct of the Democratic party.[73] A few of the Democratic papers received Brown's letter calmly. The Jackson *Clarion,* although dissenting entirely from Brown's views, published Brown's letter "with due respect for his experience and sincere convictions frankly expressed." [74] The editor of the *Columbus Democrat,* to whom the letter was addressed, declared that "the fact is, Mr. Brown's true place has been in the Republican party

[72] *Ibid.,* Aug. 21, 1877, quoting Brown's letter to Jas. A. Stevens, editor of *Columbus Independent.* The *St. Louis Journal* suggested that Brown felt acutely the stigma of the intolerant resolution passed at the Democratic State Convention to the effect "that all Independent candidates are inspired solely by a lust for office; that they shall be treated as common enemies to the welfare of the people and avowed enemies to the Democratic party of the State of Mississippi."—Quoted in *Jackson Times,* Aug. 27, 1877. The next year Brown made clear that he was incensed because the Democrats in Hinds County had, by a process of political jugglery, chosen all their candidates from one roads district. (*Jackson Times,* July 6, 1878, quoting letter Brown to *Magnolia Herald.*)

[73] *Ibid.,* Aug. 21, 1877.

[74] *Clarion,* Aug. 22, 1877.

ever since 1865," but that Brown did not join that party because of the wholesale corruption and plunder which it countenanced. The *Holly Springs Reporter* treated with respect the latest warning of Brown and admired his independence in continuing to differ publicly with the great majority of his party. It admitted that Brown's prediction in 1867 was true—that the carpet-baggers would dominate the Negroes because of the failure of the white population to hold out the olive branch to them. The *Vicksburg Herald* had dubbed Brown "an old gentleman with views" and now felt that he was oversensitive to criticism.[75] His own county paper, the *Raymond Gazette* was almost alone in defending Brown's latest fault-finding position. It denied that his views were influenced by the failure to have his political aspirations gratified. "Always since the year 1861," it declared, "we (Hinds County) have greatly relied upon Governor Brown's judgment and we are not yet satisfied that he has ever led us astray." [76]

Brown's letter was noticed outside the state. The *New York Times* commended it and was glad to agree with Brown that disaster would overtake the Democratic party. The *Louisville Commercial* was also favorable to Brown, while the *Memphis Herald* asserted that "if Governor Brown would only throw off this abnormal sensitiveness and come out and boldly meet the issue and show 'where the danger lies' . . . he would render Mississippi and the whole country a lasting and valuable service." [77]

It is clear that Brown had acted as spokesman for a discontented conservative group in his own and in neighboring counties. In September a conservative meeting in the southern part of Hinds County condemned the radical governments of the State by both parties since 1865. In spite of Brown's repeated statements, this meeting endorsed Brown for governor and appealed to the conservative element of the people to elect the man "who for more than ten years past, has advocated the only policy under which, we believe, our people will ever prosper, or be able to cast off the present galling yoke of oppression which has been, and is still galling us." This meeting also called a county convention at Raymond on October 15.[78] The Raymond meeting organized the "Independent People's Party," nomi-

---

[75] *Jackson Times,* Aug. 23, 29, 31, Sept. 7, 1877, quoting papers cited.
[76] *Ibid.,* Aug. 31, 1877, quoting *Raymond Gazette.*
[77] *Ibid.,* Aug. 27, 28, 1877, quoting papers cited.
[78] *Ibid.,* Sept. 11, 1877.

nated county officers, and chose W. R. Wharton for the State senate from Hinds and Rankin Counties. As Brown had not given his consent, he was not nominated for governor, but Wharton withdrew his nomination in favor of Brown. The *Jackson Times* renewed its campaign for Brown by printing appeals to the voters that Brown would be sure to advance "every interest most near and dear to all, both white and black" and by raising at the head of its editorial column, "For State Senator, Albert G. Brown." [79]

The strength of the opposition sentiment in Hinds County was indicated by the fact that Captain Montgomery, the regular candidate for the State senate, received 2,212 votes, while Brown, although not a candidate, received 1,274. In Jackson Brown also received more than half the number of votes received by Montgomery. John M. Stone, the regular candidate for governor, received 96,454 votes. Only 1,168 scattering opposition-votes for different men were cast in the State, but 1,081 of these votes were cast for Brown by his old home county of Copiah.[80] The *Jackson Times* tried to console itself by claiming that Brown, considering that he was not a candidate, ran remarkably well, and that he would have been elected by an overwhelming majority if he had chosen to run. It commended the equally partisan Jackson *Clarion,* the recognized organ of the regular Democrats, for not saying one disrespectful word concerning Brown during the campaign.[81] The *Southern Reveille* took a similar view. Since "the latent love of Governor Brown lies down in the hearts of the people, deep and fervent," it insisted that "he can beat any man in Mississippi before the people, and if ever he tries it, and takes the stump, things will howl." [82] The *Brandon Republican* was not so complimentary. It dubbed Brown "the sore-headed disorganizer, . . . the head-centre of the sore-head movement." It considered the election a well-merited rebuke to Brown and rejoiced that "the ex-Governor can now consider his political career ended." [83]

From this time on to the end of his life we catch only an occasional glimpse of the thoughts and activities of Brown. He urged the imposition of a tax for the continuation of the Natchez and Jackson railroad which had been one of his favorite projects and had

[79] *Ibid.,* Oct. 17, 29, 1877.
[80] *Ibid.,* Nov. 12, 1877. *Clarion,* Dec. 5, 1877. In Jackson Montgomery got 281 votes, Brown, 161.
[81] *Ibid.,* Nov. 8, 10, 1877.
[82] *Ibid.,* Dec. 7, 1877, quoting *Southern Reveille.*
[83] *Ibid.,* Nov. 10, 1877, quoting *Brandon Republican.*

created wealth for Copiah and Hinds Counties. At the same time he indicated that his financial status had not improved when he wrote, "If I had money, I would invest a part of it in the stock of the company, with no confident expectation of ever getting it back with interest in kind." [84]

Brown was called on to clarify the position which Mississippi's representatives in the House and Senate took during the crisis immediately following the election of Lincoln. On May 8, 1878, the Jackson *Clarion* published under the title, "Written and Unwritten History," the communication of December 14, 1860, which these representatives and Governor Pettus sent to their constituents as a result of the conference called by Pettus on November 22. This document asserted that all arguments had been exhausted and demanded "the organization of a Southern Confederacy—a result to be obtained only by separate State secession—that the primary object of each slave-holding State ought to be its *speedy and absolute* separation from a Union with hostile States." [85] The publication of this statement called forth explanations of its "unwritten history" from former Representative Reuben Davis, and from ex-Senators Jefferson Davis and Brown. Reuben Davis explained that the decisions at the meeting of November 22, 1860, were first taken by a four to three vote. Reuben Davis, O. R. Singleton, and William Barksdale had voted in favor of the calling of a State convention for the purpose of seceding by separate State action. Jefferson Davis pointed out the danger of such separate action, and Representatives Lamar and Brown voted with him against the resolution. A second resolution advised the governor of South Carolina to cause their ordinance of secession to take effect immediately after its passage without waiting for similar action by Mississippi. The same votes were cast for and against this resolution as on the first resolution. In both cases Governor Pettus cast the deciding vote in favor of the resolutions.

Jefferson Davis wrote to O. R. Singleton that his position had been correctly stated: "that secession should only be adopted as a last resort, and that a single State could not exercise the right to withdraw from the Union without most serious injury to herself, even if permitted peaceably to do so." Just as in 1851 Davis had advised

[84] *Jackson Times,* Dec. 17, 1877, quoting Brown's letter of Nov. 30, 1877, favoring added taxation for the continuation of the railroad.

[85] *Clarion,* May 8, 1878.

South Carolina and Mississippi not to secede separately since their geographical separation would prevent them from aiding each other, so in 1860, he was "in favor of waiting for the cooperation of as many Southern States as would give dignity to the measure, and the physical power to maintain it."

Brown also wrote to Singleton, confirming the position of Jefferson Davis. "Though a secessionist in theory," Brown declared, "he was never for its practical application so long as he had a hope for anything like justice in the Union." Brown did not refer to the fact that he voted with Jefferson Davis in the meeting of November 22, 1860, to take a Fabian attitude towards secession, but he claimed that Davis would have voted for the Crittenden compromise amendment to the federal constitution if the Northern senators had agreed to it. This is the only reference which we have found in which Brown refers to Davis since the end of the war. It indicated that Brown had not forgotten his early antagonism to Davis, for he neglected to state that they had voted together, and he went out of his way to insist that he (Brown) would not have voted for the Crittenden compromise.

Brown closed this letter in a spirit of disillusionment and of boredom. He seemed to want to forget the pre-war days. "I have in mind many facts to justify me in these statements and opinions, most of which can be sustained by the record, but I do not take interest enough in the subject to write them down. I write out of courtesy to you alone." [86]

But Brown did not shut himself away from current issues. He was looking forward eagerly to the local elections of 1879 and warned that "I shall in a more pronounced manner than at any period of my life advise rebellion all along the line" if all the candidates in Hinds County were again chosen from one district. This aggressive attitude was immediately interpreted by the *Brandon Republican* as meaning that Brown was "preparing for an independent race next time." [87]

A letter of Thomas Dabney, the old-line Whig planter, informs us that Brown had a serious illness in the late summer of 1878. This letter shows clearly that the closest personal relations now existed

[86] *Ibid.,* June 5, 1878, letter of Reuben Davis; June 12, 1878, letters of Jefferson Davis and Brown.

[87] *Jackson Times,* July 6, 1878, quoting Brown's letter to *Magnolia Herald* and editorial of *Brandon Republican.*

between the Browns and their neighbors, the aristocratic Dabney family, now in straitened circumstances. It would be instructive if we could know how long these social relations had existed, but only one passing reference is made to Brown before 1878 in Mrs. Smedes' noted work.[88]

In May, 1879, Brown wrote a lengthy letter to a group of over a dozen citizens who had invited him to give an expression of his opinions on the important political issues of the day. This communication, published in the Jackson *Clarion,* is important for two reasons: it is the only time after the war of which we have record when Brown expressed himself on national issues as distinct from the problems of reconstruction in the South or in Mississippi and it proved to be the last expression of which there is evidence. It may, therefore, be considered his last political will and testament. As the final stage in the evolution of his ideas, it deserves careful scrutiny.

Brown, painfully conscious that he represented no political group and that he was alienated from his own party, made it clear that he was speaking for himself alone, so that "no one need be at the trouble to disavow my sentiments that I express." He assumed that he was flattered by their assurance that his opinions would have great influence with the people, but expressed serious doubts that this was the case. He hoped his views would not be influential simply because they were his opinions. "It is one of the worst signs of the times that the people are too prone to follow blindly the opinions of others, instead of investigating and forming opinions of their own." In this over-modest mood, he even asked to be pardoned for using the personal pronoun.

Brown considered the currency problem to be the most urgent national issue, and he devoted almost half of his letter to its various phases. He reiterated the hard money position he had taken at the beginning of his political career, while admitting the need of some form of supplementary "paper money" for the necessities of trade. Although he admitted that the constitution had been "rent and torn and trampled on," he believed that it was not too late to appeal to it. It still commanded his veneration, and he asserted too extravagantly, "whatever others may say or do, I mean at all times to bow before

---

[88] Thomas Dabney gave permission for his son, Edward, to be with Brown during his illness. He sent a Mr. Douglas to inquire, after Edward also became sick at the Brown home. (Smedes, *Memorials of a Southern Planter,* pp. 88, 276–277, letter of Thomas Dabney to Emmy Dabney, Sept. 7, 1878.)

it with reverential awe." He believed the constitution justified the government in coining all the gold and silver bullion it could command, or at least, at all times, to coin enough to meet the legitimate demands of labor, traffic, and commerce. Interest-bearing bonds should be issued only as a last resort. He suggested $300,000,000 as the proper amount of gold and silver coinage. To supply the deficiency of gold and silver, he would have three times the amount issued in federal treasury notes, which should be the only paper recognized as money.

Brown attacked the fiat money advocates as he had done in the 1830s and the 1840s. He referred to this type of financing during the latter years of the Confederacy when flour sold in Richmond for $1,200 a barrel in paper money which could have been bought for $5 in silver. People did take Confederate notes, but only at ruinous rates. "Flood the country again with irredeemable paper; issue a government 'fiat,' a sort of imperial edict that the people shall take it, and they will take it, but at what rates? That is the question."

Brown started his political career by denouncing the money power behind the second bank of the United States. He retained to the end his distrust of this power, now controlled by the national banks. He did not mince his words. "I am pointedly, positively, and emphatically opposed to all national or other incorporated banks." He believed that the national bank notes should be retired as rapidly as possible. As in his early career he pictured the farmers as crushed by the financial octopus. They got only the scraps left from the banquet of the great monied corporations, received no adequate reward for their labor, and starved in the midst of plenty. Banks were of doubtful constitutionality and "of no use to anyone except the favored few in whose special interest they are generally managed." He held it intolerable that bank bonds should be tax-exempt at the same time that interest was drawn on them, that national bank notes based on these bonds should also draw interest and have the credit of the nation pledged for the final redemption of the notes. "When we look at the practical working of these pilfering shops, the human mind is aghast at their perfidy." Besides giving double interest on any real money value they possess, bankers deny all credit to the laboring masses. While the government can borrow hundreds of millions at four percent interest, the laboring man, "through the blundering or something worse of that same government, is paying at an average rate of certainly not less than twenty percent." Brown opposed the making of treasury notes or any other notes a legal tender in payment of debts. People would take the notes voluntarily at par, but, Brown threatened unconvincingly, "command us, and that too without much showing, and we rebel."

Brown next discussed the distribution of the $900,000,000 which he proposed as a suitable amount of currency. In doing so he threw his earlier strict-construction views to the winds. Indeed, we have seen that Brown gave up these State-rights principles during the War of Southern Nationalism because he knew that a powerful central government was essential to the continued existence of the Confederacy. Brown now showed that he had retained his belief in the necessity of a strong central government when he took a paternalistic position so advanced that it was rejected by the nationalistic Republican party in 1932, when in the midst of a national economic emergency. Only with the establishment of the principle of granting loans directly to individuals as a part of the New Deal of his own party in 1933 did any national government accept the far-reaching powers which Brown proposed in 1879.

Brown would distribute $600,000,000 among the States on compound ratio of territory and population. Such distribution has become commonplace during the last twenty years in matching-the-federal-dollar legislation. But far more radical was his proposal to loan $400,000,000 of this sum to individual farmers at not more than 3 percent interest and the remaining $200,000,000 to individuals engaged in other pursuits. He would guard particularly against any speculation with these funds, but would "loan directly to the man who needed the money for his own use in carrying on his agricultural or mechanical pursuits, or business of like kind." He insisted that every one receiving a loan must give the amplest security, and "would even make it a penal offense for a man who had borrowed the national credit, not to meet his obligations."

Brown, who rose to political power as the champion of the poor-white farmers of southern and of eastern Mississippi, found it easy to sympathize with the granger movement of the day [89] and used language which might be put into the mouths of the discontented farmers of recent years. Brown explained that he would give most

[89] This movement gained its greatest vigor in the Middle West and in the South. In 1875 there were 6,400 granges in the South. Mississippi was one of the four States within the nation in which it first rose to maturity. (Allan Nevins, *The Emergence of Modern America, 1865-1878*, p. 170.)

of these loans to agriculture because "it is the foundation, the mud-sill, so to speak, upon which the whole superstructure rests; disturb it, and you shake the whole business fabric of the country." Yet this basic industry was "the very one which has received the least of the fostering care of the government." The government should rescue the farmer "from the grasp of the money dealers, vampires, who are slowly sucking away his life-blood and the life-blood of the country." If the government can find men to collect and disburse its hundreds of millions annually, ranging from a petty postmaster to the collector of the port of New York, and can loan its credit, after a fashion, to national banks, "it can find trustworthy men enough to loan its credit directly to the people who are after all the government."

Just as remarkable as his dependence upon the central government for direct aid to individuals was the extension of his views on the subject of internal improvements. Here again his pre-war strict-construction views have vanished away. He specifically stated that internal improvements were desirable and should be encouraged as a means of enlarging the volume of commerce and thus of improving the general prosperity of the country. However, he was sceptical of the value of giving immediate relief to the paralyzed industries of the country, or of making improvements in advance of the demands of commerce because "contractors generally get the lion's share of the appropriation," while the men who do the work get very little, and "the general public who pay the money, nothing at all."

Brown applied these principles to specific projects. He declared that he was emphatically in favor of the construction of new levees, jetties, and outlets on the Mississippi River as soon as the demands of national commerce required them. The public interest alone should be consulted, and not the advantage of any economic group. His old antagonism to the rich Mississippi River planters flared up in his assertion that he had "too long combatted the idea of protection for the sake of protection, to take the ground now that the whole country should be taxed simply to improve the value of the estates lying on the banks of the Mississippi."

Although he admitted that he had hesitated to vote either land or money to aid in the construction of transcontinental railroads "as an original proposition," he now favored the subsidizing of the Southern Pacific. If constitutional scruples were disregarded when Congress voted hundreds of millions for the Union and the Northern Pacific roads, "we should not consider it an affront if the same thing is done when it comes to voting like subsidies for a Southern road. If we went outside the Constitution to build a Northern road, let us stay out until we have built a Southern road."

Brown not only favored internal improvements; he urged federal subsidies for aiding external trade by steamship lines to South America. He was convinced that a million or two millions of subsidy would draw to us commerce worth hundreds of millions. He realized the dangers of political jobbery and fraud in a subsidy system, but did not propose to let this danger frighten him from what he considered a great duty to the public.

Although Brown admitted that "my views on internal improvements have been expanded under the present regime," he denounced the abuses of pork-barrel legislation "to deepen puddle holes and improve the navigation of spring branches." In the days of Jackson and of Van Buren Democrats were taught to believe that one national bank was unconstitutional and that Congress could not improve the navigation of a river unless it served as a great inland sea like the Mississippi. Now there were nearly 3,000 national banks and "the government is called upon to improve the navigation of every little stream where a good sized catfish can swim." Brown declared that he still stood with the fathers of his party in opposing the appropriation of vast sums for purposes which would primarily "improve the private property of private individuals." Times had changed radically since he had entered politics, but he asked, "who is it that has the right to declare me a traitor to principle because I do not follow the changes?" He had held Democratic principles to be immutable, but added satirically, "I suppose I was wrong in this."

In the remainder of his letter Brown continued to show how disillusioned he had become over party principles and practices. Self-seekers in the North used the party slogan that "the government must not be allowed to pass into the hands of Confederate brigadiers." They had no fear that these brigadiers would actually use their power to inaugurate another war, but found the slogan valuable to rally their adherents to the defense of the spoils of office, the especial property of party leaders. In the solid South the magic word is "Democracy," in whose name "we must stand together to keep the government out of the hands of the carpet-baggers and 'niggers.' " Brown was convinced that not a single Democrat believed that there was more to be feared from a revival of Radical rule "than there is from the materialized spirits of Egyptian mummies." What they really mean is to keep themselves in office—"that is what the office-holders and nine-tenths of office-seekers mean."

Brown launched into an attack against his party which had now had undisputed control of the State for nearly four years. He was "getting weary" in waiting for the "good time a coming." He charged that conditions had not improved, that taxes had not been decreased in proportion to the decline in incomes. When Brown had mildly protested, he had been answered, "Whoop up the Democracy!—any man is a traitor who don't (*sic*) stand by the nominees!" It was high time for the members of the political concert to stop tuning their fiddles and begin to play. If the Democratic party did not soon give relief, he believed the people of the State would turn to another party.

The passage of laws and resolutions, such as the recent liberal Vicksburg resolutions, were not sufficient. "We need an earnest, energetic public sentiment that will see to it that laws are obeyed to the letter, and resolutions without equivocation or mental reservation." All else is of no avail "until in fact there is created an overwhelming public opinion which shall proclaim in tones of thunder—the rights of the colored man must and shall be respected. Allow me to add, resolutions may be treated as forms, platforms disregarded, and laws circumvented. But a united, determined, energetic public opinion is always efficient and never suffers defeat." Brown admitted that he was not in accord with any existing party, but did not want to leave his own party. "If I leave, I shall go feeling like a father who has been driven from his home by his own children."

Brown summed up his advice "to the people at large, both white and colored. Deal more justly with one another. 'All men are born free and equal' says the Declaration of Independence. The Constitution says, 'all men are equal before the law.' Observe these rules closely and in perfect faith, and all jarring between the races will cease." He ended this long political testament by forewarning his critics that his motive in writing was "not where you will be most likely to look for it," and he reiterated for the last time his familiar unequivocal denial of office-seeking in the words, "there is no office in the gift of the people that I desire, none that I would accept." [90]

The *Clarion* discussed Brown's letter in a lengthy editorial in the

[90] *Clarion*, May 28, 1879, quoting Brown's letter of May 13, 1879.

same edition in which it appeared. It agreed with many of the policies which Brown advocated: opposition to irredeemable paper money, the use of treasury notes instead of national bank notes, federal subsidies to aid South American trade, and the construction of a Southern trans-continental railroad with the aid of federal funds. It agreed with Brown that levees should be built along the Mississippi River, but believed that there should be no delay in their construction. If Brown included in "deepening mud puddles and cleaning out spring branches" what it considered legitimate public improvements such as the deepening of harbors like Pascagoula and Ship Island, or tributaries of the Mississippi, or streams like the Pearl and the Tombigbee, then the *Clarion* differed from Brown. The *Clarion* maintained that it would be suicidal for the South to object to a system which had contributed so much to the commerce and wealth of the North "at the very time when there is a prospect of securing a fair share of these benefits."

Although the *Clarion* was willing to adjust its views to the times and to go Brown one better in its acceptance of internal improvements, it was astounded at the scheme to use the government for loaning money to individuals on security. It called it "the most stupendous centralizing project that has not been conceived by the most extreme consolidationist." If writing today, this journal would have denounced it as socialistic. It was certainly correct in saying that Brown's scheme would require a stretching of the general welfare clause "which the Alexander Hamilton school of politicians in their wildest visions never dreamed of." The corruption, patronage, and pensioners that it would inflict upon the country was "a picture the imagination grows weary in attempting to paint." Instead of becoming banker for the people, the *Clarion* believed that the government should expand the currency and leave to the States the regulation of the domestic concerns of their citizens and to the citizens themselves the business of loaning money.

The *Clarion* dealt very leniently with Brown's bitter criticism of the Democratic party. The solid South, it insisted, was not to be deprecated as a menace to the North, for it was inevitable that the weaker and proscribed section would unite against the oppression of the stronger section. It pleaded for patience in the stupendous work of recovery from the Radical saturnalia, admitting that "everything may not have been done as required by the public interest." It had confidence that the Democratic Conservative party was equal to the task "of cleansing the Augean stables and lifting the good old commonwealth out of the slough of despond." [91]

One of Brown's life-long friends, L. O. Bridewell, in an open letter, also made a friendly plea to Brown to be more patient with his party. He admitted the difficulty of remaining patient in critical times and declared that Brown was no less a true Democrat than he had always been. Like the *Clarion*, Bridewell was more severe in his condemnation of Brown's grand scheme of financial paternalism, which he dubbed "violative of every idea of constitutional free government and perfect societary organization." [92]

We know nothing about Brown after this (except the reference in note 94) until his death a year later on Saturday evening, June 13, 1880. That afternoon he had gone to Terry to get a doctor to visit Mrs. Brown, who was suffering with a chill. Thomas Dabney, writing to his daughter Emmy two days later after his return from the Brown home, gives the most reliable account of the strange death of "our admirable friend." Dr. Rawls left Terry immediately, "the governor following soon after. Arriving at the gate opening upon his lawn, he dismounted to open it, and leading through, he again mounted the horse and proceeded to the pond to water him. In about ten minutes afterwards the cook observed the horse loose, and gave the alarm. The carriage-driver went to the pond immediately, saw the hat floating and the governor's shoulders and the back of his head protruding above the water, which was two feet deep at that place. He was in a crouching posture, his arms thrust forward and downward, embracing his legs, and his face submerged. Neither his shoulders nor the back of his head had been in the water. How the equilibrium was maintained is a mystery. A doctor was there, who pronounced him dead. He was in the water not exceeding fifteen minutes, perhaps ten. His lungs could not have acted since the moment of the submergence of his face, as not a drop of water issued either from his mouth or nose. He therefore did *not* drown, neither did he fall from his horse. Had he fallen, he must have gone clear under. It is supposed, as the only tenable conjecture, that he lost his hat, and in attempting its recovery by means of his cane, he lost his balance, and, finding he must go, he clung to the horse's neck and mane until he got his feet into the water, and then sunk down dead. He had been complaining for some days of an undue determination of blood

[91] *Ibid.*
[92] *Ibid.*, June 18, 25, 1879, quoting Bridewell's letter of May 30, 1879.

to the head. . . . As he was not wet all over, he did *not* fall, and, as not a drop of water was in his stomach or lungs, he did *not* drown. After satisfying myself on these points, I told Mrs. Brown that the governor must have been dead by the time he struck the water, to which she said yes." Dabney therefore concluded that Brown had died "of apoplexy, or something of that nature." [93]

Four citizens of Terry took the body of Brown to Jackson on Sunday night where a group met them at the station and accompanied his body to the rotunda of the capitol building. There it lay in state and was viewed by hundreds of citizens. At noon on Monday he was buried in Greenwood Cemetery while the Supreme Court adjourned and business in Jackson was suspended as a mark of respect. Robert Lowry, the State historian, and Ethelbert Barksdale, the editor of the *Clarion,* were among the pallbearers.

Barksdale, who had been a close personal friend,[94] paid a fitting tribute to the services and character of Brown. He recounted the numerous offices which Brown had filled before the war, but far overshot the mark when he said that undoubtedly "the great-minded and big-hearted statesman . . . would have reached the crowning honor of the Presidency of the United States but for the sectional issue which put the South and her statesmen under the ban." Due credit was given to Brown's military career in the early part of the war.

The most discerning part of the tribute dealt with Brown's attitude

[93] Smedes, pp. 287–288, letter Thomas Dabney to Emmy Dabney, Burleigh, June 15, 1880. Brown was one of Thomas Dabney's three "old and valued friends" who died in 1879 and 1880. The friendship continued with Mrs. Brown, who was urged to make her home at Burleigh until she moved to Washington. Upon the death of Thomas Dabney in 1885, Mrs. Brown wrote: "Many and many a time in our lonely home has he cheered us with his bright, hopeful conversation. We always felt better for his coming."—Smedes, pp. 282, 288, 339. The Dabney account of Brown's death is substantially the same as that of the Jackson *Clarion* of June 16, 1880. The author is not inclined to accept the tradition that, in as much as Brown had become a heavy drinker during his last years, he had fallen from his horse, dead-drunk, into three feet of water and had been unable to extricate himself. This tradition was reported to the author by citizens of Jackson, including Dr. Dunbar Rowland, State historian, and Edgar S. Wilson, at one time secretary to L. Q. C. Lamar. It is believed by citizens of Terry, and on Brown's estate itself, which the author visited.

[94] The last reference to Brown of which the author has evidence was a letter of Brown's of March 20, 1880 to the *Clarion,* renewing his subscription. Brown had been a constant reader of the *Clarion* and of its predecessor, *The Mississippian,* for over forty years and proposed to continue for the remainder of his life because he found in its editorials "vastly more to approve than to condemn." The *Clarion* announced that it would enter him on the books as a paid up life-time subscriber. (*Clarion,* Mar. 31, 1880.)

after the war. Just as he had taken an advanced position on the slavery issues in the decade before the war and the Southern people did not recognize, until the very eve of the conflict, the implications of the principle of Southern nationalism which Brown espoused, so after the War of Southern Nationalism he sought to lead the people to accept the national policy of reconstruction and urged a moderate and conciliatory approach to the Negro problem. But "for once only, his prescience and wisdom were not appreciated. He was wiser than his generation. His admonitions and teachings in '67 and '68 have since seemed like inspired prophecy." His deep and disinterested activities in public affairs during this period when he sought no public office were highly commended. He continued to be the counselor and sage of the people even when they turned a deaf ear. "If his people did not justly appreciate his policy, so much the worse for them. He had discharged his duty by them. He feared no obloquy. He wanted no thanks. When he died, time had amply vindicated the wisdom of his counsels." [95]

In November, 1880, public recognition was given to the memory of Brown. The citizens of Terry adopted resolutions which, although pitched in a tone of fulsome exaggeration, expressed the great personal affection which Brown had always been able to inspire in his immediate friends and neighbors. On November 17 a public meeting was held in the House of Representatives in Jackson to pay tribute to Brown. Ethelbert Barksdale called Governor J. M. Stone to the chair, and the governor, in spite of the severe criticism which Brown had given to his administration, said that "no son of Mississippi had ever won in larger measure the admiration, love, and confidence of the people of the State" than had Albert Gallatin Brown. The following resolution was passed: "Few men have ever been trusted so much, very few have so deserved trust. In the bestowal of public honors and trusts through the many years when they were heaped upon him there is no mystery. There was no infatuation, no delusion. The people possessed in him, and they were quick to discern it, a public servant whose chief ambition was to be worthy and capable of serving them, and his ambition was never stronger than was his earnest desire to promote their welfare and happiness."

The memorial address was delivered by General J. Z. George, who had conducted the Democratic campaign which culminated in the Revolution of 1875. He traced Brown's career from the time his father brought him, as a boy, to Copiah County to help build a log cabin on a "squatter's patch" of public land. He emphasized the fact that Brown's political career was important because it was so closely intertwined with the history of his State during the same period. With pardonable exaggeration he declared that "there never lived a citizen of any State whose life and services were so closely interwoven with her history. A great man—the late Chief Justice Smith, said in 1858 that the history of Mississippi could not be written so as to be recognized if the name of Albert Gallatin Brown was omitted from it. The remark has even more force now than then."

George reviewed the course of Brown's career from the year 1841 when he was elected circuit judge over Judge Thomas A. Willis, an able and popular incumbent who was reelected judge when Brown was elected governor in 1843. He vividly described the disastrous period of reckless speculation which preceded his governorship. It was an era when banks without capital had been chartered and the State had been flooded with irredeemable and worthless currency. Lands and slaves were bought at enormous prices on credit, and worthless railroad schemes were projected while "the sure means of acquiring wealth by steady and persistent industry and economy were despised as too slow." By the time Brown came to the governorship the bubble had burst, public and private credit had been destroyed, and the State treasury was empty. "During his first term," continued George, "by his splendid administrative abilities, without an increase in taxation, all this was changed. Before the close of his second term the State had started on a new career of prosperity and progress."

George touched lightly on his career in Congress during the critical years before the war, but praised his gallantry at the battles of Bull Run and Leesburg during the first year of the war. At the same time, he regarded it as a great misfortune that Brown was not a member of the Provisional Congress of 1861–1862 where "his thorough knowledge of people in all sections of the Union, his keen insight in political matters, might have materially aided in the adoption of a policy which, though it could not have averted what seemed predestined failure, might yet have diminished the evils of defeat."

The orator merely mentioned Brown's senatorship in the permanent Confederate Congress. He had nothing but praise for Brown's "full, free, manly, and honest acceptance of the new order of things" after the war. "He saw that the North and South were indeed to be one people, inhabiting one country, and he was therefore for reconciliation and harmony—for making the lately hostile camps one in sentiment and feeling, one in devotion to the great work of advancing the people to the highest degree of prosperity and happiness. . . . The contest being over, he retained no bitterness and cherished no resentments."

In summing up the chief characteristics of Brown, George stressed above all others the personal devotion which he inspired in the people. He declared that the news of Brown's death had caused "a wider and deeper sorrow than has followed the death of any citizen of this commonwealth." Mississippi admired as much and was as proud of the fame and achievements of others, "but she has had none whom her people loved so well, or whom they so implicitly trusted." Those who knew Brown best almost idolized him. "His own nature was affectionate in the last degree; he had more personal friends than any man I ever knew. . . . He never forgot nor deserted a friend, and he was rewarded for his fidelity by a like devotion to himself."

He praised Brown's judgment, which he termed singularly clear, sure, and penetrating. His logic discarded scholastic rules and long trains of reasoning, but was based on the "irresistible process of common sence [sic], . . . was short—almost intuitive, but the end was certain." He did not attempt the impossible and was so honest with himself that he was willing to acknowledge his own errors in judgment.

Brown was a sincere democrat who appreciated the necessity of education in a democracy. "He was, therefore, an advocate of the common school system long in advance of his contemporaries." He believed in the argument and discussion of problems with the people and respected their sober second thought as the true voice of the people. Brown constantly discussed political questions and became a clear, eloquent, and instructive speaker. Possessing neither the magnetic vehemence of Clay, nor the grand magnificence of Webster, nor the polished elocution of Preston, he nevertheless had "the power to please, and at the same time to instruct the great mass of the people. His language was terse and strong; his manner earnest and graceful; his delivery fluent and pleasing. . . . He had the habit of using homely illustrations which made his meaning evident, and laid bare to the common comprehension the true nature of problems in political science. . . . His was not a different philosophy from that of the mass of the people; but the same, better understood and more fully developed; the difference was in degree only."

George next gave his estimate of Brown as a party man. Brown was a Democrat from conviction and respected the decisions of the regular organization, but he was not a slave to his party and did not make the success of his party the ultimate end of political action. When he believed that his party was in error he had the strength of character to maintain his own convictions without severing party ties. He illustrated Brown's independence by his support of the indigent insane bill which the Pierce administration opposed and his refusal to join in the ostracism of Douglas by the Buchanan administration— and George might have mentioned his severe criticism of the Democratic party during the last few years of his life. Brown's political independence was all the more creditable because he was ambitious of distinction and renown.

George ended his address by appealing to his hearers to follow the example of Brown by serving the State "all the more faithfully and lovingly for the desolation and woe in her borders caused by war and the terrible agencies of the abnormal period which succeeded active hostilities," and he urged citizens to remember, as Brown did, "that we are citizens of a renewed Union" and "that no sense of wrong inflicted, no feeling of disappointment, shall prevent us from discharging fully the high duties of American citizenship." [96]

The *Clarion* gave the highest praise to this address as a true portrayal of the character of Brown. It declared that J. Z. George "knew every attribute and aspiration of the illustrious man he essayed to describe. It was a labor of love and of patriotic duty, and he performed it with the hand of a master." [97]

[96] *Clarion*, Nov. 18, 1880, containing the resolutions of the citizens of Terry and George's memorial address. A five stanza poem on Brown by Maggie A. Downing of Raymond had appeared in the *Clarion* of Aug. 25, 1880.

[97] *Ibid.*, Nov. 18, 1880. A few years later Mrs. Brown died at Grass Lawn near Mississippi City and was buried in Jackson with her husband and elder son. (MSS. Ruth Burnett Papers, clipping, no date.) She was a woman of much culture and refinement and was especially noted for her liberal hospitality as mistress of the executive mansion during her husband's governorship. A few years after the death of Mrs. Brown, her remaining son, Joseph A. Brown, moved to Seattle, Washington, where he lived until his death in 1910. [Letter of Mrs. T. B. (Lottie Brown) Waller, daughter of Joseph Brown, to author, May 23, 1931, from Seattle, Wash.]

BIBLIOGRAPHY

I. Manuscript Sources

Manuscripts consulted in the Department of Archives and History, State
of Mississippi, Capitol building, Jackson, Mississippi:
J. F. H. Claiborne Collection, Vols. A, B, C.
John A. Quitman Papers, 1851–1858.
William N. Whitehurst Papers, Vol. N, Nos. 7–13.
Governors' Archives, Series E, Nos. 35, 36.
Executive Journal, Governors McNutt, Tucker, Brown.
Executive Journal, 1838–1845.
Executive Journal, Governors Brown-McRae.
Secretaries of State Archives, Series F, Nos. 51, 58, 65, 68, 71, 85.
Auditors' Archives, Series G, Nos. 67–217.
Ruth Burnett Papers, Terry, Mississippi.
Zachariah Chandler MSS., Vol. IV, 1866–1870, Library of Congress.
J. F. H. Claiborne MSS., I, II, III, Library of Congress.
Stephen A. Douglas MSS., University of Chicago.

II. Printed Official Documents

Congressional Globe, 26th Congress, 2nd session; 30th–36th Congresses
    (Washington, 1841, 1849–1861).
Mississippi Election of 1875, 2 Vols., 44th Congress, 1st session (Washington, 1876).
Richardson, James D., editor, *The Messages and Papers of the Presidents, 1789–1897*, 10 Vols., (Washington, 1896–1899).
Statistical View of the Population of the United States from 1790 to 1830, Inclusive, Department of State (Washington, 1835).
Official Records of the Union and Confederate Armies in the War of the Rebellion.
    Series I, Vols. I, II (Washington, 1880).
    Series I, Vol. V (Washington, 1881).
    Series I, Vol. LII, Part II (Washington, 1898).
    Series II, Vol. IV (Washington, 1899).
    Series II, Vol. VI (Washington, 1899).
    Series IV, Vols. II, III (Washington, 1900).
Official Records of the Union and Confederate Navies in the War of the Rebellion. Series II, Vol. II (Washington, 1921).
Abstract of the Returns of the Fifth Census, House Document No. 263, 22nd Congress, 1st session (Washington, 1832).
Tenth Census of the United States, I (Washington, 1883).

Journal of the Senate of Mississippi, 1841 (Jackson, Miss., 1841).
Journal of the Convention of the State of Mississippi, 1851 (Jackson, Miss., 1851).
Journal of the Senate of Mississippi, 1854 (Jackson, Miss., 1854).
Journal of the Senate of Mississippi, 1857 (Jackson, Miss., 1857).
Journal of the Senate of Mississippi, Special Session, March–April, 1864 (Jackson, Miss., 1864).
Journal of the Congress of the Confederate States of America, 1861–1865, Vols. II, III, IV, Senate Document No. 234, 58th Congress, 2nd session (Washington, 1904).
Pamphlet, "Address of the Committee of the Mississippi Convention to the Southern States, 1849" (Library of Congress, no date).
Auditor's sheet, Assessment of Persons and Personal Property, Mississippi, 1853.

III. Other Primary Works

Cluskey, M. W., editor, *The Speeches, Messages, and Other Writings of the Hon. Albert G. Brown, a Senator from the State of Mississippi* (New York, 1859). [Smith, in his work, *Parties and Slavery*, p. 310, in listing "the only writings of ultra-southern men of this period which have been published," omits Cluskey's work.]

Jameson, J. Franklin, editor, "The Correspondence of John C. Calhoun," *Annual Report of the American Historical Association, 1899*, Vol. II (Washington, 1900).

Jones, John B., *A Rebel War Clerk's Diary at the Confederate States Capital*, 2 Vols., (Philadelphia, 1866).

Moore, John Bassett, editor, *The Works of James Buchanan*, 12 Vols., (Philadelphia, 1910).

Phillips, Ulrich B., editor, "The Correspondence of Robert Toombs, Alexander H. Stephens, and Howell Cobb," *Annual Report of the American Historical Association, 1911*, Vol. II (Washington, 1913).

Rowland, Dunbar, editor, *Jefferson Davis, Constitutionalist. His Letters, Papers and Speeches*, 10 Vols. (Jackson, Miss., 1923).

Rowland, Dunbar, *The Official and Statistical Register of the State of Mississippi* (Nashville, Tenn., 1908).

Southern Historical Society Papers, Vols. XLIV, XLV (Richmond, 1923, 1925).

The Whig Almanac and United States Register (New York, 1852).

IV. Newspapers

Newspapers consulted in the Department of Archives and History, State of Mississippi, Capitol building, Jackson, Mississippi, and in the Library of Congress, Washington, D. C.:
The Mississippian, 1834–1865 (Jackson).
Mississippi Free Trader, 1835–1861 (Natchez).
Natchez Courier, 1837–1867 (Natchez).

Southern Star, 1837–1840 (Gallatin).
Piney Woods Planter, 1838–1839 (Liberty).
Aberdeen Whig, 1839 (Aberdeen).
Independent Journal, 1839 (Jackson).
Sentinel and Expositor, 1839 (Vicksburg).
Whig Advocate, 1839 (Madison).
Yazoo Banner, 1839–1840 (Benton).
Statesman, 1843 (Jackson).
True Democrat, 1845–1847 (Paulding).
Sentinel, 1847–1851 (Vicksburg).
Vicksburg Whig, 1847 (Vicksburg).
Columbus Democrat, 1848–1853 (Columbus).
Port Gibson Herald, 1848–1851 (Port Gibson).
Hinds County Gazette, 1849–1862 (Raymond).
Southron, 1849–1850 (Jackson).
Flag of the Union, 1850–1853 (Jackson).
Monroe Democrat, 1850–1852 (Monroe).
Woodville Republican, 1850–1853 (Woodville).
Yazoo Democrat, 1850–1854 (Benton).
Independent, 1851–1853 (Aberdeen).
Southern Standard, 1851–1853 (Columbus).
Primitive Republican, 1852 (Columbus).
Southern Reveille, 1852–1854 (Port Gibson).
Eastern Clarion, 1858–1861 (Paulding).
Washington Constitution, 1859 (Washington, D. C.).
Richmond Whig, 1861–1865 (Richmond, Va.).
Richmond Dispatch, 1862–1865 (Richmond, Va.).
Richmond Enquirer, 1862–1865 (Richmond, Va.).
Richmond Examiner, 1863–1865 (Richmond, Va.).
Clarion, 1865–1880 (Jackson).
Jackson Times, 1876–1878 (Jackson).
Jackson Daily News, 1929 (Jackson).
New York Times, 1932 (New York).

V. Secondary Sources

Alexander, DeAlva Stanwood, *The History and Procedure of the House of Representatives* (Boston, 1916).
Aughey, John Hill, *The Iron Furnace: or, Slavery and Secession* (Philadelphia, 1863).
Baldwin, Joseph G., *Flush Times in Alabama and Mississippi* (New York, 1853).
Bartlett, David V. G., *Presidential Candidates: Containing Sketches, Biographical, Personal and Political, of Prominent Candidates for the Presidency in 1860* (New York, 1859).
Beale, Howard K., *The Critical Year: A Study of Andrew Johnson and Reconstruction* (New York, 1930).

Bowers, Claude G., *The Tragic Era: The Revolution after Lincoln* (New York, 1929).

Brown, William Garrott, *The Lower South in American History* (New York, 1903).

Buck, Paul H., "The Poor White in the Ante-bellum South," *American Historical Review*, XXXI, 1 (October, 1925).

Buckley, J. M., *A History of Methodism in the United States* (New York, 1896).

Butler, Pierce, *Judah P. Benjamin* (Philadelphia, 1907).

Carpenter, Jesse, *The South as a Conscious Minority* (New York, 1930).

Cate, Wirt Armistead, *Lucius Q. C. Lamar: Secession and Reunion* (Chapel Hill, N. C., 1935).

Catterall, Ralph C. H., *The Second Bank of the United States* (Chicago, 1903).

Chadwick, French Ensor, "Causes of the Civil War," *American Nation Series*, XIX (New York, 1906).

Chesnut, Mary Boykin, *A Diary from Dixie* (New York, 1905).

Claiborne, J. F. H., *The Life and Correspondence of John A. Quitman*, 2 Vols. (New York, 1860).

Claiborne, J. F. H., *Mississippi as a Province, Territory and State, with Biographical Notices of Eminent Citizens*, Vol. I (Jackson, 1880).

Clay, Mrs. Clement C., *A Belle of the Fifties* (New York, 1904).

Cole, Arthur C., "The Irrepressible Conflict, 1850–1865," *History of American Life Series*, VII (New York, 1934).

Cole, Arthur C., *The Whig Party in the South* (Washington, 1913).

Craven, Avery Odelle, *Edmund Ruffin, Southerner: A Study in Secession* (New York, 1932).

Craven, Avery Odelle, editor, *Essays in Honor of William E. Dodd* (Chicago, 1935).

Cutting, Elizabeth, *Jefferson Davis, Political Soldier* (New York, 1930).

Dabney, Virginius, *Liberalism in the South* (Chapel Hill, N. C., 1932).

Davis, Jefferson, *Rise and Fall of the Confederate Government*, 2 Vols., (New York, 1881).

Davis, Reuben, *Recollections of Mississippi and Mississippians* (Boston, 1891).

Davis, Varina Howell (Mrs. Jefferson), *Jefferson Davis, Ex-President of the Confederate States of America; a Memoir by His Wife*, 2 Vols. (New York, 1890).

De Leon, Thomas Cooper, *Belles, Beaux, and Brains of the 60's* (New York, 1909).

————, Thomas Cooper, *Four Years in Rebel Capitals: An Inside View of Life in the Southern Confederacy from Birth to Death* (Mobile, Ala., 1890).

Dictionary of American Biography, Vol. III, Allen Johnson, editor (New York, 1929).

Dodd, William E., *The Cotton Kingdom* (New Haven, 1921).

Dodd, William E., *Jefferson Davis* (Philadelphia, 1907).

Dodd, William E., *Robert J. Walker, Imperialist* (Chicago, 1914).

Du Bose, John W., *The Life and Times of William Lowndes Yancey* (Birmingham, 1892).

Dumond, Dwight Lowell, *The Secession Movement, 1860–1861* (New York, 1931).

Dumond, Dwight Lowell, editor, *Southern Editorials on Secession* (New York, 1931).

Dunning, William Archibald, *Essays on the Civil War and Reconstruction* (New York, 1898).

Duval, Mary V., *History of Mississippi and Civil Government* (Louisville, Ky., 1892).

Eckenrode, H. J., *Jefferson Davis, President of the South* (New York, 1923).

Everett, John S., "John A. Quitman's Connection with the Cuban Filibusters" (Typewritten thesis for the Master's degree at George Peabody College for Teachers, in archives of the Department of Archives and History, Jackson, Mississippi).

Fleming, Walter L., *Documentary History of Reconstruction,* 2 Vols. (Cleveland, 1906, 1907).

Fleming, Walter L., editor, *The South in the Building of the Nation,* 13 Vols. (Richmond, 1909).

Flippin, Percy Scott, *Hershel V. Johnson of Georgia: State Rights Unionist* (Richmond, 1931).

Foote, Henry S., *Casket of Reminiscences* (Washington, 1874).

Foote, Henry S., *The War of the Rebellion* (New York, 1866).

Garner, James W., *Reconstruction in Mississippi* (New York, 1901).

Garner, James W., "The First Struggle over Secession in Mississippi," *Publications of the Mississippi Historical Society,* Vol. IV, (University, Miss., 1901).

Gordon, Armistead C., *Jefferson Davis* (New York, 1918).

Gray, Lewis Cecil, *History of Agriculture in the Southern United States to 1860.* Vol. I (Washington, 1933).

Greeley, Horace, *The American Conflict,* 2 Vols. (Hartford, Conn., 1864–1866).

Gross, Alexander, *A History of the Methodist Church, South* (New York, 1894).

Hardy, W. H., "Recollections of Reconstruction in East and Southeast Mississippi," *Publications of the Mississippi Historical Society,* Vol. VIII (University, Miss., 1904).

Harris, Wiley P., "Autobiographical Sketch" (Typewritten, presented to Department of Archives and History, Jackson, Miss., 1929).

Harrison, Mrs. Burton, *Recollections Grave and Gay* (London, 1912).

Hart, Albert Bushnell, "Slavery and Abolition, 1831–1841," *American Nation Series,* XVI (New York, 1906).

Hart, Albert Bushnell, *The Southern South* (New York, 1910).

Hearon, Cleo, "Mississippi and the Compromise of 1850," *Publications of the Mississippi Historical Society,* Vol. XIV (University, Miss., 1914).

Hearon, Cleo, "Nullification in Mississippi," *Publications of the Mississippi Historical Society,* Vol. XII (University, Miss., 1912).

Helper, Hinton R., *The Impending Crisis of the South: How to Meet It* (Enlarged edition, New York, 1860).

Herndon, Dallas Tabor, "The Nashville Convention of 1850," *Transactions of the Alabama Historical Society,* Vol. V (Tuscaloosa, Ala., 1904).

Howland, Louis, *Stephen A. Douglas* (New York, 1920).

Johnson, Allen, *Stephen A. Douglas: A Study in American Politics* (New York, 1908).

Kline, Allen Marshall, "The Attitude of Congress toward the Pacific Railway, 1856–1862," *Annual Report of the American Historical Association, 1910* (Washington, 1912).

Lonn, Ella, *Desertion During the Civil War* (New York, 1928).

Lowry, Robert, and McCardle, William H., *History of Mississippi* (Jackson, Miss., 1891).

McCutchen, Samuel Proctor, "The Political Career of Albert Gallatin Brown," Typed dissertation (University of Chicago, 1930).

MacDonald, William, Jacksonian Democracy, 1829–1837, *American Nation Series, XV* (New York, 1906).

McGuire, Mrs. Judith W. B., *Diary of a Southern Refugee During the War* (New York, 1867).

McLaughlin, Andrew C., *A Constitutional History of the United States* (New York, 1935).

McNeily, J. S., "Climax and Collapse of Reconstruction in Mississippi, 1874–1876," *Publications of the Mississippi Historical Society,* Vol. XII (University, Miss., 1912).

Mayes, Edward, *History of Education in Mississippi* (Washington, 1899).

Mayes, Edward, *Life of Lucius Q. C. Lamar* (Nashville, Tenn., 1896).

Milton, George Fort, *The Eve of Conflict: Stephen A. Douglas and the Needless War* (Boston, 1934).

Montgomery, Frank A., *Reminiscences of a Mississippian in Peace and War* (Cincinnati, 1901).

Moore, Albert Burton, *Conscription and Conflict in the Confederacy* (New York, 1924).

Nevins, Allan, "The Emergence of Modern America, 1865–1878," *History of American Life Series,* VIII (New York, 1927).

Nichols, Roy Franklin, *Franklin Pierce: Young Hickory of the Granite Hills* (Philadelphia, 1931).

Norwood, John Nelson, *The Schism in the Methodist Episcopal Church, 1844: A Study of Slavery and Ecclesiastical Politics* (Alfred, N. Y., 1923).

Oberholtzer, Ellis Paxson, *A History of the United States Since the Civil War,* Vols. II and III (New York, 1922).

Owsley, Frank L., *State Rights in the Confederacy* (Chicago, 1925).

Paxson, Frederic L., *History of the American Frontier, 1763–1893* (Boston, 1924).

Pearce, Haywood J., Jr., *Benjamin H. Hill: Secession and Reconstruction* (Chicago, 1928).

Phillips, Ulrich B., *American Negro Slavery* (New York, 1918).

Phillips, Ulrich B., "Georgia and State Rights," *Annual Report of the American Historical Association, 1901*, Vol. II (Washington, 1902).

Phillips, Ulrich B., *Life and Labor in the Old South* (Boston, 1928).

Pollard, Edward A., *Life of Jefferson Davis, with a Secret History of the Southern Confederacy* (Philadelphia, 1869).

Poore, Ben Perley, *Perley's Reminiscences of Sixty Years in the National Metropolis*, I (Philadelphia, 1886).

Pryor, Mrs. Roger A., *Reminiscences of Peace and War* (New York, 1904).

Putnam, Mrs. Sallie A. Brock, *Richmond During the War: Four Years of Personal Observation* (New York, 1867).

Rhodes, James Ford, *History of the United States, 1850–1909*, 8 Vols. (New York, 1892–1919).

Riley, Franklin L., "Life of Col. J. F. H. Claiborne," *Publications of the Mississippi Historical Society*, Vol. VII (Oxford, Miss., 1903).

Riley, Franklin L., *A School History of Mississippi* (Richmond, 1900).

Robinson, William Morrison, Jr., *The Confederate Privateers* (New Haven, 1928).

Rowland, Dunbar, *Encyclopedia of Mississippi History Comprising Sketches of Counties, Towns, Events, Institutions, and Persons*, 2 Vols., (Madison, Wis., 1907).

Rowland, Dunbar, "Political and Parliamentary Orators and Oratory of Mississippi," *Publications of the Mississippi Historical Society*, Vol. IV (Oxford, Miss., 1901).

Savage, John, *Our Living Representative Men: From Official and Original Sources* (Philadelphia, 1860).

Schaff, Morris, *Jefferson Davis: His Life and Personality* (Boston, 1922).

Scharf, J. T., *History of the Confederate States Navy* (New York, 1887).

Schlesinger, Arthur Meier, *New Viewpoints in American History* (New York, 1922).

Schwab, John C., *The Confederate States of America, 1861–1865: A Financial and Industrial History of the South During the Civil War* (New York, 1901).

Shannon, Fred A., "The Homestead Act and the Labor Surplus," *American Historical Review*, XLI, 4, July, 1936 (New York, 1936).

Shields, Joseph D., *The Life and Times of Sergeant S. Prentiss* (Philadelphia, 1884).

Shryock, Richard Harrison, *Georgia and the Union in 1850* (Philadelphia, 1926).

Simms, Henry Harrison, *Life of Robert M. T. Hunter* (Richmond, 1935).

Smedes, Susan Dabney, *Memorials of a Southern Planter* (New York, 1887).

Smith, Theodore Clarke, "Parties and Slavery," *American Nation Series*, XVIII (New York, 1906).

Stephenson, Nathaniel W., *The Day of the Confederacy* (New Haven, 1919).

Stephenson, Nathaniel W., "The Question of Arming the Slaves," *American Historical Review*, XVIII, 2, January, 1913 (New York, 1913).

Stephenson, Nathaniel W., "Southern Nationalism in South Carolina in 1851," *American Historical Review,* XXXVI, 2, January, 1931 (New York, 1931).

Sydnor, Charles S., "Life Span of Mississippi Slaves," *American Historical Review,* XXXV, 3, April, 1930 (New York, 1930).

Sydnor, Charles S., *Slavery in Mississippi* (New York, 1933).

Tate, Allen, *Jefferson Davis, His Rise and Fall* (New York, 1929).

Tatum, Georgia Lee, *Disloyalty in the Confederacy* (Chapel Hill, N. C., 1934).

Timberlake, Elise, "Did the Reconstruction Regime Give Mississippi Her Public Schools?" *Publications of the Mississippi Historical Society,* Vol. XII (University, Miss., 1912).

Tribune Tracts 2. "Democratic Leaders for Disunion" (New York, 1860).

Turner, Frederick Jackson, *The United States: 1830–1850, The Nation and Its Sections* (New York, 1935).

VanWinkle, H. E., *Nine Years of Democratic Rule in Mississippi* (Jackson, Miss., 1847).

Wells, W. Calvin, "Reconstruction and Its Destruction in Hinds County," *Publications of the Mississippi Historical Society,* Vol. IX (University, Miss., 1905).

Wender, Herbert, "Southern Commercial Conventions, 1837–1859," *Johns Hopkins University Studies in Historical and Political Science,* Series 48, 4 (Baltimore, 1930).

White, Laura Amanda, *Robert Barnwell Rhett: Father of Secession* (New York, 1931).

Wilson, Henry, *The Rise and Fall of the Slave Power in America,* 3 Vols., (Boston, 1872–1877).

Winston, Robert W., *High Stakes and Hair Trigger, The Life of Jefferson Davis* (New York, 1929).

Woods, Thomas H., "The Mississippi Secession Convention of 1861," *Publications of the Mississippi Historical Society,* Vol. VI (Oxford, Miss., 1904).

Wright, Mrs. D. Giraud (Louise Wigfall), *A Southern Girl in '61* (New York, 1905).

INDEX

Abolitionists, denounced by Brown, 13, 20-21, 33, 148; opposed in Kansas, 141; doctrine accepted by South if Negroes in Southern army, 243, 246, 248

Acee, General E. L., favored for Congress, 1837, 9

Adams, John Quincy, denounced rejection of Prentiss and Word, 12

Adams, Stephen, Union Democrat, chosen senator, 102

African slave trade, opposed by Brown, 162, 171-172, 173; legislature of Mississippi declined to force issue, 190

Alabama, favored submission to Compromise of 1850, 84

Alabama Platform, 1848, opposed by Brown, 54; theory favored by Brown, 55

Alcorn, General James L., commander of Eighteenth Regiment, 211; nominated and elected governor, 1869, 261-262; defeated for governor, 1873, 263; debated with Brown, 277

Ames, Adelbert, extravagant administration as governor, 32; appointed provisional governor, 260; elected governor, 263; drew color line against whites, 264; indirect attack by Brown on personal extravagance, 268

Andrew, Bishop James O., defended by Rev. Winans, 61

Arizuma, protection of slavery sought by Brown, 203-204

Aughey, Rev. John H., views on poor whites, 208

Baldwin, Joseph C., characterization of frontier, 3

Ball's Bluff, battle of, Brown cited for bravery in, 211

Bank, United States, denounced by Brown, 10-11; recharter demanded, 4; popularity of, 9

Banks, Nathaniel Prentiss, elected speaker of House, 1856, 142-143

Banks, denounced by Brown, 18, 40; opposed by Democratic Association of Jackson, 34; see Planters' Bank, Union Bank

Bankruptcy bill, 1840, favored by Brown, 20

Barbecue, described, 36; in honor of Brown in 1859, 173

Barksdale, Ethelbert, editor of *The Mississippian*, 141; criticized Brown's position in 1860, 195-196; urged additional troops to relieve Vicksburg, 227-228; supported Davis in Confederate House of Representatives, 237; introduced bill for Negroes in army, 247-248; favored acquiescence in reconstruction measures, 255-256; urged cooperation with conservative Republicans, 260-261; accepted Negro suffrage, 262; pallbearer and speaker at Brown's funeral, 294-295; at memorial service, 295

Barksdale, William, nominated congressman-at-large, 1853, 112; discussion of conference in 1860 on State secession, 284-285

Barnwell, Robert Woodward, Confederate senator from South Carolina, 215

Barry, W. S., urged for Senate, 1857, 152; president of Mississippi secession convention, 206

Barton, Roger, favored for Congress, 1838, 12

Bell, John, favored by Unionists in Mississippi in 1860, 190; not discussed by Brown, 194; votes won in Mississippi, 199

307